Organisational Anthropology

Anthropology, Culture and Society

Series Editors:
Professor Vered Amit, Concordia University
and
Dr Jon P. Mitchell, University of Sussex

Recent titles:

ORGANISATIONAL ANTHROPOLOGY

Doing Ethnography in and among Complex Organisations

Edited by Christina Garsten and Anette Nyqvist

PlutoPress
www.plutobooks.com

First published 2013 by Pluto Press
345 Archway Road, London N6 5AA

www.plutobooks.com

Distributed in the United States of America exclusively by
Palgrave Macmillan, a division of St. Martin's Press LLC,
175 Fifth Avenue, New York, NY 10010

British Library Cataloguing in Publication Data
A catalogue record for this book is available from the British Library

ISBN   978 0 7453 3247 5   Hardback
ISBN   978 1 8496 4916 2   EPUB eBook
ISBN   978 1 8496 4917 9   Kindle eBook

Library of Congress Cataloging in Publication Data applied for

This book is printed on paper suitable for recycling and made from fully managed and
sustained forest sources. Logging, pulping and manufacturing processes are expected to
conform to the environmental standards of the country of origin.

10   9   8   7   6   5   4   3   2   1

Typeset from disk by Stanford DTP Services, Northampton, England
Simultaneously printed digitally by CPI Antony Rowe, Chippenham, UK and
Edwards Bros in the United States of America

Contents

Acknowledgements

This book has materialised as the result of a long-term and intimate connection between two spheres of interest and two organisations – social anthropology and organisation studies, as they appear at the Department of Social Anthropology at Stockholm University and at Score (Stockholm Centre for Organizational Research) jointly run by Stockholm University and Stockholm School of Economics. Both these spheres of interest and both these organisations have played a large part in shaping us and our minds, and we believe we have helped to shape them. Many thrilling, productive and improbable ideas are assessed in these organisations, and we have often found ourselves spirited away by the mind-blowing landscapes that spread out before us in anthropological studies of organisations.

Many colleagues in the Department of Social Anthropology and at Score have contributed fertile ideas to this book. We wish to thank Göran Ahrne, Nils Brunsson, Staffan Furusten, Ulf Hannerz, Adrienne Sörbom and Renita Thedvall for sharing our curiosity in how to understand organisations anthropologically. In the wider academic community, we are thankful to the vast numbers of organisation scholars, regardless of disciplinary bent, who have contributed their ideas. Thanks to Melissa Fisher and Janine Wedel for fun and undogmatic conversations on the topic, to Mikkel Flyverbom for encouragingly checking up on analytical progress, to Kerstin Jacobsson for intellectual and friendly support and to Brian Moeran for clever insights and good advice. We also wish to thank Tor Hernes for insisting that this book should be written in the first place and Hervé Laroche for sharing our interest in the seemingly mundane and boring. To our contributing authors – it has been a true adventure to work with you all! Thank you for sharing your research and your stories with us, for constructive conversations and for moving the field ahead. A large chunk of the work for this book has meshed in various ways with life in another kind of organisation: the family. To our respective families – our loving thanks.

Christina Garsten and Anette Nyqvist
Stockholm, Midsummer 2012

Series preface

Anthropology is a discipline based upon in-depth ethnographic works that deal with wider theoretical issues in the context of particular, local conditions – to paraphrase an important volume from the series: *large issues* explored in *small places*. This series has a particular mission: to publish work that moves away from an old-style descriptive ethnography that is strongly area-studies oriented, and offer genuine theoretical arguments that are of interest to a much wider readership, but which are nevertheless located and grounded in solid ethnographic research. If anthropology is to argue itself a place in the contemporary intellectual world, then it must surely be through such research.

We start from the question: 'What can this ethnographic material tell us about the bigger theoretical issues that concern the social sciences?' rather than 'What can these theoretical ideas tell us about the ethnographic context?' Put this way round, such work becomes *about* large issues, *set in* a (relatively) small place, rather than detailed description of a small place for its own sake. As Clifford Geertz once said, 'Anthropologists don't study villages; they study *in* villages.'

By place, we mean not only geographical locale, but also other types of 'place' – within political, economic, religious or other social systems. We therefore publish work based on ethnography within political and religious movements, occupational or class groups, among youth, development agencies, and nationalist movements; but also work that is more thematically based – on kinship, landscape, the state, violence, corruption, the self. The series publishes four kinds of volume: ethnographic monographs; comparative texts; edited collections; and shorter, polemical essays.

We publish work from all traditions of anthropology, and all parts of the world, which combines theoretical debate with empirical evidence to demonstrate anthropology's unique position in contemporary scholarship and the contemporary world.

Professor Vered Amit
Dr Jon P. Mitchell

1
Entries
Engaging organisational worlds

Christina Garsten and Anette Nyqvist

INTRODUCTION: ENTANGLED IN ORGANISATIONS

Our contemporary world is an organised world. Whether in Stockholm, Singapore or Santiago de Chile, we live most of our lives within and among organisations. We grow up in kin groups of one sort or other; we attend schools; we are employed in firms or public agencies; we join the local athletic clubs, trade unions, secret societies or international human rights organisations. In any corner of the world, people organise. In fact, we would face great challenges if we were to free ourselves from the opportunities and clutches of organisational life.

Some of the most pervasive forms of organisations, such as families, state agencies and business corporations, play critical roles in shaping our individual and personal lives. We need only think of the many intricate ways in which our citizenship in a nation manages to penetrate our lives through passport routines, tax regulations, and public (i.e. state) schools and health care, for instance, to realise that, whether we like it or not, the state is part of our personal and social lives. Similarly, the business corporation weaves itself into our everyday existence through the food we eat, the clothes we wear, the values that are communicated to us by the management of our workplace and the payment we receive for our labour. Whereas the human propensity to organise is universal, how we organise, and why and when we organise, vary across historical and cultural contexts. Anthropologists have always geared themselves to understanding how social forms are shaped by human actions, and how we, in turn, are shaped by them. The study of social organisations lies at the very core of the anthropological enterprise.

This book is about doing ethnography in and among complex organisations. Rather than trying to define how fieldwork is done and access gained, the book focuses on the processes of *engaging* with the field, and the challenges, dilemmas and opportunities involved when the field is an organisation. The notion of 'engaging' implies ways of approaching and researching, but also ways of analysing and producing knowledge. It entails both a methodological and a theoretical process. More specifically, this book addresses how the organisational context influences the research process, the methodological adjustments and innovations that may be needed and the openings that may be entailed in the fieldwork in such milieux. The contributing authors discuss the process of initiating contact, establishing rapport and gaining the trust of organisational members. The book also examines more closely the knowledge that may be gained, the assemblage of ideas and resources that influence the construction of that knowledge, and the blind spots that may emerge from restricted access and trust.

The book is based upon the premise that processes of gaining entry into and doing fieldwork in an organisation share essential characteristics with fieldwork in more classical anthropological environments. But the ethnographer is also faced with specific challenges related to the boundaries that organisations are prone to maintaining: exclusive membership, protection of ideological or financial interests and secrecy around key resources. These challenges are also related to constant restructuring, change and transformation, and to distributed localities and mediatised discourses and forms of interaction. Furthermore, informants or interlocutors are often well-educated, highly skilled professionals (sometimes with advanced academic degrees) who challenge or engage the skills of the ethnographer in ways that differ from the conventional perception of what it is like to 'engage with the locals'. Doing anthropology in complex settings therefore requires a different set of skills, a readiness for 'polymorphous engagements' (Gusterson 1997), for 'studying sideways' (Hannerz 1998, 2006) and 'studying through' (Wright and Reinhold 2011), for 'following' (Marcus 1995), and for doing ethnography 'at the interface' (Garsten 2009) of organisational structures.

For us to understand better the challenges and opportunities involved in doing anthropology in and among organisations, we invite the reader to explore the distinct characteristics of organisation that give rise to these challenges, and to examine some courses of action that anthropologists take in order to deal with them. The contributing authors share their experiences and insights into ways of engaging anthropologically with professional elites, experts and high-level managers in government organisations, business corporations, and non-governmental organisations. Our aim is for the book to provide an inspirational and reflexive contribution to contemporary discussions on the challenges and opportunities of doing anthropological fieldwork in complex organisational settings.

FROM TRIBES TO CORPORATIONS

There was a time when we could claim with some confidence that the anthropological study of formal organisations was young and innocent. This is no longer the case. Anthropology now has a relatively long and well-established record of researching state agencies, business corporations, multilateral institutions and non-governmental organisations. It is now close to a century since anthropologists and other social science scholars engaged in the path-breaking Hawthorne studies at the Western Electric Hawthorn Plant studies in western Chicago and Cicero, Illinois, and discovered workers' 'social system' or 'social organisation'.[1,2] Elton Mayo, who played a central role in the project, was himself a psychologist, sociologist and organisation theorist. He was as well acquainted with the work of anthropologists Bronislaw Malinowski and Alfred Radcliffe-Brown and their studies on social organisation. At a critical point, he was introduced to one of Radcliffe-Brown's students, William Lloyd Warner, who had just returned from fieldwork in Australia, studying the Murngin. Warner, intrigued by the insights that could be brought to bear on the informal social organisation of the plant, consulted with the Hawthorne researchers in designing and conducting the next phase of their experiment. 'With this act', Marietta Baba (2006: 87) writes, 'he fathered industrial or organizational anthropology'.

As Marietta Baba (2006) and Helen Schwartzman (1993) recount in vivid detail, the Hawthorne researchers conducted the final phase of the Hawthorne project, known as the Bank Wiring Observation Room (BWOR) experiment, with W. Lloyd Warner on board as design consultant. This portion of the project was aimed at exploring what workers actually *did* on the job, in contrast with what they *said* during the interviews. Hawthorne management, working in the spirit of Scientific Management, had accepted Frederick W. Taylor's concept of 'economic man' as a baseline.[3] However, the piece rate system installed to motivate workers had exactly the opposite effect to what the managers envisioned. Workers had their own notion of a 'fair day's work', which was considerably below that which management envisioned as desirable. The workers had their own informal standard, minutely calculated and translated into a certain number of units to be produced by each man during the day.

The Hawthorne findings thus defied the dominant management theory of the day. In Taylor's vision of the economic man, individuals would respond positively to incentive structures, give their maximum effort, and push their peers to do the same. What the management ideology failed to consider was that the workers did not respond as individuals, but as a social group. They had developed their own informal organisation, their own perceptions of what constituted a good day's work, and their own local response to management ideology. The BWOR study was the first to demonstrate empirically the perspectival gaps between management and the workers. In Baba's (2006: 88) words:

> Here was the first solid empirical evidence of informal organization (what we might call an occupational subculture or counter-culture), defined as the actual patterns of social interaction and relationships among the members of an organization that are not determined by management.

This informal organisation could be and was mapped by quantifying interactions among workers and by graphically depicting networks of relationships among the various work groups or cliques. It was seen to differ remarkably from the formal organisation, as laid out in the rules and policies of the corporation and that management had established to enable pursuit of corporate goals (Baba 2006). In this spirit of discovery of the social system, the informal organisation and its relation to the formal, the networks and local ideologies, anthropologists have continued to venture into organisations.

Ever since the days of the Hawthorne studies, many anthropologists have contributed to the feeding of trajectories of organisational anthropology.[4, 5] We say trajectories in the plural, because this is, first of all, a highly varied and rich field of research and, more important, we have no wish to stake out yet another sub-discipline in anthropology.[6] On the contrary, our aim is to zoom in on researching organisations, while maintaining the position that the study of organising is at the core of mainstream social anthropology. We wish to highlight some theoretical strands and lines of interest in the anthropological study of organisations.

Organisational anthropology in its contemporary versions can be traced back to essential concerns in anthropology – the study of social relations and social forms, in comparative perspective. As such, it embraces the study of social processes of organising and social forms of organisation in their entirety, and is not to be equated merely to the study of western formal organisations. In his seminal work, *Argonauts of the Western Pacific* (1922), Malinowski demonstrated how the *kula ring* of exchange was predicated upon and contributed to the shaping of the social and political organisation of the groups involved. In today's business corporations, exchange is also at the very core of the organisation, and structures much of the climate of social interaction and perspectives on both politics and competitors. Exchange was also at the heart of Fredrik Barth's (1966) interest in how social groups were formed. In his influential collection of essays on 'models of social organisation', he advances the view that social structures are formed by the strategic transactions of individuals, and thus by an unfolding of interactive social processes.

The study of organisation from an anthropological point of view also builds on classic insights gained from studies on the linkages between kinship systems and organisation. Such early anthropologists as Alfred Radcliffe-Brown (1922, 1931), Claude Meillasoux (1975) and Edmund Leach (1954, 1968) have demonstrated the pivotal role of kinship in structuring systems of exchange and political systems. Contrary to official standpoints, and as every ethnographer of contemporary organisations knows, kinship continues to play a role in recruiting, promoting and sharing resources. Think, for example, of the meaning of family ties in the *mafia*, the *camorra* and similar organisations (Blok 1988; Pine 2012), the significance of affinity in big business (Marcus and Hall 1992) and in charity organisations (Harr and Johnson 1991). While our contemporary organisations may embrace ideals of meritocracy, neutrality and formalism, in daily practice it is often the case that affinity, personal preference and improvisation gain the upper hand.

Organisations may be seen as circuits of power, in which normative frameworks are produced and globally diffused, where knowledge is crafted and circulated and from where packages of ideas are diffused. A prevalent view in the history of anthropology has been that systems of meaning and symbolic universes are shaped by or generated in systems of social relations (Hannerz 1992). Paraphrasing Marshall Sahlins, one could say that organisations emerge as 'dominant sites of cultural production' (1976: 211). In this view, organisations are sites where systems of meaning are cultivated, shaped, diffused and contested. Mary Douglas (1978), inspired by sociologists Durkheim and Fleck, proposed that the symbolic order represents the social order through the forms of 'group and grid'. In brief, 'group' referred to an individual's social position as inside or outside a bounded social group and 'grid' referred to an individual's social role within networks of social privileges and obligations. Individuals are expected to move across the dimensions, according to choice or circumstances. As the model developed, the mapping of cultures upon types of social organisation was transformed into a dynamic theoretical system, challenging methodological individualism (Douglas 2006).

Perhaps more starkly, Douglas's (1970) perspective on institutions as legitimised social groupings has been highly influential in shaping our understanding of how it is that institutions shape our ways of thinking and acting, and how thinking itself is dependent upon institutions, and continues to be so. There is a great deal of confusion around the terms 'institution' and 'organisation' and how they relate to each other. Sometimes, anthropologists and sociologists use the term 'institution' or 'institutional order' synonymously with organisation. Usually, though, an institution does not denote an organisation. In a general sense, institutions refer to a set of cultural rules that regulate social activities in patterned ways. In Ahrne's (1994: 4) words, '[o]rganizations are materialized institutions'. In the new institutional theory in organisation studies, institution represents 'a social order or pattern that has attained a certain state or property' (Jepperson 1991: 45). Douglas, however, used the word 'institution' in a way that overlaps largely with organisation, to mean a legitimised social grouping. With Douglas, we learn that different types of organisations prompt us to think different thoughts and respond to different emotions. Douglas did not suggest that we are merely mindless cogs in a machine; she convincingly demonstrated how institutions, the way we conceive of them, and the categories and rationalities they foster have significant implications for human agency.

If Douglas's notion of institution is one key entry point of anthropological interest in organisations, another is the notion of 'corporation', which may connote to an anthropologist any collective of individuals who act as one unit for one or several purposes. In common parlance, the most common conception of the corporation is a limited-liability joint-stock company. This legal person is now the dominant organisational and institutional form of our time, with characteristics that cannot be reduced to the individuals who own, manage and work for it (Bashkow 2012; Micklethwait and Wooldridge 2005). Through the production and dissemination of corporate ideology and normative ideals, it powerfully shapes the ways its members – its employees – think and act. It also moulds public discourse and practice through its public relations and marketing efforts, and contributes to the ideological transformation of the individual from producer to consumer. The limited-liability joint-stock company has become an agent *par excellence* of cultural production and, as Sahlins would have it, a site of cultural production. A thorough understanding of the corporation as an organisational form is essential if we want to understand the workings of organisations, and their implications for the lives of people.

As James Dow (1973) demonstrates, the concept of corporation has been the focus of a long-standing muddle over its meaning in anthropology. It has been used to connote various types of 'corporate groups' in the Parsonian-Weberian (Weber 1947: 145) sense of the term, as in *Verband* – a group that was characterised by closedness, an internal set of institutionalised norms and a norm-enforcing subgroup of leaders headed by a single individual (see, for example, Nadel 1951). It has also been used to connote special social units endowed with special rights and obligations, such as the segmentary lineage (see, for example, Fortes 1953; Fried 1957) or the system of landholding in village communities (Wolf 1955). At one point, the muddle reached such a thickness, Dow (1973: 906) recounts, 'that Befu and Plotnikov concluded that the structural properties of corporations, as they were conceived of in anthropology, were so common that "we do not regard them as critically important in the concept of corporation, since almost any social group will, according to these criteria, manifest "corporateness"' (1962: 314). Later, Cochrane (1971) wanted to eliminate the concept altogether unless it replicated the Anglo-American legal concept of corporation, while Goodenough (1971) argued that the word should be used as an emic symbol, in whatever way accords with the author's intuition (Dow 1973: 904). In anthropological terms, therefore, the business corporation of late industrialism, as a legal person with distinct rights and duties, is only one version of many varieties of the social and organisational form of the corporation. In the remainder of this book, it is this version of corporation that will be in focus.

A conduit for the anthropological study of business corporations has been the concept of culture. In the 1980s, after decades of silence, anthropology and organisation studies resumed a dialogue around the notion of culture (Wright 1994). The peak of interest in corporate culture and organisational culture in the 1980s and 1990s attracted large numbers of anthropology, organisation studies and management scholars to the study of systems of meaning and meaning-making in organisations.[7] In this whirlpool, anthropological contributions shed light on the 'native' taxonomies or classification schemes of professionals and how they were used to mark occupational boundaries within and across firms (Gregory 1983). The 'ways of knowing' of high-energy physics were uncovered (Traweek 1992), indicating how, almost imperceptibly, the lab site elicits certain forms of knowing and acting and discourages others.

Through their focus on culture, anthropologists have been able to uncover how actors in corporations have worked on managing meaning to construct a sense of organisational community and identity and to erect boundaries towards the outside and the 'other', all the while extending their communities across national borders. Culture may figure as an agile and alluring dimension in the creation of communities of belonging that fashion the understanding of corporate identity and the identity of workers, thereby exerting subtle ideological control (Finn 1998; Garsten 1994, 2008; Krause-Jensen 2011; Kunda 1992).

Evident in all these contributions is a keen eye to the organisation as a site of cultural production and diffusion and to the seductions and snares of organisational ideology. While organisational culture in organisation theory was generally seen as one factor among many in organisations, and one that glued the organisation together harmoniously, anthropologists have tended to see organisational culture as continuously negotiated and contested. Through anthropologists' recognition of the larger structures of influence and the asymmetries of power among various positions in organisations, anthropological contributions to the study of organisations were set apart from the general tendency in organisation theory.

IRON CAGES INSIDE OUT

'[A]nthropology,' Michael Herzfeld (1992: 45) writes, 'with its propensity to focus on the exotic and the remarkable, has largely ignored the practices of bureaucracy.' As he further notes, 'this silence is ... a remarkable omission. It is also suggestive.'

As the administrative aspects of an organisation, bureaucracies have much to offer in terms of oddities and discoveries for anthropologists. While we may think of them, in Weber's ideal sense (Lassman and Speirs 1994), as markers of modernity and rationality, freed of delusory rituals and cosmologies, it has been asserted that western bureaucracies are, in fact, havens for ritualistic practices, for the construction of taxonomic systems and for the crafting of cosmologies in ways that make them amenable to anthropological analysis (Britan and Cohen 1980; Handelman 1978, 1981; Riles 2006). Herzfeld (1992) demonstrated the symbolic roots of western bureaucracy, asking how it is that 'some people apparently become humourless automatons as soon as they are placed behind a desk?' Demonstrating how indifference is not a given emotional state, but is socially produced in certain organisational contexts, he questioned the underlying assumptions of rationality upon which western bureaucratic organisations are built. In doing so, Herzfeld simultaneously and playfully challenged the notion of 'western' bureaucracy. In his view (1992: 16):

> it is not at all clear what 'the West' is, even though its existence and its association with bureaucratic rationality are often assumed. By making central such a problematical identity, I seek the sort of productive discomfort that characterizes anthropology through continual realignments of cultural and social comparison. This is an approach that offers a perspective on how people contend with the forces that try to control who they are.

It is this productive discomfort that we believe to be essential in engaging with seemingly mundane and familiar organisational contexts. Indeed, we should be bewildered when bureaucrats appear forced to deny their own moral judgement, when codes of accountability appear as evidence of actual practice, or when classificatory systems tell us who is 'employable' and who is not. Understanding bureaucracy as a social phenomenon is largely to understand how conventions of rationality, formalism and indifference come into play, but also to understand people's ways of relating to bureaucracy as expressions of collectively moulded feelings and conventions. The Weberian 'iron cage' (Weber 1991 [1904]) thus traps individuals in systems based on ideas of rational calculation, efficiency and control, but also provides collective ground for recognised tensions and sentiments of outrage, frustration or comfort.

With reference to what is perhaps the pivotal example of an ideal-type bureaucracy – the state – Tim Mitchell (2006) has argued that 'the appearance of the state as a discrete and relatively autonomous social institution is itself a reification that is constituted through everyday social practices' (cited in Sharma and Gupta 2006: 8). The mundane arrangements of setting up and policing a frontier (one of the central tasks of the modern state) involves, in Mitchell's (2006: 180) words, 'a variety of fairly modern social practices – continuous barbed-wire fencing, passports, immigration laws, inspections, currency control, and so on'. These practices help manufacture something that becomes much more than the sum of the powers that constitute it, appearing as a structure containing and giving order and meaning to people's lives. The state, Mitchell (2006: 180) maintains, should not be studied 'as an actual structure', but as 'the powerful, apparently metaphysical effect of practices that make such structure appear to exist'.

This view invites us to study the state as an effect of structure, yet one that, in turn, has a structuring effect on practice. It invites us to think of the state as an effect of power and not automatically distinct from other organisational forms through which social relations are created and maintained – such forms as non-governmental organisations and business corporations. From this perspective, we do not assume a priori that the state is the central locus of power. Instead, as eloquently suggested by Sharma and Gupta (2006: 9), we need to figure out 'how "the state" *comes to assume* its vertical position as the supreme authority that manages all other institutional forms that social relations take' (italics in original).[8] If the state is perceived as differentiated from other institutional and organisational forms, then the question is: how did it come to be so?

The state has its own ways of seeing things, distributing people into slots, developing classificatory systems and interventions in accordance with defined problems and opportunities. Bureaucrats are trained to think in particular ways and to see the world accordingly. The great advantage of such tunnel vision, in James C. Scott's (1998) view is that it brings into sharp focus certain limited aspects of an otherwise far more complex and unwieldy reality. 'This very simplification, in turn, makes the phenomenon at the centre of the field more legible and hence more susceptible to careful measurement and calculation' (Scott 1998: 11). This aggregate, synoptic view of selective reality makes possible a schematic kind of knowledge, control and manipulation. Scott has shown how large-scale, modernist state projects of planning in various parts of the world have been made possible by a narrowing of vision, and by making legible the subjects of intervention. In Scott's opinion, legibility is a central problem of statecraft, because the state is, in many regards, blind to the realities it is set to govern. Technologies that render citizens, land or other resources legible make large-scale social engineering possible.

A central concern of anthropologists has been the examination of the ways in which bureaucracies in large-scale organisations make use of technologies that render subjects governable at a distance. A vast scholarly body of research has been produced by investigating the technologies of audit in public organisations, such as universities, hospitals and government agencies (see, for example, Shore et al. 2011). Bureaucracy orders and 'reads' social worlds through the technological toolkit it produces. It does this 'by moving persons among social categories or by inventing and applying such categories' (Handelman 1995: 280). As Barnett and Finnemore (2001: 412) have it, the power of bureaucracies and of international organisations generally resides in the fact that 'they present themselves as impersonal, technocratic, and neutral – as not exercising power – but instead as serving others; the presentation and acceptance of these claims is critical to its legitimacy and authority' (see also Ferguson 1990; Nyqvist 2008; Shore and Wright 1997).

Bureaucratic power is intimately connected to knowledge. An organisation's claim to knowledge rests largely on whatever information and expertise it can muster (see, for example, Rose and Miller 1992). Organisations are highly skilled in developing tools and technologies that assist them in the creation, administering, analysis, representation and dissemination of knowledge. Statistics, censuses, indexes, social security numbers and DNA profiles come to mind. One of the principal instruments of knowledge representation is the document. As noted by Annelise Riles (2006: 6), 'Many of the buzzwords of the moment – from transparency to accountability – are in practical terms calls to documentation' (Rosga 2005). Documents are 'artefacts of modern knowledge practices' (Riles 2006: 7), and they have a great deal to tell us about utopian visions of organising, of what is at stake, what is deemed worthwhile to document and what is not. Documents can teach us about the ways of knowing of people in the field, but also how people, objects and events are sorted into categories, visualised and made legible and therefore auditable.

ORGANIS-*ING*, ORGANIS-*ATION*

Despite the power of formal organisations to govern almost all aspects of our social lives, anthropologists have tended to ignore them, focusing attention on the transversal examination of anthropological problems, such as the construction of categorical identities, the negotiation of policy, decision-making procedures, and the asymmetries of influence between local and global levels of hierarchy. This has turned out to be both an advantage and a disadvantage. It allows for a tighter analytical focus on mainstream social science problems that may or may not have to do with organisations. It also allows for a process view on organisation, emphasising the social processes that tie actors, objects and ideas into assemblages and render some into more durable social figurations. On the flip side, it places anthropologists in a comparatively uncomfortable situation in relation to more systematic comparative analysis, and puts the advancement of anthropologically informed organisational theory on trial.

The general viewpoint in this volume is that of organisations as continuously in the process of formation, under constant modification and reproduction, although they can be temporarily stabilised, and show varying degrees of 'tightness'. The concept of organisation, as a 'social figuration' or a social order is thus broader than the concept of 'formal organisation'. When we speak here of formal organisation, we mean a social figuration that has achieved a degree of stability.[9] Chester Barnard (1968: 3), a management theoretician with a significant influence on organisation theory, put it simply when he described formal organisation as 'the concrete social process by which social action is largely accomplished'. Recent developments in organisation theory have pushed this processual view of organisation further, stressing the continuous modification and reproduction (Hernes 2008).

Ahrne and Brunsson (2011) suggest that organisation is a particular kind of social order, one that includes one or more of the elements of membership, hierarchy, rules, monitoring and sanctions. This view makes the distinction between organisation and environment less dramatic. Organisation can be found not only within, but also outside and among formal organisations.

Following Ahrne and Brunsson (2011), one of the key characteristics of a formal organisation is its membership. Members may be employees of a business corporation or a bureaucracy, elected representatives of a non-governmental organisation or individuals who have chosen to enter a voluntary association or a charity organisation as members. Members have differential access to the resources of the organisation – to its financial resources, central tenets of ideology, core body of knowledge or innermost secrets.

As the locus of connections between individuals, organisations are sites where individual actions can be transformed into social processes (Ahrne 1994). Organisations are typically stronger than individuals or networks and more persistent than either of them. By affiliation to an organisation, individuals can accomplish things they could not achieve alone. Organisations are circuits for transforming individual action into social action, and may empower people beyond their capacities as individuals. On the other hand, members of an organisation are also substitutable, albeit to varying degrees. Essentially, this means that the organisation does not stand or fall with single individuals, but tends to survive them. Consequently, there will usually be a degree of competition for positions among members, as evidenced in recruitment procedures, promotions, restructurings and layoffs. The management of an organisation is usually well aware of this aspect, and will use various forms of influence to spur a sense of competition and insecurity among members.

To be a member of an organisation, therefore, is to live with some measure of built-in friction. Barnard posits the 'zone of indifference' as the dimension of the relationship between management and individual members that animates authority relationships and cooperation within an organisation (Barnard 1968; Stewart 1989). In his view, cooperation depends on the individual accepting being controlled to some degree without questioning authority. We should add that the zone of indifference is also where resistance takes hold, as we start to question the very nature of the social contract between ourselves and the organisation. For the anthropological eye, this is an intriguing space for inquiry.

The formal organisation creates power, but also authority, and authority and organisation tend to go hand in hand. The authority of an actor typically relies to a large extent on the organisation's resource base and membership base, and extends authority founded on these. On the other hand, in cases in which there is no authority, there is hardly any degree of organisation. Authority – along with the exercise of power and control – is one of the most significant dimensions of organisation.

Moreover, the formal organisation is typically characterised as having its own norms or rules of social behaviour: there are expectations as to what one can, should and ought to do. In the words of March et al. (2000: 15), rules are 'the talk' of organisations. The formal organisation also dictates procedures to be followed by its members, thereby creating levels of conduct that are seen to be appropriate to that organisation. We can expect people to deal with these procedures in various ways: with acceptance, resistance, translation or ignorance. The rules and procedures are perhaps most clearly visible in a bureaucracy (think of the intricate web of rules and procedures in state bureaucracies). Yet, they are equally influential in other organisations, such as non-governmental organisations and business corporations – the many rules and procedures of global fast-food chains being a case in point (see Whitelaw, chapter 2 in this volume).

In the new institutional perspective of Meyer and Rowan (1977), formal organisations are systems of coordinated and controlled activities that arise when work is embedded in complex networks of technical relationships and boundary-spanning exchanges. In contemporary and complex societies, formal organisational structures are rooted in highly institutionalized contexts. Organizations must continuously deal with incorporating, editing or resisting the prevailing rationalised ideas by which they are influenced. New management trends, conceptions of work and employment, and understandings of social responsibility must be negotiated. They are producers of assemblages of ideas, norms and rules (Brunsson and Jacobsson 2000). Several chapters in this volume reveal the normative force of transnational management trends and universal bureaucratic norms, how they are wrestled with in the organisation, and the articulation and diffusion of assemblages of ideas.

The contributors to this volume have all had reason to inquire into the organisational dimensions of the organisations under study and to reflect upon their implications. Moreover, the volume includes different types of formal organisations, in which various dimensions of organisation can be seen to influence fieldwork as well as analysis. Membership, for example, implies different requirements for European Union (EU) bureaucrats than it has for Freemasons (see Thedvall, chapter 7, and Mahmud, chapter 12, in this volume).

A further qualification is that this book deals with so-called complex organisations. Although the notion of complexity may be a bit unwieldy and elusive, it captures some of the distinctive features of the type of organisations that attract our interest. Complexity in this context captures the high degree of internal differentiation of social positions and roles. The internal distribution of labour tends to be highly intricate, with spheres of expertise linking with each other.

Moreover, complex organisations tend not to be easily confined in spatial terms, but to be dispersed across space and to figure as translocalities, in Appadurai's (1996) terms; or as frameworks for flows of people, ideas, meanings and material objects (Hannerz 1992). We can also see that the organisations under scrutiny reveal a dense and nested pattern of social networks, with social ties criss-crossing units, departments, office locations, regions and nations. Forms of connectivity may appear at both formal and informal levels. Complexity also reveals itself at the cognitive level. The systems of knowledge, ideas and norms are highly differentiated, with systems of meaning only partly overlapping and congruent. Some organisations have larger inventories of differentiated ideas and meanings than others, and more or less complicated modes of handling them, by way of practices, routines and rules.

Anthropologists have tended to rebel against taking the organisational boundaries for granted, so as not to confine their ethnographic studies. There is often a wedge of dissociation between the emic understandings of the organisational boundaries and those of the anthropologist. Boundaries are not to be taken for granted in the delineation of the field and the unit of analysis, but as something to be empirically investigated. While this may have placed anthropologists at an analytical disadvantage in relation to the field of organisation theory, in which the boundaries of the formally defined organisation are often congruent with the empirical object of study, it has facilitated the questioning and problematising of boundaries. With Marc Augé (2009), we maintain that the notions of the frontier and the boundary are good to think with, as they create meaning in an otherwise unruly universe. And, critically, they provide leads to what there is to protect – what is really at stake.

FORMALITY IN BRACKETS

Our interest in formal organisations should not be understood merely as an interest in formality. Formal organisations house a great deal of informal social interaction. Anthropological studies of organisations are often credited with keeping a keen eye on the everyday happenings of organisational life. Recognition that the informal processes and structures of an organisation are as significant, if not more significant, than the formal processes and structures is one of the primary contributions of anthropology to the study of organisations. The Big Man of the formally recognised organisation may not be the same as the Big Man of the informal structure.[10] The informal, the personal and the intimate may promote, create, undermine or overthrow formal structures, and thus play a critical role in organising processes (Britan and Cohen 1980; Wright 1994). Because of their careful ethnographic practices, anthropologists have been credited with the ability to reveal and lay bare the everyday workings, the inner lives and the back stages of organisations. Intimacy, trust, deceit, small talk and gossip have all been the subject of scholarly contributions (see, for example, Ybema et al. 2009), testifying to the influence of Goffman's (1959) dramaturgical rendering of public life and life in 'total institutions' as being performed both front stage and back stage. The twin concepts suggest that we have (at least) two modes of presenting our selves: one when we are aware of the visibility of our actions for others and another when we let down our guard. Back stage is not a space relegated to secondary importance, however, but is as infused with meaning as is front stage. With present-day electronic forms of communication, switching between back and front stage takes on further complexity. Texting, emailing, Facebooking and Tweeting may seem like private ways of interacting, but with an errant keystroke (like hitting 'reply all'), back-stage communications can easily enter front stage. The interest in the informal, the unscripted and the intimate also bears witness to the general anthropological inclination to dig deeper into the great significance of small issues.

While the anthropological toolkit lends itself to fruitfully uncovering the intricacies of the informal, the back stage and the secret, we should not work on the assumption that what is less easily accessible is more likely to be true or authentic. Organisations continuously need to balance between front stage and back stage, the scripted and the authentic. Authenticity may be bestowed on that which is scripted and appears on front stage, as symbols of the 'true self' of the organisation. The trend in managerial rhetoric toward 'just being yourself' becomes an issue when it is turned into a managerial attempt to overcome a lack of joy, community and life inside organisations (Fleming 2009 and chapter 4 in this volume). And the transparent 'glass cage' of a corporate office building may work in tandem with more secretive organisational agendas (Krause-Jensen 2011).

The anthropological study of organisations thus brings to the fore the variability of organisational forms, the character of social relations that constitute and overthrow them, the forms of connectivity that bind them together and dissolve them, the norms underlying social interactions, the sanctions used to keep behaviour in its place, and the ways in which the distribution and exchange of resources contribute to the stabilising and ordering of social activities. The comparative dimension of anthropology alerts us to the variability and multiplicity of organisational forms, and allows for the identification of the universal.

Organisational anthropology is not to be seen as a sub-discipline of anthropology, then, but as deploying, adjusting, and advancing mainstream anthropological concepts and research tools for the study of organisations and processes of organising. How then, do we study such organisations?

WHERE THE ACTION IS

The anthropological study of complex societies, transnational processes, and global flows has led to an adaptation of ethnographic practices. Established modes of ethnographic practices have been adapted to the study of dispersed and shifting forms of organisation and to the study of professionalised, expertise-based communities. Ethnography has moved from its conventional single-site location, with a view to engaging with broader contexts of social, political and economic change, to multi-site observations and participation that trace the linkages among sites, people, ideas, money and products. By 'tracking' strategies, ethnographers are now tracing such processes as capitalist production, policy-making and social mobilisation across a multitude of sites and spheres. Macro- and micro-levels of observation are twinned not only by theoretical concerns, but also by ethnographic practices.

Laura Nader's (1974) invitation to 'study up' alerted anthropologists to the need to see connections among groups in society and to link groups and individuals to larger processes of change. Her call played a significant role in mobilising anthropologists to engage in the study of people in power, the privileged and people with resources. It recharged the linking of micro-structures to macro-structures through careful attention to 'vertical slices' of influence and the varying forms of social stratification and layering of society (Nader 1980). In the study of organisations, studying up can enhance our understandings of power relations and forms of dependency and control. As many anthropologists have experienced, studying up also challenges taken-for-granted understandings of our relationships with informants and requires a rethinking of the interrelated issues of access, methodology, attitudes and ethics (Nader 1974: 301).

Because power in contemporary forms of governance tends to be nomadic (Agamben 1998) and move along distributed networks in all directions, we need to look in all directions. Anthropologists are now following social processes by studying horizontally or 'sideways' (Hannerz 2006) – by 'studying through' (Reinhold in Shore and Wright 1997; Wright and Reinhold 2011). Studying sideways enables the ethnographer to engage with peers in related areas of expertise to examine the epistemological and ontological assumptions and practices of their peers as well as themselves. Sideways studies have facilitated the study of professional groups, across field sites, organisations and nation-state boundaries (see, for example, Hannerz 2004; Plesner 2012). By studying through, the ethnographer seeks to trace 'the ways in which power creates webs and relations between actors, institutions and discourses across time and space' (Shore and Wright 1997: 11). Studies of policy processes are particularly amenable to this type of approach, and such studies have been used to reveal how the motivations and assumptions of policy-makers inform the dominant ways that policy problems are identified (Wedel et al. 2005: 34). Similarly, negotiation processes and decision-making processes within and across organisations may be examined and understood by careful studying through.

The ethnographic tradition of following people around to figure out exactly 'what the devil they think they are up to' (Geertz 1983: 57–58) becomes all the more challenging given the globalised distribution of organisations and practices, and the increasingly dynamic nature of organisational roles. The trick, according to Marilyn Strathern (1995), is to keep an eye on 'where the action is'. Rather than assuming that the 'local' and the 'global' indicate orders of magnitude or scales of importance, we should attend to the ways in which people change their contexts of action, and thus endow phenomena with varying levels of significance. The local may not be firmly set and immobile, but may be situationally defined, temporarily spatialised.

In a world of shifting contexts, ethnographers have been creative in inventing ways of following people in their mobile contexts without separating them from their contexts. With mobile groups of professionals, 'shadowing' has assumed special importance in the field of organisation studies (Czarniawska 2007). Czarniawska maintains that ethnography needs to become more mobile, in order to grasp knowledge about people, objects and ideas that circulate globally. Static concepts of culture, organisation and society do not serve us well in studying people on the move.

Approaches to studying sideways and through, and tracing shifting contexts, allow for the tracking of forms of influence, but also introduce another set of concerns in relation to the forms of engagement with informants. In situations in which researcher and researched occupy similar social positions and share some degree of professional background, situations in which negotiations replace a researcher-imposed dialogue and the circulation of common concepts messes up an orderly division between the vocabularies of researcher and informant, emic and etic intermingle. This situation introduces another set of considerations, pertaining to reflexivity about one's position in social space and in relation to the informant – that has implications for interpretation and analysis. To be able to observe critically, to reflect upon and grapple with one's social position, is a crucial dimension of ethnographic fieldwork. Reflexivity, in Charlotte Aull Davies's perspective, is essentially 'a turning back on oneself, a process of self-reference' (1999: 4). Issues of reflexivity are particularly salient in ethnographic research, in which the relationship between the researcher and those being studied is particularly close, and the researcher's self is deployed as the primary research tool. Social anthropology, like social science in general, involves a series of mediations among different constructions of reality, in order to increase understanding of these various constructions of the social world in which they are situated (Aull Davies 1999: 214). In these mediations, reflexivity is central to ensuring a degree of accuracy and accountability in interpretations. Studying sideways and through, engaging with educated elites and professionals with related repertoires of knowledge, often embed the researcher in an illusion of 'cultural intimacy' (Herzfeld 1997) that may lessen her sensitivity to the implications of her positioning in the field. All the more reason, then, to take the reflexive analysis seriously and to recognise the collective understandings, the tacit agreements and the sources of bias that derive from the fields in which we operate (see also Bourdieu 2004).

In a general sense, as noted by Marcus, anthropology has been designed for 'a focus on the low rather than the high, on the ordinary rather than on the event' (Rabinow et al. 2008: 73). With the movement of anthropology into complex forms of organisations, into finance, technoscience, media and policy, the concepts and tools available for studying and analysing these new terrains are sometimes not attuned to them. As Rees (2008: 12) has it: 'The inevitable result is a profound mismatch between old concepts and new analytical requirements.' To some extent, the concepts and tools of the ethnographer need to be calibrated to the study of more complex, shifting and dispersed types of organisations. Hugh Gusterson notes that 'participant observation is a research technique that does not travel well up the social structure' (1997: 115). He suggests, rather, that ethnographers involved in studying elites and experts, power and politics, de-emphasise anthropology's defining research technique in favour of 'polymorphous engagements' (1997: 116). Such an approach to ethnographic fieldwork, Gusterson holds, would involve interaction with informants across a number of dispersed sites and sometimes in virtual form, and would require the connection of data eclectically from a disparate array of sources in many ways.

In addressing the challenges and opportunities of contemporary anthropology, Westbrook (2008: 23) contends that the enterprise of ethnography may need to be re-imagined. As part of this process, he advocates a 'conversational ethnography', by which conversation becomes a key form of engagement with the informant.

> Why cannot conversations, organized in some academically respectable fashion and branded 'ethnography', be used to confront, think through, the chaos of contemporary social life? If that is a possibility, then the effort to refunction ethnography ... is largely the effort to think through a practice of fostering certain kinds of conversation with people who know something, or perhaps exercise power, in such a way that we learn something about their world? (Westbrook 2008: 23)

Whether conversational or not, ethnography in complex organisations raises the question of the possible, conceivable and reasonable forms of engagement between researcher and researched. The affinity that often exists among bureaucrats, officials, managers and scholars may be disturbing to the scholars, but is something we need to consider in the study of organisations. Douglas Holmes and George Marcus (2005) have coined the term 'para-ethnography', to describe the knowledge practices of actors that, in many ways, are similar to those of the ethnographer. People in organisations try to make sense of their environments, to reduce equivocalities and to find metaphors to guide them in their daily work. To some extent, they engage in ethnography-like types of knowledge seeking. This affinity may engender new forms of collaboration and new insights.

We subscribe to the value of attentiveness to the polymorphous and shifting forms of social engagements. We also believe that the more classic version of participant observation is useful in understanding the social worlds of elites and managers in complex organisations. The study of organisations should not, by definition, lead us into contentment with single-stranded and one-dimensional relationships with our informants or with short-term and restricted access. Several of the authors in this book have undertaken what we would describe as long-term, intense fieldwork and have cultivated multi-dimensional relationships with people in the field. We need to adapt and sharpen our analytical tools, however, in order to capture what we are looking for in organisational contexts. How we engage with the field should ideally be a question of the nature of the questions we ask. What do we want to know?

The main themes in this book revolve around the process of gaining access to and moving ahead in organisational fieldwork and the ways in which our contributing authors have engaged with these themes in a variety of organisational settings as they address a variety of questions. What are the challenges and opportunities involved in doing anthropology in complex organisational settings? How have these challenges been engaged in, solved or circumvented? How have anthropologists capitalised on their opportunities? What forms of relationships and types of engagement have developed between the fieldworker and informant/interlocutor? What types of knowledge are gained? And, not least, what are the blind spots?

OUTLINE OF THE BOOK

Section one, entitled 'Corporate corridors', provides us with insights into the construction of intimacy and authenticity, identity and culture in various business settings. The chapters in this section show how engaging with private corporations requires the researcher to learn the ropes, both cognitively and physically. They reveal how conversations with actors in corporations often entail layers of reflexivity and calls upon the ethnographer to employ a repertoire of forms of engagements. They also demonstrate the holding power of corporate ideology, and how it can be used by managers to make claims on life at large.

One form of engagement is the embodied ethnography of going to work. In chapter 2, Gavin Whitelaw reports his conducting of 'observant participation' (Wacquant 2003) from behind the counter of a Japanese convenience store. Such an endeavour enables an emphasis on both appearance and practice. Working as a convenience store clerk, he learned, step by step, the productions of impersonal familiarity and acquired an understanding of the complexities of power, intimacy and trust.

The familiarity that Jakob Krause-Jensen describes in chapter 3 is the fine line between insider and outsider. From his position in the human resource department of a corporation, where notions of values and culture are central, Krause-Jensen notes a deceptive familiarity with environment, informants and the issues at stake. He discusses the benefits and challenges not only of participation, but also of contributing to the field of ethnography, and upholds the position that active participation and contribution was, in fact, seen as a condition for his access and presence.

Peter Fleming argues in chapter 4 that the quest for expressions of authenticity in corporate business may be seen as processes of co-optation. He suggests that in the 'just be yourself' management philosophy now in vogue, the symbolic boundary between work and non-work is manipulated and blurred so that productivity may be increased. At contemporary workplaces, efforts are made to capture 'life itself' and put it to work, to the extent that both work and life become increasingly managed.

Emil A. Røyrvik sheds light in chapter 5 on the corporation as a social institution with a social mandate. In his study of managers in a Norwegian transnational corporation, Røyrvik holds multiple roles and positions as both researcher and adviser, which he uses in his collaborative approach to fieldwork. He suggests that, as ethnographers, we enact the boundaries that co-construct the worlds we seek to understand; he calls such sideways-glancing fieldwork 'oblique ethnography'.

In the second section, 'Policy arenas', policies in and of formal organisations are conceptualised as powerful tools for governance. Here the authors describe how policies both connect to *and* cut through organisations. The chapter demonstrates that following the trajectory of policies in and between organisations provides us with crucial insights into the workings of the organisation itself.

In chapter 6, Anette Nyqvist proposes that doing ethnography in a culture of accessibility calls for enhanced sensibilities regarding the nuances and degrees of access. Studying through policy issues in a Swedish bureaucracy may seem like access heaven, given that the first act on public accessibility to government documents and officials in Sweden was passed in 1776. Nyqvist notes that access is processual and relative: front stage has back stages and back stages have front stages. She suggests that studies of the official and formal may be seen as ethnography from the sidelines of centre stage.

In chapter 7, Renita Thedvall provides 'thick descriptions' of Weberian-type bureaucratic decision-making processes in the EU – where formal rules and defined hierarchies aim at developing politically neutral policies. Thedvall's meeting ethnography provides insights into the ways a particular policy-making culture works in the EU setting and how 'cultural intimacy' plays a significant role. She must continuously negotiate her access and suggests that her 'punctuated entries' into the field mirror the diversity of organisations that comprise EU.

Halvard Vike's contribution in chapter 8 provides insights into the workings of an organisation that experienced a failed reform. Vike explores the social life of organisations and notes that these formally organised worlds are actually simplified cultural models and representations that denote given social patterns and specific ideas and interests. Vike conceptualises the ethnographer of such complex organisations as an 'organisational nomad' who moves around within the organisation and dives in and out of it and, in doing so, helps us to grasp the complex workings of the organisation.

In 'Working the network', the third section of the book, the notion of 'network' is conceptualised not as a contrast to organisation, but rather as a pivotal part of human organisation and a necessity for gaining access and engaging in ethnographic fieldwork. Networks are seen as nurturing organisational ties and connections, and as undermining and challenging them, because they cut across organisational boundaries.

In chapter 9, Christina Garsten describes an intricate and intertwined 'economy of connections' at work within the organisational world of think tanks. Through the story of her struggles to find a way into the nebulous field of think tanks in Washington, DC, Garsten analyses the importance of personal ties and shows how the vast network can be viewed as a contemporary 'gift economy', in which connections and the exchange of information serve as gifts – key components in the ways in which think-tank professionals work.

Brian Moeran shows how the practice of networking, of making connections, can pave the way for ethnographic fieldwork in and of organisations. He demonstrates how connections may reveal power and open up fields of local knowledge. Moeran's argument in chapter 10 is that connections constitute a crucial aspect of the organising of organisations and that interpersonal connections imply a certain cultural style. The power of social connections may thus be manifested as the power of cultural styles.

Åsa Boholm sheds light on bureaucratic social interaction and the social aspects of decision-making in chapter 11. Her study reveals the complexity of seemingly simple decision-making, how networking in and among organisations shapes decision-making processes, and the way in which such processes may be seen as shared cooperative activities. Decisions, Boholm argues, absorb uncertainty about future courses of action, and serve to establish and construct temporarily stable organisational alignments.

The final section of the book is called 'Opaque worlds'. Here we examine the visible and the obscured, transparency and opacity. The authors attempt to catch a glimpse of that which is difficult to see and examine what is revealed. The chapters also demonstrate that being on the margin or on the outside may be just as fruitful as being at the centre of the organisation. At the margins, key issues may be highlighted and underscored, and knowledge may be gained about what is guarded, valuable or secret.

In her study on Freemasons described in chapter 12, Lilith Mahmud makes use of her outside position and status as a 'profane ethnographer'. Mahmud conceptualises Masonic lodges as legal and secretive organisations. She returns to classical anthropological debates and links the anthropology of secret societies to more contemporary studies of secretive practices within bureaucratic organisations. In the process of becoming the profane ethnographer, Mahmud sheds light on the organisation's complex negotiations of power, intimacy and belonging.

In his research on the particular constellation of communicative values of the European Central Bank in chapter 13, Douglas R. Holmes aligns his ethnographic inquiry with the organisational anthropology of the organisations that he studies, and he shows how they address questions of contemporary culture and political economy. Holmes sheds light on the efforts made to materialise the values of and within the European Central Bank, and demonstrates how organisational design may be derived from systems of ideas. Transparency, Holmes asserts, sustains the collaborative regime; indeed, in most banks, transparency is considered crucial.

In her contribution, chapter 14, Tara Schwegler shows how the inability to engage in direct observation can be productive, and she uses a method of 'strategic absence' to shed light on power struggles within the formal structure of Mexican bureaucracy. Bureaucracy, she argues, is in constant motion, and ethnographers cannot stand still to observe it. Anthropological studies of organisations therefore require heightened ethnographic agility and flexibility. Schwegler holds that the binary opposition of absence versus presence obscures permutations of long-term participant observation and mobile inquiry.

Finally, in chapter 15, 'Momentum', we return to the initial claims of this book and the contributions that anthropological research on organisations can make to the discipline and to the advancement of organisation studies. Maintaining that the study of social processes of organising are at the heart of anthropology, there are both methodological and theoretical advances to be made in venturing into this terrain. It is to these contributions we now turn our attention.

NOTES

1. See F. J. Roethlisberger and W. J. Dickson, *Management and the Worker* (1939). The Hawthorne studies still invigorate debate around their results. See for example Lewitt and List (2009).
2. Long before the Hawthorne studies, at the beginning of the 19th century, anthropologists were involved in the British colonial administration (Baba 2006). The expansion of administrative services and trade to India and West Africa meant that anthropological expertise was sought by the colonial government to offer knowledge about local cultures. While working for the colonial administration provided early experiences in organisational anthropology, we do not go into detail on this topic here. See Baba (2006), Baba and Hill (2006), Kuper (1983) and Pels and Salemink (1999) for elaborations on the early connections of anthropology to colonial administrations.
3. Frederick Winslow Taylor published his influential book, *The Principles of Scientific Management*, in 1911. The monograph laid out the principles of Scientific Management – what was then considered modern organisation and decision theory – and has had a huge impact on shaping organisations and managerial ideals. Taylor's influence rendered him 'The Father of Scientific Management' and his approach is also often referred to as 'Taylorism'. See, for example, Waring (1991), for an extended overview of the impact of Scientific Management.

4. Susan Wright (1994) identifies three periods when anthropologists made particular contributions to organisational studies: the 1920s, when both disciplines were in their early stage of development; the 1950s and 1960s; and the 1990s.

5. A range of works testifies to the ambitions to capture contours of the field of organisational anthropology. See, for example, Jiménez (2007), Hamada and Sibley (1994), Wright (1994) and Ybema et al. (2009). Some contributions have had a stronger focus on providing insights into ethnographic approaches to organisations. See, for example, Cefkin (2009), Gellner and Hirsch (2001), Neyland (2008), Schwartzman (1993) and Moeran (2005).

6. Organisational anthropology denotes, in our view, that the organising processes and organisational dimensions of social interaction are the focus of interest. It does not entail articulating clear boundaries of a sub-field. From this viewpoint, it shares areas of interest with the anthropology of work, the anthropology of business and applied anthropology.

7. In the field of organisation studies, Alvesson (1993), Brown (1995), Czarniawska-Joerges (1992), Frost et al. (1985), Hatch (1997), Martin (2002) and Schultz (1994), among others, contributed works aimed at capturing organisational culture. Gender dimensions in organisations have been highlighted e.g. by Mills and Tancred (1992), Gherardi (1995), and Acker (2006). See also Fisher (2012) and Blomberg (2009).

8. From early on, anthropologists have contributed to uncovering the workings of the state and its bureaucracies. Scholars like Radcliffe-Brown (1940) and Sahlins (1963), and later Ferguson and Gupta (2002), Hansen and Stepputat (2001), Mitchell (1991) and Troullot (2003) have critically challenged the assumption that the state is a fixed, a priori given unity and empirical object, entailing a concentration of power.

9. Norbert Elias's (1978) concept of 'figuration' provides a link between the individual and society. It posits figuration as a network of interdependencies formed by individuals. Figuration is a dynamic, shifting set of connections and relationships that achieve varying degrees of stability.

10. A Big Man typically refers to a highly influential person in a tribe in Melanesia and Polynesia. As Marshall Sahlins (1963) demonstrated, the authority of a Big Man is not always formally recognised, but rests primarily on the power of persuasion and on acquired wisdom. The Big Man, as the term suggests, has a large group of followers, both from his own community and from the outside. In return for their support, which is essential in enhancing his status, he provides protection and assistance on various matters.

REFERENCES

Acker, J. (2006) 'Gender and organizations', in J. S. Chafetz, *Handbook of the Sociology of Gender* (New York, NY: Springer).

Agamben, G. (1998) *Homo Sacer. Sovereign Power and Bare Life* (Stanford, CA: Stanford University Press).

Ahrne, G. (1994) *Social Organizations: Interaction Inside, Outside and Between Organizations* (London: Sage).

Ahrne, G. and N. Brunsson (2011) 'Organization outside organizations: The significance of partial organization', *Organization*, Vol. 18, No. 1, pp. 83–104.

Alvesson, M. (1993) *Cultural Perspectives on Organizations* (Cambridge: Cambridge University Press).

Appadurai. A. (1996) *Modernity at Large: Cultural Dimensions of Globalization* (Minneapolis, MI: University of Minnesota Press).

Augé, M. (2009) *Pour une anthropologie de la mobilité* (Paris: Éditions Payot et Rivages).

Aull Davies, C. (1999) *Reflexive Ethnography* (London: Routledge).

Baba, M. L. (2006) 'Anthropology and business', in H. J. Birx, ed., *Encyclopedia of Anthropology* (Thousand Oaks, CA: Sage).

Baba, M. L. and C. E. Hill (2006) 'What's in the name "applied anthropology"? An encounter with global practice', in C. E. Hill and M. L. Baba, eds, *The Globalization of Anthropology*. NAPA Bulletin 5 (Washington, DC: American Anthropological Association).

Barnard, C. (1968) *The Functions of the Executive*, Thirtieth Anniversary Edition (Cambridge, MA: Harvard University Press).

Barnett, M. and M. Finnemore (2001) 'The politics, power, and pathologies of international institutions', in L. A. Martin and B. A. Simmons, eds, *International Institutions: An International Organization Reader* (Cambridge, MA: Massachusetts Institute of Technology and the IO Foundation).

Barth, F. (1966) *Models of Social Organization*, Occasional Paper No. 23 (London: Royal Anthropological Institute).

Bashkow, I. (2012) *An Anthropological Theory of the Corporation* (Chicago, IL: Prickly Paradigm Press).

Befu, H. and L. Plotnikov (1962) 'Types of corporate unilineal descent groups', *American Anthropologist*, Vol. 64, No. 2, pp. 313–327.

Blok, A. (1988) *The Mafia of a Sicilian Village 1860–1960: A Study of Violent Peasant Entrepreneurs* (Oxford: Blackwell).

Blomberg, J. (2009) 'Gendering finance: Masculinities and hierarchies at the Stockholm Stock Exchange', *Organization*, Vol. 16, No. 2, pp. 203–225.

Bourdieu, P. (2004) *Science of Science and Reflexivity* (Cambridge: Polity Press).

Britan, G. and R. Cohen, eds (1980) 'Toward an anthropology of formal organizations', in *Hierarchy and Society: Anthropological Perspectives on Bureaucracy* (Philadelphia, PA: Institute for the Study of Human Issues).

Brunsson, N. and B. Jacobsson (2000) *A World of Standards* (Oxford: Oxford University Press).

Cefkin, M., ed. (2009) *Ethnography and the Corporate Encounter: Reflections on Research in and of Corporations* (New York, NY: Berghahn Books).

Cochrane, G. (1971) 'Use of the concept of the "corporation": A choice between colloquialism or distortion', *American Anthropologist*, Vol. 73, No, 5, pp. 1144–1150.

Czarniawska, B. (2007) *Shadowing and Other Techniques for Doing Fieldwork in Modern Societies* (Malmö: Liber).

Czarniawska-Joerges, B. (1992) *Exploring Complex Organizations: A Cultural Perspective* (Newbury Park, CA: Sage).

Douglas, M. (1970) *How Institutions Think* (New York, NY: Routledge).

—— (1978) *Cultural Bias* (London: Royal Anthropological Institute).

—— (2006). 'A history of grid and group cultural theory', http://projects.chass.utoronto.ca/semiotics/cyber/douglas1.pdf (accessed 3 July 2012).

Dow, J. (1973) 'On the muddled concept of corporation in anthropology', *American Anthropologist*, new series, Vol. 75, No. 3, pp. 904–908.

Elias, N. (1978) *What is Sociology?* (London: Hutchinson).

Ferguson, J. (1990) *The Anti-Politics Machine: 'Development', Depoliticization, and Bureaucratic Power in Lesotho* (Cambridge: Cambridge University Press).

Ferguson, J. and A. Gupta (2002) 'Spatializing states: Toward an ethnography of neoliberal governmentality', *American Ethnologist*, Vol. 29, No. 4, pp. 981–1002.

Finn, J. L. (1998) *Tracing the Veins: Of Copper, Culture, and Community from Butte to Chuquicamata* (Berkeley, CA: University of California Press).

Fisher, M. S. (2012) *Wall Street Women* (Durham, NC: Duke University Press).

Fleming, P. (2009) *Authenticity and the Cultural Politics of Work: New Forms of Informal Control* (Oxford: Oxford University Press).

Fortes, M. (1953) 'The structure of unilineal descent groups', *American Anthropologist*, Vol. 55, No. 1, pp. 17–41.

Fried, M. H. (1957) 'The classification of corporate unilineal descent groups', *Journal of the Royal Anthropological Institute*, Vol. 87, No. 1, pp. 1–29.

Frost, P., L. F. Moore, M. R. Louis, C. C. Lundberg and J. Martin, eds (1985) *Organizational Culture* (Thousand Oaks, CA: Sage).

Garsten, C. (1994) *Apple World: Core and Periphery in a Transnational Organizational Culture*, Stockholm Studies in Social Anthropology 33 (Stockholm: Almqvist and Wiksell International).

—— (2008) *Workplace Vagabonds: Career and Community in Changing Worlds of Work* (Basingstoke: Palgrave Macmillan)

—— (2009) 'Ethnography at the interface: "Corporate social responsibility" as an anthropological field of enquiry', in M. Melhuus, J. Mitchell and H. Wulff, eds, *Ethnographic Practice in the Present* (Oxford: Berghahn Books).

Geertz, C. (1983) *Local Knowledge* (New York, NY: Basic Books).

Gellner, D. and E. Hirsch, eds (2001) *Inside Organizations: Anthropologists at Work* (Oxford: Berg).

Gherardi, S. (1995) *Gender, Symbolism and Organizational Cultures* (London: Sage).

Goffman, E. (1959) *The Presentation of Self in Everyday Life* (New York, NY: Anchor Books).

Goodenough, W. H. (1971) 'Corporations: Reply to Cochrane', *American Anthropologist*, Vol. 73, pp. 1150–1152.

Gregory, K. (1983) 'Native-view paradigms: Multiple cultures and culture conflicts in organizations', *Administrative Science Quarterly*, Vol. 28, pp. 359–376.

Gusterson, H. (1997) 'Studying up revisited', *Political and Legal Anthropology Review*, Vol. 20, No. 1, pp. 114–119.

Hamada T. and W. E. Sibley, eds (1994) *Anthropological Perspectives on Organizational Culture* (Lanham, MD: University Press of America).

Handelman, D. (1978) 'Introduction: A recognition of bureaucracy', in D. Handelman and E. Leyton, eds, *Bureaucracy and World View: Studies in the Logics of Official Interpretation*, Social and Economic Studies No. 22 (St John's: Institute of Social and Economic Research, Memorial University of Newfoundland), pp. 1–14.

—— (1981) 'Introduction: The idea of bureaucratic organization', *Social Analysis*, Vol. 9, pp. 5–23.

—— (1995) 'Comment', *Cultural Anthropology*, Vol. 36, No. 2, pp. 280–281.

Hannerz, U. (1992) *Cultural Complexity: Studies in the Social Organization of Meaning* (New York, NY: Columbia University Press).

—— (1998) 'Other transnationals: Perspectives gained from studying sideways', *Anthropology and the Question of the Other*, special issue, ed. T. Maranhão, *Paideuma* 44, pp. 109–123.

—— (2004) *Foreign News: Exploring the World of Foreign Correspondents* (Chicago, IL: Chicago University Press).

—— (2006) 'Studying down, up, sideways, through, backward, forward, away and at home: Reflections on the field worries of an expansive discipline', in S. Coleman and P. Collins, eds, *Locating the Field: Metaphors of Space, Place and Context in Anthropology* (Oxford: Berg).

Hansen, T. B. and F. Stepputat, eds (2001) *States of Imagination: Ethnographic Explorations of the Postcolonial State* (Durham, NC: Duke University Press).

Harr, J. E. and P. J. Johnson (1991) *The Rockefeller Conscience: An American Family in Public and in Private* (New York, NY: Scribner Brothers).

Hatch, M. J. (1997) *Organization Theory: Modern, Symbolic and Postmodern Perspectives*. Oxford: Oxford University Press.

Hernes, T. (2008) *Understanding Organization as Process: Theory for a Tangled World*. (London: Routledge).

Herzfeld, M. (1992) *The Social Production of Indifference: Exploring the Symbolic Roots of Western Bureaucracy* (Chicago, IL: University of Chicago Press).

—— (1997) *Cultural Intimacy: Social Poetics in the Nation-state* (New York, NY: Routledge).

Holmes, D. and G. E. Marcus (2005) 'Cultures of expertise and the management of globalization: Toward the refunctioning of ethnography', in A. Ong and S. J. Collier, eds, *Global Assemblages: Technology, Politics, and Ethics as Anthropological Problems* (Oxford: Blackwell).

Jepperson, R. L. (1991) 'Institutions, institutional effects, and institutionalism', in W. W. Powell and P. J. DiMaggio, eds, *The New Institutionalism in Organizational Analysis* (Chicago, IL: University of Chicago Press).

Jiménez, A. C., ed. (2007) *The Anthropology of Organisations* (London: Ashgate).

Krause-Jensen, J. (2011) *Flexible Firm: The Design of Culture at Bang & Olufsen* (London: Berghahn Books).

Kunda, G. (1992) *Engineering Culture: Control and Commitment in a High-tech Corporation* (Philadelphia, PA: Temple University Press).

Kuper, A. (1983) *Anthropology and Anthropologists: The Modern British School* (London: Routledge and Kegan Paul).

Lassman, P. and R. Speirs, eds (1994) *Weber: Political Writings*. Cambridge Texts in the History of Political Thought (Cambridge: Cambridge University Press).

Leach, E. R. (1954) *Political Systems of Highland Burma: A Study of Kachin Social Structure* (London: Bell and Sons).

—— (1968) 'Social structure: The history of the concept', in *International Encyclopedia of the Social Sciences*, Vol. 14 (New York, NY: Macmillan).

Lewitt, S. D. and A. List (2009) *Was There Really a Hawthorne Effect at the Hawthorne Plant? An Analysis of the Original Illumination Experiments*. Working Paper 15016 (Cambridge, MA: National Bureau of Economic Research).

Malinowski, B. (1922) *Argonauts of the Western Pacific: An Account of Native Enterprise and Adventures in the Archipelagos of Melanesian New Guinea* (London: Routledge and Kegan Paul).

March, J. G., M. Schultz and X. Zhou (2000) *The Dynamics of Rules* (Stanford, CA: Stanford University Press).

Marcus, G. (1995) 'Ethnography in/of the world system: The emergence of multi-sited ethnography', *Annual Review of Anthropology* Vol. 24, pp. 95–117.

Marcus, G. and P. D. Hall (1992) *Lives in Trust: The Fortunes of Dynastic Families in Late Twentieth-century America* (Boulder, CO: Westview Press).

Martin, J. (2002) *Organizational Culture: Mapping the Terrain* (Thousand Oaks, CA: Sage).

Meillasoux, C. (1975) *Femmes, greniers et capitaux* (Paris: Librarie François Maspero); trans. as *Maidens, Meal and Money: Capitalism and the Domestic Community* (Cambridge: Cambridge University Press, 1981).

Meyer, J. W. and B. Rowan (1977) 'Institutionalized organizations: Formal structure as myth and ceremony', *American Journal of Sociology*, Vol. 83, No. 2, pp. 340–363.

Micklethwait, J. and A. Wooldridge (2005) *The Company: A Short History of a Revolutionary Idea* (London: Phoenix).

Mills, A. J. and P. Tancred, eds. (1992) *Gendering Organizational Analysis* (London: Sage).

Mitchell, T. (1991) 'The limits of the state: Beyond statist approaches and their critics', *American Political Science Review*, Vol. 85, No. 1, pp. 77–96.

—— (2006) 'Society, economy, and the state effect', in A. Sharma and A. Gupta, eds, *The Anthropology of the State: A Reader* (London: Blackwell).

Moeran, B. (2005) *The Business of Ethnography: Exchanges, People and Organizations* (London: Berg).

Nadel, S. F. (1951) *The Foundations of Social Anthropology* (New York, NY: The Free Press).

Nader, L. (1974 [1969]) 'Up the anthropologist: Perspectives gained from "studying up"', in D. Hymes, ed., *Reinventing Anthropology* (New York, NY: Random House).

—— (1980) 'The vertical slice: Hierarchies and children', in G. M. Britan and R. Cohen, eds, *Hierarchy and Society: Anthropological Perspectives on Bureaucracy* (Philadelphia, PA: Institute for the Study of Human Issues).

Neyland, D. (2008) *Organizational Ethnography* (Thousand Oaks, CA: Sage).

Nyqvist, A. (2008) *Opening the Orange Envelope: Risk and Responsibility in the Remaking of Sweden's National Pension System*. Stockholm Studies in Social Anthropology 64 (Stockholm: Stockholm University).

Pels, P. and O. Salemink, eds (1999) *Colonial Subjects: Essays on the Practical History of Anthropology* (Ann Arbor, MI: University of Michigan Press).

Pine, J. (2012) *The Art of Making Do in Naples* (Minneapolis: University of Minnesota Press).

Plesner, U. (2012) ' Studying sideways: Displacing the problem of power in research interviews with sociologists and journalists', *Qualitative Inquiry*, Vol. 17, No. 6, pp. 471–482.

Rabinow, P. and G. E. Marcus, with J. D. Faubion and T. Rees (2008) *Designs for an Anthropology of the Contemporary* (Durham, NC: Duke University Press).

Radcliffe-Brown, A. (1922) *The Andaman Islanders: A Study in Social Anthropology* (Cambridge, MA: Cambridge University Press).

—— (1931) *The Social Organization of Australian Tribes* (London: Macmillan).

—— (1940) 'On joking relationships', *Journal of the International African Institute*, Vol. 13, No. 3, pp. 195–210.

Rees, T. (2008) 'Introduction: Today, what is anthropology?', in P. Rabinow and G. E. Marcus, with J. D. Faubion and T. Rees, *Designs for an Anthropology of the Contemporary* (Durham, NC: Duke University Press).

Riles, A., ed. (2006) *Documents: Artifacts of Modern Knowledge* (Ann Arbor, MI: University of Michigan Press).

Roethlisberger, F. J. and W. J. Dickson (1939) *Management and the Worker* (Cambridge, MA: Harvard University Press).

Rose, N. and P. Miller (1992) 'Political power beyond the state: Problematics of government', *British Journal of Sociology* ,Vol. 43, No. 2, pp. 172–205.

Rosga, A. (2005) 'Transparency and accountability: Trafficking in the rule of law', paper presented at Cornell Law School, 7 February.

Sahlins, M. D. (1963) 'Poor man, rich man, big man, chief: Political types in Melanesia and Polynesia', *Comparative Studies in Society & History*, Vol. 5, pp. 285–303.

—— (1976) *Culture and Practical Reason* (Chicago, IL: University of Chicago Press).

Scott, J. (1998) *Seeing Like a State* (New Haven, CT: Yale University Press).

Schwartzman, H. B. (1993) *Ethnography in Organizations* (Thousand Oaks, CA: Sage).

Schultz, M. (1994) *On Studying Organizational Cultures: Diagnosis and Understanding.* (Berlin: Walter de Gruyter).

Sharma, A. and A. Gupta, eds (2006) *The Anthropology of the State: A Reader* (London: Blackwell).

Shore, C. (2011) 'Studying governance: Policy as a window onto the modern state', in C. Shore, C., S. Wright and D. Peró, eds, *Policy Worlds: Anthropology and the Analysis of Contemporary Power* (New York, NY: Berghahn Books).

Shore, C. and S. Wright, eds (1997) *Anthropology of Policy: Critical Perspectives on Governance and Power* (New York, NY: Routledge).

Stewart, D. W. (1989) 'Barnard as a framework for authority and control', *Public Productivity Review*, Vol. 12, No. 4, pp. 413–422.

Strathern, M. (1995) 'The nice thing about culture is that everyone has it', in M. Strathern, ed., *Shifting Contexts: Transformations in Anthropological Knowledge* (London: Routledge).

Taylor, F. W. (1911) *The Principles of Scientific Management* (New York, NY: Harper and Winslow).

Traweek, S. (1992) *Beamtimes and Lifetimes: The World of High Energy Physicists* (Cambridge, MA: Harvard University Press).

Troullot, M. R. (2003) 'The anthropology of the state in the age of globalization: Close encounters of the deceptive kind', in *Global Transformations: Anthropology and the Modern World* (New York, NY: Palgrave Macmillan).

Wacquant, L. (2003) *Body and Soul: Notebooks of an Apprentice Boxer* (Oxford: Oxford University Press).

Waring, S. P. (1991) *Taylorism Transformed: Scientific Management Theory Since 1945* (Chapel Hill, NC: University of North Carolina Press).

Weber, M. (1947) *The Theory of Social and Economic Organization*, trans. A. Henderson and T. Parsons (New York, NY: Bedminster Press).

—— (1991 [1904]) *The Protestant Ethic and the Spirit of Capitalism* (London: HarperCollins).

Wedel, J., C. Shore, G. Feldman and S. Lathrop (2005) 'Toward an anthropology of public policy', *Annals of the American Academy of Political and Social Science*, Vol. 600, No. 1, pp. 30–51.

Westbrook, D. A. (2008) *Navigators of the Contemporary: Why Ethnography Matters* (Chicago, IL: University of Chicago Press).

Wolf, E. (1955) 'Types of Latin-American peasantry: A preliminary discussion', *American Anthropologist*, Vol. 57, pp. 452–471.

Wright, S., ed. (1994) *Anthropology of Organizations* (London: Routledge).

Wright, S. and S. Reinhold (2011) '"Studying through": A strategy for studying political transformation. Or sex, lies and British politics', in C. Shore, S. Wright and D. Peró, eds, *Policy Worlds: Anthropology and the Analysis of Contemporary Power* (New York, NY: Berghahn Books).

Ybema, S, H. Wels, D. Yanow and F.H. Kamsteeg, eds. (2009) *Organizational Ethnography: Studying the Complexities of Everyday Life* (Thousand Oaks, CA: Sage).

Section one
Corporate corridors

2
Counter intelligence
The contingencies of clerkship at the epicentre of convenience culture

Gavin Hamilton Whitelaw

INTRODUCTION: CONVENIENT ACCESS

Convenience stores epitomise easy entry. They must. As a franchise business format predicated on round-the-clock availability, high customer volume and rapid product turnover, convenience stores emphasise speed over specialisation and place 'function before fuss' (Iyer 2009: 140). In doing so, they constitute a class of competitive global retail which has carved a niche for itself on street corners and roadsides. In Japan in particular, these stores are now ubiquitous. A business template introduced to Japan less than four decades ago, convenience stores (or *konbini*) are now an ¥8 trillion yen ($10 billion)[1] industry (JFA 2012). The nation's 43,000 stores are visited by the equivalent of one-third of Japan's population on a daily basis.

In this following chapter, I discuss my process of entry into the organisational life of a particular convenience store in Tokyo. I reveal how work – a combination of observation, training, and labour – established my credibility within a store while providing me with valuable practical knowledge of day-to-day store operations and large issues affecting the industry. Moreover, access to these stores through work challenges assumptions of franchises as merely monolithic outlets devoid of cultural meaning. By serving behind the counter, I came to better understand the semi-autonomous character of franchises and, in the case of Japan, how owners of the stores work to maintain a particular level of standardised service while actively engaging with the company headquarters to which they are contractually bound. Clerking at a *konbini* provided me with this important organisational 'interface' (Garsten 2010) and allowed me to see more clearly the dynamics of power, intimacy, and trust that undergird the most mundane of contemporary institutions.[2]

INITIAL ENTRIES: SHOPPING FOR A STORE

When I arrived in Tokyo to begin my research in the fall of 2004, I wanted to combine structural and institutional analyses of these stores with 'observant participation' (Wacquant 2003, 2005) as a clerk behind the counter. My proposed approach was not novel. From Chicago School studies in the

1930s to recent ethnographies in organisations as diverse as slaughterhouses (Pachirat 2011), boxing gyms (Wacquant 2003), and sweatshops (Prentice 2008), researchers consciously employ work as a method and means for understanding how 'culture is lived, and in the living of it, constituted' (Turner 2000: 52). Post-war ethnographic research on Japan is particular rich in organisational and workplace studies that utilise work in this way. From the corporate offices and the service sector (Allison 1994; Creighton 1992; Goldstein-Gidoni 1997; Matsunaga 2000) to artisan workshops (Kondo 1990; Moeran 1984; Singleton 1989) and volunteer organisations (Nakano 2005; Stevens 1997), ethnographers have frequently turned to work and embodying a certain form of labour in order to more fully explore the construction of identities, ideologies, and power structures in contemporary Japanese society.

While the meaning of embodiment may vary from researcher to researcher and study to study, the value of embodying the labour anthropologists seek to understand is clear. As one anthropologist puts it, 'without that visceral experience, we do not know what questions to ask, nor what the meaning of the response is, nor can we fully understand the complexities of difference in the work setting, and how they interact' (Roberts 2008: 76). Moreover, the very negotiations and questions that accompany an embodied approach invigorate the ethnographic writing that follows. An embodied approach provides monographs with potential compelling narrative structures while casting fresh light on old methodological questions (Whitelaw 2008: 62–63).

Although committed to working in a *konbini*, once in Tokyo the prospect of finding an appropriate field site suddenly seemed more daunting. As a customer, I had access to more than enough stores. But finding a *konbini* where the owner or manager would allow me behind the counter to conduct research was not straightforward. First, there was the question of what kind of *konbini* should be the focus of my efforts. Within a 15-minute stroll of my apartment were several dozen *konbini* alone. They ran the gamut from major national chains and regional franchises to independent local shops. Furthermore, the conditions of the stores varied considerably depending on their location. Some stores slumbered on quiet back streets in residential neighbourhoods. Others buzzed with activity in the midst of business districts. One thing was clear, despite the *konbini*'s homogeneous image, there was not an 'average' or 'typical' store.

To get started, I selected six *konbini* in my immediate neighbourhood and patronised them on a regular basis. I often made several visits a day in hopes of learning a bit more about how the stores operated and the kinds of people who used them. My technique might best be described as 'hanging out' (Spradley 1980), a layman's term for 'participant observation' used by some anthropologists. A Japanese friend gave my approach a less neutral emic gloss: '*tamuro*' (loitering). Loitering had its limits, though. The least obtrusive places for me to position myself in a store were in front of the magazine rack or beside the photocopier. In both cases, my back was typically to the aisles and counter – the two zones of the store that held the most interest and activity. When possible, I used one of the convex store security mirrors to keep an eye on the activity going on behind me. Seeing my reflection staring back at me within the store did less to unsettle my identity than to remind me of how suspicious what I was doing probably appeared to others.

In truth, usually there was not much going on in these stores for me to observe. The store staff remained distant, at times as stationary as the products on the shelves. My attempts at engagement did not get very far. To strike up a conversation at the counter was predicated on me spending money and resulted in little more than a few words being exchanged. Even after several weeks of regular visits, I found little indication that the people working behind the counter differentiated me from the rest of the customers who used the store. An aisle-based approach, I realised, left me with only a partial perspective on these stores.

The conditions and limits I encountered in hanging out at *konbini* galvanised my interest in finding another position. The 'help wanted' (*sutaffu boshū*) notices taped to store windows were an obvious avenue for me to explore, but I was initially hesitant. I was uncertain about walking in cold off the street and effectively communicating my research objectives to a complete stranger. My trepidation wore off enough to make some initial inquiries, but these attempts fizzled, again at the counter. In one *konbini*, a sullen clerk simply told me that the owner wasn't in and asked me to 'come back later'. At another store, the posted position had been filled a week earlier. 'I forgot to take down the advertisement,' the manager apologised.

I also toyed with a more 'top-down' approach: directly contacting the corporate headquarters of a particular *konbini* chain and requesting to carry out research as a clerk. My interactions with the corporate side of the industry until that point were always open and amicable but remained at arm's length and filtered through the measured smiles of public relations department representatives who met me armed with glossy brochures and references to company websites. A top-down approach had certain advantages, but it also had the potential of restraining me and influencing the direction of the project.

Instead of writing to companies, I chose to talk with friends. I turned to my acquaintances and the association and networks with which I was involved to help assist me in searching for a store in which to carry out my research. This rather conventional approach has proven successful for a number of anthropologists (see Bestor 2003: 315). At every opportunity, I asked people I knew if they had an acquaintance who owned or operated *konbini* and to whom they could introduce me. It was this approach that eventually put me behind the counter of a *konbini* called Daily Yamazaki.

A FOOT IN THE DOOR

My path into Daily Yamazaki began in October, when my landlord told me about the Wakamatsus.[3] The Wakamatsu family owned a local Daily Yamazaki franchise. At the time of my research, Daily Yamazaki was Japan's fifth largest convenience store chain and belonged to Yamazaki Baking, Japan's largest bread manufacturer. The convenience store division had grown from

Yamazaki Baking's bread distribution network. Many of the early Daily Yamazaki franchisees were the former owners of bread stores and pastry shops who decided to shift, expand, or revitalise their businesses through converting to a convenience store format. The Wakamatsu family belonged to this category and had expanded a former family business in the 1990s. The convenience store franchise they owned was located not far from where I was living.

My landlord accompanied me to my meeting with the store's chief supervisor (*senmu*), the younger brother of the franchise owner. We crowded into the narrow, cigarette smoke-suffused confines of the *konbini*'s backroom, or 'backyard', to talk with *senmu*. My landlord's introduction was brief: 'This is Gavin. He wants to study *konbini*. Thanks for your help.' His job now over, he squeezed past me and ducked out the service door leaving me on my own to handle the rest. My research 'pitch' felt more like a fumble. The space was so cramped that standing up to hand my business card to *senmu*, my knee struck the trashcan and I nearly dropped my card on the floor. Confidence draining with each passing minute, I talked about my lack of knowledge, understanding and experience with the actual day-to-day functioning of convenience stores and said that I wanted to know how these stores were understood and used by customers and workers as well as the community around them. *Senmu* lit another cigarette and scoffed.

'I don't think this is the right place for you then,' he said. 'There isn't much "community" around here…This is a business district (*bijinesu-gai*)… It's empty (*gara gara*) on the weekends. Even the coffee shops are closed.'

Unsure if this was an indirect way of telling me 'no', I persisted by saying that I would be happy to 'volunteer' at the store. Our conversation lurched forward again.

'This isn't a typical convenience store (*futsū no konbini ja nai*),' he warned pulling a shopping basket half-full of packaged food to the foot of his desk. He began scanning the contents of the basket. He passed a handheld device over the bar code of each item then hit a button on a computer keyboard in front of him. '*Konbini* research …' he huffed, gesturing to the basket of food beside him with disgust. 'Look at this waste (*haiki*)! Shameful (*Mottainai*).' Lighting his third cigarette, he rotated in his chair to look at the store's work-shift schedule on the board behind him. 'We just hired a few new people. But if all you want to do is learn about store operations and are OK working without pay, it's fine for you to get some experience here for a few months. Don't let your research get in the way of the customers, though.' Fifteen minutes later, I left the store with a dog-eared photocopy of the store's service manual to read, a new plastic wrapped uniform and instructions to return to the shop at 7:30 a.m. on Saturday for training.

A VOLUNTARY BEGINNING

From my first Saturday morning shift onward, I was treated much the same way that any new employee would be. The understanding was that when in uniform, I would be ready to do the tasks expected of other part-time staff. I even punched in and out on a timecard when I was on duty, a requirement of all staff and an easy way for the management to keep track of my comings and goings.

For training, *senmu* put me in the care of the store manager (*tenchō*). *Tenchō* was a heavy-set woman in her early fifties, who wore faded blue jeans, baggy t-shirts and tied colourful bandanas on her head to keep her hair out of her face. Like *senmu*, she, too, was a heavy smoker. *Tenchō* assigned me weekend morning shifts initially, because they were the slowest and the customers more forgiving. During my four days of in-store training, counterwork was a primary focus: greeting customers, running the register, bagging purchases and counting money. A certain level of competence and efficiency was required with each of these tasks in order to ensure that the store ran smoothly.

Each shift began in a similar fashion: I arrived at the store 15 minutes early, punched in, and then pulled on my uniform – a basic short-sleeve zippered jacket with generous pockets. The fabric was a grey and white gingham with red and yellow piping. The new uniform gave off the faint smell of popcorn. A tiny silver tag on the sleeve reminded me that the material I was wearing was made from recycled plastic, a fact that made me feel strangely close to many of the store's products.

Five minutes before the shift began, *tenchō*, another part-time worker and I gathered in front of a yellowing poster in the store's backyard and repeated the 'Seven Fundamental Service Phrases' (*Sekkyaku Nana Daiyōgo*). *Tenchō* led the chorus.

'*Irasshaimase, ohayōgozaimasu* (Welcome, good morning),' *tenchō* said.

'*Irasshaimase, ohayōgozaimasu*,' we repeated.

Tenchō said the phrase, this time boosting her voice and stretching out the penultimate syllable as if trying to wrap it around some fictitious customer at the other end of the backyard.

'*Irasshaimase, ohayōgozaimaaasu*,' we responded, this time with greater emphasis.

Learning to produce and reproduce such service phrases, first in the *konbini*'s back stage then at the counter, forced me to reflect on how curious some of these now standard expressions actually were. The greeting, '*Irasshaimase, ohayōgozaimasu*', for example, is now the hallmark of the *konbini* service model, yet it is an interesting socio-linguistic turn of phrase as well. It fuses two different forms of greeting that in standard Japanese are usually kept distinctly separate. '*Irasshaimase*' (welcome) is typically used by merchants when greeting customers in a transactional environment. No verbal response is expected from the customer. '*Ohayōgozaimasu*', (good morning) on the other hand, is an everyday greeting exchanged between friends, acquaintances, co-workers, students and teachers. Saying *ohayōgozaimasu* establishes a particular reciprocal context for a relationship and etiquette dictates that the receiver should promptly answer with the same greeting (Whitelaw 2008: 67). During conversations with industry experts, it was suggested that such hybrid phrases date back to the 1960s and 1970s when Japanese companies began establishing American franchises on native soil. Faced with translating English operation manuals and transposing an American concept of 'friendliness' into a Japanese retail context, a decision was made to combine existing expressions and create something grammatically new and yet culturally familiar. Whether intentional or not constantly repeated phrases like '*irasshaimase, ohayōgozaimasu*' shift the atmosphere of the selling space in subtle ways. *Tenchō* revealed to me another benefit to these greetings. While dissolving some of a store's uniqueness and intimacy, their repeated usage combined with a turn of the clerk's head or a lifting of the eyes help keep shoplifting down.

At the counter, the first task of a fresh shift of clerks was to confirm all the money on hand, machine by machine, a procedure known as *rejitenken* (register check), or in Daily lingo, *rejiten*. Clerks squared those amounts with how much the registers indicated the drawers should contain. Any discrepancy, even a single yen, was dealt with immediately. The register greatly aided in these calculations and adjustments. *Konbini* cash registers are highly sophisticated data collection and processing machines. They gather consumer data, archive transactions and can even be used to place product orders or check on store stock. With the turn of a key, the registers become calculators ready to regurgitate reams of sales data on receipt paper or allow the clerk to add up the money in the drawer, coin by coin. During training, *tenchō* instructed me on the order of operations. 'It takes practice,' she warned me. Standing to one side, I observed her glide through the task of logging onto the machine and counting the money in the drawer. Counting numerous yen notes quickly required a technique that seemed mechanically simple from a distance. But when I tried to repeat what I had seen, the task demanded choreography of the fingers that my hands refused to master. *Tenchō* took to physically positioning my fingers in the correct configuration for counting bills.

I was also trained on how to ring up and bag a customer's purchase. Once again, *tenchō* made the task look simple and basic, but with the move from observation to practice, I floundered. Finding the location of the bar code for some products was challenging. Before a transaction could be processed, consumer data had to be collected with the press of one of eight clientele keys (*kyakusō kī*). The clientele keys were coloured coded by gender (pink for female, blue for male) and broken down by age category: 'senior' (50 or older), 'adult' (30–49), 'young adult' (15–30), 'child' (0–15). Bagging required sensitivity to the kinds of items being purchased. The first rule was to check to see if the customer wanted any food, like *obentō*, warmed. On the label of each *obentō* was a number that corresponded with a setting on the store microwave. Hot and cold foods needed to be kept separate. Heated *obentō* were placed in light brown plastic bags with wider bottoms so that products remained flat. Chopsticks, spoons and forks must accompany the purchase when appropriate. The necessary utensils were to be placed in the bag, preferably on top of the heated food. Only napkins were self-service. 'Personal' products like sanitary napkins and condoms should be treated with care and placed in brown paper bags and taped closed. Products with strong odours or that might leak – *tofu*, shampoo and dishwashing detergent – were first put in thin, clear plastic bags before being placed in the larger plastic bag with other items. Finally one had to judge the appropriate size and number of plastic bags necessary to accommodate a given purchase. The store stocked six different sizes and shapes of plastic bag. *Tenchō* pointed out each size and gave an example of what kind of purchases each bag was appropriate for.

Further training also took place during my lunch break in the store's backroom. On my first day, *tenchō* gave me permission to take as much 'loss' (*rosu*) as I wanted from the shopping basket next to the trashcans. 'Loss', also known as *haiki shōhin* (waste products) – or simply *haiki*, was food that was near or past its selling date (*shōmikigen*) and, according to the industry and government regulation, needed to be removed from the shelves and disposed of by the store. As I turned to see what was on the *haiki* menu, *tenchō* added that eating such food was not 'standard' convenience store practice. From the looks of the empty spaghetti *obentō* package, wrapping, and fork lying in the garbage, it was obvious that one co-worker had already gleaned and consumed her meal from the basket of loss. The food remaining for me included a couple of misshapen *onigiri*, an *obentō* made with deep fried chicken, and another wrapped plastic platter of day-old 'filling' spaghetti haphazardly leaning on its side. I took the deep fried chicken. *Tenchō* appeared worried that I might be holding back and scooped up several *onigiri* to tempt me. 'You are living alone, aren't you? How do you eat? Take them home.' I declined her kind offer.

She gave me permission to heat the *obentō* in one of the microwaves at the front counter, reminding me, though, that while in the store, loss should always be eaten in the backyard. When I returned, I found *tenchō* standing beside the trash methodically destroying the unclaimed food items that remained in the basket. In the backyard, it seemed, loss had an even shorter shelf life. My appetite wilted as she tore into spaghetti *obentō*, poured its contents into one garbage can and threw the plastic plate, lid, and cellophane wrapping into another. *Tenchō* shifted her body so that my heated lunch and I could return to the chair. After the spaghetti, she set upon the *onigiri*. She handled the doomed food in the backyard with far less concern than the same food at the counter when a customer was purchasing it. Her movements were quick and efficient. She rotated her fist and stripped the *onigiri* of its plastic covering. The mound of rice plummeted into the trashcan with a muffled smack. The smell of tomato sauce mingled with stale cigarette smoke and I half-heartedly ate my lunch.

THE CHRISTMAS SHIFT

My training ended in early October and by December I began to feel settled as Daily Yamazaki's volunteer clerk. I had grown accustomed to the store's operative flow. *Tenchō* no longer reminded me about what to do or when to do it, nor did she emerge from the backroom whenever a customer approached my register. Working the register also came to feel more natural. I no longer fumbled with change, forgot to give out receipts, or made mistakes in selecting the proper bag size. The faster and smoother my transactions at the counter became, the fewer stares I seemed to receive from customers.

One afternoon, *tenchō* introduced me to a part-time housewife who had been hired recently and asked me to help train her at the register. I accepted. A few mornings later, *tenchō* again asked for my assistance, this time it was filling in an evening shift because one of the other clerks had an appointment and the store would be shorthanded. Again I accepted, and refused an offer to be paid, feeling it was the least I could do for the assistance the store was giving me with my research. The following day, I sensed a shift in backyard relations. *Tenchō* treated me to a cup of hot coffee and the co-worker I assisted began to share with me his passion for American motorcycles. Later that month I received two more emergency requests and similar offers to be compensated. I took the extra shifts but continued to refuse money party out of principle: I had agreed not to be paid and was doing fine without a wage. Moreover, my voluntary status provided me with freedom and flexibility. But an arrangement that I found to be convenient was growing more uncomfortable for the people I was assisting. By filling in shifts for actual workers and refusing pay I was throwing a delicate, reciprocal relationship with the store and its management out of kilter.

On Christmas Eve, balance was restored when I agreed to dress in a synthetic Santa Claus suit and hock Christmas cakes in front of the store. Christmas cake selling is annual industry-wide sales event. The practice pits chain against chain, store against store. *Senmu* was traditionally in charge of Daily Yamazaki's seasonal cake campaign and the job of wearing a Santa suit and selling cakes on the sidewalk outside the store typically fell in his lap. Despite his love of pastry, he had come to loathe Christmas. When I accepted the request to become Santa and take to the sidewalk Christmas Eve, *senmu* look visibly relieved.

There were three varieties of Daily Yamazaki Christmas cakes that year. The cheapest was a no-frills chocolate cake that sold for ¥1050 ($13.17). The most expensive was the ¥2200 ($25.24) double-layer whipped cream (*namakurīmu*) deluxe cake with candles and a plastic Father Christmas face perched at the top. While the rest of Daily Yamazaki's regular store staff remained warm inside the store, I spent a cold, blustery nine hours manning a table on the sidewalk outside the store selling cakes. Nakata, the store's Operation Field Consultant, or OFC, joined me in the early evening during the peak hour of sales. OFCs are service representatives dispatched by the chain headquarters to assist franchisees with the operating of their shops. Thanks to the collective effort on both sides of the store's glass doors, by 10 p.m. we had sold 147 of the 150 cakes *senmu* ordered. My efforts on the exterior contributed to nearly half of those sales, placing our store among the top Christmas cake selling Daily Yamazaki franchises in the Tokyo metropolitan area that year.

Upon returning the nylon beard and red suit to the store's backroom near midnight on Christmas Eve, *senmu* gave me one of the unsold deluxe cakes to take home, followed with an envelope of cash to reimburse me for my nine hours of work and a formal request that I consent to being hired part-time by the store. He stressed the difficulty he and *tenchō* were having finding dependable help to properly fill shifts. With *senmu* making the offer, it was difficult to decline. And so, on Christmas Eve, I shed my position as volunteer and went on the books as part-time staff.

ENTERING THE OFF STAGE

In becoming a paid, part-time clerk, my work-shift load increased. Not only was there greater incentive for me to work, but I also felt more obliged to fill in shifts and reciprocate for the three months of assistance that *senmu* and *tenchō* had given my research. As a result of the extra hours, I began to see Nakata more often as well. Nakata visited the store twice a week, usually in the afternoon. Nakata maintained an energetic air, whisking into the store in his suit, tie and jacket. He drove a butter yellow Volkswagen Beetle with the Daily Yamazaki emblem on its doors. He was often late for his appointment at the store and would apologise, usually with the excuse that parking caused him problems. Occasionally Nakata donned a store uniform when he was required to be outside of the backroom working on something, but normally he simply took off his coat and sat down with *senmu* to look at sales data. *Tenchō* seemed to keep her contact with Nakata to a minimum. At best, there was a general ambivalence toward Nakata. No particular care was taken in preparing for his visits. The crew was not reminded on the days he was scheduled to appear, no attempt was made to ensure that the floors were especially clean or that the backyard was in order. Even the gleaning of unsold packaged food continued as usual.

On the fourth Monday of each month, Nakata and *senmu* paid a visit to *senmu*'s older brother's restaurant in a neighbouring ward to look over the store data from the preceding month. To my surprise, I was invited to attend their January meeting. 'It's time for you to meet *shachō*,' as *senmu* referred to his older brother in the context of the store. 'Your help selling Christmas cakes was very appreciated and *shachō* wants to thank you personally.'

Nakata didn't learn about my being invited until minutes before we were to depart and he seemed less than pleased with the arrangement, but he also didn't have much choice. He himself had seen me stamping off the December cold in a synthetic Santa suit outside the store's entrance.

Senmu, Nakata and I left Daily Yamazaki at 1:40 p.m. We piled into Nakata's butter yellow VW Beetle that was illegally left parked outside the store with its hazard lights flashing. Not expecting an additional passenger, Nakata had to make room in the back seat of the car for me to sit by restacking piles of folders and advertisements. *Senmu* didn't take much notice of the chaos in the back seat. Sitting down in the front seat, he immediately asked Nakata about how much a car like this cost. Nakata deflected the question with some statistical data about the VW's dimensions and turning radius. The most important fact about the vehicle was that it was easy to park.

A picture of Nakata's baby son sat on the dashboard of the car. *Senmu* asked about the photo and Nakata admitted that it was a New Year's greeting card that he had not sent and was planning to give in person to one of his clients. 'Didn't I send you one of these cards?' he asked *senmu*.

'Probably', *senmu* responded. 'My wife deals with all that stuff.'

The car ride over to *shachō*'s restaurant gave *senmu* a chance to give me an informal tour of the neighbourhoods where *senmu* and his siblings grew up. Nakata, acting like a chauffer, remained silent. The restaurant was empty when we arrived and we were greeted first by the chief, then by *shachō* himself wearing his white chef's uniform. At university, *shachō* belonged to the school's judo team and his body retained that low centre of gravity. He ushered us to a table at the far end of the restaurant then disappeared into the back kitchen returning with a tray of coffee, which he passed to those seated at the table, keeping one cup for himself. Around us on the walls hung maps of Italy and empty bottles of grappa in wicker baskets suspended from nails. *Senmu* sat beside his brother. *Shachō* owns both the restaurant and convenience store. Rather than asking about the franchise's fiscal health, *shachō* first inquired about his younger brother's health. *Senmu* was struggling with high blood pressure and high cholesterol.

'Go easy on the sugar,' *shachō* admonished his sibling. *Senmu* just sneered and tore open the packet, flicking every last grain into the hot beverage in front of him. Heaving his thick arm over the chair next to him, he toyed with the paper sugar packet while listening to Nakata and his brother beginning to talk.

Nakata produced a thick stack of printouts on the store's quarterly earnings from his bag. December was a bad month despite the high sales in Christmas cakes. Nakata ran his fingers over a page of data. Things appeared to be picking back up, but the store needed to do close to a million yen in average daily sales to make up for a sluggish December. Nakata handed the stack of paper to *shachō* to look at himself.

Nakata felt the solution to improving sales lay in the types of products being sold. He started with the topic of alcohol. The store needed to do more to increase alcohol sales. Data suggested that evening alcohol sales at the store were uncharacteristically low given the area. Nakata suggested putting another glass case in the store to feature beers and sweetened wine coolers. *Senmu* grimaced and asked where they would find room. Having worked evenings, I could visualise *senmu* thinking that more alcohol would increase his nightly work. At 9 p.m. every evening, he sighed as the dollies containing heavy boxes of beer and soda rolled off the truck. *Senmu* bore a deep grudge against alcohol. Drinking beer had been eliminated from his diet but he still had to get on his hands and knees to organise and stock the refrigerated shelves.

Nakata countered that on the contrary, more alcohol and display space was needed to catch the latent demand of the evening crowds. *Senmu* frowned. Only a few nights before he mentioned how much business the store was now doing between 9 p.m. and 10 p.m. 'Overtime (*Zangyō*),' he surmised. 'Companies are not hiring new people and making those who have jobs work longer hours.'

The discussion grew livelier when Nakata started discussing the data on the store's losses. Nakata pointed out that the store was having some shrinkage as a result of shoplifting (*manbiki*). Sales figures indicated that women's fashion magazines were disappearing from the shelf without being paid for. *Senmu*, however, seemed unconcerned with the *manbiki*. The topic only made *senmu* grow more frustrated.

Senmu redirected the discussion and started asking if Nakata had any information about the rumours that a competing *konbini* chain was about to launch a new competitive menu. Nakata leaned back in his chair. He, too, seemed to sense a shift.

'I wouldn't worry much,' Nakata responded, almost annoyed but still trying to smile. 'Next month Daily...' *Senmu* grimaced, 'Frankly, Daily's *beihan* (rice-based food) tastes poor. The *onigiri*... the *obentō*... the rice is hard. Seven's[4] and Lawson's *onigiri* (rice balls) are soft. Seven's *obentō* are really tasty.' With this last comment, *senmu* threw his hand in the direction of the door. Just around the corner from the store stood one of Japan's veteran 7-Eleven franchises. Nakata scribbled a few words in a notebook open on the table. 'You have a point. There are some foods we need to work more on. But we are doing well with bread. Bread is something Daily has confidence in.' *Senmu* lashed out again, 'Then why is there some bread that we can't stock?' He pointed out that the Lawson chain can order certain Yamazaki bread products, but Yamazaki's own convenience store cannot. Nakata grew defensive and tried to put the Lawson's long-standing account with Yamazaki Bread in perspective. He noted that Daily Yamazaki has access to more products that Lawson cannot order.

At last *shachō* stepped in to cool tensions down. Turning to his brother he said that the store crew needed to work on *maedashi* – making sure products are visible and shelves look filled. The important thing was not to make customers disappointed (*gakkari sasenaiyōni*). He then questioned the OFC about product loss and was updated that the store was averaging ¥10,000 a day loss with a little less on weekends when fewer prepared foods are ordered.

Shachō did not end the conversation there, however. He wanted some straight talk from Nakata on the condition of the Daily Yamazaki chain itself. Nakata started to discuss conditions at some of the other stores in Daily's vicinity, but *shachō* rephrased the question saying he was interested in store numbers nationwide. Nakata shifted in his seat and admitted that the chain was facing greater competition. Yamazaki was phasing out its old franchise contracts and offering these owners new franchise packages. The old franchise arrangement was simply not profitable for the chain or the owner. With the new contract fees came more services that customers demanded. It was the way the industry was headed. *Senmu* and *shachō* listened quietly.

Shachō responded to Nakata's update with an update of his own: the family was considering not renewing their store contract. *Senmu* wanted to return to the issue of *konbini* competition, but focused on the current Daily location. There were new *konbini* opening around the area. Could a 'Seven' appear soon? It wasn't likely according to Nakata. *Senmu* agreed but then added that Shinsengumi, a competing chain, seemed more aggressive and willing to set up a store almost anywhere. 'They're springing up all over.'

The discussion of competition quieted spirits. Nakata downed the last of his coffee in a gulp and we prepared to leave. Walking to the door, Wakamatsu quizzed Nakata about the Daily Yamazaki's new Hot Daily, a new model of Daily Yamazaki with a bakery attached. Nakata appeared to have recovered from the intense questioning and said that there was one being built a few subway stops away. 'You should take a look.'

On our way back to the store, I again squished myself in the back seat next to Nakata's suit jacket, a large Daily Yamazaki paper bag that read: 'We assist in supporting friendly lifestyles.' Pointing at the new high rises Nakata said he wanted to live in a new building like that. It would be OK to have a *konbini* or a supermarket nearby for shopping, he said, but he disliked living on a shopping arcade (*shōtengai*). 'It's too tightly knit (*komakai*).' We took a back street to the store in hopes of avoiding afternoon traffic. *Senmu* guided Nakata past a small corner bakery. *Senmu* pointed out that this bakery also used to belong to the Yamazaki Bread production *keiretsu* (subsidiary chain).

'Is that right?' said Nakata.

Senmu huffed, 'There really is a lot you don't know.'

A few weeks later, am/pm *konbini* introduced its new *obentō* series, a joint venture product with Gyūkaku, a popular restaurant chain specialising in barbecue dishes. The tie-up made national news when it was announced. Shortly after that, Daily Yamazaki headquarters dispatched a team from their service division to the Wakamatsu's store to rearrange product locations and boost store sales. For a month or two, there was some noticeable improvement, but in June two new *konbini* opened within a block of Daily Yamazaki's door and sales began to weaken once again.

IMPERSONAL FAMILIARITY AND THE INTIMACIES OF CONVENIENCE CULTURE

My involvement with Daily Yamazaki and its various points of interface revealed the training, effort, concerns and struggles that lie behind the store's seemingly seamless functioning (Whitelaw 2008). Through clerking, I participated in an ongoing production of impersonal familiarity that gives convenience stores speed and appeal. While in uniform, I contributed to an atmosphere that releases store staff and customers from certain obligations and which differentiates the *konbini* from other species of local retail. In the back stage of store operations, my presence offered an occasion to exert a bit of leverage in contractual relations with the chain headquarters.

The convenience store's emphasis on efficiency, standardisation and calculability sharply contrasts with prevailing notions of Japanese society and, in particular, neighbourhood commerce. Store contracts and proprietary distributions channels wed the *konbini* to larger corporate interests while disembedding their operations from local economies and community concerns. The *konbini*'s competitive global retail format places this commercial outlet in league with fast food chains and hypermarts – the very genre of late capitalist 'nonplace' (Augé 1995) that robs main street of its distinctive character (Kunstler 1993; Ritzer 1993) while undermining conventional modes of ethnographic inquiry. However, approaching *konbini* from behind the counter complicates such readings. Furthermore, the convenience store's success cannot simply be laid at the feet of demographic shifts and technological advances. The persistence of difference and the layers of negotiation within a seemingly standardised store format and retail experience help highlight the critical and creative role that owners and store managers play in grafting this national marketing node and global retail model to the routines and sensibilities of particular main streets, neighbourhoods and other commercial spaces.

Working behind the counter reveals that the cultural integration of this particular institution is not seamless, nor are its notions of convenience uncontested or universally embraced. Although *konbini* support an increasingly divergent range of lifestyles, their expansion generates new discourses and anxieties about the nature of this success and its wider social implications. The super-saturation of convenience stores in urban areas and fierce competition contribute to the demise of less competitive stores, large and small, and expose fissures in long-standing merchant alliances and customer relationships. As family-run franchises and, in some cases, the last remaining local corner store, *konbini* nourish the masses and dreams of middle-class entrepreneurship. Yet the *konbini*'s pre-packaged single portion meals and reliance on round-the-clock part-time labour further disrupt a post-war social ideology based on family, stability and life-long employment.

In reaction to earlier provocations about the importance of flows (Appadurai 1996, 2001), scholars have begun to call for greater attention to points of interface (Garsten 2010) and sites of contact (Condry 2011) when studying global organisational forms and mass culture. This shift is a welcome one. The *konbini* connects interests in mass culture and organisations. An approach to understanding them, and the ways human beings learn to perform, manipulate and manoeuvre within the convenience they provide may be as intimate – and conventional – as putting on a uniform.

NOTES

1. The yen to dollar rate used for this chapter is ¥100 = $1.25.
2. This chapter has been developed from doctoral fieldwork conducted between 2004 and 2006 and draws on data previously presented in a 2008 article, 'Learning from small change: Clerkship and the labors of convenience', published in the *Anthropology of Work Review*.
3. Keeping with standard ethnographic practice, all informant names used in the text are pseudonyms.
4. Seven is short for 7-Eleven, Japan's largest convenience store chain. Lawson is the second largest *konbini* franchise in Japan.

REFERENCES

Allison, A. (1994) *Nightwork: Sexuality, Pleasure, and Corporate Masculinity in a Tokyo Hostess Club* (Chicago, IL: University of Chicago Press).

Appadurai, A. (1996) *Modernity at Large: Cultural Dimensions of Globalisation* (Minneapolis, MI: University of Minnesota Press).

—— (2001) *Globalisation* (Durham, NC: Duke University Press).

Augé, M. (1995) *Non-places: Introduction to an Anthropology of Supermodernity* (London: Verso).

Bestor, T. C. (2003) 'Inquisitive observation: Following networks in urban fieldwork', in T. C. Bestor, P. G. Steinhoff and V. Lyon-Bestor, eds, *Doing Fieldwork in Japan* (Honolulu, HI: University of Hawaii Press).

Condry, I. (2011) 'Touching Japanese popular culture: From flows to contact for ethnographic analysis', *Japan Studies*, Vol. 31, pp. 11–22.

Creighton, M. R. (1992) 'The Depatō: Merchandising the west while selling Japaneseness', in J. Tobin, ed., *Re-made in Japan: Everyday Life and Consumer Taste in a Changing Society* (New Haven, CT: Yale University Press).

Garsten, C. (2010) 'Ethnography at the interface: "Corporate social responsibility" as an anthropological field of inquiry', in M. Melhuus, J. P. Mitchell and H. Wulff, eds, *Ethnographic Practice in the Present* (London: Berghahn Books).

Goldstein-Gidoni, O. (1997) *Packaged Japaneseness: Weddings, Business, and Brides* (Surrey: Curzon).

Iyer, P. (2009) 'Eat, memory: Our lady of Lawson', in A. Hesser, ed., *Eat, Memory: Greater Writers at the Table: A Collection of Essays from the New York Times* (New York, NY: W. W. Norton).

JFA (2012) *Convenience Store Statistics* (January 2011–December 2011) (Tokyo: Japan Franchise Association).

Kondo, D. K. (1990) *Crafting Selves: Power, Gender, and Discourses of Identity in a Japanese Workplace* (Chicago, IL: University of Chicago Press).

Kunstler, J. H. (1993) *The Geography of Nowhere: The Rise and Decline of America's Man-made Landscape* (New York, NY: Simon and Schuster).

Matsunaga, L. (2000) *The Changing Face of Japanese Retail: Working in a Chain Store* (London: Routledge).

Moeran, B. (1984) *Lost Innocence: Folk Craft Potters of Onta, Japan* (Berkeley, CA: University of California Press).

Nakano, L. Y. (2005) *Community Volunteers in Japan: Everyday Stories of Social Change* (Oxford: Routledge Curzon).

Pachirat, T. (2011) *Every Twelve Seconds: Industrialized Slaughter and the Politics of Sight* (New Haven, CT: Yale University Press).

Prentice, R. (2008) 'Knowledge, skill, and the inculcation of the anthropologist: Reflections on learning to sew in the field', *Anthropology of Work Review*, Vol. 29, No. 3, pp. 54–61.

Ritzer, G. (1993) *The McDonaldization of Society: An Investigation into the Changing Character of Contemporary Social Life* (Newbury Park, CA: Pine Forge Press).

Roberts, G. (2008) 'Commentary – Embodying labor: Work as fieldwork', *Anthropology of Work Review*, Vol. 29, No. 3, pp. 76–77.

Singleton, J. C. (1989) 'Japanese folkcraft pottery apprenticeship: Cultural patterns of an educational institution', in M. W. Coy, ed., *Apprenticeship: From Theory to Method and Back Again* (Albany, NY: State University of New York Press).

Spradley, J. P. (1980) *Participant Observation* (New York, NY: Holt, Rinehart and Winston).

Stevens, C. (1997) *On the Margins of Japanese Society: Volunteers and the Welfare of the Urban Underclass* (London: Routledge).

Turner, A. (2000) 'Embodied ethnography: Doing culture', *Social Anthropology*, Vol. 8, No. 1, pp. 51–60.

Wacquant, L. (2003) *Body and Soul: Notebooks of an Apprentice Boxer* (Oxford: Oxford University Press).

—— (2005) 'Carnal connections: On embodiment, apprenticeship, and membership', *Qualitative Sociology*, Vol. 28, No. 4, pp. 445–447.

Whitelaw, G. H. (2008) 'Learning from small change: Clerkship and the labors of convenience', *Anthropology of Work Review*, Vol. 29, No. 3, pp. 62–69.

3
Counter-espionage
Fieldwork among culture experts in Bang & Olufsen

Jakob Krause-Jensen

INTRODUCTION: DECEPTIVE FAMILIARITY

In studying organisations, we straddle insides and outsides, the familiar and the unknown. The point of this chapter is to reflect on the challenges of ethnographic fieldwork in a deceptively familiar environment. Based on my own experience of fieldwork in a human resource department in Bang & Olufsen, I want to untangle some of the complexities of doing ethnographic research in a business organisation among people who shared much of my social and cultural background (two of them were even anthropologists). The human resource consultants who worked as 'culture experts' also occupied an ambiguous role between management and workforce, which in many ways resembled the 'insider-outsider' position of the participant observer; and they worked with similar concepts (religion, values, culture, complexity). In some practical sense those similarities made fieldwork a lot easier, but in other important ways they made fieldwork more complex. In its early days the discipline of anthropology was associated with 'the comparative method'. This method was tied to an evolutionist programme and, together with this agenda, it has been long discredited. I want to argue, however, that the ethnographic study of complex organisations invites us to reactivate in a different form 'comparison' as an important element in the anthropologists' reflexive methodology.

My fieldwork in Bang & Olufsen epitomises a situation where it is very hard to draw a clear line between ethnographer and informant. I want to argue that it is important to try to draw the line, which implies keeping an eye on both similarities and differences between our informants and ourselves, and my chapter thus contributes to recent discussions on methodology centred around concepts of 'studying sideways' (Hannerz 2006) and 'para-ethnography' (Holmes and Marcus 2006) all trying to come to terms with the fact that the distinction between 'participant observer' and 'observing participant' is sometimes difficult to uphold. These resemblances provide new opportunities for engagement because the insider-outsider dialectic – our in-between position – resonates with key experiences of working in complex organisations.

BANG & OLUFSEN: 'COOLBRAND' AND 'CORPORATE RELIGION'

Bang & Olufsen – or B&O as every adult Dane knows it – is a producer of luxury home electronics. Along with Lego, Royal Copenhagen and Carlsberg, the company is one of the crown jewels of the Danish manufacturing industry. Originally influenced by Bauhaus functionalism and the softer Scandinavian versions of it expressed in Danish furniture classics from the 1950s and 1960s, for about half a century Bang & Olufsen has built its world-wide reputation around its user-friendly, minimalist designs (Krause-Jensen 2012). In 2011 Bang & Olufsen was number five on Centre for Brand Analysis' global ranking of 'coolbrands'.[1]

As a company that produces luxury items for the world's elite, Bang & Olufsen has felt the financial crisis in a particular way. This is reflected in the financial reports: The company saw an instant drop in turnover from DKK 4.1 billion in 2007/08 to 2.8 billion in 2008/09. As Birger, who is a concept developer, told me in 2011: 'We experienced the crisis before anybody else, because the people who have an ear to the ground in the banking world, they are our core customers.' Following dismal results and dire prospects, Bang & Olufsen has been forced to cut down on its workforce in recent years. In 2007/08 the company employed 2579 people, whereas in 2011 this number had dropped to 2008. However, after years of negative results in 2011 the annual account reported a small increase in turnover – and profits of DKK 40 million (Bang & Olufsen 2011: 12) – and, under the newly appointed CEO Tue Mantoni, Bang & Olufsen has launched a plan, 'Leaner, Faster, Stronger', to 'realise the company's brand potential'.

During the period of my field research in 1999–2000, however, the company was very successful: stock prices were at their peak, and Bang & Olufsen was widely portrayed in the Danish media as a positive example of value-based management. With the help of internal and external consultants, Bang & Olufsen defined and communicated its values, vision and mission in an attempt to attract customers and investors and to fire up the passion and commitment of its employees. This made me curious: coming out of a business enterprise – supposedly the heartland of utilitarian rationality – the fact that the CEO publicly announced that 'the company sold values and not electronics' and that the company's chief consultant spoke about the importance of establishing a 'corporate religion' (Kunde 2000) sounded engagingly exotic.

A CULTURE CLASH: FIELDWORK SERENDIPITY AND BOTTOM-LINE LOGIC

Doing ethnographic fieldwork in business organisations involves particular methodological opportunities and difficulties. Often, anthropologists who study organisations (myself included) do their studies close to 'home'. Since the *raison d'être* of doing anthropological analysis in organisations is to shake the reader out of mundane understandings and conceptual complacency, 'anthropology at home' is a tricky venture. 'Home', however, should be looked at as an experiential category independent of the physical location of the field site, and so 'anthropology at home' is simply a misleading and unnecessary category – strangeness does not start at the other side of the ocean but at the tip of your nose. Furthermore, previous experiences of ethnographers suggest that getting permission to do fieldwork in an organisation can be as hard and time-consuming as getting around reluctant border authorities in remote countries. It took Robert Jackall ten months and rejection from 36 corporations before he eventually – by chance and through a friend's connections – obtained the necessary permissions that led to *Moral Mazes* (1988: 3). And his experience is not singular. Other ethnographers report on the rejections suffered, the wait involved and the anxieties raised in trying to get access to business organisations (see Smith 1997: 425–426; Thomas 1994: 34). Vicki Smith (2009: 230) mentions the 'notorious difficulty of making person-to-person contact with organisational gatekeepers – middle managers and personnel staff', trying to get past reluctant secretaries, writing carefully calibrated emails and pinning your hopes to meetings scheduled weeks down the road. And when the ethnographer has made the necessary appointment, convincing the gatekeepers is not an easy task. An organisation is defined as 'an organised group of people with a particular purpose' (*New Oxford English Dictionary*), and the distinguishing purpose of the *business* organisation is to produce and trade services and goods to consumers, or, as management thinker Peter Drucker famously put it: 'the purpose of business is to create and keep a customer' (1993 [1954]: 37). An organisation, then, is a group of people doing things in coordinated ways, and '[e]ven the smallest organisations necessarily involve conscious monitoring and control of the relationship between means and ends on a fairly regular basis' (Gellner and Hirsch 2001: 3).

Organisations are thus theoretically defined by instrumental means–ends thinking, and consequently we would expect business organisations to be sites where efficiency and bottom-line logic are ever-present concerns. From this perspective, organisations do not seem to be particularly easy places to be allowed to do ethnographic fieldwork, as such means–ends rationality runs counter to some fundamental ideas of what ethnographic research is all about. One major obstacle lies in the fact that ethnographic results cannot be counted or quantified. Another problem is that our final research question is not given in advance, but emerges as we go along. How could you explain the value of serendipity to leading organisational members whose prime concern is logistics and productivity? How do we account for the fact that our data cannot be used as 'benchmarks' for organisational improvement? And how about the point that our research question is not a hypothesis to be verified or falsified, and that our initial inquiry often takes the form of questions, such as 'Who are these people, and what are they doing here?' rather than 'How can this particular problem be solved?' In short, how do we defend the merit of open-ended 'curiosity' questions that invite thick description, critical reflection and contextualised answers, rather than questions that depend on isolating variables to establish tight causal connections? From the outset, fieldwork at

Bang & Olufsen seemed to be an uphill battle. Fortunately, reality does not always live up to expectations.

ETHNOGRAPHY AND ESPIONAGE

Nine months before I started the fieldwork, I had an appointment with the personnel manager at Bang & Olufsen. I had written a letter explaining my interest in the use of concepts of culture in company discourse, and he had invited me for a meeting to discuss my project. Realising that I had left the world of 'academic quarters' and was about to enter one where 'logistics' – demanding that the right things and the right people be at the right place at the right time – were likely to have a high priority, I was in very good time when I entered main office building on a sunny August morning. My blazer jacket felt hot and uncomfortable as I took a seat in the empty lobby. The only sound came from a receptionist frequently announcing into her headset: 'Hello, this is Bang & Olufsen'. I was leafing aimlessly through the pink pages of one of the business papers on display when I suddenly heard a familiar voice: 'Jakob – what are *you* doing here?' To my joy and surprise it was Soren, a fellow anthropologist, who had graduated a few years before me. He told me that he had been employed for seven months in the human resource development department, a small independent strategic unit working very closely with senior management. He described the curious coincidences that led him to the job, and he revealed that to him the biggest 'culture shock' had been to realise the role played by money: first in the sense that the 'business perspective' was an ever-present social fact, and second he was stunned by the amount of resources (the fees paid to management consultants, the cost of leadership training, etc.) spent on 'strategic development'. He went on to note that, curiously enough in this world of bottom-line logic and benchmarks, 'anthropologists' had quite a name – both because of their research strategy of participant observation and because their other-worldly experience (Soren had done fieldwork in rural Tanzania) presumably gave them an ability to see things from odd, unexpected angles. Soren told me about his job as human resource consultant working as a relay 'between management and the organisation', and he confided that he considered himself 'a sort of undercover agent'. I was just about to ask him to elaborate when a smiling man came forward and introduced himself as Ib Hansen, the head of the personnel department.

Ib was surprised to discover that Soren and I knew each other and immediately asked Soren to take part in the meeting – as a kind of 'litmus test' as he exclaimed with a twinkle in his eye. When we entered his office, he asked me to take a seat and offered coffee. He then leaned forward, put his elbows on his desk and his fingertips contemplatively together, looked at me and asked in an affected rural accent: 'Well, what do you want to sell us?' The humorous use of accent was a reference to the fact that Bang & Olufsen is located in a small town, Struer, in the rural periphery of Denmark, where people are stereotypically known to be earthbound and prudent. The accent allowed Ib to articulate his concern without seeming too business-like – and also defined the situation as an informal one. The question was perfectly reasonable: of course a case had to be made to explain why he, the gatekeeper, should open the door to an uninvited stranger. I told him that, just like other anthropologists doing fieldwork, I intended to do 'participant observation', which implied a wish to get first-hand experience of the working lives of the people I studied. Thus, I argued that as the university would be paying my salary I could be looked upon as six months of free labour. I also emphasised that although I wished to participate, I was *not* a consultant, but that I would eventually produce an outsider's account of social and cultural processes in the company, which I hoped would be eye-opening to employees in Bang & Olufsen and to people interested in human resources and management practices more generally. He then wanted to hear more about my research interests. I told him that as an anthropologist I was interested in 'culture' or, more specifically, how notions of culture were used in the organisation, and I explained why I thought Bang & Olufsen was a particularly interesting place to explore issues of culture management.

Since the beginning of the 1980s the notion of culture has played a key role in management discourse and practices in the western world. Bang & Olufsen's work in this regard was highly profiled in the Danish media and, as an anthropologist, I was curious: Bang & Olufsen had a particular position, which enabled them to draw on many dimensions of the culture concept in their attempt to articulate their identity and appeal to employees. First, Bang & Olufsen connected with *national culture*. As mentioned earlier, over the years the company had come to be seen as a showcase of Danish manufacturing, since its signature of 'the flat line', a slim, functionalist aesthetic, linked it to a particular modernist *Danish* design tradition. Furthermore, because the company produced what in marketing jargon was called 'high involvement' products, that is expensive electronics with an emotional appeal, the company could also play on the *elite* notion of culture as 'refined taste', 'distinction' and 'exclusivity' in their effort to attract customers and mobilise employees.

At this point Ib suddenly got up from his chair, strolled across the office, opened the door and exclaimed with a mock frown: 'Sorry. The meeting is over – Bang & Olufsen is *not* exclusive. It is EXCELLENT.' He smiled in the direction of Soren and returned to his desk explaining that Bang & Olufsen had just defined a new set of fundamental values, which were currently being presented to employees, and that one of them was 'excellence', which was *very* different from 'exclusive'. Apart from 'excellence' the values were 'synthesis' and 'poetry', and, as I later learned, the ironic keying – 'let's-not-take-this-too-seriously' – was widespread, also among the consultants and high-placed employees, who were meant to communicate the values. Among other things, such a humorous subtext pointed to a reflexive or analytical distance, and thus created a particular space of understanding, rapport or, in George Marcus's (1998) apt phrase – 'complicity' – between my informants and me. We finally agreed that the best place for me to start fieldwork would be either the personnel or human resources department. I was told that autumn was peak season, and we arranged for me to start fieldwork nine months later in April, when things were likely to be a bit quieter.

In the corporate world, however, some things tend to change quickly, and when I returned, Ib had moved to a managerial position in another company, and a more comprehensive *human resource department* had been born, fusing the smaller human resource *development* unit with the personnel department. As mentioned above, Ib had been the head of the more classical personnel department. And even though he had acted as my gatekeeper, the interest in the strategic uses of 'culture' had clearly placed me outside the limits of his jurisdiction and within the province of human resource development. Some of my informants later suggested that he had probably opened the gate just to annoy the head of human resource development, and in the hope that I might challenge the consultants' work and use my ethnographic methods and anthropological expertise on culture to come up with a competing description of Bang & Olufsen values.

This first meeting highlights some of the intricacies of doing fieldwork in a rapidly changing, radically reflexive environment marked by power plays, different interests and hidden agendas. As these circumstances indicate, any claim to discover an unambiguous set of fundamental values must be taken with a grain of salt. Like most other anthropologists, I was very cautious with the culture concept. Right from the outset I knew that I was not going to write 'an ethnography of Bang & Olufsen', much less identify an immutable corporate cultural essence in the form of a body of shared values. I was interested in 'why-they-were-interested-in-culture' in this sense: how that interest unfolded, how notions of culture and value were used as an integral part of management practice, and how different groups of employees responded to that.

HOW NOT TO THINK ABOUT METHOD

Often, when I supervise students writing their field reports on organisations, they want to know how much space to devote to 'methods' and how much space to devote to 'analysis'. My answer is deliberately vague, and I sometimes offer the following tirade from Roland Barthes:

> Method inevitably disappoints; posing as a pure metalanguage, it partakes of the vanity of all metalanguages. Thus, a work that unceasingly declares its will-to-methodology always becomes sterile in the end. Everything takes place inside the method, nothing is left to the writing. The researcher repeats that his text will be methodological, but this text never arrives. There is nothing more sure to kill research and sweep it off into the left-overs of abandoned works, nothing more sure, than method. (quoted in Czarniawska-Joerges 1998: 76)

The point is not to disqualify any talk of 'method', but to avoid treating it as 'a pure metalanguage' – something reified and rational that can be dealt with in safe isolation from personal experience and analysis. Organisational environments, with their built-in instrumentality, might predispose us to think about methods in such empiricist terms, as an essentially technical affair, as something to be 'applied' or 'taken up' as one would solid items from a toolbox (Davies and Spencer 2010: 8). Anthropologists are involved with their fieldwork material, however, in a particular way, as ethnography depends on person-to-person encounters, or, to draw on the metaphors of John Weeks:

> The advantage of ethnography as a method is that it forces us to shed the metaphoric white lab coat and live among the people we are studying. Ethnography offers insights unattainable by other means. But that white coat and the claims of objectivity and distance it represents is the armour of the social scientist. Without it, we researchers are implicated in our research. (2004: 29)

This 'implication' refers to the fact that fieldwork is to a large extent a personal experience that requires us to be aware of our own position and connections to the world we describe. Fieldwork is not only an intellectual endeavour but also an emotional one. The ethnographer's changing states of being during fieldwork and how these states may either enable or inhibit the understanding that fieldwork aims to generate should be made part of the analysis (Davies and Spencer 2010: 1). Furthermore, as testified by the arrival story above, method and analysis are inextricably interwoven, and the often-arduous process of negotiating entry – the 'distractions' – can be analytically revealing as they tell you something about power and organisational sensibilities and priorities. Or, as Michael Burawoy described it when reflecting on his difficulties of getting access to Hungarian firms: 'Resistance to novel and potentially threatening research ... exposes deeply held values and interests of the actors – both the ties that bind and the lines that divide' (quoted in Smith 2009: 228; see also Hannerz 2006: 32).

POSSIBILITIES AND OBSTACLES OF PARTICIPANT OBSERVATION

One general problem that confronts the ethnographer wanting to do participant observation in organisations is that these settings often involve activities requiring expert knowledge and highly specialised skills. Such requirements make *participation* difficult and put severe limits on the ethnographer's hope of grasping 'the native's point of view' (Geertz 1974), that is, capturing the professional's experience, even in a situation where you share language and broader cultural background with your informants. Another problem is that doing fieldwork in organisations often involves 'studying up' (Nader 1972; Wright 1994), and that powerful people are often less accessible and unlikely to be available to the traditional ethnographic way of participation or 'hanging out' (Davies and Spencer 2010: 44). So, in organisations access to informants is often limited, regulated and timed (Gusterson 1997: 116).

Considering these methodological cautions, the human resources department seemed to be a happy choice of field location as it was the department where I actually did *not* have any trouble blending in, and where my methodological intentions of taking part in the daily work – of doing *participant* observation – could most easily be accomplished. The majority of my 'colleagues' were academics, two of them with a background in anthropology. There was no outward difference between my 'colleagues' and myself. I had my own workspace: a large, grey, adjustable desk with a telephone and computer. I was left free to roam around, move in and out of projects and define my own level of engagement. In a sense, my loose mandate and freedom of movement was no different from that of other human resource employees: They were encouraged to be 'self-managing', to develop their own jobs, to get involved where they saw fit, and to establish connections and cultivate their organisational network across departmental divisions. Although I did not act as an independent consultant, I assisted my human resource consultant-colleagues/informants in their work. I helped to facilitate team-talks, took part in the human resource department's strategy meetings, helped to arrange retailer visits, planned and participated in residential seminars arranged by my consultant-colleagues in the human resource department and offered to departments across Bang & Olufsen; and I was sometimes given small assignments, like giving a brief talk on corporate culture or writing a memo on 'taboo' in the organisation (see also Krause-Jensen 2010: 108–109). When I did not have any meetings or other work tasks, I spent my time reading reports and corporate magazines, taking field notes, transcribing interviews and having informal chats with people.

The semi-open office gave me opportunities both to 'participate' and 'observe' – a near perfect environment in which to conduct ethnographic research. First of all, the open office layout made it easy for me to watch and listen and get involved in small talk and informal interaction. Handling a notebook normally requires a great deal of discretion and tact (Emerson et al. 1995: 23–25). But the fact that I looked and sounded like any other busy clerk when I took notes on my computer often allowed me to avoid the potentially embarrassing 'frame-break' (Goffman 1974: 345) caused by intense scribbling and to take field notes as events and conversations took place.

REFLEXIVITY AND COMPARISON

I was often told that if I wanted to be present at meetings, I had to contribute. Retreating into a fly-on-the-wall observer position was not an acceptable option. Thus, active participation was a necessary condition for my presence as much as the result of any methodological choice on my part. Of course, my participation should not be exaggerated. Even though an unspecified level of contribution was a condition for my presence, I was not responsible for the outcome. I was independent in the sense that I was not paid by the company, and generally I was left free to get involved wherever my research interest took me. My analysis had to contribute, not to the bottom-line of the organisation, but to a theoretically embedded discussion, and so my stakes and interests were ultimately clearly different from theirs. I related to many corporate events not as issues that had direct and practical bearings on my life, but as objects of possible research interests. But as every fieldworker knows, such practical detachment did not mean that fieldwork was free from worry. As expressed by Crapanzano (2010: 60):

> the anthropologist's sense of time, marked as it is by a beginning and an ending [...] is 'telic'. It has a goal. In fact a moving goal. To come up with an array of findings that will eventually become a text. [The goal] affects the field experience in multiple ways. Among the most important of these is rendering it suspenseful and anxiety provoking (Will I get the data?).

My perspective on the human resources department reflected my research interest, but what struck me as peculiar about life in Bang & Olufsen was coloured by my personal history, in ways that I was both aware and unaware of, including my own organisational experience and background in a university department of almost equal size to the human resource department. A human resources department in a private company and a department of ethnography in a university are different. In one organisation, turbulence and change was enormous. When I came back one year after fieldwork, more than one-third of the employees in the human resources department had moved, either to other departments in the organisation or to other more attractive jobs elsewhere – or because they were simply fired or 'freed' (*fritstillet*), which is the common organisational euphemism. When I returned five years later *none* of my 17 'colleagues' were there. The other system was characterised by social stability and continuity: academic 'capital' is slowly accumulated and tied to specific fields, and does not invite rapid exchanges with the larger job market. At Bang & Olufsen, things happened at a speed that made life in my university department seem slow. This slower academic rhythm, for example, is reflected in the fact that my monograph (Krause-Jensen 2010) took such a long time to complete, at least from a corporate perspective. To the surviving Bang & Olufsen organisational member, the things I am writing now would most likely seem to belong to a very distant past; after all, my fieldwork took place in the last millennium. It provides some sort of consolation to know that apparently I am not the only lead-footed ethnographer. In her article on ethnographies of work, based on 53 research monographs, Vicky Smith writes that:

> [t]he average length between the start of fieldwork and publication of the fifty books for which information was provided was 8.14 years. (To be sure, this length of time is extended by the nine anthropologists in the sample; their average was 10.7 years ...). (Smith 2009: 228)

In one system, people came from different educational backgrounds, but they were engaged in continuous and extensive collaboration in networks and projects in open office landscapes. In the other system, people came from the same educational background, but generally worked on a variety of different, independent research projects and had their own offices. In one system, identifying and talking about culture and values was a common, practical concern. In the other system, the collective identity was not given the same attention, and 'culture' was a theoretical concept that was continuously questioned. The point of listing these differences is to stress the fact that my perspective on the human resource department of Bang & Olufsen is shaped by the anthropology department I came from, not only in the intellectual sense that this department is the place were my concepts were developed and my theories refined, but also in the sense of shaping a more general cultural, organisational background implied in the differences above.

But our similarities far outweighed these differences. This was not only due to the fact that I was conducting fieldwork in a human resource department, where people often used concepts of culture identical or similar to my analytical concepts and abstractions. It was also, and probably more important, a similarity that was grounded in the fact that I was conducting field research in Denmark among people with whom I shared a middle-class background and many concerns. For instance, the transience that normally separates the ethnographer from his or her informants (Emerson et al. 1995: 4) was a condition that characterised many employees' relation to their workplace. Many of the topics that came up during the interviews and conversations resonated with my own experience. For instance, being a university employee with no fixed working times and a relatively uncertain future, I shared the freedom and the worries of many of my informants: the ever-present temptations of the email (this was before anyone knew of Facebook); the balance of being accessible, and the necessity and difficulty of carving out private space to get your work done; the administration of the boundary between family life and organisational commitments; and the ambivalence between great freedom and unclear organisational demands (see also Krause-Jensen 2010).

Having noted these differences and similarities, I will now return to the fact that I was allowed a high degree of participation, thus contributing to the production and reproduction of the phenomena I was studying. As an anthropologist, I was presumed to have interesting things to say on matters of culture, so a few days into fieldwork, the human resource manager asked me to write a memo on 'organisational taboos' to the senior management group. I took part in arranging seminars and meetings and tried to contribute creatively with ideas, and my thoughts and practices thus fed into the reality I was describing and analysing. As the previous examples indicate, this 'double hermeneutics' (Giddens 1994 [1990]: 15) was not an abstract process, but rather a concrete and immediate one. In the early stages of my fieldwork, in an attempt to get an overview of the formal organisation of Bang & Olufsen Ltd, I once sketched an organisational diagram in the form of a 'mind-map'. Birte, one of the recruitment officers, saw my drawing, and she showed it to her colleagues. She told me that she liked 'the web-like character of the diagram instead of the old square boxes organised in pyramids'. Eventually an official version was made on the basis of my sketch.

Furthermore, the human resources department was an obvious vantage point to explore issues around culture management, as it was the department most directly involved in identifying, developing and communicating corporate identity to the rest of the organisation. As Garsten (1999) points out in her investigation of temporary workers – the emblematic employment category of flexible capitalism – they were in some sense 'betwixt and between'. Similarly, yet in another sense, the human resource consultants were betwixt and between, cultural intermediaries meant to act as brokers between managerial interests and worker concerns. As 'culture experts' they embodied what Robert Jackall has called 'ambiguous expertise': 'that is, their clients possess at least experientially the basic knowledge that management consultants claim' (1988: 37). This is clearly different from the expertise of a software engineer or a corporate accountant, and it means that the human resource area is not protected from non-expert opinion – who hasn't got something to say about 'culture'?

FIELDWORK AMONG CULTURE EXPERTS

The concept of 'culture' is an important bridge between ethnographic/anthropological research and the world of organisations (Bate 1997). But it is a treacherous one, for, as Raymond Williams pointed out some time ago, along with 'nature', 'culture' is probably the most complex concept in the English language (Williams 1976: 8). Studying the work of culture experts therefore makes it obvious that the ethnographer is not discovering pristine lands, but, in the words of Marcus and Fischer (1986: xx): '[steps] into a stream of already existing representations produced by journalists, prior anthropologists, historians, creative writers, and of course the subjects of the study themselves'.

I wanted to describe and analyse how notions of culture were produced and distributed in an attempt to realise the idea of a flexible organisation of self-managing employees. But, as mentioned, this constructivist way of understanding the work of the human resources department ran counter to native interpretations. It was emphasised time and again that the three new values – 'poetry, excellency and synthesis' – were 'fundamental' in the sense that they were *not* invented or produced, but 'discovered' or 'recognised'. The existence of such shared, deep-seated subconscious value-essence, however, seemed implausible in a world where employees were becoming ever more mobile and organisational boundaries were increasingly difficult to draw: Who shared the values of Bang & Olufsen? Was it the factory workers? Senior management? The engineers and designers? The customers? The shop owners? The outsourcing partners? The shareholders? In short, I was interested in the 'values', yes, but not as a stable essence that described a firm community. Instead, I wanted to track a process, and to situate and contextualise the role of this 'lay ethnography' in the on-going working life of Bang & Olufsen employees as they do their jobs, advance their careers, and make sense of organisational life.

For some of the employees in human resources development, notions of culture thus had a double significance: organisational values were both the context and the object of their work – they were both agents and subjects of corporate culture. As mentioned, my understanding of culture was different from that of my colleagues in the human resource department. When I introduced and explained my project to the employees in the department, they often told me that I was on the wrong track: if, as I said, I was interested in 'culture', the human resources department was simply the wrong place to look for it. True enough, the department was a key player in identifying corporate values and communicating the corporate vision, but people here saw themselves as consultants and mediators who helped to describe and uncover a tradition they were only marginally part of. In spite of official claims that the company was selling 'not televisions but *values*', Bang & Olufsen culture was associated with the factories and product development. Bang & Olufsen culture was seen to exist in the departments and among the people who worked with the actual product. 'If you are looking for the culture, you should go down there', Yvonne from the human resources department said nodding through the window towards the roof of the factory below the administrative building.

The human resources department was clearly 'meta' in the sense that it was not directly involved in the development and manufacturing of the actual products. In another sense, however, it is very much a part of organisational reality: it is the explicit strategy of Bang & Olufsen to move from being 'product-driven' to being a 'vision and value-driven' company. This implies an organisational prioritisation of the less tangible and concrete, an insistence on developing the 'Brand', and a corresponding emphasis on 'communication' and marketing as areas of strategic importance. The three values had just been identified and the strategic importance of the human resource area was reflected in the fact that the department was situated on the top (third) floor of the administrative building, just outside CEO Anders Knutsen's office, and 'communication' (including human resources) was now his direct responsibility.

As mentioned above, the department was involved in the work of uncovering and communicating the values. Thus, participant observation was not only an ambivalent methodological privilege of the anthropologist; it also covered much of what was going on in the department. Like me, the human resource employees were skilled observers of their own organisational reality. In her analysis of corporate culture in Apple Inc., Christina Garsten remarks:

> the concept of culture, and organisational culture in particular, is not only a key analytical concept; it also has a significant emic dimension. In other words, the employees' theorising about the subject was in some instances very close to mine. (Garsten 1994: 40)

As Garsten suggests, the concept of culture is not just a copyright concept of the anthropologist: the study of corporate culture is an examination of practical, scientifically informed attempts to design and manage culture, an ethnography of lay ethnographers – an effort to describe and interpret the culture of culture management. Looked upon from a methodological angle, then, the most immediate problem is not to 'go native' or drown in the unreflexive *Lebenswelt* of the locals. The difficulty is not that it is impossible to extract oneself from the immediacy of sheer participation. The problem is that the experience and organisational life of the employees is radically reflexive and theorised. Life is tied up with conceptual description and self-reflection (Krause-Jensen 2010).

In reflecting on his fieldwork among foreign correspondents, Ulf Hannerz used the term 'studying sideways' to capture the work of ethnographers like himself, who '[focus] their ethnographic curiosity on people with practices not so unlike their own' (2006: 24). Researching human resource consultants represents a paradigmatic case of such a study as my fieldwork was taking place among 'native anthropologists' or lay ethnographers. Like me, they were 'symbolic analysts' (Reich 1992) sharing an interest in capturing, describing and communicating matters cultural. The fact that we used concepts that were nominally identical, and the fact that in terms of qualifications and educational background, I was no different from any other human resource employee, meant that fieldwork was characterised by an ever-present ambiguity with regard to my position in relation to the company and my 'colleagues'.

The fact that some human resource consultants referred to themselves as spies both testifies to their own sense of the intricacy of their organisational involvements, and pointed to their critical reflexive stance. If Soren, as previously mentioned, confided to me that he saw himself as an 'undercover' agent – who was I, spying on the spy? My informants and I not only shared a common middle-class background and an interest in culture, but also a precarious position. Douglas Holmes and George Marcus (2006) suggest the phrase of the 'para-ethnographic' to capture that we must take into account the highly reflexive or self-critical stance of our informants living in an ambiguous world they, like the ethnographer, struggle to make sense of. The distinction between the ethnographer and employees cannot be drawn easily. It is crucial, however, that the fact that it is impossible to maintain a clear-cut separation does not imply that we should abandon the attempt to draw the line and make the distinction. On the contrary, being aware of the similarities and overlaps, as well as acknowledging the differences, is a component of a form of reflexivity which should be part and parcel of participant observation. It is exactly our straddling position – the betwixt and between – from which our research proceeds that provides us with an opportunity to grasp an often contradictory, fuzzy and ambiguous organisational reality. To make Kenneth Burke's statement my own: 'what we want is not terms that avoid ambiguity, but terms that clearly reveal the strategic spots where ambiguities necessarily arise' (1962: xx).

NOTE

1. See: http://tinyurl.com/d9ljjgp.

REFERENCES

Bang & Olufsen (2011) Årsrapport 2010/11 (Struer: Bang & Olufsen A/S koncernen).

Bate, S. P. (1997) 'Whatever happened to organizational anthropology? A review of the field of organizational ethnography and anthropological studies', *Human Relations*, Vol. 50, No. 9, pp. 1147–1175.

Burke, K. (1962) *A Grammar of Motives, and A Rhetoric of Motives* (Cleveland, OH: World Pub. Co).

Crapanzano, V. (2010) 'At the heart of the discipline', in J. Davies and D. Spencer, eds, *Emotions in the Field: The Psychology and Anthropology of Fieldwork Experience* (Stanford, CA: Stanford University Press).

Czarniawska-Joerges, B. (1998) *A Narrative Approach to Organization Studies* (Thousand Oaks, CA: Sage).

Davies, J. and D. Spencer (2010) *Emotions in the Field: The Psychology and Anthropology of Fieldwork Experience* (Stanford, CA: Stanford University Press).

Drucker, P. F. (1993 [1954]) *The Practice of Management* (New York, NY: HarperCollins).

Emerson, R., R. Fretz and L. Shaw (1995) *Writing Ethnographic Fieldnotes* (London: University of Chicago Press).

Garsten, C. (1999) 'Betwixt and between: Temporary employees as liminal subjects in flexible organizations', *Organization Studies*, Vol. 20, No. 4, pp. 601–617.

—— (1994) *Apple World: Core and Periphery in a Transnational Organizational Culture*, Stockholm Studies in Social Anthropology 33 (Stockholm: Almqvist and Wiksell International).

Geertz, C. (1974) '"From the native's point of view": On the nature of anthropological understanding', *Bulletin of the American Academy of Arts and Sciences*, Vol. 28, No. 1, pp. 26–45.

Gellner, D. N. and E. Hirsch (2001) *Inside Organizations: Anthropologists at Work* (Oxford: Berg).

Giddens, A. (1994 [1990]) *The Consequences of Modernity* (London: Polity).

Goffman, E. (1974) *Frame Analysis* (Cambridge, MA: Harvard University Press).

Gusterson, H. (1997) 'Studying up revisited', *PoLAR: Political and Legal Anthropology Review*, Vol. 20, No. 1, pp. 114–119.

Hannerz, U. (2006) 'Studying down, up, sideways, through, backwards, forwards, away and at home: Reflections on the field worries of an expansive discipline', in S. Coleman and P. J. Collins, eds, *Locating the Field: Space, Place and Context in Anthropology* (Oxford: Berg).

Holmes, D. and G. Marcus (2006) 'Fast capitalism: Para-ethnography and the rise of the symbolic analyst', in M. S. Fisher and G. Downey, eds, *Frontiers of Capital: Ethnographic Reflections on the New Economy* (Durham, NC: Duke University Press).

Jackall, R. (1988) *Moral Mazes: The World of Corporate Managers* (Oxford: Oxford University Press).

Krause-Jensen, J. (2010) *Flexible Firm: The Design of Culture at Bang & Olufsen* (Oxford: Berghahn Books).

—— (forthcoming) 'Creativity, innovation and design at Bang & Olufsen', in B. Moeran and B. Christensen, eds, *Exploring Creativity* (Cambridge: Cambridge University Press).

Kunde, J. (2000) *Corporate Religion: Building A Strong Company through Personality and Corporate Soul* (London: Financial Times/Prentice Hall).

Marcus, G. (1998) *Ethnography Through Thick and Thin* (Princeton, NJ: Princeton University Press).

Marcus, G. and M. M. J. Fischer (1986) *Anthropology as Cultural Critique: An Experimental Moment in the Human Sciences* (Chicago, IL: University of Chicago Press).

Nader, L. (1972) 'Up the anthropologist: Perspectives gained from studying up', in D. Hymes, ed., *Reinventing Anthropology* (New York, NY: Pantheon).

Reich, R. B. (1992) *The Work of Nations: Preparing Ourselves for 21st-century Capitalism.* (New York, NY: Vintage Books).

Smith, V. (1997) 'Ethnography bound: Taking stock of organizational case studies', *Qualitative Sociology*, Vol. 20, No. 3, pp. 425–435.

—— (2009) 'Ethnographies of work and the work of ethnographers', in P. A. Atkinson, A. J. Coffey, S. Delamont, J. Lofland and L. H. Lofland, eds, *Handbook of Ethnography* (London: Sage).

Thomas, R. J. (1994) *What Machines Can't Do: Politics and Technology in the Industrial Enterprise* (Berkeley, CA: University of California Press).

Weeks, J. (2004) *Unpopular Culture: The Ritual of Complaint in a British Bank* (Chicago, IL: University of Chicago Press).

Williams, R. (1976) *Keywords: A Vocabulary of Culture and Society* (London: Fontana/Croom Helm).

Wright, S., ed. (1994) *Anthropology of Organizations* (London: Routledge).

4
When life goes to work
Authenticity and managerial control in the contemporary firm

Peter Fleming

INTRODUCTION: AUTHENTICITY AT WORK

Traders wearing anti-capitalist T-shirts on the floor. Entrepreneur icons like Mark Zuckerberg using his 'hoodie' as a key symbolic trademark. Call-centre employees with bright green hair, tattoos and face-piercings. Snooze zones and gaming areas in a software firm. Gay-friendly workplaces and open sexuality in the office. Flight assistants telling jokes over the intercom. These examples all point to a major change in the way contemporary managerialism operates today to enlist the efforts of workers. As many commentators have noted, management ideology has often demanded various types of conformity in order to achieve its economic goals. In the factory or bureaucratic office of yesteryear, uniformity and collective adherence to the rhythm of rationality usually characterised the workplace. In many organisations today, however, there is something quite different about the employee compared to what Whyte (1956) memorably called the archetypical 'organizational man'. The dull uniformity of this character was particularly definitive of the corporate realm and the bureaucratic office: he or she exuded a one-dimensional personality, and it was difficult to distinguish between one worker and another. With respect to the so-called high-commitment organisational cultures of the 1980s and 1990s, it is no wonder that O'Reilly and Chatman (1996) draw parallels between extremist cults and the modern corporation. Both represent 'greedy' (Coser 1974) institutional forms that isolate the individual from the rest of their *Lebenswelt*, since family, leisure and other lifestyle signifiers that indicated a life outside the firm were viewed as possible contaminants. The ultimate ideological goal back then was internal coherence, uniformity and homogenization with individual quirks and idiosyncrasies kept to a minimum.

A new management ideology (which we might call neo-managerialism) can now be observed in many workplaces, which opens up significant anthropological areas of interest for us. This approach to human resource management displaces the conventional concern with personnel uniformity. The 'just be yourself' corporate philosophy (Fleming and Sturdy 2010) attempts to include the 'whole person' in the labour process. Be authentic, real and bring to work those aspects that are unique and different about you. This aspect of the 'just be yourself' business management is interesting since authenticity or 'who I really am' is presumed to be something that is generally experienced more *outside* the organisation (when the workday is over). Thus there is an attempt to both practically and symbolically evoke private sphere associatives such as consumption, sexuality, leisure and so forth. The assumption that we are more 'ourselves' outside of work than within the confines of the factory or office reflects the continuing importance of the wider division between the public and private, home and labour that emerged in the first tumult of the Industrial Revolution.

How do we account for this shift in the way corporate managerialism approaches the employee and what are its social anthropological implications? More specifically, why has personal authenticity become so important for the way work is organised and performed? Rather than viewing such 'liberation management' (Peters 2003) techniques as the arrival of new freedoms in our jobs, this chapter will argue that they are linked to the changing relations of power between managers and the managed. More precisely, they are indicative of the contemporary corporation's drive to create moments of what I call *existential exposure*. By inviting more aspects of the 'whole person' (which include many qualities that make us individuals in the private setting), the working subject is further appropriated into the production process towards capitalistic ends. In the 'just be yourself' firm, the symbolic boundary between work and non-work is manipulated in order to incorporate more of aspects of self in the name of increased productivity. To explain how this might be so, I want to develop the theoretical insights of Hardt and Negri (1994, 2009), including the 'the social factory' and 'the commons' to argue that this prompt to be authentic at work entails a moment of co-optation. Because so many workplaces require the genuine and non-feigned emotions and personalities of its employees, more efforts are made by firms to capture 'life itself' and put it to work. In employment settings such as the modern call-centre, for example, the task requires the use of our discretion, ability to emote and personality.

To make this argument, the chapter is organised as follows. First I discuss the classic boundary between work and non-work, and its disruption with arrival of 'flexible capitalism' and the aforementioned 'just be yourself' management philosophy. Then I counter the widespread assumption that this shift represents new freedoms at work. I do this by using the critical theory of the Italian Autonomist tradition, which links these permutations to the deepening of managerial control – in which 'life itself' is put to work. Finally, some observations are made about the significance these shifts have for understanding the politics of organising today.

THE DISMANTLING OF WORK/LIFE BOUNDARIES

The most striking facet of the 'just be yourself discourse' in firms today is the way it emphasises the non-work realm as a key reference point. As others have also argued, the split between the public and private is important in liberal political thought. The expressive individualism encouraged by organisations like South-Western Airlines and Google dovetails with the axiomatic assumption that the authentic person can be found in the private back-stage recesses of the subject – which usually are expressed in leisure, consumption and the home. The workplace has generally been viewed as a site of alienation and regimentation in which the individual quirks of the individual are downplayed in favour of unifying control systems. This is the 'lack of life' that invariably pervades our experience of work, even if it offers limited enjoyments and pleasures occasionally. With the transformation of labour into an end in itself – a coercive role bound by a fundamental antagonism rather than an expression of creativity and life – it became something that we would avoid like the plague, to paraphrase Marx.

The definition of authenticity as something private is shored up by two important historical achievements in western societies. The first is the inauguration of the public/private division and the second is the material split between work (a place where we forego life) and non-work (where we hope to attain 'a life' apropos sex, leisure, relationships and so forth). The notion of the public and private has already been alluded to and is a cornerstone feature of western socio-political thought (Arendt 1958). It first emerges in the wake of the monumental advent of the nation-state, society and public life whereby one engages in political dialogue and reflection. The *polis* provides the conditions for the private, but in liberalist thinking a kind of tense symbiosis emerges between the private individual and our social lives. As Sennett (1976) argues, the appearance of the liberal state co-emerges with the idea of a private person that is often set against the state or public collective in relation to his/her views, feelings and practices (the invention of the modern family was not far behind). Marx after Hegel saw this as a founding moment of alienation. Within the flows of an extreme individualism, personal authenticity now occluded any display of self in the public sphere – be it the market, the street or the workplace (also see Taylor 1992).

The second important historical achievement that underlies the equation of authenticity with private individualism relates to the establishment of the work and non-work division. The shift from feudalism to capitalism in Europe during the eighteenth and nineteenth centuries witnessed a major reorganisation of both the physical and conceptual spatiality of working life (Braudel 1961). Under feudalism peasants and artisans were usually located in close proximity to home, family and what today we might call leisure; what Mills (1956) called the 'craftsman' configuration of an integrated life. With the emergence of capitalism and factory production, however, the spatial characteristics of the 'putting-out' system in particular were unsuitable due to the lack of worker discipline and control (Thompson 1963). Factories were fenced off like prisons and the urbanisation of the industrial proletariat created a new geography of work that was markedly different from previous systems. But this division also involved important temporal and subjective elements. As time became the source of wealth under the aegis of capitalist production, the working day was dichotomised between company time and private time

(Clegg and Dunkerly 1980). And depending on whether one was at home or at work, quite different selves were exhibited (Scott and Storper 1986).

Although the division between work and non-work life was certainly not watertight, with the work ethic (Thompson 1963) and industrial paternalism (Bendix 1956), for example, playing a major role outside the factory gates, the spatial division did represent a significant shift from the previous economic regime. For sure, this division between work and life, public and private is fragile (especially with changing employment patterns), but it still has great symbolic sway over the way in which we carve up our lives. The phenomenological minutiae of the work required to maintain this boundary has been mapped by Nippert-Eng (1996). Work and home mean different things to us regarding self-identity and the emotional geography we expect to occupy. In relation to the scientific lab workers she studied, Nippert-Eng summarises the micro-management of this spatial division pertaining to one of the more 'life giving' activities, that of sex:

> From the time they begin their apprenticeships, machinist folklore, contractual disputes, equipment requirements, and sexually homogeneous environments continually reinforce the idea that time and space is either dedicated to work or home, public or private pursuits. The lesson is that, ultimately, these cannot be the same. Because of its learned, exclusive mental association with one realm and not another, then, the more we are like Ed (a lab worker), the more even the thought of sex in the workplace is outrageous. (Nippert-Eng 1996: 3)

Nippert-Eng (1996) points out that this boundary is, of course, imaginary, in that it is breached constantly during the vagaries of everyday working life. But as an associative imaginary (with strong masculine connotations regarding its differentiation from the home/family), it still organises our lives in meaningful ways. The home is often romanticised, considered a kind of sanctuary, a place of intimacy, where rest and leisure are enjoyed outside the deadening rhythms of work. Home is a place of freedom and choice and work is dominated by hierarchy and rule: 'As a private realm ... home ideally is a place where we can "be ourselves", "put up our feet", "let down our hair" and relax among those who see us "warts and all"...' (Nippert-Eng 1996: 20). In other words, the imaginary boundary and its respective associations have for many years remained strong for understanding 'who we are' in these different settings.

Separating Work and Life in Management Thought

Given the connotations outlined above it is not surprising that the boundary between work and non-work has been a perennial concern in management thought and practice. The associations noted by Nippert-Eng (1996) are certainly accurate for many, but she forgets that they arose from a long struggle between capital and labour that perhaps stretches back to the enclosure movement in the early phases of industrialism. More recently, the factory space was clearly considered a zone of discipline and 'work' as opposed to leisure and freedom. As Weber (1948) also highlighted in his description of the bureaucratic office, depersonalisation was a paramount objective in order to achieve efficiency. The office had to be evacuated of life and made a structure reminiscent of a machine or disciplined army. Weber identified a process of 'eliminating from official business love, hatred and all purely personal, irrational, and emotional elements' (Weber 1948: 216). Moreover, in illustrating the 'rules of separation' in administrative bureaucracies, Weber states that there is usually a complete:

> separation of the property belonging to the organisation, which is controlled within the sphere of the office, and the personal property of the official, which is available for his [sic] own private use. There is a corresponding separation of the place in which official functions are carried out, the 'office' in the sense of premises, from living quarters. (Weber 1948: 331–332).

There are exceptions to this boundary maintenance behaviour in work organisations – such as the activities of Ford's Sociological Department and the interest shown in the influence of extra-employment attitudes on task performance by early Human Relations theorists (see Roethlisberger and Dickson 1933). But by and large the influence of non-work was considered something to be avoided.

This fear of 'contamination' was no more pronounced than in the 1980s and early 1990s attempt to build 'strong' high-commitment corporate cultures. As many commentators have observed (see Barker 1999; Casey 1995; Van Maanen 1991), culture management aims to 'marry' the employee emotionally and subjectively to the company. Under the auspices of unitary values, the organisation becomes a community or collective in which the 'old' divisions between capital and labour are outwardly superseded. The organic solidarity that underpins cultural control is succinctly explained by Barley and Kunda – committed employees 'make no distinction between their own welfare and the welfare of the firm' (1992: 382). In this sense, then, *employees become part of the company*. Kunda's (1992) ethnographic analysis of cultural control at 'Tech' – a computer engineering firm – follows Goffman's (1959) classic dramaturgical front stage and back stage demarcation. Kunda depicted an organisation in the throes of a chronic struggle between *role embracement* and *role distancing*. Employees were constantly exhorted to absorb the designed membership role as their own and become a 'company (wo)man'. But at the same time, they wanted to maintain a private reserve that was truly theirs and beyond the corporate collective. Employees adopted a number of tactics to cope with this, including depersonalisation or distancing of self. As a result, 'the emotions experienced as part of the organisational self are presented as distinct from other aspects of emotional life and at some remove from one's "authentic" sense of self' (1992: 183). According to Kunda, such depersonalisation requires that:

one control and even suppress personal and spontaneous reactions to the work environment, thus purging them from the organizational self and leaving only appropriate 'emotions'. Failure to do this is noticed by others. (1992: 184)

This purging process is no more evident than in the externalisation of the emotional injuries incurred at Tech. Given the intense work effort that was required to signal loyalty to the company, marriage break-ups, burnout, alcohol abuse and other pathologies were a common occurrence. However, there are limits to what Tech wants to know about this more harmful side of its culture. An engineer speaks of a departed manager: 'One day he stood up and told us he was going to a detox center ... he didn't have to tell us. Some people were quite upset. Keep that kind of shit to yourself.... He's gone now' (Kunda 1992: 202–203).

Be Authentic ... Or Else!

The current quest to 'authenticise' the employee in the 'just be yourself' management philosophy is, in part at least, characterised by the ideological displacement of the traditional symbolic boundary separating work from non-work. This fetishisation of the extra-employment sphere as a kind of productive device to impute some 'life' into work and motivate employees was well under way before the arrival of so-called 'liberation management'. More holistic approaches to human resource management (Heuberger and Nash 1994) have used imagery sourced from the private realm, especially in relation to emotional labour where employees attempt to give customers a more homely and genuine service. Hochschild's (1983) classic study of airline attendants recorded a striking application of this in her ethnographic analysis. In order to facilitate their emotional labour in the aeroplane cabin, employees were encouraged to use a 'living room analogy' and act 'as if' the airplane cabin was their home.

The idea of replicating the private inside the firm finds its fullest expression in the 'just be yourself' business philosophy. The appropriation method of the 'greedy' corporation is different to that of, say, culture management simply encroaching upon the private lives of employees through overwork or stress (see Gregg 2011; Scase and Goffee 1989). Here, the inverse seems to be the case: positive experiences and emotions recognised to be associated with the non-work sphere (such as relaxation, recreation, fun, etc.) are actively evoked in organisations rather than suppressed or prohibited. Most importantly, non-work and its attendant rituals of authentication represents a kind of 'kingdom of individuals' that fits well with the hyper-individualised notion of authenticity we have delineated. Real and genuine selves are often defined within the collective categories – race, sexual preferences, consumption patterns, etc. – but are firmly sited and embodied at the monadic level of the 'original' person. Hence the importance of an expressive or aesthetic difference, diversity, and even dissenting 'cool'.

An important mechanism for evoking the self-styled private self inside the organisation is simulation and the mimicking of themes, motifs and activities that are mentally and symbolically associated with the non-work sphere, and most commonly that of the private individual. Consumption, lifestyle factors, sexuality and humour, for example, are not externalised in favour of a collective normative alignment nor barred from the organisation in the bureaucratic tradition, but celebrated as a useful organisational resource. The title of Semler's (2004) best-selling book is telling of the general concern here – *The Seven-day Weekend: Changing the Way Work Works*. The idea is that work can be a space that resembles non-work, or, in this case, the weekend, since the deadening uniformity of previous corporate regimes no longer fits the needs of a more dynamic and knowledge-hungry economic environment. Semler argues that by injecting into labour the authentic experiences and identities that we might enjoy outside the firm, more flexible and positive employees are likely to result.

Post-industrial Patterns of Authenticity

While authenticity is usually considered to be that which makes us real, different and unique, as it enters the parlance of management it (ironically) takes on some predictable forms. There are some emblematic themes that count as 'authentic', which seem to appear quite regularly in companies that I have researched as well as those studied by others. Sexuality is an obvious 'source' of authenticity that I have noted being promoted in rather stereotypical ways in the call-centres I have studied through ethnographic methods (see Fleming 2009). As Nippert-Eng (1996) suggests in her ethnographic study, work and sex are conventionally considered mutually exclusive activities (although many commentators have observed that sex was probably always present in the informal work sphere in the form of games, harassment and so forth). The formal acceptance of sexuality and sexual identities associated with gay and/or lesbian identities is interesting. In the call-centre I studied during a one-year semi-ethnographic investigation, open sexuality and sexual fraternising were openly promoted by the organisation as a way of creating a less boring and more fun environment. In particular, management celebrated gay sexual identity, making this workplace very different from the homophobic organisational structures in which gay workers have to hide their identities.

Many workplaces have approached diversity legislation as an opportunity for increased synergies rather than a restraint on effectiveness (Janssens and Zanoni 2005). Raeburn's (2004) study of US organisations that embrace sexual diversity, for example, indicates that they generally benefit from more motivated and dynamic work environments. Similarly, diverse lifestyles and identities are also a major source of perceived authenticity, something more likely to be expressed outside of the organisation. Management commentators suggest that this diversity should be harnessed and used to make the organisation a more dynamic, creative and enjoyable place to be. Deal and Key (1998: 25) argue that celebrations at work foster diversity and 'provide social support for being yourself and believing that you matter'.

This celebration includes the expression of alternative lifestyles, different dress codes and various ways of living 'against the system' – as Ross (2004) points out in his ethnographic research, chic slacker 'underground cool' is a favourite self-identity promoted in the IT industry. This enables workers to feel that they are remaining true to their cyber-punk, do-it-yourself roots even as they are 'working for the man'. Fun and play in the workplace is similarly a major theme, which goes against the grain of much industrial ideology wedded to the notion of unemotional rationalisation. The assumption is that only once the workday is over can play enter the social scene. Its transposition inside the regime of work in the 'just be yourself' management approach is thus unsurprising.

THE CORPORATE EXPLOITATION OF 'LIFE ITSELF' AT WORK

This systematic incorporation of 'life itself' (or all that is putatively authentic about us that we once suppressed when at work) into the corporate form is often said to herald new workplace freedoms. Now we can be ourselves in a setting that once chided formal displays of our unique personhood. I want to argue, however, that it is connected to shifting strategies of corporate control. A two-fold articulation of managerial power is operating when the organisation attempts to utilise non-work themes in the workplace. First is a kind of 'existential exposure', in which more of the employees' selfhood is made available to the managerial gaze in order to enhance motivation, sell the firm to the customer and push responsibility for collective production onto the worker and so forth. In this sense, we must not take the symbolic blurring too seriously, since there are obvious limits: the employee can fulfil their personal authenticity by being themselves, but only up to a point, and that point represents the limit of capital. Second, the simulation underlying the attempt to foster non-work modes of 'life' in the organisation works to detract attention from the traditional controls already in place. And this mimetic transposition often fails, becoming a locus of antagonism in and of itself (e.g. cynicism towards the 'just be yourself' management philosophy).

In order to argue that authenticity at work is an extension of managerial control (rather than its relaxation), I draw on the Italian Autonomist ideas of Hardt and Negri (1994, 2009) among others. For them, the current appropriation of aspects of subjectivity and practice that apparently lie outside of the traditional sphere of labour would exemplify the coming post-industrial 'social factory' (also see Tronti 1979 [1966]). This concept describes the nature of capitalist development in the West, in which the logic of production and consumption has become a *social universal*. Production becomes abstracted from any fixed and isolatable task and permeates the entire social body:

> ... labouring processes have moved outside the factory walls to invest the entire society. In other words, the apparent decline of the factory as site of production does not mean a decline of the regime and discipline of factory production, but means that it is no longer limited to a particular site in

society. It has insinuated itself throughout all social forms of production, spreading like a virus. (Hardt and Negri 1994: 9–10)

The conspicuous role played by 'non-work' themes in the discourse of authenticity at work points to this virus-like quality of recent management thinking. Many workplaces today parasitically turn to non-work for ideas, cues and subjective efforts – all of which formally fall outside the zone of production – in order to enhance the production process. This is especially so in jobs that require a high degree of sociality, which prior management ideology frowned upon as a dangerous realm of worker autonomy. For Hardt and Negri (2009), a rich stratum of informal sociality is increasingly required for corporate capitalism to reproduce itself (since it could never do this of its own accord). It needs an outside point of cooperative and creative labour – what they call a non-corporate *commons* – to sustain its otherwise untenable principles (see also Crouch 2011). This is what Hardt and Negri call the ironic communist underbelly of capitalism, a rich constellation of communication, shelter, creativity, emotional frames and a priori mutual aid. For how else can we account for the wealth in society that is qualitatively above and beyond the surplus harnessed by financial markets, wage-labour relations and private property?

I evoke Hardt and Negri because I think that the 'just be yourself' discourse (and its icon of personal authenticity) is a vehicle to prospect and enclose those social qualities (related to non-work) that the for-profit enterprise cannot engender itself. An immediate implication here is that our understanding regarding the source of authenticity changes from one based on a private non-work self to a radically socialised one. That is to say, sexuality, lifestyle, fun, play and so forth are not individual characteristics of an isolated identity but features of an 'elemental communism' – perhaps bolstered by networks of family, friends, spontaneous acts of cooperation and other formally non-work associations – that organisations want for themselves (in their own form). The public/private dichotomy is eschewed for a thoroughly social understanding of the working subject. This conceptualisation of work stems from the early nineteenth-century arguments regarding the centrality of labour for the development of capitalism. Rather than posit capital as an ontological 'first principle' and labour a reactive outcome of organised work, the spontaneous cooperation of workers, their communication and social antagonism shape the contours of capitalist development. This is especially so since the commons is first and foremost antithetical to the principles of commodification, and especially capitalist exploitation. In this sense, corporate capitalism has always been parasitical on the living labour that it autonomously gathers around itself in the form of a commons. Capital aims to appropriate this unvalorised labour of cooperation and is a reactive response to the resistance it meets when it seeks to harness that commons:

Operaismo builds on Marx's claim that capital reacts to the struggles of the working class; the working class is active and capital reactive. Technological development: Where there are strikes, machines will follow. 'It would be possible to write a whole history of the inventions made since 1830 for the sole purpose of providing capital with weapons against working-class revolt.' (*Capital*, Vol. 1, Chapter 15, Section 5). Political development: The factory legislation in England was a response to the working-class struggle over the length of the working day. 'Their formulation, official recognition and proclamation by the State were the result of a long class struggle.' (*Capital*, Vol. 1, Chapter 10, Section 6). *Operaismo* takes this as its fundamental axiom: the struggles of the working class *precede* and *prefigure* the successive re-structurations of capital. (Hardt and Negri 1999: 101)

The quotation above extrapolates from a little excerpt in Marx's *Grundrisse* and the chapter on social cooperation in *Capital* (Marx 1976 [1867]). It argues that our ability to spontaneously self-organise *despite* the anti-social precepts of economic rationality precedes the corporate form. Our social intelligence, ability to share knowledge and love of being together makes up the immaterial wealth so necessary to capitalism today, especially when it is so dependent on the human qualities of workers. Hardt and Negri use the term 'immaterial labour' (and more recently 'cognitive capitalism') to understand this cooperation, creativity and invisible 'good will' that underlies the corporate form. The term 'immaterial labour' is certainly not a synonym for rather tenuous notions of the 'service worker' or the 'symbolic analyst'. Instead it points to a dimension of labour that has probably been always present under capitalist conditions. A good example can be found in the classic sociological research of Peter Blau (1955). In the office he studied, workers resisted in a strange manner – by doing exactly what they were told to do. They followed the rules to the letter. As a result, an invisible wealth of informal relations, discretion and non-codified knowhow was withdrawn and the enterprise came to a grinding halt. This is the commons that formal economic rationality depends upon, seeks to capture, but can never allow to be fully realised (for that would be communism). The injunction to exude authenticity and its concomitant transfer of non-work modes of sociality onto the firm is one such vehicle for tapping this immaterial labour.

Putting 'Life itself' to Work

We can begin to see how the ostensible 'freedom' to be yourself in the authentic workplace might be a foil for extending the logic of exploitation ever deeper into the social lives of workers. It is the way recent managerialism celebrates the qualities of non-work that makes me suspicious. One only has to look at the kind of social skills and personable abilities that are needed in many firms today, from creative innovation to artisanal amateurism and heightened social aptitudes. The immaterial labour here revolves around the evocation of those aspects of self that were once prohibited in the realm of work. This feature of corporate valorisation is most evident in the 'liberation management' ideas promoted by Tom Peters (2003) and others. When we think of the quest for authenticity via the replication/appropriation of non-work from this perspective, it is important to overcome the ideological division between the private individual and the public organisational space. We must think of the 'private' and non-work signifiers – lifestyle, fun, sexuality and so forth – as indicators of *the commons* residing both inside the firm and beyond the sphere of production. This is why it is of such utility to the contemporary firm that wants people continuously poised for the demands of contemporary production.

Some exemplary cases of this parasitical foray into non-work (via the discourse of authenticity) are evident in the literature. Recall Hochschild's (1983) ethnographic observation regarding how airline attendants were encouraged to use a 'living room analogy' and act 'as if' the aeroplane cabin was their home. The home space is directly called upon – including the family network, the feelings one has when relaxing in the living room, the polite rituals and kindness of entertaining guests and other kinds of 'social labour'. A particular assumption of cooperative work at home involving tacit knowledge and associative communicative rituals is being appropriated in terms of its symbolic worth when the company aims to have it replicated in the cabin. The negative side of much domestic life, however, is not included this discourse.

In his anthropological study of an IT firm that also aimed to interconnect productive work and play, labour and leisure, the public and private, Ross (2004) found very good examples of what we might call immaterial labour and the appropriation of the commons. The firm placed great emphasis on being authentic, true to yourself and speaking one's mind. He observes that:

> in knowledge companies that trade in creative ideas, services and solutions, everything that employees do, think, or say in their waking moments is potential grist for the industrial mill. When elements of play in the office or at homesite/offsite are factored into creative output, then the work tempo is being recalibrated to incorporate activities, feelings and ideas that are normally pursued in employees' free time. (Ross 2004: 19)

The company that Ross ethnographically studied also turned to 'resistance' and 'rebellion' to infuse work with a sense of personal authenticity. Indeed, according to the guru of 'liberation management', Tom Peters, corporations need to absorb the spirit of resistance and revolt in a rapidly changing economic landscape. We therefore witness a somewhat counter-intuitive celebration of anti-managerialism by management itself. The message reads like this: 'turn management on its head', make organisations fun and subversive, and employees will be more motivated and engaged in their jobs. Peters is not alone here. Management consultant Bains (2007) suggests that employees ought to simply 'be themselves', express their lifestyle difference, however radical they might be. Elsewhere, the 'tempered radical' (Meyerson 2001) is celebrated as an agent of authentic change. More serious academic scholarship has similarly noted a shift in the employment practices of corporations. Ross (2004), mentioned above, observed what he calls the 'industrialization of bohemia' in Silicon Alley dot.com companies, in which anti-capitalist values and an underground counter-culture were fostered to give firms a more authentic flavour. The key evaluative categories for team leaders are not obedience or complete uniformity, but authenticity, dissent, anti-hierarchy and difference (also see Boltanski and Chiapello 2005).

CONCLUSIONS

In this chapter, I have attempted to place the recent turn to authenticity in management discourse within a political framework in order to enhance our appreciation of new modes of corporate power from a social anthropological perspective. Rather than see the opportunity to display real selves ('warts and all') in the realm of work as a moment of freedom, perhaps the opposite is the case. In an era in which private enterprises require social qualities that it cannot create on its own terms, then it needs some kind of vehicle to capture them on the job. The massive amount of emphasis placed on 'non-work' in the 'just be yourself' corporate discourse is telling about this. Moreover, this is why the milieu of many organisations today looks so radically different to those of yesteryear. Workers with face-piercings and tattoos, managers in informal attire and Zuckerberg-like 'hoodies', and stockbrokers wearing anti-capitalist T-shirts with an image of Lenin giving the finger. Again, while this difference, colour and 'buzz of life' is heralded by pro-business observers of new freedoms in the workplace, I argue that it is indicative of 'cognitive capitalism' that parasitically draws upon non-work or 'the commons' in order to reproduce its unsustainable tenets. Social anthropological methods are especially useful for tracking this type of power because they get under the official veneer to access the often hidden structures of everyday power at work.

The management discourse of authenticity points to the striking horizontalisation of production as it parasitically encloses the non-work activities and aptitudes of employees. The corporation today views free time inside and outside the workplace to be abundant with potential moments of exploitable value. If we think of the appropriation of the non-work sphere as the underlying rationale of managed authenticity, extending the 'social factory' to ever more spheres of life, then we need to redefine what work 'is' and 'where' it is happening in contemporary capitalism. In organisations that aim to enhance authenticity among workers by allowing them to 'just be themselves', the immaterial labour of exploiting the commons outside of production displaces the imagined boundaries between spaces of consumption, personal and family life, and the conventional workplace. With this displacement, or even dissolution of the boundary between life and labour in the 'just be yourself' discourse, the realm of non-work becomes marginalised (as it becomes functional) since more and more of the social landscape is constituted as a space of (potential) labour power.

But we also need to be attentive to what might be called the 'vertical' search for instances of social labour when dissecting the management of personal authenticity. For example, some have shown this with regard to humour and play, which has long been a feature of the informal organisation, under the governance of workers themselves. In the past games and jokes were often considered sources of disruption by management. But now new management approaches seek to promote fun and games (even those that parody the enterprise), parasitically commandeering employee initiatives with the hope of creating more productive performances. Social anthropological techniques – such as the ones I utilised in my study of everyday life in a call-centre – are integral for observing these emergent patterns of power. The ethnographies of Ross (2004), among others, reveal the darker side of modern management techniques because they allow researchers to experience first-hand the rituals and roles that the 'just be yourself' discourse entails 'on the ground'.

The official managerial ideology looks very different here, especially the assumption that authenticity is something primarily 'out there' in the world of non-work. Indeed, we still find that work itself is a source of identity, of dignity and various other forms of 'psychological and social needs'. Hoschschild (1997) remarks in her ethnographic investigations that, for many female workers, employment is an escape from the home, offering a temporary chance for self-affirmation that is otherwise denied them: 'one reason workers may feel more "at home" at work is that they feel more appreciated and more competent there' (Hochschild 1997: 200). How do these workers feel when they see motifs reminding them of their private worlds appearing in the office? This question flags an important internal limitation to the 'just be yourself' discourse, one that might become an important point of conflict as work and life become increasingly blurred, and increasingly managed.

REFERENCES

Arendt, H. (1958) *The Human Condition* (Chicago, IL: University of Chicago Press).

Bains, G. (2007) *Meaning Inc.: The Blue Print for Business Success in the 21st Century* (London: Profile Books).

Barker, J. R. (1999) *The Discipline of Teamwork: Participation and Concertive Control* (London: Sage).

Barley, S. R. and G. Kunda (1992) 'Design and devotion: Surges of rational and normative ideologies of control in managerial discourse', *Administrative Science Quarterly*, Vol. 37, pp. 363–399.

Bendix, R. (1956) *Work and Authority in Industry: Ideologies of Management in the Course of Industrialization* (Berkeley, CA: University of California Press).

Blau, P. (1955) *The Dynamics of Bureaucracy* (Chicago, IL: University of Chicago Press).

Boltanski, L. and E. Chiapello (2005) *The New Spirit of Capitalism*, trans. G. Elliott (London: Verso).

Braudel, F. (1961) *Chapters in Western Civilization* (New York, NY: Columbia University Press).

Casey, C. (1995) *Work, Self and Society: After Industrialism* (London: Routledge).

Clegg, S. and D. Dunkerley (1980) *Organization, Class and Control* (London: Routledge and Kegan Paul).

Coser, L. A. (1974) *Greedy Institutions: Patterns of Undivided Commitment* (New York, NY: Free Press).

Crouch, C. (2011) *The Strange Non-death of Neoliberalism* (Cambridge: Polity Press).

Deal, T. and M. Key (1998) *Celebration at Work: Play, Purpose and Profit at Work* (New York, NY: Berrett-Koehler).

Fleming, P. (2009) *Authenticity and the Cultural Politics of Work* (Oxford: Oxford University Press).

Fleming, P. and A. Sturdy (2010) 'Being yourself in the electronic sweatshop: New forms of normative control', *Human Relations*, Vol. 64, pp. 177–200.

Goffman, E. (1959) *Presentation of Self in Everyday Life* (Harmondsworth: Penguin).

Gregg, M. (2011) *Work's Intimacy* (Cambridge: Polity).

Hardt, M. and A. Negri (1994) *The Labor of Dionysus: A Critique of the State Form* (Minneapolis, MI: University of Minnesota Press).

—— (1999) *Empire* (Cambridge, MA: Harvard University Press).

—— (2009) *Commonwealth* (Cambridge, MA: Harvard University Press).

Heuberger, F. and L. Nash, eds (1994) *A Fatal Embrace? Assessing Holistic Trends in Human Resources Programs* (New Brunswick, NJ: Transaction).

Hochschild, A. R. (1983) *The Managed Heart: Commercialisation of Human Feeling* (London: University of California Press).

—— (1997) *The Time Bind: When Work Becomes Home and Home Becomes Work* (New York, NY: Holt).

Janssens, M. and P. Zanoni (2005) 'Many diversities for many services: Theorizing diversity (management) in service companies', *Human Relations*, Vol. 58, No. 3, pp. 311–340.

Kunda, G. (1992) *Engineering Culture: Control and Commitment in a High Technology Corporation* (Philadelphia, PA: Temple University Press).

Marx, K. (1976 [1867]) *Capital*, Vol. 1 (London: Pelican).

Meyerson, D. (2001) *Tempered Radicals: How Everyday Leaders Inspire Change at Work* (Cambridge, MA: Harvard University Press).

Mills, C. W. (1956) *The Power Elite* (New York, NY: Free Press).

Nippert-Eng, C. (1996) *Home and Work: Negotiating Boundaries through Everyday Life* (Chicago, IL: University of Chicago Press).

O'Reilly, C. and J. Chatman (1996) 'Culture as social control: Corporations, cults, and commitment', in B. Staw and L. Cummings, eds, *Research in Organizational Behavior* (Greenwich, CT: JAI Press).

Peters, T. (2003) *Re-imagine! Business Excellence in a Disruptive Age* (London: Dorling Kindersley).

Raeburn, N. C. (2004) *Changing Corporate America from Inside Out: Lesbian and Gay Workplace Rights* (Minneapolis, MI: University of Minnesota Press).

Roethlisberger, F. and W. Dickson (1936) *Management and the Worker* (Cambridge, MA: Harvard University Press).

Ross, A. (2004) *No-collar: The Humane Workplace and its Hidden Costs* (Philadelphia, PA: Temple University Press).

Scase, R. and R. Goffee (1989) *Reluctant Managers: Their Work and Lifestyles* (London: Unwin Hyman).

Scott, A. and M. Storper (1986) *Production, Work and Territory* (London: Unwin Hyman).

Semler, R. (2004) *The Seven-day Weekend* (New York, NY: Penguin).

Sennett, R. (1976) *The Fall of Public Man* (London: W. W. Norton).

Taylor, C. (1992) *The Ethics of Authenticity* (Cambridge, MA: Harvard University Press).

Thompson, E. P. (1963) *The Making of the English Working Class* (Harmondsworth: Penguin).

Tronti, M. (1979 [1966]) 'The strategy of the refusal', in B. Roseer and P. Saunders, eds, *Working Class Autonomy and the Crisis: Italian Marxist Texts of the Theory and Practice of Class Movement: 1964–1979* (London: Red Notes and CSE Books).

Van Maanen, J. (1991) 'The smile factory: Work at Disney Land', in P. Frost, L. Moore, M. Lewis, C. Lumberg and J. Martin, eds, *Reframing Organizational Culture* (Newbury Park, CA: Sage).

Weber, M. (1948) *From Max Weber: Essays in Sociology*, ed. and trans. H. Gerth and C. W. Mills (New York, NY: Oxford University Press).

Whyte, W. H (1956) *The Organizational Man* (New York, NY: Doubleday).

5
Oblique ethnography
Engaging collaborative complicity among globalised corporate managers

Emil A. Røyrvik

INTRODUCTION: CROSSING BOUNDARIES

Calls for more ethnographic research in the context of organisational and management research appear from time to time. For example, an interesting point-counterpoint exchange appeared in the *Journal of Management Studies*, where the editors voiced the need for the unique ethnographic approach, and challenged two notable anthropologists of the corporate worlds to discuss the contributions and role of ethnography in organisation and management studies (Editors 2011; Van Maanen 2011; Watson 2011). Independent of such calls, a substantive catalogue of ethnography in and of corporations has been published (see, for example, Baba 1986; Garsten 1994; Jordan 2003; Krause-Jensen 2010). There is also an adjacent, more applied tradition of corporate ethnography (Cefkin 2009). Nevertheless, a comprehensive review of anthropology and the corporation concludes that: 'To date, one cannot discern a coherent set of research questions or competing schools of thought characterizing the anthropology of corporations' (Welker et al. 2011: 5). The authors acknowledge all the important ethnographic research into corporate worlds, yet assess the overall corpus on the subject to be small in comparison to the significance and weight afforded to research on the nation-state.

While keeping this background in mind, this chapter engages in reflections on ethnography in corporate worlds, and in particular among globalised corporate managers. As such it addresses June Nash's (1979) early call for an anthropology of the multinational corporation that would, among other things, include managers. By using some illustrations from my own multi-sited and multi-temporal research in this area, I want to focus on some constructive dilemmas, challenges and opportunities these sites of research might offer. As part of this effort I want to free ethnography from its relegation to a form of method, and reaffirm the importance of theorising and engaging in ontological reflection in ethnographic practice.

While corporate worlds share many of their constitutive characteristics with other social worlds and fields, their goal-oriented purposefulness, their decisive instrumentalism, stands out as a particularly important premise of corporate organisation. Whereas corporations to a large extent are defined by efficacy, the management of corporations is similarly defined by idioms of usefulness and instrumental rationality. The inception of the management tradition(s) can be traced back to the American discourse among engineers in the US in the years from 1880 to 1932 (Shenhav 1999), the latter year being when Berle and Means (1991 [1932]) announced the 'managerial revolution'. Shenhav exposes the 'process by which managerial rationality crystallized to become the unquestioned pacemaker of the modern social order', while playing a critical role in 'diffusing repertoires of instrumental rationality worldwide' (1999: 2). Studying corporate management is thus a study of key aspects of modernisation and modern forms of instrumental rationality.

The constitutive instrumentalism of corporate organisation and management is instantiated in various ways in corporations, from profit seeking and production goals, to ownership structures, audit practices, reward systems and wage relations, and, not least, laws that invest corporate actors with jurisprudential obligations, responsibility and accountability. The management ideology in Hydro, a leading global supplier of aluminium, where my fieldwork was conducted, is also, as we shall see, strongly influenced by a tradition of 'democratic capitalism' that emphasises the corporation as a social institution with a broad social mandate.

In this chapter I choose to explore these worlds from their defining characteristics in terms of boundary construction, maintenance and re-definition. From membership regulation to mechanisms of work organisation, to facilitating efficiency, control, and also forms of empowerment, formal boundaries are actively created, maintained, changed and moved in corporate worlds. In conjunction with the broad trends of globalisation, external and internal corporate boundaries are reshaped, transcended, unmade and made anew. And in my particular ethnographic focus on corporate investment projects, the creation and management of new boundaries and bounded entities, and the re-drawing and erasing of the old ones, are critical activities. In investment projects new corporate entities are created, first as various projects and sub-projects with power and resources made available, which may then lead to a new production plant with the status of a legal person. This new 'corporate person' also has numerous newly created boundaries, interfaces and organisational entities within it, for example departments, and it is also created with multiple boundary interfaces to other parts of Hydro, to customers and to other stakeholders.

I argue that by traversing and being positioned *at* the boundaries – mainly through various techniques of following people, objects and concepts in the organisational worlds we study in a 'sideways' (Hannerz 1998), non-linear, abductive way – we enact the boundaries and borders that co-construct the worlds we want to understand. Through this boundary transgression and confirmation, the social world of corporations stands out, affords empiric observation, and might be stitched together through ethnographic description (Garsten 2009). This oblique ethnography is challenging and rewarding in terms of access, entries and exits, and might be considered, in some senses, as a continuous process of entries/exits, yet offers novel research opportunities.

As will be unfolded more in detail below, 'oblique' here signifies both the methodological dismantling of the 'ethnographic trilogy' (of one researcher, studying in one place and at one time) and studying neither up nor down but rather sideways, with interlocutors 'who are, like anthropologists, in a transnational contact zone, and engaged there with managing meaning across distances' (Hannerz 1998: 109). Further, the term signifies the utilisation and juggling of several research roles, and the traversing of multiple corporate boundaries that makes the entries of the ethnographer 'into' the various subfields indirect. Typically the presence of the ethnographer in different corporate arenas and situations was legitimated by a rather complex, not easily communicated or traceable, history and chain of events, yet at other times there were hardly any 'good reasons' for the ethnographer's presence. And in corporate worlds, and especially among managers, just hanging around is not necessarily appropriate. But because of the obliquity, in the sense of the multiple and cross-boundary ties to corporate members and stakeholders, some vague yet quite reasonable reason could be concocted. Still, in some situations one of the roles, in particular the contract research and advisory role, had a more easily understandable mandate related to some specific research activities and deliverables attached to it that could be communicated to corporate members.

A part of the notion of oblique ethnography is a suggestion that rather than searching for the valued ideal of insider anthropology, of gaining good rapport, organisational ethnographers may, to sustain productive working relationships in fieldwork, engage in various forms of collaborative complicity with the organisational actors who benefit from or are put at a disadvantage by the ethnographic projects. In this sense corporate ethnographies can provide value both to the academic community in terms of published ethnographies and to the corporate world by possibly contributing to changing the terms of both discourse and practice with and within corporations.

FROM RAPPORT TO COLLABORATIVE COMPLICITY

A premise of the practices that occur in my ethnographic field, what Trouillot calls 'the ethnographic trilogy' (2003: 125), is dismantled. This trilogy is the notion of one researcher spending a prolonged continuous period doing fieldwork in one separate and discrete geographical location. My entrance to the field was through a focus on investigating management practices in a set of industrial investment projects in the Norwegian-based globalised corporation Hydro. The company is a leading actor in the aluminium industry. In 2012, Hydro employed 23,000 people in more than 40 countries worldwide. In 2010 revenues were NOK 75.754 billion.

My fieldwork was conducted at ten geographical locations in Europe, China and Qatar, sometimes in between them, at airports, hotels, seminars, etc. Some of the work took place in a collaborative mode with another research colleague and with members of the company. And although I have had a collaborative research relationship with the company for ten years (2001 to

2011), I have been 'in and out of the field' constantly. This expression itself evokes the notion heralded in much anthropological conceptualisation, that culture resides in discrete geographical places (Gupta and Ferguson 1997). And, for me, each 'continuous batch' of 'localised' fieldwork has hardly been longer than two weeks. My research collaboration with the company also started out as contract-based research through my role as a research scientist at SINTEF, a large research foundation, and continued, partly in parallel, through my four-year PhD project in social anthropology, using the company as the ethnographic case. In my research relations with the company I thus sustained a dual role, on the one hand as a research scientist in contract-based research, sometimes including action research (Greenwood and Levin 1998) and research-based advisory work; and, on the other hand, as a more traditional PhD student working on an ethnography of corporate management (Røyrvik 2008). The dual role entailed dilemmas but offered the possibility of conducting participant observation in these fields.

For example, in addition to writing research reports and providing research summaries in presentations to company interlocutors, participative collaboration between Hydro managers and myself in the role of the SINTEF researcher consisted in engaging collaboratively as an adviser in the planning phase of a new investment project. In the Qatalum project, for example, the SINTEF researchers participated in providing concepts and models for planning and implementing the enrolment and training of employees for the new production plant. One such concept was the 'Dream-team', outlining how experienced Hydro managers and employees in their global network could form a flexible team to support the new organisation both on site and through virtual means with all kinds of competences in the start-up phase. Another related concept developed was the 'Training trail', outlining an 'itinerary' of training modules new (groups of) managers and employees at the new plant should experience, as well as visiting various relevant sister plants in the Hydro network. These concepts had various intended and unintended side effects in terms of, for example, experience sharing, 'culture building' and motivation. Sometimes the families of the new employees were invited along on Training trail trips. The Training trail was presented by the executive vice president as part of Hydro's overall concept in the Qatalum project at a management board meeting. This advisory function was grounded in research insights and results gained in former research projects with Hydro, not only in the domain of investment projects but in other business units in the company, and thus with other people as partners. The researchers' experiences from across various internal businesses and organisational boundaries enabled a role with a broad view of the capacities in the overall network. This is also an aspect of the 'obliquity' of such ethnography.

A few more words about the Hydro field are necessary. Hydro was founded in 1905, the same year as Norway achieved its national independence. Being global in outlook from its inception, the histories of Hydro and of Norway are intimately connected, and Hydro, with its engineering culture, has been a key locomotive in the development of the modern Norwegian industrial nation and, consequently, the welfare state. Historically, managers and employees in Hydro have a perception of their company as a vital social institution that has a much broader social and democratic mandate and justification than pure profit-making – yet also as being fiercely market oriented (Andersen 2005; Johannessen et al. 2005; Lie 2005). A few quotes illustrate this. One corporate executive said: 'I would like to resolve the stupid tension between money and society because they are one and the same.' An employee voiced a similar perspective: 'We see the world through one lens where there is no distinction between business performance and social contribution. They are mutually supportive.' Another executive said: 'We helped build a country not just a company. It is in our blood to see the world of business through the lens of society,' and another employee stated: 'the very premise of our existence was to help found a nation, not just make money.'

In general terms the management ideology and corporate culture in Hydro instantiates a primary example of what is known as democratic capitalism (Røyrvik 2011; Sejersted 1993), where a strong state combines with strong communalism and connects with the broadly based *petit bourgeois* and its ideals of equality and democracy. A core question regarding this model has been how the economic domain can enable democratically participatory citizens and democratic societal development. In this view democracy is the overarching system value of capitalism (Slagstad 2001: 527). This system has come under increasing pressure during the last decades (Byrkjeflot et al. 2001), including in Hydro where neoliberalism and the financialisation of the economy have led to changes in their managerial rationality. In short, these changes have been a move, especially since 1999, from 'industrial management' to 'money management', for example through an intensified focus on shareholder value, the bottom line, and the invention and implementation of top to bottom financial performance, control and incentive structures (such as stock options schemes).

With my particular focus on the management of investment projects in Hydro, I consider this multi-sited and multi-temporal field of projects to make up a network of 'global assemblages' (Ong and Collier 2005); the projects and their connections are emergent, decentred, ephemeral and fundamentally characterised by movement, while nonetheless exhibiting orderliness and structuredness in quite an extreme sense. Such a field could be seen in light of Hannerz's (2003) reflections about the translocal field, or Faubion's (2009) notion of fieldwork as a topology of connectivity.

It is in the context of this kind of mobile ethnography across boundaries, multi-sited and multi-temporal, that the figure of complicity (and betrayal) becomes most relevant. While anthropologists arguably more often than not have understood themselves as being both inside and outside of the sites and social relations they study, as Marcus discusses, they have maintained a faith and, in a sense, a fictional hope that 'they could be relatively more insiders than outsiders if only by mastering the skills of translation, sensitivity, and learned cultural competencies – in short, that they could achieve rapport' (1998: 118). Getting 'inside' by achieving rapport, that is, a close and harmonious relationship with subjects, in which understanding of each other's feelings and ideas prevails, has been the (fictional) ideal.

Marcus (1998) develops the figure of complicity in contrast to rapport, and also in contrast to the type of complicity discussed by Geertz, where complicity leads to rapport. The paradigmatic case in point was when Geertz (1973) had to flee from a Balinese cockfight that was raided by the police, and the ensuing handling of the situation and his complicity with the other participants present 'opened the doors' for rapport and getting on the 'inside' with people in the village. Geertz elsewhere (1968) adopts a subtle perspective on the doubleness of the insider/outsider positioning, in that the kinds of rapport achieved entail an 'anthropological irony', where both ethnographer and informants engage in mutual fictions to overlook their different positions. However, Marcus's version of complicity works in contrast to the kinds of complicity that aim to achieve rapport. Although it 'begins from the same inside-outside boundary positioning' (1998: 118) as the classical 'getting on the inside' ideal of good rapport, this figure of complicity does not posit the same faith in being able to probe the 'inside' of a culture, and, given the entanglement of the local in the global, it also does not presuppose the subjects themselves as 'insiders'.

Moreover, the complicity that Marcus advocates stresses the productivity of retaining a kind of outsider position: 'The idea of complicity forces the recognition of ethnographers as ever-present markers of "outsidedness"'(1998: 118). Here one might evoke Duerr's (1985) analogy of the researcher as a witch (*hagazussa*), who is actively positioned on the fence, with one foot on the inside and one on the outside of the social order. 'Never stirring from the boundary', Marcus writes, the ethnographer's presence 'makes possible certain kinds of access that the idea of rapport and the faith in being able to get inside (by fiction à la Geertz, by utopian collaboration à la Clifford, or by self-deception à la Rosaldo) does not' (1998: 118–119). Marcus argues that it is only when both the ethnographer and subject do not try to escape the 'outsidedness' of the situation, but on the contrary makes the outsidedness the common ground between them, that ethnography can begin to accommodate the new multi-sited research contexts.

Complicity here underscores that both ethnographer and subject entertain an awareness of 'existential doubleness' deriving from 'a sense of being *here* where major transformations are underway that are tied to things happening simultaneously *elsewhere*, but not having a certainty or authoritative representation of what those connections are' (1998: 118). In this sense we can interpret the boundary between the ethnographer and her counterparts in the same double sense, as constituting both a barrier and a bridge, establishing a relationship and a connection. And what ethnographers are seeking from their interlocutors in these new scenes is not so much local knowledge as:

> articulation of the forms of anxiety that are generated by the awareness of being affected by what is elsewhere without knowing what the particular connections to that elsewhere might be. The ethnographer on the scene in this sense makes the elsewhere *present*. (1998: 119)

Rather than seeking rapport through various means, so as to 'forget' their differences, the point of complicity, as argued by Marcus, is the exact opposite: that the anthropologist and his subject do *not* engage in fictions that achieve rapport, but rather engage each other in exchanges of outsidedness and elsewhereness. As I will describe in more detail below, my dual role as a PhD student and a contract researcher with accumulating experience from across the company's different business areas, facilitated this common outsidedness with interlocutors.

As argued by Marcus, this recognition of a common predicament is the primary motivation behind developing the notion of complicity to accommodate the new forms of contexts and fields in which ethnography is currently being conducted. As emphasised in the ethnographic extended case method (Burawoy 2009; Evens and Handelman 2006), unfolding the figure of complicity rests on highlighting the external origination and connection of local discourses to other sites and networks. In the particular fieldwork event this externality might be marked and set off by the fieldworker's outsider presence, but it transcends the ideal of insider rapport and collaboration. This joint predicament in outward extended complicity and concern with outsidedness, for both ethnographer and subject, affords a methodological push that moves the research project into the realm of multi-sited fieldwork, 'a trajectory that encourages the ethnographer literally to move to other sites that are powerfully registered in the local knowledge of an originating locus of fieldwork' (Marcus 1998: 120). In this sense, the figure of collaborative complicity offers a potential for collaborative ethnography in complex modern contexts such as corporations, but in the mode of complicity positioned at the boundaries of insideness/outsideness, free of the demands of rapport, to pursue a grounded – ethnography-from-below – approach to the complex connectivity of the 'global age' (Røyrvik 2012). Outlined in more detail below, this kind of boundary position was enacted in my own fieldwork, and also reflected the increasing and more subtle investigation of organisational boundaries in the social sciences.

CORPORATE BORDERWORK

In recent years the ideas of 'boundaries' and 'borders' have achieved a key role across the humanities and social sciences (Lamont and Molnár 2002; Tilly 2005). We might turn to the classical social scientists as a point of departure in understanding the dynamic and dual quality of boundaries as something that both divide and connect. Simmel (1957) described the dynamics of social groups and forms in terms of drawing, maintaining, reinforcing and crossing boundaries. He linked the human preoccupation with parting and connecting with our fascination for bridges and doors, and notions like the 'boundaries of something' versus the 'boundaries between something' highlight this duality. Since Durkheim and Mauss's original work on social classification there has been a broad consensus that human beings and cultures order the world by drawing and re-drawing boundaries, both conceptual or figurative, and physical or literal/material. People think and talk of borders and boundaries because they have been inscribed in and are inscribing the imagination and consciousness of people (Flynn 1997; Paasi 1999; Rösler and Wendl 1999).

In the context of organisation and management research, an increasing awareness of boundaries has also recently emerged. In opposition to a mainstream view of organisational boundaries as given, fixed and unambiguous, organisational boundaries are thematised as becoming blurred (Marchington et al. 2005), fluid and more complex (Leng and Dahles 2005), and even obsolete. Paulsen and Hernes (2003), however, provide multiple perspectives and case studies on organisational boundaries and managing boundaries in organisations, and show that while boundaries certainly function to stabilise and order the organisation, they also facilitate mobilisation and the capacity to reach out and influence processes in the external environment. This notion of organisational boundaries is in dialogue with Garsten's (2009) concept of 'ethnography at the interface' of organisations. Her study of the field of corporate social responsibility comprised of traversing the interfaces and connections of this translocal field by 'tracing the relationship of capitalism and social responsibility, across cultural, national and geographical boundaries' (2009: 66). The concept of boundaries as 'interfaces' highlights the doubleness of boundaries as both barriers and bridges. 'Interface' signals both something that cleaves and connects, something that both divides and establishes relationships. Both Paulsen and Hernes' (2003) and Garsten's (2009) approach to boundaries also highlights the necessity and possibility of extending out of the organisational confinement of the one rigorously defined organisation, when focusing on organisational boundaries. The very notion of an organisational boundary suggests a connected outside.

Useful in the context of organisational boundaries, the multivocality of boundaries and their multiple functions are captured by the concept of 'borderwork' (Rumford 2008), which emphasises the role of citizens and non-citizens in imagining, making and breaking borders. 'Bordering' processes are not solely practised by nation-states, and should rather be conceived of as a set of highly asymmetric and unequal processes. A central question is who does most of the bordering, and who is mostly 'bordered'? This question is related to the debate about the concept of culture, between Geertz, who famously stated that culture is a web of significance man himself has spun, and Keesing who, quoting Scholte, noted that few do the actual spinning; the majority are simply caught up in it (Keesing 1987: 161–162). Ethnographers of corporate worlds should investigate this tension: while everybody is involved in bordering and borderwork, some actors' borderwork is clearly more consequential than others'. Notably, corporate managers are among those groups in organisations doing a lot of border and boundary spinning.

COMPLICITY AMONG ELITES

In my own mobile, translocal and multi-temporal fieldwork among managers in multiple sites of the global Hydro corporate network, numerous organisational boundaries and interfaces were enacted; nation-state boundaries, boundaries demarcating hierarchical levels in the organisation; interfaces between functions and business areas (for example the various R&D departments versus the numerous business functions and the differentiation between the business areas); boundaries between corporate staff and operations, and between human resource and other support functions, and production. My own specific focus on investment projects (Røyrvik 2011) exposes numerous project boundaries that, among other things, divide the project owners from the project proper, and distinguish between the owner function and the operations function; and boundaries demarcating organisational entities along value chains and timelines: upstream, midstream and downstream, or in projects according to phases, with institutionalised decision gates that the project must pass through to move forward.

The corporate managers I studied were intensely preoccupied with borderwork, and to gain access to and working relationships with such elites, I nurtured my double role as contract research scientist and PhD student. Several of the research projects at SINTEF are conducted as action research (Greenwood and Levin 1998), where the interventionist side of research is accentuated. In my work with Hydro the activist side has been played out in my role as SINTEF researcher, whereas it has been actively downplayed in my role as PhD student. What makes the activist desire somewhat special in this case, is the elite and expert context of the field. Although one executive in Hydro at one point jokingly said that the success of my PhD education was dependent upon the success of Hydro in their new projects, at the end of the day, the 'activism' which the SINTEF projects brings to the table, 'making a difference' in this kind of a system, as it were, is both highly ambivalent and marginal.

One key implication of the dilemmas outlined above has been the issue of in which role I participated in social events during fieldwork: the SINTEF researcher and science-based adviser role or the anthropological student role. Some of my key collaborators frequently saluted me with variants on the theme of 'How is the student doing?' The greeting was an explicit way of jesting with my (at least) double status. 'When are we going to get anything useful from these students?' was another favourite. This double role was, I argue, more of a strength, not least because it facilitated a space for open-ended communication. In gathering data this doubleness could be problematic, however, in terms of which themes to focus on in discussions and interviews. As a PhD student my interests in the people I was collaborating with was in general more open-ended and unspecified than in my role as a SINTEF researcher. Thus, under the omnipresent time pressures in many fieldwork situations there had to be a trade off between focusing on themes, actions and getting information that was more instrumentally needed in the SINTEF projects versus more open-ended communicative interaction favourable to my PhD project. Similarly, when visiting, interviewing, observing and to a limited extent participating, at the investment project and production field sites, or rather in the oblique 'fieldflows', the management of this double role had to be carefully improvised and handled. To get the attention of members and access to meetings the role of SINTEF researcher in utility-based collaboration with Hydro often had to be performed. However, this role could easily lead to an image of being 'sent from headquarters to audit the local operation', so the emphasis on independent research also had to be stressed in some contexts. And at local sites I wanted to downplay the formal role of 'adviser' as quickly as possible and rather incorporate the role of a curious and interesting dialogue partner.

Although this juggling of statuses at times was far from straightforward, it seemed to work. One reason might be that corporate managers and other members themselves are very familiar with professional status shifts and role-playing, based upon their multiple roles, according to circumstances. An illustration of this could be in the opening of an interview I did with a high-level corporate manager. During the first minutes, he felt the need to clarify his own role related to the interview situation and topical circumstances, so he started out by saying:

> Who am I now? Well, as far as it goes I am the same as I have always been. For what I am going to talk about now, however, I think we should see me as a manager who has experience in restructuring plants, closing down or transforming companies.

Following Nugent's (2002) distinction between 'accessible' and 'effective' elites, anthropologists may be able to get access to the former while the latter are difficult to approach and have no structural need to consent to being studied. Also, Kunda, in his study of engineers in a high-tech company, discusses the difficulties with access and describes access as inversely related to hierarchical level. As a result he spent most of his time among staff 'largely because contact with staff was easier, and my role as observer–confidant– interesting guy seemed to work' (1992: 236). He complains about 'continuous and often frustrating contact with protective secretarial gatekeepers' (1992: 236). Similarly, ethnography of an elite organisation, Marcus (1986) writes, can most likely be done with the out-of-power, the retired, among the elites in decline or those of marginal importance. Without my double status including one that also could play on utility, addressing the imperative of usefulness in corporate settings (Blomberg 2009), of being useful among the managers by bringing into the dialogue cross-boundary outsidedness and elsewhereness (research perspectives from multiple investment projects in Hydro and from other companies), access would have been very difficult and, I believe, *participant* observation even more so. Another notable feature of the work has been that I have not gained a particularly deep, personal and intimate relationship with many of the actors in the company. Except for two or three people, my relationship with them has been restricted to the professional sphere. In several cases, however, I think largely due to my status as an anthropologist, we have jointly explored this sphere far beyond the borders of how they among themselves in daily interactions would define it. Leaving aside several restaurant dinners and an occasional party, we have not spent a lot of time informally 'out of office'.

This prompts reflections about ethnography in elite and expert social environments. Why do anthropology under such circumstances at all? 'Is the point of doing fieldwork among experts to do a conventional ethnography of them?', Holmes and Marcus ask (2005: 236). I concur with the answer they provide:

> The anthropologist does not study the lives of central bankers, for instance, because they have the same kind of interest that the everyday lives of the Tikopia, the Tongans, or the Nuer have had for anthropologists. Indeed, rarely do ethnographers have access to the details of the everyday lives of expert subjects.... We believe it is highly unlikely that a robust ethnography of 'everyday life' can be done within these cultures of expertise ... (2005: 236)

On the other hand, anthropology's signature must be found in the inquiry one way or the other. The solution of Holmes and Marcus (2005) is a kind of re-functioning of ethnography, which they label 'para-ethnography', where another kind of a native's point of view remains in the domain of experts. This is a space where the concept of experience is central, both as an anthropological signature and as a bridge towards the dominant forms of knowledge production in the expert domains of study. The para-ethnographic dimension is the identification and engagement with the 'self-conscious critical faculty that operates in any expert domain as a way of dealing with contradiction, exception, facts that are fugitive' (Holmes and Marcus 2005: 237). This self-reflective mode suggests a social sphere that is not in perfect alignment with the experts' formally accepted representational models. Critical to this mode of doing ethnography is its status as a kind of marginal social thought, in 'genres such as "the anecdotal", "hype", and intuition – within practices dominated by the technocratic ethos ... ' (2005: 237). The anecdotal as a form of representing and enacting the 'native point of view' of corporate members, in relative tension to official accounts, plays a crucial role in this kind of ethnography. In my perspective, the anecdotal is a sub-genre of narrative modes of signification and knowing. In relation to the narrative modality, much of my fieldwork is based upon interviews. Most of them are conducted with single subjects. Some have been conducted alone, and some in collaboration with colleagues. The romantic ideal of rapport, of becoming friends with the ones you study, of nurturing deep emotional and morally contingent relationships, is more difficult in a multi-sited study, and becomes considerably intensified in a complex capitalist elite context.

Again, a possible downside needs to be mirrored against what kinds of relationships are fostered by the members of the company themselves. Managers change positions frequently, project teams are formed from a global pool of people and dissolved after project completion. Although long-term personal networks exist and are important in many respects, few foster any deep relationships outside the work context. In these kinds of studies, as

Hannerz (1998) notes, personal relationships with the informants are not of particularly great importance, as long as one is on good speaking terms. Carrying out interviews as the most common fieldwork technique is also modelled upon the scripts of communicative interaction of the organisational members themselves. Managers regulate their interactions through systematic procedures of scheduling meetings. Conversational interviews, of approximately one hour each, fit in nicely with this socialising regime as a legitimate way of interaction.

A final characteristic of the types of fieldwork discussed here, with general interest to ethnographic research, is the use of an abundance of diverse material simply not available or existing in the idealised naturalist studies of 'primitive life' in ethnography (see, for example, Gupta and Ferguson 1997). Once access is secured, and even without, this type of field offers a range of highly significant but untraditional 'ethnographica': from newspaper articles, TV-debates and internet presentations, and a variety of official reports (for example annual reports) to intranet web-pages, internal interactive net-cafés, company information and communication technology systems of diverse types, pictures and movies, internal and confidential documents such as minutes of meetings, reports and evaluations, email exchanges, presentations and forecasts. The significance of media and media materials is strong because they partly constitute and hold these translocal fields together, mediating the managing of meaning across boundaries and distances, both for ethnographers and interlocutors.

TROPES OF TRANSGRESSION

If a 'brave new world' of multi-sited, multi-temporal and collaborative para-ethnography, studying modern institutions and global assemblages, studying up and sideways has been installed in mainstream anthropology, it is worth probing whether these practices of constructing anthropological objects are aligned or not with the deeper historical currents of such object construction practices (see, for example, Gupta and Ferguson 1997). Do forms of oblique ethnography represent continuity and/or a radical break with anthropological object construction practices?

As with any discipline, anthropology might be considered as a specialised form of rhetorical 'object construction practice', and Tord Larsen (2006) analyses anthropology as such through four distinct phases. In all phases 'the primitive' is the anthropological object *par excellence*: the primitive as (1) nature (both the savage and the noble savage), as (2) pre-rational, as (3) authentic and (4) the lost primitive re-primitivised. The question is whether oblique ethnography instantiates or represents a break with the last phase of re-primitivising the lost primitive. For example, exoticisation practices in anthropological studies of management have been noted by Linstead (1997). Larsen writes that modern objects are prepared for the anthropological gaze in ways that make them appear as 'primitive', and thus makes possible the 'discovering [of] magic at the factory, totemism in the bureaucracy ...

fetishes in the commodities, metaphors in marketing, and heaps of rituals hidden in all the instrumentality' (2006: 14, my translation). In the figure of collaborative complicity in corporate worlds, does the ethnographer re-primitivise the lost primitive? Each of the four phases emerges, according to Larsen, out of a rhetorical situation bringing forth its own classification mechanism. The scientific revolution de-animates nature and establishes the dominant categorical dichotomy of subject and object (mind and nature); the enlightenment adds the opposition between rationality and irrationality; and the Industrial Revolution institutionalises the contrast between the authentic and the alienated (organic and mechanical). These dichotomies constitute at a fundamental level the relation between the knower and the known. The prototypical, and most legitimate, anthropological objects are, thus, those phenomena we as ethnographers have evolved 'away' from: 'ontological hierarchies, the analogue relationship between micro and macro-cosmos, magic, sacrificing, totemism, clan organization, animism, ancestor worship' (2006: 6, my translation).

It is against such a background that we must understand the postcolonial discourse claiming that anthropological descriptions embody a historicisa-tion of their objects, confining them to the past, which in turn establishes a hierarchical asymmetry between knower and known. In this reading 'the primitive' as the exemplary anthropological object is taken hostage as the manifestation of the discipline's melancholic yearning for that which is lost, positioning *melancholy* as the ethos or feeling that singles out the anthro-pological object. As Larsen writes: 'the lost is the prototypical object of anthropology. [The] desire for what is lost ... attracts us to the authenticity from which we have become alienated in our attempts to gain reflexive control over it' (2006: 12, my translation). We might say that the anthropological gaze is forever searching for the past in the present, whether it is on live, public display with 'the most other of others' in remote and discrete geographical locations, or whether it is hidden in small pockets of modern institutions.

The rhetorical devices embedded in our anthropological descriptions seem to deceive us, even in the postcolonial period, which supposedly has forever purged the asymmetrical relations and 'pith-helmet procedures of colonial ethnology' (Gupta and Ferguson 1997: 26, referring to Geertz). When talking about urgent anthropology, anthropology at home or applied anthropology, or when I have described my fieldwork as multi-sited and multi-temporal, our language re-inscribes the same basic categories and fundamental dichotomies we want to free ourselves from. Urgent anthropology implies something almost lost is really about to become extinct; anthropologists at home are recommended to employ defamiliarisation techniques; applied anthropology rests upon a notion of a pure, romantically innocent, non-interventionist anthropology; and multi-sited and multi-temporal fields and fieldwork presuppose 'ideal' singular field sites and field times. We do not speak of 'single-sited' or 'single-temporal' studies. While conducting fieldwork through the figure of collaborative complicity, the question of whether an anthropology without radical alterity is possible still seems to remain unresolved. In the new anthropological/ethnographic studies of modern institutional elites, however, it is arguably difficult to sustain a rhetoric that primitivises the 'other'. The asymmetries are to some degree turned upside down, in such a way that the subject matter coerces our descriptions away from the objectifying languages of the monological rhetoric of colonial discourse. In these studies we might rather appreciate a discursive 'fight' between two different forms of hegemonic language, a tension that could prove fruitful in modifying the rhetorical object construction practices of anthropology.

If we agree with Larsen (2006), that we have witnessed a shift from objectifying to subjectifying languages on a large scale (in relation to the oriental, the primitive, to women, children and the mentally ill), this is a result of a broad decolonisation of the world. The 'other' has increasingly become an agent, a fellow subject independent of our representations. And in conjunction with this process of independence, our descriptions change form. In this perspective there seems to be a major self-reflexive mission in the studies of modern corporations and elites, providing an opportunity to dethrone and transform the rhetorical worshipping of primitivisation. Nevertheless, a reinvented ethnography should continue a tradition where the universal and the particular need not be opposed. This kind of position is summarised in Bloch's description of his book *From Blessing to Violence*, where he characterises it as an example of anthropology's hybrid commitment to write about 'specific events in specific places at specific times' (1986: 2), while also engaging in theoretical reflection with its general conclusions.

A reconfiguring of ethnography as a sideways oblique ethnography of collaborative complicity, positioned at and through the boundaries, might contribute towards reinstating ethnography as constituting 'fieldwork, headwork, and textwork' (Van Maanen 2011: 218). Doing so could also possibly re-inscribe the difference between anthropology and ethnography as voiced, for example, by Timothy Ingold (2007). He draws on Radcliffe-Brown's distinction between ethnography as an ideographic practice of describing particularities, and anthropology as a nomothetic science searching for general insights, laws and generalisations. While arguing for the reinvention of an anthropology with room for philosophy, an 'outdoor philosophy', he suggests that ontological reflection should be brought back into the anthropological enterprise.

Then anthropology should be recast as a study *with*, not *of*, and it could be perceived as both a way of knowing and being. And in grounding knowing in being, anthropology can be seen as educating our perception of the world. As such, argues Ingold (2007), theory and method come together as both arts and crafts in a way that opens up rather than closes, and anthropology is in this perspective framed as a 'sideways glance'. And with this move we are approaching something like the essence of oblique ethnography. I suggest that organisational anthropology can fruitfully pursue this mode of doing mobile ethnography, while exploring the dilemmas and possibilities it may afford as exemplified, in my case, by globalised corporate managers.

In my fieldwork I followed managers and investment projects as they traversed, created and transformed the multiplicity of organisational boundaries that construct their professional social world. And in the mode I call collaborative complicity my ethnographic engagement in the field was also positioned, in some senses ambivalently, at these organisational interfaces that connect members and ethnographer through common outsidedness and elsewhereness. This form of oblique ethnography enacts the boundaries that constitute internal and external organisational fields, and marks up the landscapes of inner and outer social worlds from where the anthropological gaze can find valuable vantage points – for both particular organisational descriptions and general insights.

REFERENCES

Andersen, K. G. (2005) *Flaggskip i fremmed eie: Hydro 1905–1945* [Flagship in foreign hands: Hydro 1905–1945] (Oslo: Pax Forlag).

Baba, M. L. (1986) *Business and industrial anthropology: An overview. NAPA Bulletin*, No. 2. (Washington, DC: American Anthropological Association).

Berle, A. Jr and G. Means (1991 [1932]) *The Modern Corporation and Private Property* (New Brunswick, NJ: Transaction).

Bloch, M. (1986) *From Blessing to Violence* (New York, NY: Cambridge University Press).

Blomberg, J. (2009) 'Insider trading: Engaging and valuing corporate ethnography', in M. Cefkin, ed., *Ethnography and the Corporate Encounter* (New York, NY: Berghahn Books).

Burawoy, M. (2009) *The Extended Case Method: Four Countries, Four Decades, Four Great Transformations, and One Tradition* (Berkeley, CA: University of California Press).

Byrkjeflot, H., S. Myklebust, C. Myrvang and F. Sejersted, eds (2001) *The Democratic Challenge to Capitalism: Management and Democracy in the Nordic Countries* (Bergen: Fagbokforlaget).

Cefkin, M., ed. (2009) *Ethnography and the Corporate Encounter* (New York, NY: Berghahn Books).

Duerr, H. P. (1985) *Dreamtime: Concerning the Boundary Between Wilderness and Civilization* (Oxford: Basil Blackwell).

Editors (2011) 'Ethnography in the context of management and organizational research: Its scope and methods, and why we need more of it', *Journal of Management Studies*, Vol. 48, No. 1, pp. 198–201.

Evens, T. M. S. and D. Handelman, eds (2006) *The Manchester School: Practice and Ethnographic Praxis in Anthropology* (New York, NY: Berghahn Books).

Faubion, J. D. (2009) 'The ethics of fieldwork as an ethics of connectivity, or the good anthropologist (isn't what she used to be)', in J. D. Faubion and G. E. Marcus, eds, *Fieldwork Is Not What It Used to Be: Learning Anthropology's Method in a Time of Transition* (Ithaca, NY: Cornell University Press).

Flynn, D. K. (1997) '"We are the border" – Identity, exchange, and the state along the Bénin–Nigeria border', *American Ethnologist*, Vol. 24, No. 2, pp. 311–330.

Garsten, C. (1994) *Apple World: Core and Periphery in a Transnational Organization. Stockholm Studies in Social Anthropology 33* (Stockholm: Alqvist and Wicksell International).

Garsten, C. (2009) 'Ethnography at the interface: "Corporate social responsibility" as an anthropological field of inquiry', in M. Melhuus, J. Mitchell and H. Wulff, eds, *Ethnographic Practice in the Present* (Oxford: Berghahn Books).

Geertz, C. (1968) 'Thinking as a moral act: Ethical dimensions of anthropological fieldwork in the new states', *Antioch Review*, Vol. 28, No. 2, pp. 139–158.

—— (1973) 'Deep play: Notes on the Balinese cockfight', in C. Geertz, *The Interpretation of Culture* (New York, NY: Basic Books).

Greenwood, D. and M. Levin (1998) *Introduction to Action Research* (Newbury Hills, CA: Sage).

Gupta, A. and J. Ferguson, eds (1997) *Anthropological Locations: Boundaries and Grounds of a Field Science* (Berkeley, CA: University of California Press).

Hannerz, U. (1998) 'Other transnationals: Perspectives gained from studying sideways', *Paideuma*, Vol. 44, pp. 109–123.

—— (2003) 'Several sites in one', in T. H. Eriksen, ed., *Globalisation: Studies in Anthropology* (London: Pluto Press).

Holmes, D. and G. Marcus (2005) 'Cultures of expertise and the management of globalization: Toward the re-functioning of ethnography', in A. Ong and S. J. Collier, eds, *Global Assemblages: Technology, Politics, and Ethics as Anthropological Problems*. (Malden, MA: Blackwell).

Ingold, T. (2007) 'Anthropology is not ethnography', Radcliffe-Brown Lecture in Social Anthropology (London: The British Academy).

Johannessen, F. E., A. Rønning and P. T. Sandvik (2005) *Nasjonal kontroll og industriell fornyelse: Hydro 1945–1977* [National Control and Industrial Renewal: Hydro 1945–1977] (Oslo: Pax Forlag).

Jordan, A. T. (2003) *Business Anthropology* (Long Grove, IL: Waveland Press.)

Keesing, R. M. (1987) 'Anthropology as interpretive quest', *Current Anthropology*, Vol. 28, No. 2, pp. 161–169.

Krause-Jensen, J. (2010) *Flexible Firms: The Design of Culture at Bang & Olufsen* (New York, NY: Berghahn Books).

Kunda, G. (1993) *Engineering Culture: Control and Commitment in a High-tech Corporation* (Philadelphia, PA: Temple University Press).

Lamont, M. and V. Molnár. (2002) 'The study of boundaries in the social sciences', *Annual Review of Sociology*, Vol. 28, pp. 167–195.

Larsen, T. (2006) 'Melankoli og retorisk heroisme. Om former for antropologisk gjenstandsdannelse' ['Melancholia and rhetorical heroism: The forms of anthropological objectification'], *Rhetorica Scandinavica*, Vol. 40, pp. 8–26.

Leng, L. W. and H. Dahles (2005) 'Conclusions: Organizational boundaries reconsidered', *Asia Pacific Business Review*, Vol. 11, No. 4, pp. 593–598.

Lie, E. (2005) *Oljerikdommer og internasjonal ekspansjon: Hydro 1977–2005.* [Oil wealth and international expansion: Hydro 1977–2005] (Oslo: Pax Forlag).

Linstead, S. (1997) 'The social anthropology of management', *British Journal of Management*, Vol. 8, pp. 85–98.

Marchington, M. P., D. Grimshaw, J. Rubery and H. Willmott, eds (2005) *Fragmenting Work: Blurring Organisational Boundaries and Disordering Hierarchies* (Oxford: Oxford University Press).

Marcus, G. E. (1986) 'Contemporary problems of ethnography in the modern world system', in J. Clifford and G. E. Marcus, eds, *Writing Culture* (Berkeley, CA: University of California Press).

Marcus, G. (1998) 'The uses of complicity in the changing mise-en-scène of anthropological fieldwork', in *Ethnography through Thick and Thin* (Princeton, NJ: Princeton University Press).

Nash, J. C. (1979) 'The anthropology of the multinational corporation', in G. Huizer and B. Mannheim, eds, *The Politics of Anthropology: From Colonialism and Sexism Toward a View from Below* (The Hague: Mouton).

Nugent, S. (2002) 'Gente Boa: Elite cultures in Amazonia', in C. Shore and S. Nugent, eds, *Elite Cultures: Anthropological Perspectives* (London: Routledge).

Ong, A. and S. J. Collier (2005) *Global Assemblages: Technology, Politics, and Ethics as Anthropological Problems* (Malden, MA: Blackwell).

Paasi, A. (1999) 'Boundaries as social practice and discourse: The Finnish–Russian border', *Regional Studies*, Vol. 33, No. 7, pp. 669–680.

Paulsen, N. and T. Hernes, eds (2003) *Managing Boundaries in Organizations: Multiple Perspectives* (Basingstoke: Palgrave Macmillan).

Røyrvik, E. A. (2008) *Directors of Creation: An Anthropology of Capitalist Conjunctures in the Contemporary.* PhD dissertation, Department of Social Anthropology, NTNU, Trondheim.

—— (2011) *The Allure of Capitalism: An Ethnography of Management and the Global Economy in Crisis* (New York, NY: Berghahn Books).

—— (2012) 'Ethnography of globalization', in G. Ritzer, ed., *Wiley-Blackwell Encyclopedia of Globalization* (Malden, MA: Wiley-Blackwell).

Rösler, M. and T. Wendl, eds (1999) *Frontiers and Borderlands: Anthropological Perspectives* (Frankfurt: Peter Lang).

Rumford, C. (2008) *Cosmopolitan Spaces: Europe, Globalization, Theory* (New York, NY: Routledge).

Sejersted, F. (1993) *Demokratisk kapitalisme* [Democratic capitalism] (Oslo: Universitetsforlaget).

Simmel, G. (1957) *Brücke und Tür*. Stuttgart: Köhler (English translation 1994 by M. Ritter: 'Bridge and door', *Theory, Culture & Society*, Vol. 11, No. 5, pp. 5–10).

Slagstad, R. (2001) *De Nasjonale Strateger* [National Strategies] (Oslo: Pax Forlag).

Shenhav, Y. A. (1999) *Manufacturing Rationality: The Engineering Foundations of the Managerial Revolution* (New York, NY: Oxford University Press).

Tilly, C. (2005) *Identities, Boundaries and Social Ties*. (Boulder, CO: Paradigm Publishers).

Trouillot, M. R. (2003) *Global Transformations: Anthropology and the Modern World* (New York, NY: Palgrave Macmillan).

Van Maanen, J. (2011) 'Ethnography as work: Some rules of engagement', *Journal of Management Studies*, Vol. 48, No. 1, pp. 218–234.

Watson, T. (2011) 'Ethnography, reality, and truth: The vital need for studies of "how things work" in organizations and management', *Journal of Management Studies*, Vol. 48, No. 1, pp. 202–217.

Welker, M., D. J. Partridge and R. Hardin (2011) 'Corporate lives: New perspectives on the social life of the corporate form', *Current Anthropology*, Vol. 52, No. S3, pp. 3–16.

Section two
Policy arenas

6
Access to all stages?
Studying through policy in a culture of accessibility

Anette Nyqvist

INTRODUCTION: THE RELATIVITY OF ACCESS

In this chapter, I describe and discuss access as an ongoing situational and relational process of ethnographic fieldwork. I have two interrelated goals for this chapter, both concerning processual aspects of accessibility. Based on various research projects on the performativity of policy in such diverse fields as national social insurance politics and the financial market, I begin by proposing a contextualised view of access. I argue that a culture of accessibility has evolved within the Swedish public administration system, such that access has become the norm and that access policies are organising principles that shape the way 'we live, act and think' (Shore and Wright 1997: i) – and, not least, they affect the civil servants working within government authorities. I then discuss how a problematising perspective on access processes can help shed light on methodological aspects concerning forms of engagement with and within formal organisations. In doing this, I hope to contribute to a more complex and nuanced conceptualisation of access, a key concern of any ethnographic inquiry. After describing accessibility as a culture and organising principle, I stop to ask four questions. Access to what? Where? To whom? For what purpose? As we all know, access is not merely a matter of getting through the door.

Anthropological inquiry in and among organisations is no longer novel research; rather it is at the stage of young adulthood and is coming of age – a good time to discuss issues of access in explicit detail and to focus on problematising issues of access. It seems also to be a good time to steer away from some of the pitfalls that an overly generalised and taken-for-granted conceptualisation of access leads to if the concept is left unspecified. Ethnographers who choose to study complex organisations sometimes assume what I have called elsewhere 'an anthropologetic stance' (Nyqvist 2003), in which they are constantly excusing themselves for not addressing issues in more traditional settings. And, after completion of the research, ethnographies of complex organisations are sometimes met with critical questions from within the discipline – questions about the quality and depth of research. Has the researcher been able to go far enough and deep enough, for example, for it to be considered strong ethnography?

The broad aim of this chapter, then, is to problematise issues of access – to examine access as diversified and multidirectional processes rather than as a problem and potential obstacle for good ethnography, a stance that reifies access, or rather the difficulty of access, as a monolithic condition and as a prerequisite for ethnographic research in and of organisations. With particular focus on conducting ethnographic fieldwork in public and semi-public bureaucratic organisations in Sweden, in this chapter I look at forms of engagement and their boundaries by asking the seemingly simple questions: Access to what? Where? To whom? And why? Revisiting Erving Goffman's (1959) famous metaphor of drama to understand social organisation, I shed light on the relative aspects of front and back stages and argue that, for ethnographers interested in policy processes in and of complex organisations, a pass to access all stages is perhaps not always something to wish or strive for.

POLICY AT THE NEXUS

My research interest lies in what transpires at the nexus of statecraft and market-making (see Peck in Nyqvist 2008: 19), and I view policy as a structural artefact and intriguing object of study. Policies are viewed here from an anthropological perspective, seen as ideological vehicles and powerful tools for governance and are, as such, studied as fundamental organising principles of society (Shore and Wright 1997; Shore et al. 2011). From this perspective, they are conceptualised as instruments of power through which governments and such other organisations as corporations and non-governmental organisations organise and seek to govern spaces, ideas and, ultimately, subjects. The metaphors of 'window' and 'lens' have been used to describe how the analytical focus on a particular policy process enables critical discussion of broader and sometimes disguised political issues of power structures and transformations (Shore 2011; Shore and Wright 2011).

Policies are processes that run through and touch upon actors at all levels within the boundaries of an organisation. Policies also link organisations of various types and sizes, thus bridging gaps between various forms of organisations and creating interconnectivity across large-scale arenas. By studying policies as 'political technologies' (Foucault 1977, 1991), their often disguised, or at least understated, transformative aspects – the performativity (Austin 1976; Butler 1997; Callon 1998) of policies – are placed at the centre of attention. As ideological vehicles, policies advance a preferred and often idealised vision aimed at governing and impacting in certain directions.

The ethnographic study of policy processes entails 'studying through' (Wright and Reinhold 2011) – following the trajectory of the process through and among organisations, tracking the meaning of key concepts, attending and analysing various meetings, and tracing decisions. Decision-making is a fundamental and formative function in all types of formal organisations, and an in-depth understanding of the structure and temporality of decision-making is at the core of studies in and of policy arenas.

In this chapter, I draw from two of my fieldwork experiences. In one of these studies I researched the workings of Sweden's revised national pension system; part of the fieldwork was conducted at the two government authorities in charge of administering the national pension system. I also draw from current fieldwork, in which I am examining the investment strategies of institutional owners – large mutual funds, insurance companies and pension funds – and studying how these organisations position themselves as role models and, in various ways, work toward shaping other market actors and organising financial markets.[1] As for my attempts at understanding occurrences at the nexus of statecraft and market-making, one could say that the pension system study is aimed at illuminating statecraft at that nexus, whereas the ongoing research focuses on market-making. My interest in both these studies has been to shed light on the organising capacity of policies as political technologies. I study policies at the nexus of statecraft and market-making as official and formal discursive vessels of ideas, containing aims and visions with a certain directionality and a great deal of agency. It is, then, the performativity of organisations, both public and private, that has been my main object of study.

CULTURE OF ACCESSIBILITY

Quite to my surprise and the surprise of others, I seem to have made Weberian-type ideal models of a hierarchical, impersonal and rational administrative system (Weber 1958 [1946]) my preferred sites for conducting ethnographic inquiry. These seemingly neutral and objective organisational settings, governed by formal rules in hierarchical decision-making structures could, at both first and second glances, seem utterly boring and uneventful. And they often are. But for those of us interested in the contemporary workings of power and new forms of governance, the endless corridors of state authorities are real hot spots, the meeting rooms of public and private organisations are *the* places to be, official documents provide intriguing reading, and people in business suits are *the* people to hang around.

Sweden is a great place to indulge in such interests. On 2 December 1766, King Adolf Fredrik signed Sweden's first Freedom of the Press Act, which included the novel constitutional principle of Public Rights of Access, which, in the name of enlightenment, granted the general public access to read and voice their opinion on official documents:

I, Adolph Friedrich with God's grace, King of Sweden, Göthes and Wendes, etc., Heir of Norway and Count of Schlesswig, Hollstein, etc., [...] give each one of my faithful servants increasingly abundant opportunity to know better and evaluate a wisely constituted form of government. (*Tryckfrihetsförordningen* 1766, as reprinted in Hirschfeldt 2010: 69–78, my translation)[2]

The 250-year-old Swedish Freedom of the Press Act is the world's first legislation of what is commonly known today as Freedom of Information

(FOI) legislation or 'Right to Know' policies implemented, to various degrees, by a majority of nations around the world. The Swedish legislation has been revised and reformed a number of times over the years and now grants everyone, citizens and non-citizens alike, free access not only to any and all official non-classified documents, but also to 'civil servants and others who work in the central government sector or for local authorities' who 'have the right to tell outsiders what they know'.[3]

Public Access as a Norm and an Organising Principle

After 250 years of such generous access to people, places and papers within the Swedish state apparatus, access and openness have become the norm within Swedish society in general and an organising principle for the way public administration and statecraft is conducted. Annelise Riles presents an insightful discussion and reflections on the way documents can be seen as new agents and 'artifacts of modern knowledge practices' (2006: 2) and not merely ethnographic material, but, and perhaps more important, objects in which both researchers and informants have a shared interest.

All public documents in Sweden must be filed and kept in archives, a task that has become professionalised and performed by registration officers (registrars) at departments of registration of government authorities. A document is considered official and therefore public when it is received by a public authority, drawn up by a public authority or held by a public authority. A document is not merely paper with something written on it; it can refer to writings, pictures or recordings which can 'be read, listened to or otherwise comprehended using technical aids'.[4] All types of decisions, minutes from meetings, travel documents, receipts, pay cheques, emails and tweets, and anything received, written or recorded by public officers in their line of duty is to be registered, archived and made available for scrutiny by anyone. Public officials are also to make themselves available to the public – to answer letters, phone calls and emails from citizens without undue delay. There is no doubt that the Principle of Public Access (Government Offices of Sweden 2004) affects the way Swedish bureaucratic work life is organised. And imagine the abundance of empirical material the broad definitions of 'official document' entail for researchers inclined to trace processes of policy-making in Sweden.

Over the past 250 years, public access has become the norm and the open relationship between the Swedish state and its citizens is taken for granted. In 1767, a year after the inauguration of the Principle of Public Access, a local judge denied a common citizen in a small town in Sweden access to the minutes of a court meeting. The commoner provided a copy of the new Public Access policy, and the local judge was himself brought to court, where the supreme court judge strongly reprimanded him and recommended that he be discharged (Hirschfeldt 1998).

It is now a simple matter for Swedish citizens to order copies of any public document or contact state employees at any level. The right to do so, and information on how to go about doing it, is taught at school. I remember my class repeating, in chorus, after the teacher what we should say to a public official who denied us access to a document: '*Beslut med besvärshänvisning!*' (Literally, 'Decision with complaint reference', meaning: 'Give me an official document that states who denied me access to what, and where to file an official complaint of the denied access.')

A culture of accessibility has evolved over the past 250 years not only within the Swedish state apparatus, but also as a taken-for-granted citizens' right (Swedish Government 1983). This culture of accessibility affects the organisation of public organisations – the two government authorities and the national pension fund company in which I conducted ethnographical fieldwork, for example – and how the employees within these organisations conduct their tasks and everyday work-related routines. In the next section, I provide some ethnographic examples of the way employees within Sweden's public administration navigate in – and, not least, around – this culture of accessibility.

Navigating within a Culture of Accessibility – the Informants

My 15-month fieldwork took place at *Försäkringskassan* (the Social Insurance Agency) and *Premiepensionsmyndigheten* (the Premium Pension Authority), the two government authorities that were in charge of administering the national pension system in 2005.[5] I participated in a vast assortment of pre-scheduled meetings held at various stages and levels of policy processes dealing with public communication of the pension scheme. The meetings varied in size, significance and level of formality, outlining the contours of a pyramid-shaped Weberian bureaucratic hierarchy. The smallest of these were interview situations, with a state employee and I being the only meeting participants. Outside of these interviews, the smallest, least significant and informal, yet still official and pre-scheduled meetings, were those held in a tiny, barren meeting room at the end of a corridor or in the basement of either bureaucracy building; these meetings consisted of three or four individuals, including myself. The largest, most significant and strictly formal meetings of this fieldwork were those held in the bright executive boardrooms, with comfortable chairs, thick carpets and fresh flowers, with prominent participants, an official chairman and a meeting secretary writing minutes.[6]

More informal and unofficial meetings, also of varying size and significance, were held outside the official and hierarchical bureaucratic meeting structure and therefore outside of public access. An example of such a meeting is the common *bensträckaren* ('leg stretcher'), in which there is a break in an official meeting for a few minutes, but meeting participants continue to talk – now 'off record' around the coffee machine, water cooler or restroom queue. There are numerous other, more organised ways of avoiding the production of official documents within the culture of accessibility, most often instituted at small or mid-sized working-group meetings. The convening participant usually opens the meeting by asking the other participants if what follows can be called a 'work meeting', upon which the documents produced during the meeting are defined as 'working notes' and therefore not official documents that must be registered, filed and made publicly available.

Yet another way to duck public access is through the practice of calling for and scheduling *förmöten* (preparatory meetings) – meetings at which a select group of individuals meet to talk through important issues expected to be raised at an upcoming formal meeting. But was business being conducted even before these preparatory meetings? During my time at the state authorities, I heard several times about *pre-preparatory* meetings but was never invited to participate in one in which an even smaller group met to prepare for the preparatory meeting. These pre-meetings and pre-pre-meetings were, to my knowledge, not considered official and accessible but were conceptualised as work meetings, and therefore off the public record.

Such unofficial gatherings before, during and after official meetings, together with practices of renaming meetings and the documents produced there, are examples by which employees within formal and hierarchic bureaucratic organisations develop strategies and work practices to navigate in and around a prevailing culture of public accessibility that has become the norm and is taken for granted. At best, they can be seen as harmless practices that have evolved in order to make everyday routines easier for civil servants to work within a 250-year-old culture of public access. At worst they can be seen as strategies of power used to get around the public right to access principle and hide documents and processes from civil servants further down the bureaucratic hierarchy and from the scrutiny of the general public. Others have written about what may be obscured behind discourses of transparency (Garsten and Lindh de Montoya 2008). Either way, accessibility is the norm in the context of Swedish public administration, and public access is an organising principle.

Navigating within a Culture of Accessibility – the Researcher

When planning the fieldwork for my current research on policy processes within the world of institutional owners, I, too, made choices that can be seen as navigating manoeuvres within a culture of accessibility. At the outset of the current research project on institutional investors and well aware of my right to access official documents and civil servants, I knocked on the door of one of the national pension funds – a hybrid organisation of government authority and pension fund company. Apart from the fact that the organisational form epitomises the very nexus of statecraft and market-making and thus makes for the perfect organisation to zoom in on, I also realised that they would be bound by law to open the doors to their offices and archives. So, based on the fact that this was a two-year project and that I have a pathological respect for – if not fear of – deadlines, for strategic reasons and in order to speed up the fieldwork process, I contacted the department heads of one of the national pension funds instead of one of the private pension funds. This strategy allowed me to wave in front of them the first paragraph of the second chapter of the Swedish Rights of Access principle of the constitution in order to get a foot in the door. It turned out that I did not have to plead with or wave anything at the public officers cum fund managers at the national pension fund. They, of course, had their organisation and routines established in accordance with the culture of accessibility, and I was welcomed in through the door. But to where? To whom? And for what purpose?

STAGES OF STAGES

Erving Goffman (1959) famously applied the metaphors of drama and performance to the understanding of human social organisation. His conceptualisations of front stage and back stage, together with the less commonly referenced 'region' of 'outside' (1959: 135), are still valuable tools for those of us conducting ethnographic studies in and among complex organisations. Goffman's analysis of how context, position and purpose shape the way individuals engage with each other is intriguing and relevant to a methodological discussion of access and positionality of ethnographic fieldwork. Thinking about front- and back-stage performances points straight to issues of inside/outside (Marcus 1998; see also in this volume Krause-Jensen, chapter 3; Mahmud, chapter 12; Røyrvik, chapter 5; on being in between, at the threshold of or straddling the positions of inside and outside see Krause-Jensen, chapter 3) whether we are conducting participant observation or observing participation (Moeran, this volume chapter 10; Wacquant 1995). Taking Goffman's conceptualisation and metaphor seriously forces us to consider the different degrees and stages of front and back stages while contemplating relational aspects of intimacy and distance, of adaptability and boundary setting. In short, in order 'to figure out what the devil they think they are up to' (Geertz 1984), we must first figure out what the devil we think *we* are up to. If what I am studying is a performance, then, where am I situated? The simple yet fundamental question here is: 'Access to what?' When, as previously discussed, access has become the norm and in many ways taken for granted, it is time to complicate the picture and try to discern how access is negotiated, contested and managed *within* a culture of accessibility.

The study of policy entails analytical attention to the official version of things – to what is presented and why – and to the performance and enactment of an organisation. The goal is to shed light on what policy does and discern the directions it points to, which paths it opens and which are closed. With Goffman's analogy, policy is the performance, the public is the audience, and the ethnographer is moving around on stage, sometimes watching the performance from the sidelines, where audience reactions can also be studied. At other times the ethnographer is looking at the enactment of policy from behind centre stage, where not only the actual show can be observed, but also the work done behind the scenes that allows the performance to take place. From this angle, back stage is as much in view, and part of the performance, as front stage is. What matters is the performance; it is the official and formal enactment of policy that is in the limelight.

Being Where?

Geertz famously wrote about the important difference and textual connection between 'the Being Here and Being There sides of anthropology' (1988: 144) – of the pivotal importance of creating a distance between where ethnography is gathered in the field and where it is analysed behind a desk in the academic environment. This is undoubtedly a significant and valuable insight: distance from the field, from there, is crucial. The lingering question is 'where is there?' or perhaps rather 'what is *there*?' What does 'there' entail? (Bradburd 1998).

As Lynne Hume and Jane Mulcock have stated, 'Good participant observation thus requires a self-conscious balance between intimacy with, and distance from, the individuals we are seeking to better understand' (2004: xi). True – but this assertion is based on the assumption that the ethnographer's main interest is in understanding 'the individuals'. Again, I do not argue against the general assertion – on the contrary – but my aim here is to discuss what lies, more specifically, in some of our most taken-for-granted and generally accepted notions of what it is that anthropologists set out to do and discover out there.

For the sake of the argument, and at the risk of portraying myself as antisocial or asocial and non-empathic (a recurring topic of discussion among those close to me) I would say that I am not a people person, I am not really interested in or curious about individuals per se, and in my research to date I have not set out to understand individuals. When conducting fieldwork my object is not to attempt to understand them but rather to 'figure out what the devil they think they are up to' (Geertz 1984). Call me picky, but there is an important shift of focus between approaching fieldwork with the object of studying a group of individuals and setting off to examine what that group of individuals does.

Front and Back, On and Off, In and Out

Goffman's metaphor is based on the dramatic performance, and his definition of 'performance' is: 'all the activity of a given participant on a given occasion which serves to influence in any way any of the other participants' (1959: 15). With intention or not, the result of such activity is that others are influenced by it. In my reading, the purposefulness of the activity is key, and for those of us interested in studying processes of power, this seems like an appropriate point of departure. Goffman goes on to define and discuss three different 'regions' connected to each performance: the *front stage*, the *back stage* and the *outside*. The front stage is where the individual displays and enacts the performance before observers; it is the official, arranged, intentional and rehearsed performance (1959: 17–30).

The relative aspects of Goffman's regions, or positions, are brought forward with the 'back region', or back stage, which is defined as 'a place, relative to a given performance, where the impression fostered by the performance is knowingly contradicted' (1959: 112). It is here, behind the scenes and away from the view of the audience, that 'stage props' and personal items are kept, where costumes are adjusted, masks removed and characters abandoned. It is back stage that the performer relaxes and 'drops his front' (1959: 112). Back stage, therefore, is dependent upon and connected to the front stage, and relates intimately to the performance that is enacted before an audience. Back stage, then, is still on stage, and back-stage activities are inevitably linked and directly related to the official performance. For there to even be a back stage there needs to be a front stage.

Goffman introduces a third, 'residual', and less well remembered, region in his analysis: 'the outside' (1959: 135). The outside region refers to all that does not relate to the performance. There are, of course, innumerable fascinating things going on off stage, outside the theatre and at other theatres; but in Goffman's analogy, all of that is 'outside' and thus irrelevant for the study of a particular performance and the social organisation and interactions of the individuals performing it. If I am studying a policy process at a public administration or at a private corporation, therefore, it is the official presentation of the policy and, of course, all the intricate preparations leading up to the official version, the performance, that is of interest – not what all the actors and stage workers do off stage, when they are 'outside', after hours, after work, out of character and off that stage and onto another. A pass to access all stages, and stages of stages, then, is not possible or even of interest.

With Goffman's analogy, studying through a policy may involve the observation of preparations and rehearsals back stage before opening night and watching the actual performance from an array of angles: from behind the scenes back stage, from the sidelines behind the curtain and perhaps even participating as an extra somewhere in the back regions of front stage. Such research may also include sitting in the audience, observing members of the audience as they watch the performance. But it primarily entails hanging out with, talking to and observing what the actors and stage workers do in preparing for and enacting the performance.

Follow Suits

To 'follow suit' – to 'follow behind' in the sense of 'go along with' and 'imitate' – is an appropriate general description of a large part of my fieldwork of studying policy processes through formal organisations. The concept of 'shadowing' (see, for example, Czarniawska 2007) is sometimes used to describe this type of fieldwork, but to me this term implies a certain amount of 'uncandidness' with regard to the situation: that the subject is being followed without knowing it. Conversely, it suggests that the ethnographer can follow the subject without being noticed, and observe the subject like that famous fly on the wall could do. I have proposed elsewhere that this form of engagement may instead be considered 'tag-along fieldwork' (Nyqvist 2008: 29), in which the researcher asks permission to follow the informant in his or her daily activities at work, whatever this may entail and wherever it occurs. The term 'follow suit' is even more appropriate and descriptive, as it not only describes a form of engagement during fieldwork, but also pinpoints important char-acteristics of the informants – men in suits.

The people I interview and follow at work are mostly men in suits and ties, with shiny shoes and briefcases. Over the past six years and two projects I have met only a few exceptions: a handful of women in suits and scarves and a couple of daring men in suits but without ties! I meet with them, talk to them, mingle with them, have lunch and after-work drinks with them, and follow them around as much as possible. I take notes, some carefully written during meetings with various numbers of participants and levels of formality. Some notes are jotted down in haste while walking quickly down a corridor on the way to or from a meeting, yet other notes are scribbled down while balancing a plate of cold cuts, elaborate hors d'oeuvres or a glass of wine or a colourful cocktail. I sit down for hour-long, relatively formal, always recorded, interviews with key informants who have taken time out of their fully booked schedules. Put simply, I am interested in what these individuals do at work, in their role as professionals, as representatives of their organisations, whether this is a corporation or a state authority or a non-governmental organisation (Ahrne 1994). I am not interested in the private lives or personal backgrounds of these individuals; I am interested in who they are front stage and what they do there, not who they are back stage or 'outside' and what they do there.

A fair amount of mimicry seems to be useful here, and the notion of 'follow suit' points to the adaptability and attentiveness needed in this form of engagement and ethnographic experience. The ethnographer must have the ability to observe and note subtle expressions and the taken-for-granted, everyday practices of an organisational culture at play. In addition, it is necessary to mimic and imitate the observed, to be open to more experience, to engage in participatory observation from the side lines, yet still up on stage. As an extra in the play, you not only pay attention to what is being said and done during the performance, but you play along and try to fit in, don the appropriate attire, learn the 'language', go into character and improvise along with the main actors and more experienced participants. And of course you also realise that the informants are also in character, playing their parts in the official performance of policy. I think about what to wear to fit in during fieldwork and, over the years, I have expanded my wardrobe beyond jeans, T-shirts and sneakers. I put on what to me are uncomfortably formal clothes and set off to do fieldwork: attend meetings, conduct interviews, tag along behind key informants and follow suit. I do this until the interview is completed, the meeting is finished or the workday of my informants is over, which by no means is at 5 o'clock, and I then get off stage and out of character, go home and put on something comfortable. And I imagine that the people I have been following are doing exactly the same thing. That more relaxed, informal and private arena can, of course, be thought of as the back stage. But to me, and for the purposes of my research interests, it is 'outside' and thus an entirely different arena where other things, irrelevant for my research purposes, are played out at that stage's front and back spheres.

For those of us engaged in ethnographic fieldwork in and among complex organisations, several intriguing and inspiring suggestions of varying forms of engagements for ethnographic encounters and interactions have been proposed and put into practice during the last few decades: the notions of 'studying home' (see, for example, Hannerz 2001, 2006) and the concept of 'studying sideways' (Hannerz 2004) have proven to be valuable ones for organisational anthropology. Similarly, Holmes and Marcus's (2005, 2006) notion of 'para-ethnography', in which researchers engage in collaborative ethnographic fieldwork with their informants, is now further contemplated, developed and tested. A contribution of Hugh Gusterson's (1997: 116) is also relevant here. He suggests that ethnographers studying elites and experts, power and politics, rethink participant observation and interact instead with informants across a number of dispersed sites and sometimes in virtual form, and that they connect data eclectically from a disparate array of sources in many ways – what he calls 'polymorphous engagement'.

All these forms, and especially 'para-ethnography' and 'polymorphous engagements', entail a fair amount of adaptability. In biology, where polymorphism is a common concept and from where Gusterson most probably borrowed the term, it is used to describe when different life forms exist in the same population of a species and is related to biodiversity, genetic variation and adaptation. Several lingering questions are left for us ethnographers, however. What is polymorphous enough? How much do you adapt, mimic and follow suit before you begin to 'go native' and no longer see the particularities of the performance? And how far do you follow your informants? Do the 'dispersed sites' that Gusterson suggest we go to in order to interact with informants lead us off stage and to the 'outside' region? The attentive ethnographer knows when certain boundaries have been reached during fieldwork, when frames are being stepped out of, when settings are changing and when it is no longer a matter of merely following suit. Experienced ethnographers know when they are on their way to a different theatre, where an entirely different performance is being enacted. These are awkward moments (Hume and Mulcock 2004). In the next section I describe some such awkward examples from my fieldwork experience. Some of them are what Goffman calls 'backstage difficulties' (1959: 119–121), in which the boundaries between front and back stage are unclear and the back stage becomes off stage, where the private is sensed behind the official and public.

Private Matters Front Stage

There is gossip. People talk over lunch and at coffee breaks. There are stories of things that X and Y have done while competing for the same position, Y suddenly getting promoted or fired: workplace gossip. And there are stories of this and that having happened at the conference, of A and B having been seen together at a restaurant last night, and of how C is going through a tough time; a hint of alcohol or other substance abuse and, of course, accounts of more or less dramatic divorces. I take notes constantly and automatically, of everything, but I have never bothered to transcribe, much less ever found use for, my notes of these private matters. Stuff belonging to another setting – back stage or 'outside' – that pop up in instances where the official front stage momentarily becomes somewhat less official.

During my first meeting with someone who became one of the key informants in my current research, I happened to notice that we were wearing identical wedding rings – not unusual, perhaps, but they were not ordinary plain gold rings either. He became one of the individuals I followed at work and during work-related occasions and sites for two years, conducting a recurring conversational series of interviews with him. In the middle of one such interview, about a year and a half after our first encounter, I suddenly noticed that he was not wearing his wedding ring, and found myself momentarily distracted from our interview about institutional owners' investment strategies and about what had occurred on stage at a particular company's annual general meeting that we had both attended. I had just divorced and thought for a second that I should comment upon the coincidence of our similar wedding rings and the fact that they were now not worn. I quickly reflected upon how he was so collected and 'normal' – that whatever the story behind the fact that the wedding ring was no longer on his finger, it had no bearing on his official, front-stage performance – nor mine. And I cannot help but wonder if, at that moment, we had similar thoughts about each other's back-stage stuff. And then I asked him if and how he and his colleagues use the term 'fiduciary'.

Front-stage Encounter in the Back Room

Every spring my freelancing photography friends throw a thematic costume party at their offices. Guests come decked out in accordance with the theme and most of them are unrecognisable at first glance. A few years ago, the theme was 'Russia and popular culture' or some such thing. A number of Cossacks danced with *babushkas*, some Lenins worked the room and stone-faced *mafia* thugs covered with tattoos took it all in. Three friends and I came as Russian military bimbos. Short khaki skirts and high heels, glamorous platinum wigs crowned with uniform hats, lots of medals and red stars on our pushed-up uniformed breasts.

Hiding behind far too much make-up and finding comfort in the fact that everyone in the room looked just as ridiculous and vulgar as I did, I had a great time. I was not only back stage, but also at a private back-stage party in the downstairs dressing room when I saw a vaguely familiar face and posture to my right. Is it not … ? Oh my … There behind dark sunglasses, oily slicked-back hair, tight trousers in some kind of manmade material and a too-short tank top, flashing a fair amount of belly flesh, was one of my key informants from a previous project. He is the head of a large government authority and we had spent countless hours together in interviews, and in meetings at the government authorities and the Department of Health and Social Services, during my year of fieldwork. There was an awkward moment as we both acknowledged recognition, and the moment got longer and more awkward as we embarked on a polite and extremely uncomfortable conversation about front-stage stuff: greasy hairdo and naked belly, push-up bra and blonde wig, talking social reform and policy-making to the sound of loud Russian techno. Meeting like this in a private backroom, way back stage, was strange enough. To try to behave and talk as if we were front stage was just plain weird, and I am glad it did not happen during my year of fieldwork at the state authority. 'Polymorphous engagements', studying sideways and at home, can surely be challenging and awkward. Not only because 'they read what we write' (Brettell 1993), but also because they may turn up partying at the same party way off stage.

Taking a Front-stage Dive

Part of the fieldwork for my current research involves attending annual general meetings. These are intriguing performances, but at the same time frankly boring, tedious and most often predictable events. Lately I often catch myself taking a deep breath of fresh air upon leaving the site of the meeting. After one such meeting in a northern town I just wanted to go home. I left the meeting hall – stepping off the stage, so to speak – walked to the train station, and bought a coffee and the evening paper from the news stand. I climbed the stairs to the right platform for the Stockholm train and immediately spotted one of my key informants – the head of one of the large institutional investors in Sweden – further along the platform, also waiting for the Stockholm train. I should, of course, have taken the opportunity to go up to him and say: 'Hello, so you're also taking the train back home?' and politely forced him to spend three hours 'back stage' with me, talking about that day's performance, when what we both (I assume) wanted to be was off stage. I had already left the theatre, stepped out of character and did not want to go back up on stage any more that day, so instead I ran as quickly as I could in high heels and ducked down to hide behind one of the pillars on the platform. I held my breath and hoped that he would not see me. It was a small station with a deserted platform and he must have seen me, but we kept our distance and avoided eye contact. When the train came, he got on up front and I chose the last car. I suspect he, too, sat and enjoyed his three-hour ride off stage.

CONCLUSION: KNOWING WHERE TO DRAW THE LINE

In line with what Erving Goffman writes about 'backstage difficulties' (1959: 119–121) – situations in which front- and back-stage boundaries are blurred – my examples could be called 'off-stage difficulties': situations in which the boundaries between on and off stage become challenged at times and must be managed and handled. I would argue, however, that rather than seeing situations as pointing towards *unclear* boundaries between front and back stages or on and off stages, that these awkward moments highlight and *clarify* where the boundaries between the different stages are drawn in specific situations and performances. In other words, fieldwork experiences like these are not merely uncomfortable and awkward, but also informative and revealing, in that they emphasise the relative and processual character of access.

With ethnographic research focusing on the official versions of things, on presentations and performances, one must be highly adaptive *and* attentive – ready to improvise and participate in the performance, but also sensitive to the various stages of stages. Conducting ethnographic fieldwork within a culture of accessibility sharpens one's sense of the boundaries of front, back, on and off stages. For both researchers and the researched.

NOTES

1. The research project has been financially supported by the research programme Organising Markets, financed by Riksbankens Jubileumsfond.
2. Finland was then part of Sweden, and due credit must be given the Finnish priest and member of Parliament, Anders Chydenius, known as the initiator and creator of the Freedom of the Press Act and Public Access principle of 1766 (see Hirschfeldt 1998, 2010).
3. See: www.sweden.gov.se.
4. See: www.domstol.se.
5. The administration of Sweden's national pension system has undergone substantial reorganisation. Since 1 January 2010 it has been administered by one new government authority, *Pensionsmyndigheten*, rather than two, and the Premium Pension Authority was then closed.
6. For further reading of anthropological perspectives on the decision-making processes of meetings, and of meetings as social forms and powerful nodes or arenas, see, for example, Abram (2003), the volume edited by Richards and Kuper (1971), Thedvall (2006 and chapter 7 in this volume), and Boholm (chapter 11 in this volume).

REFERENCES

Abram, S. (2003) 'Anthropologies in policies, anthropologies in places: Reflections of fieldwork "in" documents and policies', in T. Hylland Eriksen, ed., *Globalisation. Studies in Anthropology* (London: Pluto Press).

Ahrne, G. (1994) *Social Organization* (London: Sage).

Austin, J. L. (1976) *How to Do Things with Words* (Oxford: Oxford University Press).

Bradburd, D. (1998) *Being There: The Necessity of Fieldwork* (Washington, DC: Smithsonian Institution Press).

Brettell, C. (1993) *When They Read What We Write: The Politics of Ethnography* (Westport, CT: Bergin and Garvey).

Butler, J. (1997) *Excitable Speech: A Politics of the Performative* (London: Routledge).

Callon, M. (1998) 'Introduction: The embeddedness of economic markets in economics', in M. Callon, ed., *The Law of Markets* (Malden, MA: Blackwell).

Czarniawska, B. (2007) *Shadowing and Other Techniques for Doing Fieldwork in Modern Societies* (Malmö: Liber).

Foucault, M. (1977) *Discipline and Punish: The Birth of the Prison* (Harmondsworth: Penguin).

—— (1991) 'Governmentality', in G. Burchell, C. Gordon and P. Miller, eds, *The Foucault Effect: Studies in Governmentality* (Chicago, IL: University of Chicago Press).

Garsten, C. and M. Lindh de Montoya, eds (2008) *Transparency in a New Global Order: Unveiling Organizational Visions* (Cheltenham: Edward Elgar).

Geertz, C. (1984) '"From the native's point of view": On the nature of anthropological understanding', in R. Shweder and R. Le Vine, eds, *Culture Theory: Essays on Mind, Self, and Emotion* (New York, NY: Cambridge University Press).

—— (1988) *Works and Lives: The Anthropologist as Author* (Stanford, CA: Stanford University Press).

Goffman, E. (1959) *The Presentation of Self in Everyday Life* (New York, NY: Anchor Books).

Government Offices of Sweden (2004) 'The Principle of Public Access', http://www.sweden.gov.se/sb/d/2184/a/15521 (accessed 20 April 2012).

Gusterson, H. (1997) 'Studying up revisited', *Political and Legal Anthropology Review*, Vol. 20, No. 1, pp. 114–119.

Hannerz, U. (2001) 'Anthropology', in N. Smelser and P. Baltes, eds, *International Encyclopedia of Social and Behavioral Sciences* (Oxford: Elsevier).

—— (2004) *Foreign News: Exploring the World of Foreign Correspondents* (Chicago, IL: University of Chicago Press).

—— (2006) 'Studying down, up, sideways, through, backward, forward, away and at home: Reflections on the field worries of an expansive discipline', in S. Coleman and P. Collins, eds, *Locating the Field: Metaphors of Space, Place and Context in Anthropology* (Oxford: Berg).

Hirschfeldt, J. (1998) '1766 års Tryckfrihetsförordning och offentlighetsprincipens utveckling', *Förvaltningsrättslig tidskrift*, Vol. 61.

—— (2010) 'Tryckfriheten – från 1700-talsidé till konstitutionellt grundvärde', in Öppenhetsarvet *från Anders Chydenius. Vad gör vi med det idag?* [Open Access from Anders Chydenius: What Do We Do with It Today?] (Karleby: Anders Chydenius stiftelse).

Holmes, D. and G. Marcus (2005) 'Cultures of expertise and the management of globalization: Toward the re-functioning of ethnography', in A. Ong and S. J. Collier, eds, *Global Assemblages: Technology, Politics and Ethics as Anthropological Problems* (Malden, MA: Blackwell).

—— (2006) 'Fast capitalism: Para-ethnography and the rise of the symbolic analyst', in M. Fisher and G. Downey, eds, *Frontiers of Capital: Ethnographic Reflections on the New Economy* (Durham, NC: Duke University Press).

Hume, L. and J. Mulcock, eds (2004) *Anthropologists in the Field: Cases in Participant Observation* (New York, NY: Columbia University Press).

Marcus, G. (1998) *Ethnography through Thick and Thin* (Princeton, NJ: Princeton University Press).

Nyqvist, A. (2003) 'Thoughts on how to avoid being anthropologetic in the midst of ambiguity', unpublished paper, Department of Social Anthropology, Stockholm University.

—— (2008) *Opening the Orange Envelope: Risk and Responsibility in the Remaking of Sweden's National Pension System*, Stockholm Studies in Social Anthropology 64 (Stockholm: Stockholm University).

Richards, A. and A. Kuper, eds (1971) *Councils in Action* (Cambridge: Cambridge University Press).

Riles, A., ed. (2006) 'Introduction', in *Document: Artifacts of Modern Knowledge* (Ann Arbor, MI: University of Michigan Press).

Shore, C. (2011) 'Studying governance: Policy as a window onto the modern state', in C. Shore, S. Wright and D. Peró, eds, *Policy Worlds: Anthropology and the Analysis of Contemporary Power* (New York, NY: Berghahn Books).

Shore, C. and S. Wright, eds (1997) *Anthropology of Policy: Critical Perspectives on Governance and Power* (New York, NY: Routledge).

Shore, C. and S. Wright (2011) 'Conceptualising policy: Technologies of governance and the politics of visibility', in C. Shore, S. Wright and D. Peró, eds, *Policy Worlds: Anthropology and the Analysis of Contemporary Power* (New York, NY: Berghahn Books).

Shore, C., S. Wright and D. Peró, eds (2011) *Policy Worlds: Anthropology and the Analysis of Contemporary Power* (New York, NY: Berghahn Books).

Swedish Courts (n.d.) 'What is an official document?' http://www.domstol.se/Funktioner/English/ (accessed 20 April 2012).

Swedish Government (1983) SOU 1983:70 *Värna yttrandefriheten, Yttrandefrihetsutredningens betänkande* [Defend Freedom of Expression: Recommendations of the Swedish Government Commission on Freedom of Expression] (Stockholm: Liber).

Thedvall, R. (2006) *Eurocrats at Work: Negotiating Transparency in Postnational Employment Policy*, Stockholm Studies in Social Anthropology 58 (Stockholm: Stockholm University).

Wacquant, L. (1995) 'The pugilistic point of view: How boxers think and feel about their trade', *Theory and Society*, Vol. 24, No. 4, pp. 489–535.

Weber, M. (1958 [1946]) *From Max Weber: Essays in Sociology* (New York, NY: Oxford University Press).

Wright, S. and S. Reinhold (2011) '"Studying through": A strategy for studying political transformation. Or sex, lies and British politics', in C. Shore, S. Wright and D. Peró, eds *Policy Worlds: Anthropology and the Analysis of Contemporary Power* (New York, NY: Berghahn Books).

7
Punctuated entries
Doing fieldwork in policy meetings in the European Union

Renita Thedvall

INTRODUCTION: GREY-BEIGE-BROWNISH SURROUNDINGS

I entered one of the European Commission's conference centres in Brussels along with the Swedish delegation to the European Union (EU) Employment Committee. Ahead of us was a line of people waiting to pass through the metal detectors and have their bags x-rayed. There was a long queue for the lift, so we walked up the escalators to one of the meeting rooms on the third floor. The conference centre had at least four meeting rooms on each floor of the five-storey building, and just before 10 a.m. there were always, as today, many people rushing to their various meetings. Many languages were being spoken around us, for people were arriving from their member states to attend their respective meetings in the building that day.

The meeting room was furnished according to the stereotype of a bureaucratic institution, with old-fashioned furniture and grey-beige-brownish surroundings, wall-to-wall grey carpets, fake mahogany tables, and chairs covered with beige office-chair cloth. Along the walls of the meeting room were booths for the interpreters. Language translation is critical because the defining of concepts and the writing of opinions and policy documents are the most important and tangible parts of the EU Employment Committee's work. The languages translated on this day were the three official EU languages, English, French and German, as indicated on a board in a corner of the room. I found a seat behind the Swedish delegation. The members were seated in a circle in front of me, with the member states in alphabetical order according to the spelling of each member state's name in its language.[1] In front of each member state's row of seats was a sign stating the name of the member state. The Secretaries of the Employment Committee, the President, and the European Commission were seated between the United Kingdom and Belgium – the alphabetical ends of the circle.

I took out the policy documents to be discussed from my bag. The representatives of other member states and the Commission arrived, and the room slowly filled up. There was a constant buzz around me of members greeting and kissing each other. The interpreters were taking their places in the translators' booths, and I examined my headset to make sure it was set to 'English'. Members were starting to take their seats, and at about 10:15 the President rang the bell, clang, everyone fell silent and the meeting began.

The EU is an organisation made up of nation-states. This makes it particular in many ways. It is made up of members that act as representatives of the member states or the European Commission both in explicitly political forums such as the EU Parliament or the Council of the European Union and in bureaucratic processes such as the one in focus in this chapter. I use the term 'bureaucratic' in the traditional Weberian (Weber 1958 [1946]: 196–224) sense, in that the participants in the meetings are set to develop politically neutral and objective policies in a policy- and decision-making process that is organised by formal rules, that has clearly defined decision-making hierarchies, and whose products are archived written documents. There is also a certain amount of predictability in the decision-making process, since it takes place in predetermined arenas such as meetings (1958 [1946]: 196–224). This is especially evident in the EU where member states' representatives often travel back and forth between EU meetings in Brussels and the government offices of the member states. Thus, the actual policy process takes place to large extent in and around EU meetings, since their members rarely meet face to face apart from at these meetings (Thedvall 2006, 2009).

In this chapter, I put forward that following Eurocrats in a policy-making process in the EU reveals a particular policy-making culture.[2] The policy process is punctuated in the sense that it takes place at predetermined times during the EU organisational year. This gives the fieldwork a particular quality in that it is characterised by punctuated entries. More importantly, the study brings to light what kinds of knowledge may be produced through fieldwork in EU policy-making meetings. Fieldwork reveals what kind of organisational logics govern the policy- and decision-making process in the EU meetings. With the help of Spicer and Sewell (2010) and Friedland and Alford (1991), I propose that organisational logics are spatially and temporarily localised configurations of diverse logics visible in discourse and material practices within, in this case, the EU meetings. What becomes visible through fieldwork is how intertwined and parallel different logics are in the policy-making negotiations.

The focus of this chapter is an EU policy-making process, where state representatives are set to develop 'quality-in-work indicators' to be able to measure and compare the quality of the labour markets of member states. I began this work through an internship in the European Commission during the autumn of 2001; the bulk of the field notes are from EU committee meetings, particularly the EU Employment Committee. During 2002 I had the opportunity to continue my study as a participant in the Swedish delegation of the Employment Committee (Thedvall 2006).[3] When I came to work in the office of the Directorate General of Employment and Social Affairs (hereafter called the Directorate General) in the European Commission (hereafter the Commission) in the autumn of 2001, I had a particular interest in the European Employment Strategy, as it was the EU's first attempt to coordinate employment policies in the member states.

The European Employment Strategy includes the employment guidelines that are intended to guide policy within the member states. Every member state must then write annual reports on its plans to incorporate the guidelines in national policies. The Council of the European Union (hereafter referred to as the Council) examines the national reports annually, with help from the Commission and the Employment Committee – a committee devoted to the European Employment Strategy. The Council then makes recommendations to the member states on ways to improve their policies and shares 'best practices' and 'good examples' from those employment policies that have been considered to be worthy of following. This is also referred to as soft law (Jacobsson 2004; Mörth 2004).

One way to tease out good examples and evaluate success or failure of the member states in reaching the EU employment guidelines was to develop indicators that were used to compare them. In 2001, one of the key goals of the European Employment Strategy and the employment guidelines was 'quality in work' (CEC 2001; European Council 2000, 2001). The Employment Committee bureaucrats were given the task of preparing a decision on quality-in-work indicators. Much of the discussions, negotiations and decision-making were played out in the Employment Committee meetings.

MEETINGS AS THE FIELD

Meetings, as well as the procedures for making decisions arrived at in councils and committees, have attracted the attention of a number of anthropologists. In the volume *Council in Action* (1971), edited by Audrey Richards and Adam Kuper, decision-making and political processes are discussed in a number of contexts: in an English town council (Spencer 1971), a council among the Merina of Madagascar (Bloch 1971), and the councillor system of the Bemba in Northern Zambia (Richards 1971). These case studies bring forward a number of significant aspects with regard to the anthropological study of councils and committees. Richards (1971) shows, for example, that many African councils deal with both judicial and executive decisions, and that generally this is not the case in European councils, which as a rule have an executive function only. Therefore, councils should be defined according to their form; to the extent that there are defined members, that they are located in prescribed places, that there is a series of conventions governing behaviour and so forth, rather than merely as a forum for discussing certain issues. This motivates Richards and Kuper to compare different types of councils and committees. They conclude that the comparisons show that African councils and English town councils are constrained by the same sort of pressures (Kuper 1971), and that the activities of councils in practice also involve issues other than making the actual decisions (Kuper 1971: 28).

Schwartzman's (1989) study of meetings in an American mental health centre questions the assumption that meetings are all about making decisions (1989: 208). Instead, she argues that it is the problems that produce meetings, and that the meetings then produce the organisation. In line with March and Olsen's garbage-can theory (1976), Schwartzman argues that for decisions to have a capacity of power, they have to be goal-oriented in the first place. March and Olsen (1976) propose that the purposes behind a decision are often *post factum* constructs. Schwartzman (1989), however, diverts from March and Olsen's task-focused approach by turning to meetings themselves as a social form (1989: 214; see Richards and Kuper 1971) that produces an organisation. More recent examples in the same vein are Abram's study of rituals in Town Hall councils and committee meetings in Norway (Abram 2003: 152ff) as well as my own study, on which this chapter is based on (Thedvall 2006). Abram (2003) argues that these councils and committee meetings enact a transnational flow of ideas and concepts serving to transform policy issues into local practice. She sees meetings as arenas that perform at global/local nodes, manifesting global processes. (See also Boholm's chapter 11 in this volume.)

The policy-making process in the Employment Committee meetings enacts a transnational flow of ideas and concepts, but not with the aim of transforming policy issues into local practice. Rather, they are arenas where several local practices are to be formed into one EU practice. In the meetings, the member states put forward national positions that are to be merged into an EU position on what indicators should measure quality in work. This process is governed by a bureaucratic logic (Handelman 2004) where the members are set to form politically neutral indicators that are not culturally loaded, so to speak. Yet, the decision-making processes are also driven by what I have elsewhere named, inspired by Herzfeld (1997), the 'logic of cultural intimacy' (Thedvall 2006, 2012). This may be seen as a logic of cultural intimacy in the sense that member states want to keep culturally intimate certain results of nation-state policy that it is not in their best interests to have revealed in the context of the EU. The member states' representatives are to act in the name of their respective nation-states in the policy-making process and in the process of doing that they form postnational EU decisions. In this policy process, the members are aware that some indicators would give a better outcome for their member state than others. This logic of cultural intimacy guides the discussions and negotiations just as much as the bureaucratic logic of finding the politically neutral indicators (Thedvall 2012).

MAKING MEETINGS MY FIELD

As discussed by Nader (1972: 302), one of the difficulties in 'studying-up', as well as in studying 'sideways', as suggested by Hannerz (2004), may be the problem of access. As I have shown in my dissertation (Thedvall 2006), the problem of access was partly solved as soon as I obtained an internship, or a *stage* (*stagiaire*) as it is called, in the Directorate General.[4] To gain a *stage* was, however, no small matter. I travelled several times to the Directorate General to discuss what I could do for them. The first step towards a *stage* was when I mentioned it to one of my interviewees when we had lunch. He, being Swedish, suggested that I should contact another Swede, the assistant to the Deputy Director General. She in turn recommended that I write a letter to explain what I wanted to do, what I could do for them and that I was in no need of financial support in the form of wages or insurance. She suggested that I should send it to the Deputy General Director, who was Finnish, rather than to the General Director, who was French. This was my first encounter with the ongoing networking that takes place in the EU between nationalities that perceive themselves as somehow closely related – something that I would get drawn into continuously during my stay in the Directorate General.

As I was working on gaining access there was a reorganisation of the Directorate General and my application was lost in the process. This I discovered when I contacted them again after I had not heard from them for months. I submitted my application again and this time I was directed to the Deputy Head of Unit of the unit that I wanted to work in, the unit that was responsible for the European Employment Strategy. I met the Deputy Head of Unit and, after some negotiations, we decided that I could stay for three and a half months, rather than the six that I had suggested. He referred to the fact that the organisational year started in September and ended in the middle of December, since most of the staff were on holiday before and after that period.[5] And he was right. When I began my stage in September 2001 most of the staff had recently returned or were about to return from their holidays and when I left in the middle of December the same year they were planning to go home to family and relatives in Sweden, Italy or wherever their place of origin was. In return for the opportunity to hold a *stagiaire* position, I also had to do something for them. At the end of my stay I contributed two papers to the Commission: 'Active labour market policy or workfare' and 'What can research say on the impact of the European Employment Strategy within member states?'

I soon realised that EU institutions are accustomed to having researchers working in their corridors, which was made clear by the label *stagiaire universitaire*[6] that I received. The position made it possible for me to walk freely in the corridors, search on the intranet and talk to people informally about employment policy. It was not in the corridors, however, but in the meetings that the policy-making process became most visible for observation (Thedvall 2006). People in the Directorate General and in my unit often worked on 'their' topic, by themselves, in their offices. The (almost) weekly unit meetings informed me of what people in the unit were doing and who to ask about particular policy areas. Other meetings that were important were those that I attended as the assistant of the Commission. The meetings that stood out as most interesting were the decision-making meetings between the Commission and the member states, in particular the EU Employment Committee meetings mentioned above. It was in these meetings that I could get a sense of being in the midst of action in the EU employment policy-making process. It was also here that the most of the discussion, negotiations and in practice decisions took place, this was where the member states and the Commission could be seen arguing, disagreeing and coming to solutions in the policy-making process. In essence, it was here that the EU came to life, since all the members met face to face to agree on policy.

To gain access to the Employment Committee meetings was a negotiation in itself. Before every Employment Committee meeting I had to ask if I was allowed to accompany the Commission's representative. They always said yes, but the moments before it was decided were filled with anxieties, since I knew that I would miss an important part of the process of developing quality-in-work indicators if I was not able to attend. As soon as it was decided that I could attend I could relax and look forward to the next part of the policy process. Thus, my fieldwork was characterised by punctuated entries into the field that corresponded to the meeting dates. Doing fieldwork in meetings meant that the excitements and anxieties of entering a field were repeated at every entry.

Working in the Commission was important, since it gave me access to the meetings. It also gave me some knowledge of the processes that were taking place in different parts of the Commission in preparation for the meetings (Thedvall 2006). I became increasingly curious, however, about why members said what they did in the Employment Committee meetings. To conduct participant observation in all the member states, I would have had to be in several different places at the same or nearly the same time, in order to be able to grasp all the participants' perspectives on the same issue. For logistical reasons, this proved impossible. To get at different perspectives I aimed to work in the Swedish Ministry of Industry with the Swedish members of the Employment Committee. I had come to know them during my stay at the Commission and my hope was that they would accept me as an intern at the ministry. The staff, however, were not eager to have an anthropologist roaming around in the corridors. There seemed to be an idea that I would study their behaviour though I tried to explain that I was interested in the policy-making process. The head of unit and also one of the members in the Employment Committee suggested that I should take part in their preparatory meetings in the Swedish Ministry of Industry and then follow them to the Employment Committee meetings. This was a helpful solution since it was the EU quality-in-work indicators policy process that was my focus.

In fact, most of the Swedish members' discussions and preparations for the Employment Committee meeting on this area took place at the actual preparatory meetings, since the Commission was always very late in sending the agenda and documents before the meeting. The meetings and the preparations for the meetings continued to be my focus during 2002. I took part in preparatory meetings and I followed the Swedish members to the Employment Committee meetings when the quality-in-work indicators were discussed, which was on four occasions. It also meant that the field was not available continuously. Fieldwork took the character of what Wulff (2002) has named yo-yo fieldwork, in that I yo-yo-ed back and forth into the field from my university life. The field appeared whenever a meeting was scheduled. Even if I still was in touch with the people in the field through emails and lunches, followed what new policy areas were coming up on the agenda on the Directorate General's website and read policy documents to keep myself informed about the policy area in general and the 'quality-in-work' indicators in particular, the actual fieldwork was again punctuated. With this came the same anxieties around not being admitted to the field at the next meeting, though I always was.

OBSERVING IN MEETINGS: WHAT ESCAPES A FIELDWORKER

In the meetings, my role was primarily that of an observer. I never took part as an active member. I sometimes helped the Secretariat of the Employment Committee with handing out papers or running the overhead projector when I was working in the Directorate General, and I sometimes commented on issues in the preparatory meetings in the Swedish Ministry of Industry when I was travelling with the Swedish delegation, but I was never a participant in the way the people I observed were.

The role of an observer made it possible for me to give my full attention to all the members in the meetings instead of preparing my input or thinking of it in relation to the other members, as the regular members were doing. Nevertheless, if I had been working in the Secretariat of the Employment Committee, for example, I would have been more involved with what was happening both inside and outside the meetings. In fact, the outside of the meeting room was the most difficult place in which to do fieldwork. It was impossible for me to follow all the delegates around. There were about 100 individuals directly involved in the work of the Employment Committee at the Ministries of Labour or Industry in the member states and in the Commission. In addition, there were experts from other units in the Commission or in the ministries in the member states involved.

When I took part in the Employment Committee meetings I sat in the back row, observed and took notes of what was said. The meetings usually lasted two days and they were very hectic – not least for me, since I tried to write down everything that was said. Of course that was not possible, but at least I got a pretty good sense of what was said. There were some difficulties, however. Sometimes I did not fully understand the discussion, since they were using a terminology with which I was not familiar. At other times, I was unable to follow the discussion because I was too busy writing what had been said before, so that I missed some of the beginning of the next speaker's words. The fact that I decided to follow one question, the elaborating of 'quality-in-work' indicators, was important here. During the different meetings I came to gain a fuller understanding of the discussions and their implications, and by the end of my fieldwork in the Employment Committee meetings, I recognised arguments and sometimes knew how different member states were going to react before they even took the floor.

As I have discussed elsewhere, language was an additional problem (Thedvall 2006). When member states spoke anything but English (or Swedish, of course) I had to listen to the interpreters. As Aull Davis points out, translations are far from theoretically neutral (1999: 113). The interpreters did a remarkable job, but as I got to know the topic being discussed better I sometimes had to interpret their interpretation. They might, for example, have used another term than the one agreed upon in the Employment Committee. This was something that the representatives also had to deal with and it deepened my understanding of what it means to take part in EU meetings, where interpreters are always present, and participants have to relate to layer upon layer of possible understandings.

Another aspect that proved challenging in the field was that the informants had a similar type of language, at least on the surface – an academic language and a way of reasoning similar to mine (Thedvall 2006). Policy development in the Commission is, to a large extent, performed in dialogue with the social sciences. Concepts and ideas studied by the social sciences such as 'governance' are soaked up by the Commission and made its own through the process of writing Communications, White Papers or Green Papers, as well as the other way round. This makes it difficult to see the way the meaning is made, which in turn makes it more difficult to analyse. The fact that we often have a language similar to that of our informants may give the impression that we share perspectives (Aull Davis 1999: 108). In fact, as Garsten (1994: 41) points out, fieldwork in an environment where academic language is shared between the informants and the researcher requires an even more critical stance. To reach this critical perspective required a period of distancing from the field.

Another problem with the constant and intense note-taking was that I did not have much time to see participants' facial expressions or bodily movements as they talked. Their tone of voice, however, often revealed their state of mind. I also developed a feel for the atmosphere in the group and in the room that I would not otherwise have had. In addition, even if I did not see and analyse all the facial expressions and bodily movements in regard to what the members expressed in the meetings I was still in the midst of the action. I was able to follow the negotiations and understand the different logics that were governing the discussions. I came to understand the process of knowing how to behave in the meeting room, deal with interpreters, see the importance of the actual rules of the process for the decision-making and so forth (also see Thedvall 2006, 2008a, 2009). I discuss this further in the coming sections.

BEING IN THE MIDST OF THE ACTION OF EU POLICY-MAKING

In the EU policy-making process, the issue at hand is muddled through different national opinions, discussed and negotiated. The national opinions move and shift across the meeting room and are anchored or lost in persuasion. Below is an example that I believe to be particularly revealing with regard to the processes of shaping national opinions into a common EU postnational opinion. It is the so-called drafting sessions that take place in the Employment Committee meetings. In other policy arenas in the EU such as the Coreper,[7] these sessions are very short. The Coreper is the 'last' meeting in a hierarchy of meetings before the Council where the actual formal decision is made (also see Thedvall 2006). The Employment Committee meetings are the first in this hierarchy of meetings when it comes to the European Employment Strategy and the quality-in-work indicators. In the Employment Committee the wording of the whole document is discussed in the actual meeting room.

The drafting sessions often take place before the Employment Committee members have to send the report and their opinion of the report to the Council. As I showed in my dissertation, the 'opinions' are usually the more important political documents, since it is in them that future work or future interpretations may be included or excluded (Thedvall 2006). It is also very likely that the opinions are the only documents that ministers will have time to read. The reports, and especially the opinions of the Committee, are reviewed word by word until the member states agree. The drafting sessions are often edgy in the sense that the members have to be on their toes. On the 'quality-in-work' indicators the drafting sessions sometimes lasted almost a whole day, with the Secretariat and the President of the Employment Committee re-writing the text during the lunch break.

The first drafting session on the 'quality-in-work' indicators in the Employment Committee took place on 4 October 2001, just a few days before the Council meeting on 8 October.[8] The President of the Employment Committee, a British gentleman quick to make ironic remarks, was going to make an 'oral statement'[9] in the Council on the progress made on the 'quality-in-work' indicators. When the members became aware of this at the Employment Committee meeting on 4–5 October 2001, they insisted that the oral statement should be drafted in the Committee. This showed how politically sensitive the 'quality-in-work' indicators were. When issues were not so sensitive, the President was sometimes trusted to write an opinion by himself, but this time he was not even trusted to write an oral statement. The Secretariat, together with the President, had to draft a proposal in the evening of 4 October to be discussed the following day.

At the meeting on 5 October the President of the Committee distributed the proposal for the oral statement one and half hours before lunch, hoping that the Committee would be able to reach an agreement on it before lunch. He said with a touch of sarcasm:[10]

> Now, we return to quality in work. We have prepared a draft statement. It would be nice if we could conclude this before lunch so that we can go home, but I'm prepared to sit here all day to reach an agreement. I want to have a full agreement. (Employment Committee 5 October 2001)

The members were given a few minutes to read the statement. The room was quiet for a while and then the members started to talk to one another and there was a mumbling sound all over the meeting room. After a while the President resumed the meeting and went through the document paragraph by paragraph. The members were invited to give their comments on each paragraph. They had suggestions for changes in almost every paragraph. For example, paragraph six reads:

> Turning to the other dimensions of quality, the Committee recommends that the Indicators Group explores the possibility of a composite indicator which would measure progress from unemployment to low paid work and

from low pay into higher paid work. The possibility should also be explored of extending this concept to cover progression from unemployment into part-time and fixed-term work and from there into full-time and permanent work. (Employment Committee, draft of oral statement 5 October 2001)

Some of the member states (Germany, the Netherlands, and Spain) were not happy with the idea of mentioning a 'composite indicator', which they thought would be too complicated since it would include too many variables. It would be too complicated according to the bureaucratic logic, where the indicators are not judged based on what they may say but whether they are statistically robust. In addition, the Dutch delegate, a quick-thinking man in his forties, did not want the last sentence on the 'progression from unemployment into part-time and fixed-term work and from there into full-time and permanent work', since he believed it was biased, suggesting that full-time and permanent work was superior. This was also not in the best interest of the Netherlands because the Netherlands has a high degree of part-time and fixed-term work compared to other EU member states. In the same vein, the Dutch delegation also wanted to delete 'progress' in the previous sentence and replace it with 'transition'. The Irish delegate, a laid-back, stout and senior man, agreed with the Netherlands and said that the indicators would have to be contextualised in the member states. The Belgian delegate, a senior softly spoken man, tried to solve the problem by suggesting making a distinction between voluntary and involuntary part-time and fixed-term work, but he did not get any response from the opposing member states. For the opposing member states that all had a high degree of part-time and fixed-term work, an indicator that showed involuntary part-time and fixed-term work might be problematic, indicating that full-time and permanent work was better.

Finally, they had to break for lunch and they were far from finished. Instead, the Secretariat together with the President had to re-write the statement during lunch. After lunch the new draft was distributed and gone through paragraph by paragraph again. Once more, they stopped at almost every paragraph to change the wording. Paragraph six now read:

The Committee recommends that its Indicators Group explores the possibility of indicators to measure transition from unemployment and inactivity into work. Some Members of the Committee would like to include transition from low pay into higher paid work. Others believe that this aspect should be excluded. (Employment Committee, draft oral statement, revision one, 5 October 2001)

One of the delegates suggested putting a comma after 'inactivity into work' and include after that 'and also progression in pay and work statutes (for example part-time and fixed-term work)', and then deleting the two sentences that followed. One of the British delegates, an elegant, authoritative woman, put Britain's member state sign on its end, indicating that she wanted to speak. The President called on her. The British delegate said: 'I have a problem with the word: "work statutes"' (Employment Committee 5 October 2001). The President of the Committee answered: 'May I have two minutes to consult with the Support team [the Secretariat of the Employment Committee]'? (Employment Committee 5 October 2001).

There was a short break and the Commission's representative and one of the Italian delegates joined the Secretaries and the President to help with the formulation. The President resumed the meeting and read a new suggestion for the paragraph: 'inactivity into work, and the transition within employment'. One of the German delegates, a senior hot-headed man, objected. He wanted to have a reference to 'pay' here as well as retaining 'the progression in the employment statutes'. One of the Dutch delegates protested against the use of the wording 'progression in employment statutes'. He said: 'We should be clear on what progress and statutes mean. Progress means to go to something better. I don't want it to appear that it is better with full-time work. "Employment statutes" gives this idea' (Employment Committee 5 October 2001).

The Commission's representative, a convincing, pragmatic French woman, tried to solve the problem by using the wording: 'transitions in employment'. She also suggested, supporting Germany, having a new sentence on pay. She put forward: 'In this context the Committee will give further consideration to other issues such as pay.' The President asked the German delegate if he was happy. He replied that he was not happy with the use of 'other issues'. The President tried to suggest 'other aspects'. The German delegate said that he wanted there to be a clear connection with the sentence above, that is, the sentence on 'transitions in employment'. He said that he thought the Commission understood. One of the Commission's representatives said that his point was that it should read 'specific aspects'. In the end, the President read, before the Council, the following sentences:

The Committee recommends that its Indicators Group explore the possibility of indicators to measure the transition from unemployment and inactivity into work and the transition within employment. In this context, the Committee will give further consideration to specific aspects, such as pay. (Non-paper.[11] Oral statement at the Employment and Social Policy Council 8 October 2001)

The case makes the arguments behind policy documents visible for scrutiny. The negotiations in the meeting also show that the members are governed by certain logics, mirroring the kind of organisations that the EU and the Committee the Employment Committee are. The member states' representatives are, in their role as bureaucrats, expected to work according to bureaucratic ideals, such as political neutrality and objectivity. They are working according to bureaucratic logic. At the same time, the EU is an organisation made up of member states, which means that in every arena where members meet they represent their respective member states. Some results of state policies are best not revealed in the EU, according to the logic of cultural intimacy. Through the process of negotiating according to these logics the national opinions clash but also produce a compromise that is eventually formed into a postnational EU position. This is EU policy in the making.

CONCLUSION: THE WORKINGS OF ORGANISATIONAL LOGICS

Bureaucracies may be guided by clear rules and ideals, but in practice, they house and have to balance a great variety of priorities. In this chapter, I have aimed to make visible how ideals meet practice by way of tales from my fieldwork among Eurocrats working with developing EU quality-in-work indicators. To follow a policy-making process in the EU meant to a large extent following meetings between member states and the Commission. This gave the fieldwork a particular character, with punctuated entries to the field rather than one continuous process of entering the field; it was punctuated in the sense that I had to negotiate entrance to every meeting. The punctuated entries also corresponded with the EU policy process in the sense that the meetings were almost the only time that the member states and the Commission met face to face to discuss, negotiate and decide on policy issues. The EU policy negotiations take place at prescheduled meetings that punctuate the organisational rhythm so that decisions can be made by the Council at the end of the organisational year. There is thus a way in which the temporality of the meeting cycle of a particular organisation contributes to defining the process of entry.

The fact that the EU is an organisation made up of nation-states also confers a certain quality to the policy-making process. The Employment Committee is made up of bureaucrats and governed by bureaucratic ideals of political neutrality and objectivity, referred to as a bureaucratic logic. At the same time, the members are representatives of their member states and try to argue for indicators to measure quality in work that will make their member states look good in the EU comparisons. This speaks, I suggest, of a logic of cultural intimacy, where member states keep culturally intimate certain results of nation-state policy that it is not in their best interest to have displayed in the context of the EU. The Eurocrats thus handle two seemingly incompatible logics in order to enable the development of indicators beyond the nation-state. They juggle both logics by separating the ideal of the bureaucratic logic from the pragmatics of the logic of cultural intimacy, while using both of them situationally as it serves their interests in EU meetings (Thedvall 2012). The configurations of these logics become visible in the discourse of the EU meetings and in the material practices of, for example, performing drafting sessions. Meetings reveal themselves to be condensed field sites for the examination of the workings of organisational logics.

NOTES

1. In order: Belgium, Denmark, Germany, Greece, Spain, France, Ireland, Italy, Luxembourg, the Netherlands, Austria, Portugal, Finland, Sweden and the United Kingdom. This study took place before the ten new member states joined in 2003, and the EU-15 became EU-25, and then EU-27 in 2007.

2. The research project has been financially supported by the research programme Organising Markets, financed by Riksbankens Jubileumsfond.
3. The fieldwork and the empirical material on which the chapter is based were originally collected for my dissertation: *Eurocrats at Work: Negotiating Transparency in Postnational Employment Policy* (Thedvall 2006).
4. In Brussels internships are referred to by the French term *stagiaire* regardless of language. There is a whole culture around being a *stagiaire*, or doing a *stage* as the English say. There are *stagiaire* organisations divided into different national groups and Directorates General which organise lunches, parties and other social events. Every weekend there is most likely at least one *stagiaire* party somewhere in Brussels.
5. The organisational year in the EU is determined by the half-year EU Presidencies held by one of the member states. During my fieldwork in autumn of 2001 Belgium held the Presidency.
6. An intern who is in the European Commission as a researcher.
7. Coreper is the Council of Permanent Representatives, the members of which are the Ambassadors from the member states' permanent representatives to the EU. The Coreper discusses all policy issues, not just employment policy before it is sent to the Council.
8. The empirical case that follows is almost identical to that presented in chapter 6 in my dissertation (Thedvall 2006).
9. The 'oral statement' would be submitted to the Council in written form but it would not be included as an official document since it was only a progress report, not a written opinion of the Employment Committee.
10. The 'quotations' in the text are not exact quotations, but are taken from my field notes from the meetings. I have chosen to write the 'Italian delegate says', however, even if I do not have the exact quotation, as I believe that I have captured a way of speaking in the Committee which is not my own.
11. A 'Non-paper' is an unofficial paper. It is, if you will, a working paper that will not be registered.

REFERENCES

Abram, S. (2003) 'Anthropologies in policies, anthropologies in places: Reflections of fieldwork "in" documents and policies', in T. H. Eriksen, ed., *Globalisation: Studies in Anthropology* (London: Pluto Press).

Bloch, M. (1971) 'Decision-making in councils among the Merina of Madagascar', in R. Audrey and A. Kuper, eds, *Councils in Action* (Cambridge: Cambridge University Press).

CEC (2001) 'Employment and social policy: A framework for investing in quality', COM 2001: 313 final.

Davies, C. A. (1999) *Reflexive Ethnography: A Guide to Researching Selves and Others* (London: Routledge).

European Council (2000) *Presidency Conclusion: European Council in Nice, December 2000.* http://ue.eu.int/ueDocs/cms_Data/docs/pressData/en/ec/00400-r1.%20ann.en0.htm (accessed 20 April 2012).

—— (2001) *Presidency Conclusions: European Council in Stockholm, March 2001.* http://ue.eu.int/ueDocs/cms_Data/docs/pressData/en/ec/00100-r1.%20ann-r1.en1.html (accessed 20 April 2012).

Friedland, R. and R. Alford (1991) 'Bringing society back in: Symbols, practices and institutional contradictions', in P. Walter and J. D. Paul, eds, *The New Institutionalism in Organizational Analysis* (Chicago, IL: University of Chicago Press).

Garsten, C. (1994) *Apple World: Core and Periphery in a Transnational Organizational Culture*, Stockholm Studies in Social Anthropology 33 (Stockholm: Almqvist and Wiksell International).

Handelman, D. (2004) *Nationalism and the Israeli State: Bureaucratic Logic in Public Events* (Oxford: Berg).

Hannerz, U. (2004) *Foreign News: Exploring the World of Foreign Correspondents* (London: University of Chicago Press).

Herzfeld, M. (1997) *Cultural Intimacy: Social Poetics in the Nation State* (London: Routledge).

Jacobsson, K. (2004) 'Soft regulation and the subtle transformation of the state: The case of EU employment policy', *Journal of European Social Policy*, Vol. 14, No. 3, pp. 355–370.

Kuper, A. (1971) 'Council structure and decision-making', in A. Richards and A. Kuper, eds, *Councils in Action* (Cambridge: Cambridge University Press).

March, J. G and J. P. Olsen (1976) *Ambiguity and Choice in Organizations* (Bergen: Universitetsforlaget).

Mörth, U. (2004) *Soft Law in Governance and Regulation: An Interdisciplinary Analysis* (Cheltenham: Edward Elgar).

Nader, L. (1972) 'Up the anthropologist: Perspectives gained from studying up', in D. Hymes, ed., *Reinventing Anthropology* (New York, NY: Pantheon Books).

Richards, A. (1971) 'The nature of the problem', in A. Richards and A. Kuper, eds, *Councils in Action* (Cambridge: Cambridge University Press).

Richards, A. and A. Kuper (1971) *Councils in Action* (Cambridge: Cambridge University Press).

Schwartzman, H. B. (1989) *The Meeting: Gatherings in Organizations and Communities* (London: Plenum Press).

Spencer, P. (1971) 'Party politics and the processes of local democracy in an English town council', in A. Richards and A. Kuper, eds, *Councils in Action* (Cambridge: Cambridge University Press).

Spicer, A. and G. Sewell (2010) 'From national service to global player: Transforming the organizational logic of a public broadcaster', *Journal of Management Studies*, Vol. 47, No. 6, pp. 913–943.

Thedvall, R. (2006) *Eurocrats at Work: Negotiating Transparency in Postnational Employment Policy*, Stockholm Studies in Social Anthropology 58 (Stockholm: Almqvist and Wiksell International).

—— (2009) 'Tillfälliga byråkratier: Mötesformens betydelse för formandet av beslutsprocessen i metaorganisationer ['Instances of bureaucracy: The significance of the meeting format in shaping the decision-making processes of meta-organisations'], *NOS*, Vol. 11, No. 2, pp. 48–63.

—— (2012) 'Negotiating impartial indicators: To put transparency into practice in the EU', *Journal of the Royal Anthropological Institute*, Vol. 18, No. 2, pp. 311–329.

Weber, M. (1958 [1946]) *From Max Weber: Essays in Sociology*, trans., ed., with an introduction by H. H. Gerth and C. Wright Mills (New York, NY: Oxford University Press).

Wulff, H. (2002) 'Yo-yo fieldwork: Mobility and time in a multi-local study of dance in Ireland', *Shifting Grounds: Experiments in Doing Ethnography*, special issue, *Anthropological Journal on European Cultures*, Vol. 11, pp. 117–136.

8
The instrumental gaze
The case of public sector reorganisation

Halvard Vike

INTRODUCTION: IN THE THICK OF IDEAS

Our understanding of formally organised worlds – both in everyday forms as well as more analytical and political versions – is often based on the premise that they are supposed to be clearly delineated 'things' that can be used by those in charge of them to achieve specific goals.[1] We, as humans, conceptualise the world by means of categories that help us simplify its complex and dynamic nature, and by doing this we tend to reify our social environment. Our tendency to see formally organised worlds as some kind of hierarchically shaped instrument to be handled by leaders according to some set of clearly articulated visions and intentions is clearly at odds with the facts.

Formally organised worlds cannot be observed in all their complexity – the highly simplified cultural models we rely on in order to grasp them cognitively, are metaphorical in nature. They are, in Lakoff and Johnson's (1980) terminology, metaphors we live by. As is the case with entities such as 'western democracies', they are objectifications of specific kinds. In contrast to analytically constructed phenomena like 'kinship' or descriptive categories such as 'a house', they constitute *representations* of the kind identified by Holy and Stuchlik (1983) – names of complex phenomena that denote not only a given social pattern but also specific ideals, beliefs as well as interests. Discourses on management, leadership, governance, etc. seem to embody a particularly rich variety of what we may call multi-purpose representations, such as for example 'firm leadership' and 'efficiency'. Such categories are analytically interesting because, as cognitive mechanisms, the job they do for us, as humans, is to enable us to stick to conventional, shared default interpretations that often work even though we cannot explain precisely why (Kronenfeld 2009). The social life of organisations includes complex links between ideas, intentions, talk, action, output and interpretations among a myriad of actors which are impossible to grasp through direct experience, and thus there is reason to believe that, to the extent that they perform more or less successfully, they may do so in part for 'wrong' reasons, that is to say, reasons other than the ones to which any given intended result is attributed. This, I argue, contributes to reinforcing the idea that organisations, and in particular those who are supposed to manage them, are rational – a belief which helps to keep formal worlds together.

One of the most commonly held assumptions of modernity is that the bureaucratically regulated state societies of 'the West' are more rational – or less 'symbolic' than those of the rest of the world. This division is based on a circular argument, which provides the definitions of rationality and then finds it at home. It treats rationality as distinct from belief, yet demands an unquestioning faith not radically different from that exacted by some religions. Even critics of the state bureaucracy implicitly accept its idealised self-presentation. The nation-state represents perfect order; only the human actors are flawed. This has all the marks of a religious doctrine. (Herzfeld 1992: 17)

Herzfeld's observation – that somehow rationality rests on belief – has some important implications. One of them is that we, as analysts, should seek a deeper understanding of the relationship between rationality and belief, but at the same time keep in mind that formal organisations are not simply sets of religious doctrines and rituals (Quinn 1988).

UNDERSTANDING FORMALLY ORGANISED WORLDS

This chapter, which investigates an organisational reform in a Norwegian municipality, focuses on how such beliefs work and why, as well as on their social implications. As indicated above, it does so by paying attention to practical reifications and their significant role in organisational processes that help in establishing consensus, reinforcing values and performing essential functions that pass more or less unnoticed or, alternatively, are wrongly attributed to some external cause. The reform, which involved a long series of meetings at various hierarchical levels of the organisation, with shifting constellations of personnel, was designed as process where all actors (politicians, administrative personnel and social workers – not clients) in the municipal organisation were to be heard. These meetings were intended as means to develop a common ground among the actors and define a practical strategy for the future. They were facilitated and monitored by a supervision group, which included representatives from all three groups. The official purpose of the reform was to reorganise social services in order to provide 'better service for less money' to welfare clients (Kronenfeld and Vike 2002; Vike 1996).

One of the strengths of anthropology is that its main methodological repertoire – fieldwork – makes it possible to get access to organisations from within. What is more, the fieldworker may be able to gain first-hand knowledge of processes and experiences from a larger number of contexts, and many more different hierarchical levels, than most organisational members themselves, even leaders. In my own fieldwork in Skien municipality in south-east Norway in the mid 1990s, I did as much as I could to maximise this effect, because it enabled me to explore the organisation's extraordinary complexity in its own right, and to explore the actions and experiences of all the key actors both from within and from the outside. Since, as pointed out above, such organisational worlds are almost never observed as such by the actors themselves, but rather experienced in fragments, I wanted to understand how various actors experienced the organisation and how they perceived the organisation through available cultural models (Kronenfeld 2009; Vike 2011), as well as the consequences of using such models. As an organisational nomad I was able to move between specialised contexts, dive in and out of the reform process at many different places at different times, and even observe emergent properties in the making.

On the basis of this methodological strategy, I concentrated on the following two sets of analytical approaches. My first and primary analytical aim was to train myself in perceiving what I observed not as aspects of 'the municipal organisation', but as phenomena in the making – linked to their environments in complex and perhaps surprising ways. I looked for ways to provide insight into how systematic, coordinated attempts to realise some clearly articulated set of intentions produce many different effects – presumably only some of which the actors themselves would be able to attribute to the strength and appropriateness of the original intentions. In the same vein, I took as a point of departure the assumption that the organisational worldviews and beliefs I was exposed to during fieldwork should be dealt with as objects of analysis, both in terms of the way they represent and organise experience, and combine value and fact, as well as in terms of the effects they generate beyond the desired ones (see Anderson 1996; Brunsson and Olsen 1993; Douglas 1986; Herzfeld 1992). Furthermore, I tried to look for indications of how talk and action became conventionally woven together over time – within and between multitudes of organisational sub-worlds (Heyman 1995). I hoped thus to be able to conceptualise the ways in which complex cycles of organisational reproduction were generated – the control of which, I assumed, could be expected to be indirect as well as direct and, additionally, mediated through abstract and multivocal symbolic means (worldviews and beliefs). To give an example: leadership initiatives in organisations are never simply 'implemented'; they are always shaped by the ways in which subordinate, more or less autonomous actors, applaud, resist, sabotage or ignore them. For obvious reasons, leaders cannot know exactly how this happens or what exactly it leads to, but there is certainly a strong incentive for leaders and others who identify with them to believe that initiatives are appropriate if they somehow seem to work. Organisational analyses and manuals are often constructed on these kinds of *post hoc* insights. For such reasons, as analysts we need to try to map the processes of interaction that the actors themselves cannot fully observe or comprehend, but which they actively model cognitively and act upon. In my fieldwork in Skien I tried to do this by moving as much as I could across the organisation's internal boundaries and observing the sub-worlds which existed within it, their interconnections, the relations between the formal and the informal aspects of the organisation, as well as the mechanisms linking what was said and what was done (see Brunsson 1989; Deetz 1998; Lipsky 1980; Wright 1994).

One particular reason for emphasising the perspective outlined above is the fact that my empirical example, one version of a Nordic municipality, is characterised by a particular type of complexity that fascinates me a great deal and which seems, from a comparative perspective, highly significant. In short, municipalities are responsible for dealing with an unusually broad range of tasks, many of which are extremely hard to delineate and at the same time notoriously costly. Moreover, since municipalities are 'state servants' but at the same time autonomous organisations (responsible for making their own priorities and managing their own scarce resources), the tasks they perform often contradict each other (for instance meeting the need for much more and better elderly care and at the same time spending less money). One way to illustrate this is by looking at the municipality from the vantage point of its boundary zones. Most formal organisations – both public and private – are designed to monitor and control their own boundaries (Heyman 1995; Paulsen and Hernes 2003). If they are unable to perform this task, resources will 'leak' out. Boundaries are normally socially constructed as the interfaces where flows of resources enter and leave, permanently or temporarily. Keeping the balance or, rather, making sure that the influx of resources exceeds the amount of those flowing out, is essential for organisational survival. Normally boundary maintenance is monitored by cognitive-symbolic devices (types of value and the relationships between them) that are conventionally tied to sets of instrumental procedures, and which together enable the organisation's members both to account for the balance and, if needed, change it (Miller 2002, 2003; Shore and Wright 2000). Some public organisations are very different from this prototype, and municipalities are the typical case in point. In the context of the Scandinavian welfare state, municipalities serve two very contradictory purposes. They must balance their budgets but, as servants of ambitious states, they are supposed to satisfy needs – needs that cannot simply be ignored if resources are too scarce. Because these needs – that most often are formally legitimated by state authorities as individual rights to municipal services – have a strong tendency to increase in uncontrollable ways and become ever more expensive to deal with, a fundamental dilemma arises as to how and where to establish boundaries without undermining one or both of the municipality's key functions. Furthermore, the dilemma is reinforced by the fact that the municipality represents the end of the chain of the public service apparatus. In most areas of service provision municipalities have less access to conventional ways of preventing responsibility from becoming overwhelming, for instance by shuffling problems over to other organisations, for instance hospitals. In short, especially when it comes to providing welfare goods and educational services, municipalities are responsible for satisfying needs that cannot be easily controlled (reduced, eliminated, or simply ignored), and they are generally unable to manipulate the value ('price') of the services they provide and exclude those who cannot pay.

The second analytical approach pursued in my study of Skien municipality followed directly from reflecting comparatively on organisational boundaries (Shore and Wright 1997, 2000). It involved the attempt to develop a careful contextualisation of the organisation in question in historical and cultural terms. One of the strengths of anthropology is that its focus on social process may help us to better understand how 'culture' is shaped historically through processes of institutionalisation. Institutions – which in the modern world are overwhelmingly formalised, have a peculiar capacity to 'freeze' culture (Gregory 2003; Tilly 2005). States, political systems and public bureaucracies are most often fundamentally shaped by the social structure that existed at the time of their formalisation. The question of 'how institutions think' is essential precisely because, as Douglas (1986) argues, institutions simplify our lives by routinising the tasks we perform – thus reducing the need to constantly worry about establishing rules for interaction and critically analysing how the world around us actually works. One important 'cost' of this process is that the specific ways in which institutions not only solve problems for us but also create new ones, sometimes remain unacknowledged, unclear and/ or misunderstood. During my fieldwork in Skien municipality, it gradually became clear to me that the municipality's social policy was implemented in ways that contrasted rather strongly with politicians' and managers' models of it. As I will demonstrate in the following, municipal welfare policies are characterised by strong historical continuity and, to a large extent, the tasks they perform reflect the universalist, social democratic optimism that was institutionalised from the 1950s onwards. As such, they have contributed significantly to forming both the professional identity and the organisational autonomy of social workers within the context of the local welfare state, that is to say the municipalities. Along with the increasing emphasis on managerial ideals and models of leadership, and the introduction of the 'workfare' philosophy in social policy in Norway in the 1990s (which sought to make clients more active and responsible by linking the services they received to mandatory wage labour), the traditional social democratic optimism in social policy became less *visible* (Lødemel and Trickey 2001).

In the following I describe the reform process in Skien, a fairly large municipality by Norwegian standards, located some 130 km south-west of Oslo, which sought to innovate social policy. As a result of realising that the policy pursued so far had failed, both in terms of getting clients into the labour market and reducing municipal costs, the municipality launched a reorganisation process which sought to achieve both these two aims. This reform was part of a broader global trend of public reform. The development is often described in terms of a growth of a governance society and a proliferation of 'new public management' practices, in which decentralisation, increased self-governing and individualisation are clear reform trends (Hood 1991; Kjaer 2004; Pierre and Peters 2000; Rhodes 1997). The guiding slogan was 'Better service for less money'. At stake in the process was the municipal organisation's ability to control itself: to manipulate the flow of resources within the organisation in smarter ways. However, in the process of trying to realise these goals, the municipality ran into some major structural limitations related to the nature of the political and economic context in which it intervened; challenges which were in fact not addressed by the project. Two such structural limitations were particularly salient: first, the amount and type of municipal responsibility is fundamentally defined by the central state, which – as a welfare state of the Nordic type, oriented towards universalism – typically demands that municipalities keep their budgets balanced and simultaneously satisfy the increasing need for more and better welfare services. The state–municipality relationship is fundamentally defined by the fact that municipalities generally lack the means necessary to establish limits on their expanding responsibility to satisfy needs. These needs are exclusively defined by the central state – increasingly in the form of individual rights. The other limitation is a product of the relationship between, on the one hand, the dynamics of the labour market, and on the other, public spending. 'Better service for less money' is hard to realise in a time when increasing proportions of the labour force are forced out of the labour market, and the number of people dependent on municipal welfare is on the rise.

As indicated above, Nordic municipalities are interesting institutional forms, not least because – as parts of particularly ambitious states – they tend to absorb responsibility. As pointed out above, they become legally responsible for increasing political welfare ambitions (more often than not materialising as individual rights to services which are not specified in terms of their costs or amount, but by what they are meant to achieve, for instance 'autonomy', 'dignity', 'health') on the part of the central state and, moreover, as they get squeezed between increasing demands and capacity, they face an overwhelming 'moral majority': the alliance between (more or less) dissatisfied consumers of welfare services who have received less from the municipality than the state has guaranteed them, and a central state which increasingly assumes the role of the advocate of 'the weak' in society. Municipalities seem generally to respond to this by trying to find new ways of providing services in less costly ways, a strategy which often works because the 'grassroots bureaucracy' – which, in the health and welfare sector, is overwhelmingly female – is strongly committed to catering to needs and tends to lack the power to regulate the ratio between (the total amount of) needs on the one hand, and capacity and definitions of service quality on the other. Perhaps precisely because of this, municipalities have proven remarkably successful in being sensitive to the population's needs and in providing complex and very often costly services. Given the economic conditions and the rising amount of needs, one could reasonably expect them to fail in some fundamental way, for instance by seriously reducing the quality of service, making services inaccessible, making heavier demands on clients or all of the above. In my previous work I have emphasised that one organisational property that emerges from the way in which various actors within the municipal organisations adapt to the situation they face is that responsibility is increasingly absorbed by the lower levels of the organisation, and that the cumulative effect of scarce resources being spread across more services is a gradual reduction of quality.

One further reason why municipalities seem to be able to deal with their dilemma, I argue, may be due to the fact that leaders are relatively powerless and lack much of the control they think they need. The environment in which they act presents some serious challenges to their power and autonomy. My argument is that the municipal sector incorporates certain specifically egalitarian social forms and alliances that seriously complicate managerial ideas of how to control them instrumentally. In many cases parts of the organisation are, in fact, able to resist hierarchical control through powerful horizontal networks of trust. In order to grasp this, it is necessary to understand the historical context under which organisations of this kind came into being and how they evolved, with particular reference to the social and organisational dimensions of political conflict, and forms of reciprocity (Tilly 2005). Anthropological literature on equality in the Nordic cultural context is very helpful in this regard (Barnes 1954; Gullestad 1992; Park 1998; Vike 1997).

THE REFORMING ORGANISATION – THE BB-PROJECT

In the 1990s, politicians, leading administrators and welfare workers in the municipality of Skien joined together to form a group that set out to launch a reorganisation programme that was to provide 'better service for less money' to welfare clients. These three categories of participants, however, each understood the process and their own participation in it in different terms, and each had their points of view changed during the reorganisation process. These changes and their consequences constitute the focus of attention in the present discussion. Although the points of departure of the three categories of actors were very different, there was general agreement on the practical strategy that was developed. However, the parties' interpretations of the state of affairs after the project had been completed were again divergent and mutually contradictory.

The different perspectives of the three parties involved must of course be seen in relation to the different tasks they are assigned in the municipal organisation and in relation to the positions from which they experience their environment and look for problems to be solved. Above all, they differ in the way in which they define risk, that is, threats to the immediate environment within which they operate. In this project, politicians were pragmatically concerned with controlling the organisation and reducing costs. From their point of view, welfare workers are potentially disloyal and clients irresponsible. Although such a view was most openly expressed by the elite politicians who took part in the project, the other, politically appointed, elected members seemed to see this as a regrettable fact of life and thus a premise for action. Welfare workers, on the other hand, generally tend to identify with their clients and regard politicians and leading administrators as more or less ignorant of the deep social and individual problems welfare clients represent. Welfare workers, therefore, see politicians in particular as a threat to the meaningfulness of social work. Leading administrators are 'betwixt and between'. They tend to consider politicians suspicious because of the politicians' alleged 'lack of responsibility' as regards the problems engendered by responses to economic scarcity and the municipal organisation's attendant lack of legitimacy in the wider communal environment. At the same time, they are aware of the interest that welfare workers have in protecting their domains and they are concerned with the lack of financial responsibility that such workers, in their desire to serve their clients, can be subject to. These contrasting conceptualisations of the field contributed to a very ambiguous collective definition of the object of municipal welfare policies. The actors disagreed on what a welfare client really is and on what such a client really needs. Hence, as we shall see, a major part of the job was to achieve an understanding of the object that was sufficiently unambiguous to lend itself to operationalisation. In other words, since the project aimed at effectively and efficiently changing the state of affairs, it had to be pragmatic.

During the spring of 1994, the reorganisation programme, which was called *Bedre bruk av sosialhjelpsmidler* ('More adequate use of welfare funds'; henceforth BB-project) was discussed extensively by the supervision group (*styringsgruppa*), consisting of leading politicians, administrative personnel and welfare workers. The group evaluated a pilot project that had been carried out over a four-year period in one of the municipality's three welfare offices. As a means for improving its performance, the office had been endowed with considerable special financial support, and the group was to find out whether or not the project had been successful. Had the welfare office been able to give more welfare clients adequate and relevant help? Furthermore, did more personnel, more efficient routines and a stronger emphasis on rehabilitation of clients, as opposed to just helping them keep their heads above water, demonstrate a potential for reducing costs in the future? These questions were formulated on the basis of a perspective on administrative governance in which the relationship between goals and the means at hand was essential. According to the evaluation report, 'The main idea in the project is based on a connection between the quality of professional work and the welfare payments ("quality pays")' (Skien municipality 1994).

The group had a hard time reaching conclusions. The results as presented in the report were very ambiguous. Despite the improved personnel situation, the office in question had in fact been far less successful in terms of controlling payments and exercising budget discipline than had the other two offices that had not been endowed with special privileges or resources. Moreover, the discrepancy between client needs and the welfare office's performance had grown, particularly as far as rehabilitation work was concerned (that is, the proportion of clients weaned from rehabilitation support fell rather than rose). However, the welfare workers regarded the project as partly successful. They reported that they enjoyed their work more than before, reporting better morale and job satisfaction. Furthermore, they had improved the accuracy of classifications of activities and clients, had more control and felt that they were more efficient. Beyond such benefits to the staff themselves, they felt that they were actually giving more meaningful help to something closer to the full range of citizens who needed such help; they felt that their lowered statistical success rate in fact represented a situation in which they were finally able actually to engage the real problems instead of having to push them aside or only marginally deal with them.

From the start the social workers had been extremely hesitant to accept the ambition to achieve better service for less money, but – apparently because their relationship to the administration and leading politicians suffered from a serious legitimacy deficit due to the fact that they were under suspicion of being the clients' advocates rather than loyal municipal functionaries – they accepted the project's terms and opted for the potentially positive results of pragmatic cooperation. Yet the positive results, as the participants themselves saw it, had an ironic flavour, since the results had little to do with the overall goal of the study, which was to save money. The results, even the positive ones, were largely unintended and, from the focal perspective, extraneous. Some of the politicians and leading administrators were deeply dissatisfied, and one of them concluded bitterly that: 'quality does not pay'. As a consequence the participants looked for alternative ways to provide better services for lower costs. It was explicitly expressed that the project was in danger of becoming a collection of 'mere words', that is, a matter of good intentions without adequate means being provided for their execution.

In a conference where organisational strategy was discussed with reference to the BB-project, held a few months after the project had been evaluated, the complex relationship between rational planning and desired effects was discussed in somewhat different terms. The participants became concerned with the role of *language* and *beliefs*. The point of departure was that talk, contrasting values and beliefs, as well as a lack of loyalty, might prevent political intentions and plans from being realised. The use of 'goal structures' was the main theme in this conference. It became clear that the various participants held strongly opposed views on the meaning and importance of organisational goal structures. Some thought, for instance, that what really matters is not the content of the various goals, but rather the ability to develop 'a common vision' in the organisation, while others were strongly focused on the objective correctness of particular goals within the overall goal structure. Others thought that the goal structure had to be linked to a 'tool', that is, the budget, in order to be seriously considered. Still others were more concerned with the organisation's ability to stimulate a dialogue and normative commitment among its members.

Despite the disagreement, an overall, pragmatic consensus was achieved on the basis of the assumption that the ability to achieve organisational goals *in practice* depends on logical consistency between goals and on clearly formulated goals and budget policies. Hence this was what the rest of the conference was about. Participants were repeatedly provoked by considerations of what they considered as 'mere words', that is, the use of 'abstract' words and expressions, which were seen as lacking reference to anything but ideals. Such words, for instance 'Better service for everyone' and 'A secure life for everyone', were seen as almost meaningless because they did not have procedures attached to them. They became 'words on paper'. Some participants were also provoked when it was suggested that factors other than just logical consistency and clearly formulated policies might influence organisational processes. As one participant responded when one of the speakers mentioned that organisational sabotage might prevent planned, instrumental governance from becoming successful: 'The whole point of being here was that we should be able to estimate effects. Now we have to change our beliefs!'

In the BB-project, two main roads to a better outcome were identified. Both may be seen against the background of what we may call the linguistic ideology that seemed to prevail in the organisation, and which was illustrated in the conference example. One was to change the system according to which clients were classified, and another was to change the organisation in order to make it more efficient. The first strategy resulted in the development of an informal classification of clients as 'expensive' and 'inexpensive' (in addition to an unmarked middle category), which could be used for deciding how to arrange the queue of clients waiting for 'measures' so that municipal costs could be reduced as quickly as possible. The second strategy generated a proposal for reorganisation and was predicated on the idea that the initial reform failed because of a lack of administrative coordination and efficiency. This strategy rapidly became extremely controversial and the welfare workers opposed it vehemently. The protests revealed a considerable amount of hostility towards the departmental leadership as well as towards the municipal leaders. One welfare worker identified the situation in the organisation as a constant 'war' about which no one ever dare speak. This echoed a general complaint among grassroots bureaucrats, a complaint that was expressed to me repeatedly in interviews, that leadership dominance is too great and that the meaningfulness of work is seriously threatened. However, although the others present agreed that the war metaphor was appropriate, no one opposed the overall strategy of which the reform attempt was a product: the attempt to increase control and efficiency.

INTERPRETATIONS

On the basis of the case study, it may be noted that the need for better service for less money through increasing organisational control was never challenged in the project despite the fact that the overall goal of more service for less money clearly was not achieved. The failure was not in any way taken as an indication of a failed analysis or a failed policy; instead, it was taken as a failure of implementation, with the conclusion that what were needed were redoubled efforts along the lines which had just failed. It is in this sense that the explanatory model held by the municipal administration seems to represent a self-fulfilling prophecy (Douglas 1986; Weick 1995) – no evidence can disconfirm it and apparently negative evidence serves only to reinforce it. My concluding analytic questions concern how this apparent failure was rationalised and how intelligent and dedicated people managed to, in my view, pull the wool over their own eyes?

To some extent the vision of *pragmatism* constituted a self-fulfilling prophecy in the BB-project. It was seen as a correct model because it seemed to 'work' – by providing the solutions to the problems as they were understood. Moving money, giving orders or devising new rules – the prototypical acts which were seen as 'coming out' of this model – are more instrumental and therefore more real than other acts. The deeper problem, however, seems to be that while tautologically 'correct' and 'effective', the indicated solutions did not seem to remove the experienced conditions which triggered the perception of a problem in the first place. What bridged the relationship between the three categories of actors, who initially experienced the problems at hand quite differently, seems to be the way in which the organisation as a collective embraced a frame of discourse that was sufficiently abstract for them all to buy into, and that thereby papered over the differences among their perspectives.

The BB-project was generated by an ambition to provide more and better welfare services, but in a more inexpensive way. This ambition did not stem simply from a local belief in how things work and how the world ought to be; the premises were imposed from the outside to a great extent. The formal responsibility for the clients is a result of the policies of national authorities, as is the amount of money available to the municipality for fulfilling its tasks. The number of welfare clients and their needs are also completely out of municipal control; their decisions to seek municipal support are aggregate results of general trends in the labour market and in state unemployment policies. As I have laboured to demonstrate, when politicians, bureaucrats and welfare workers invested their efforts in trying to solve the problems that prompted the project – as well as those that were generated by it – they tried to overcome these limitations by applying their ideals concerning what welfare clients are, how they should be treated, what kind of resources were available and what limitations were imposed on them by external factors. In so doing, they encountered some major paradoxes. The politicians in fact did *not* achieve their goal, either in terms of strengthening 'welfare humanism' or in terms of efficiency. The welfare workers, although sceptical of the path chosen, took an active part in the project and in so doing they contributed to the undermining of their own sense of meaningful work (Lipsky 1980). The bureaucrats seemed to face an even less easily governable reality than the one they administered prior to the project. On top of this, it seems that all the actors agreed with the conclusion that, after all, the way the project was carried through was the best one and that more of the same – although in an improved version – is needed. In this way, it seems safe to conclude that the BB-project served to buttress the dominance of the instrumental gaze of the bureaucratic and political elite, not primarily because it was successful but because it somehow absorbed its alternatives. This is what I mean when insisting that the idea of *pragmatism* seems to carry the properties of self-fulfilling prophecies.

However, what in this case appears on the surface to be a reform failure had some other effects, too; effects that the actors did not pay much attention to. The very fact that the reform did not realise the goal of saving money was in a sense not at all bad news for the welfare workers and the many local politicians who identify with their role as representatives of 'the weak in society' (which was an expression in common use in Skien during my fieldwork). In fact, the failure to reduce expenses reflected a well-established practice among welfare workers to ignore restrictive, local welfare payment standards and instead conform to much more generous national guidelines. To defend this practice in times of economic crisis, they have established alliances with as many back-benchers in the municipal assembly as possible, as well as with the local media, so as to mobilise moral uproar when cutbacks 'hit the weakest'. As the welfare workers' chosen conformity to the discourse of realism in the BB-project indicates, the welfare workers do not seem to problematise the apparent contradiction between what they seem to say and what they seem to do. Interestingly, it may be that precisely because they do not articulate this potential problem, but instead seem to conform to whatever is in vogue among leading bureaucrats and politicians, their 'everyday resistance' is so effective. They are able to act collectively and consistently almost without any observable coordinating functions or articulated oppositional language. As noted in the introduction to this chapter, in this regard the welfare workers illustrate a common phenomenon in municipal organisations in the ambitious Norwegian welfare state. As providers of welfare service, their mandate is to do everything they can to ensure that people with rights to high-quality services actually receive them. This demands that grassroots bureaucrats be constantly on the lookout for problems to solve. On the other hand, they are supposed to be loyal to the municipal budget, which, in order to stay balanced, very often necessitates cutbacks. When caught in dilemmas of this kind, welfare workers – like other grassroots bureaucrats and many local politicians who do not identify with the political elites – are actually able to enter alliances with their users, the wider public and with the central state. The latter insists through law that needs shall be met regardless of municipal budgets, while at the same time insisting through law that municipal budgets be balanced.

Although economic considerations most often win, the analysis of the BB-project has shown that the municipal organisation seems to have some built-in mechanisms that reproduced its 'schizophrenic' nature. This organisational schizophrenia seems vital for the municipal organisation's ability to take seriously the extremely complex task of being sensitive to shifting, growing and ever more costly needs in the population. In this chapter I have tried to show that it may be precisely because the actors themselves act – or at least talk – as though they think they can achieve control by applying some highly, perhaps overly simplified instrumental organisational model, that this is made possible. Their identity is strengthened and their model of what they do together is simple enough to allow much of the substantial organisational work to be left alone, unexplained, as it were. One important, and to my mind highly interesting and perhaps even unique, property of the Nordic municipality is that it is not effectively managed in the sense of being under someone's control, primarily because there are powerful actors within the organisation who, through horizontal solidarity, are able to act according to standards other than those developed by managers (Deetz 1998; Du Gay 2000). As a result, municipalities are highly successful providers of welfare services – so much so, in fact, that what is commonly labelled 'the welfare state' in the Nordic countries is highly legitimate and extremely popular. Since, as argued above, there is reason to believe that this success is related to certain anti-hierarchical aspects of the municipal organisation, we need to understand the sources of this type of institutionalised horizontal solidarity. A key element in this part of my argument is that this type of horizontal solidarity – egalitarianism – is a modern phenomenon, inseparable from the unusually great influence which civil society organisations exerted on the Nordic states during democratic mass mobilisation. The growth and influence of egalitarianism on public life made the Nordic states much more locally embedded than other western states (Aronsson 1997; Park 1998), heavily dependent upon municipalities and the kinds of horizontal networks that often seem to dominate them, politically and professionally, thus providing them with a unique ability to modify negative effects of centralised leadership and managerial ambitions. How can we explain this?

FORMAL ORGANISATIONS, HISTORY AND CULTURE

In several later works by Norwegian anthropologists looking at aspects of 'Norwegian culture', a key assumption is that its peasant heritage is still strong, and that the ways of life of a modern class-based, capitalist society – influenced primarily by life in the metropolis – have somehow not yet found their way into the patterns of national culture. In 'Totemism, the Norwegian way – reflections on the nature of the Norwegian social democracy', Sørhaug (1984) touches on the problem of morality. Public morality in Norwegian society, he argues, is a product of the metaphorical power of the close-knit community where everyone knows everyone else. This inclines the population to see the national polity as consisting of people essentially of the same kind. The flip side of the coin is that Norwegians, so immersed in this not-yet-fully modernised cultural system, have a hard time developing a critical, distrustful attitude to their leaders and the institutions they run, as long as they seem to follow the rules and look OK. In small communities, everyone tends to think that all have identical interests, he adds. In several publications, Gullestad argues in a somewhat similar vein, emphasising that 'egalitarian individualism' has a lot to do with Norwegians' love for their home (see Gullestad 1992). Two closely related observations made by Gullestad are worth mentioning: first, that the home serves as an important metaphorical inspiration for the idea of the nation of equals, and, second, that people's love for their home makes them able somehow to resist the pressure from markets and bureaucracies dominating the public domain (Gullestad 1992: 175).

In order to establish a critical angle on the arguments proposed by Sørhaug and Gullestad we may return to Barnes' work in western Norway in the 1950s (Barnes 1954). He demonstrated that the egalitarian ethos and the organisation of trust in close-knit informal networks were intimately related to community politics. That ethos contrasted rather sharply with the much more hierarchical social system prevailing in the fishing industry and on board fishing vessels. This would indicate that the task of trying to understand egalitarian networks of trust in the Norwegian context, and of explaining their reproduction, should involve not only the study of cultural values and private life but also 'how institutions think' (Archetti 1984; Douglas 1986). As Tilly (2005) points out, political culture in nation-states does not necessarily incorporate the culture of the grassroots, but when it does, that certainly needs explanation. Thus egalitarianism and related cultural values may be fruitfully seen as emerging from power struggles and negotiations in formal arenas rather than as simply an important cultural value, an aspect of a particular worldview, a personal disposition, or all the above. The American anthropologist George Park is among the few who have actually developed and explored the potential of such a perspective. His book *The Marke of Power: Helgeland and the Politics of Omnipotence* (1998) is a remarkable contribution to the ethnography of Norway. Park is able to demonstrate not only that in Helgeland – a region on the coastal fringe of southern north Norway – local politics matter a great deal as a means for securing collective interests and egalitarian ideals at the grassroots level; he also shows convincingly that this has contributed significantly to maintaining municipal autonomy vis-à-vis the central state – without losing out in the process of national integration and the tremendous growth experienced throughout the twentieth century. The last observation is significant in light of the fact that the Norwegian state has had strong centralising ambitions on behalf of its northern periphery. More concretely, Park attributes much of this achievement to organised politics at the municipal level, which he found to be highly rationalistic, ideologically intense and pragmatically policy-oriented – and, in a non-fundamentalist way, geared to the task of preventing the central state and local elites from getting the upper hand in defining the terms of local development.

CONCLUSION: PRODUCTIVE MISUNDERSTANDINGS

In the Nordic countries, the institutional infrastructure of the state differs from that in the rest of Europe in some very important ways (Aronsson 1997; Esping-Andersen 1998, 1999; Sørensen and Stråth 1997). In the context of this article, the key element is the combination of an expansive, universally oriented welfare state and strong, democratically controlled local institutions – municipalities – which carries the main responsibility for providing essential welfare services. One particularly important aspect of this institutional infrastructure, in comparative terms, is that institutions are much too complex to be 'controlled' and 'managed' in the conventional sense. One reason for this is what we may call the fundamental dilemma of the universally oriented welfare state: the welfare policies developed by central government, which can be seen as a response to the overwhelming popularity of such policies in the population, create a demand which is very hard to delimit once launched and, notably, once the promises made are taken literally by the population at large as well as by local politicians and the welfare professions. When welfare policies get shaped in this way, much power is in practice delegated to horizontal networks far down in the institutional hierarchy, leaving managers and other organisational elites fairly powerless unless they develop compromises with those to whom the responsibility for service provision is delegated. The welfare professions, and to some extent local politicians too, are in fact partly able to act autonomously because they can always argue that they are the ones who protect the welfare state against local elites arguing instrumentally for the need to make cutbacks and balance budgets.

In this chapter, I have aimed to show how a failed reform in a Norwegian municipality can throw light not only on how the organisation works in ways that the actors themselves do not fully understand, but also that their inadequate model of understanding is a part of the explanation of *how* it works. The metaphor they live by – particularly the idea that the municipality is supposed to be controlled according to an instrumental design – does not guide their actions in any direct sense (as Lakoff and Johnson 1980 would have it); rather it stabilises a set of beliefs that is shared throughout the organisations. When coupled with a certain degree of autonomy on the part of the various organisational sub-worlds within the municipal organisations, these beliefs can be adapted rather freely to the forms of agency that are developed locally.

The idea that the municipality is supposed to be controlled according to an instrumental design does not fit well with the fact that, for at least six decades, it has served as a specialist in absorbing responsibility from the central state. The conditions upon which an organisation of this kind is founded are defined by processes far beyond the local arena, and some of them generate deep municipal dilemmas. Somehow the organisation has learned to deal with this situation, and in effect it has developed some 'schizophrenic' traits. These are normally seen as a major problem. In my analysis I have tried to demonstrate that such a view is partly a productive misunderstanding. Unlike many modern organisations encountering overwhelming complexity, municipalities often do seem to be able to correct themselves when they make grave errors, preventing bad diagnoses and misplaced reform strategies from doing as much harm as they potentially could. One important element in this, I have argued, is the institutionalisation of an egalitarian ethos – an ethos that does not stem from some inherent 'Norwegian culture', but rather from a specific interplay between cultural ideas, social forms and formal institutions in a given historical context.

NOTE

1. The case discussed in his chapter is also analysed, from a different perspective, in an earlier publication (see Kronenfeld and Vike 2002). I am grateful to the editors of the present volume for highly useful comments on earlier drafts of my chapter.

REFERENCES

Anderson, E. N. (1996) *Ecologies of the Heart: Emotion, Belief, and the Environment* (New York, NY: Oxford University Press).

Archetti, E. (1984) 'Om maktens ideologi – en krysskulturell analyse' [On the ideology of power – A cross-cultural analysis], in A. M. Klausen, ed., *Den norske væremåten* [The Norwegian Way] (Oslo: Cappelen).

Aronsson, P. (1997) 'Local politics – The invisible political culture', in Ø. Sørensen and B. Stråth, eds, *The Cultural Construction of Norden* (Oslo: Scandinavian University Press).

Barnes, J. (1954) 'Class and committees in a Norwegian island parish', *Human Relations*, Vol. 7, No. 1, pp. 39–58.

Brunsson, N. (1989) *The Organization of Hypocrisy: Talk, Decisions and Actions in Organizations* (Chichester: Wiley).

Brunsson, N. and J. P. Olsen (1993) *The Reforming Organization* (London: Routledge).

Deetz, S. (1998) 'Discursive formations, strategized subordination and self-surveillance', in A. McKinlay and K. Starkey, eds, *Foucault, Management, and Organization Theory* (Thousand Oaks, CA: Sage).

Douglas, M. (1986) *How Institutions Think* (London: Routledge and Kegan Paul).

Du Gay, P. (2000) *In Praise of Bureaucracy* (London: Sage).

Esping-Andersen, G. (1998) *Welfare States in Transition: National Adaptations in Global Economies* (London: Sage).

—— (1999) *Social Foundations of Postindustrial Economies* (New York, NY: Oxford University Press).

Gregory, R. (2003) 'Transforming governmental culture: A sceptical view of new public management', in T. Christensen and P. Lægreid, eds, *New Public Management: The Transformations of Ideas and Practice* (Aldershot: Ashgate).

Gullestad, M. (1992) *The Art of Social Relations: Essays on Culture, Social Action and Everyday Life in Modern Norway* (Oslo: Scandinavian University Press).

Hernes, T. and N. Paulsen, eds (2003) *Managing Boundaries in Organizations: Multiple Perspectives* (Basingstoke: Macmillan).

Herzfeld, M. (1992) *The Social Production of Indifference. Exploring the Symbolic Roots of Western Bureaucracy* (Chicago, IL: University of Chicago Press).

Heyman, J. M. (1995) 'Putting power in the anthropology of bureaucracy: The immigration and naturalization service at the Mexico–United States border', *Current Anthropology*, Vol. 36, No. 2, pp. 261–287.

Holy, L. and M. Stuchlik (1983) *Actions, Norms, and Representations: Foundations of Anthropological Inquiry* (Cambridge: Cambridge University Press).

Hood, C. (1991) 'A public management for all seasons?', *Public Administration*, Vol. 69, pp. 3–19.

Kjær, A. M. (2004) *Governance* (Cambridge: Polity Press).

Kronenfeld, D. B. (2009) *Culture, Society, and Cognition: Collective Goals, Values, and Knowledge* (Berlin: Mouton de Gruyter).

Kronenfeld, D. B. and H. Vike (2002) 'Collective representations and social praxis: Local politics in the Norwegian welfare state', *Journal of the Royal Anthropological Institute*, Vol. 8, No. 4, pp. 621–643.

Lakoff, G. and M. Johnson (1980) *Metaphors We Live By* (Chicago, IL: University of Chicago Press).

Lipsky, M. (1980) *Street-level Bureaucracy: Dilemmas of the Individual in Public Services* (New York, NY: Russell Sage Foundation).

Lødemel, I. and H. Trickey (2001) *'An Offer You Can't Refuse': Workfare in an International Perspective* (Bristol: The Policy Press).

Miller, D. (2002) 'A theory of virtualism: Consumption as negation', in M. Edelman and A. Haugerud, eds, *The Anthropology of Development and Globalization: From Classical Political Economy to Contemporary Neoliberalism* (Oxford: Blackwell).

—— (2003) 'The virtual moment', *Journal of the Royal Anthropological Institute*, Vol. 9, No. 1, pp. 57–76.

Park, G. (1998) *The Marke of Power: Helgeland and the Politics of Omnipotence* (St John's: Memorial University of Newfoundland, Institute of Social and Economic Research).

Pierre, J. and B. G. Peters (2000) *Governance, Politics and the State* (New York, NY: Palgrave Macmillan).

Quinn, R. E. (1988) *Beyond Rational Management: Mastering the Paradoxes and Competing Demands of High Performance* (San Francisco, CA: Jossey-Bass).

Rhodes, R. A. W. (1997) *Understanding Governance: Policy Networks, Governance, Reflexivity, and Accountability* (Philadelphia, PA: Open University Press).

Shore, C. and S. Wright, eds (1997) *Anthropology of Policy: Critical Perspectives on Governance and Power* (London: Routledge).

—— (2000) 'Coercive accountability: The rise of audit culture in higher education', in M. Strathern, ed., *Audit Cultures: Anthropological Studies in Accountability, Ethics and the Academy* (London: Routledge).

Skien municipality (1994) *Bedre Bruk av sosialhjelpsmidler* [More adequate use of welfare funds] evaluation report.(Skien: Skien municipality).

Sørensen, Ø. and B. Stråth, eds (1997) *The Cultural Construction of Norden* (Oslo: Scandinavian University Press).

Sørhaug, H. C. (1984) 'Totemisme på norsk – betraktninger om den norske sosialdemokratismens vesen' ['Totemism, the Norwegian way – reflections on the nature of the Norwegian social democracy'], in A. M. Klausen, ed., *Den norske væremåten* [The Norwegian Way] (Oslo: Cappelen).

Tilly, C. (2005) *Trust and Rule* (Cambridge: Cambridge University Press).

Vike, H. (1996) *Conquering the Unreal Politics and Bureaucracy in a Norwegian Town.* PhD dissertation, Department of Social Anthropology, University of Oslo.

—— (1997) 'Reform and resistance: A Norwegian illustration', in C. Shore and S. Wright, eds, *Anthropology of Policy* (London: Routledge).

—— (2011) 'Cultural models, power, and hegemony', in D. B. Kronenfeld, G. Bennardo, V. C. de Munck and M. D. Fischer, eds, *A Companion to Cognitive Anthropology* (Malden, MA: Wiley-Blackwell).

Weick, K. (1995) *Sensemaking in Organizations* (Thousand Oaks, CA: Sage).

Wright, S., ed. (1994) *Anthropology of Organizations* (London: Routledge).

Section three
Working the network

9
All about ties
Think tanks and the economy of connections

Christina Garsten

ENTERING: ETHNOGRAPHY BY FAILURE

I was on my way to a prestigious social club in Washington DC to meet with two 'think tankers'. The club was located in a fancy residential area near Dupont Circle, within walking distance of the apartment I rented. It was a cold and cloudy day in the middle of March, and I hugged my coat tighter around me as I made my way. After five weeks in DC, I had already learned that the weather was a more unpredictable force here than in Stockholm, and that a March day in DC could be even more inhospitable than it was back home.

At this point, my ethnographic field appeared somewhat inhospitable overall. Since arriving in DC, I felt I had achieved little progress in my strivings to enter the world of think tanks. I had sent numerous emails and received few replies. I had made a large number of phone calls, but to little avail. A lingering sense of frustration was bubbling up inside of me. At this point, I had started to recalibrate my efforts. I tried various versions of emails, tinkered with genres and modes of expression, from formal to informal, from lengthy and polite to direct and short and from respectful to what I considered intimating. I had cunningly tried to penetrate the wall of administrators occupying the phone lines and to make direct and unannounced calls. I had also begun attending seminars at various think tanks, and approaching people unabashedly after the seminar. All with meagre luck. In the meantime, I was constantly following the news, sucking in every appearance of think-tank people on the screen and making note of topics, names and frequencies. Essentially these first three weeks were ethnography by failure. As my strivings to get into the field progressed, it became clear that what it boiled down to in the end was that continuous failure was my only way forward.

It was thus with a great sense of expectation that I entered the impressive nineteenth-century mansion where the social club was housed. I was going to meet two people: a man a woman, both with extensive think-tank experience. I had been referred to them by a friend of a department chair at one of the universities around DC, and because they knew each other well, and had copied each other on their email correspondence with me, we decided that the three of us should meet together.

I pushed the heavy entrance door open with some effort. The entrance hall was wide enough to make me feel lucky just to have made it through the door.

I was greeted by a distinguished-looking elderly gentleman in what looked to me like a butler's attire; he took my coat and showed me into the tea room where, I was told, Mr Clark and Mrs Mason were already waiting for me. As we walked through the building, furnished like a British library, with dark, masculine leather armchairs, I could hear the subdued and pleasant chatting of people in semi-closed rooms, but my eyes could register only a few people.

The woman, let's call her Lynn, an elegantly dressed and attractive woman, and the tall, handsome man, let's call him Rodney, greeted me politely and offered me a drink. As we waited for my cup of tea and their mineral water to arrive, we chatted about the nasty weather. I explained my interest in think tanks, saying that I was keen to learn about the way their experts influenced political agendas and decision-making processes in Congress. I told them that I was hoping eventually to be able to spend some time inside a think tank, to learn the ropes by doing participant observation. They listened politely and enquired into the type of think tanks I was interested in – liberal or conservative, relevant policy areas and so forth. As I tried my best to provide answers to these pertinent questions, I felt my ethnographic and open-ended quest sounded slightly diffuse and soft at the edges. Rodney said I would have to make some decisions before I would be able to move on, and Lynn confirmed. Depending on the type of think tanks I decided to focus on, she said, the networks would be different. 'It's all about ties', she continued. 'We're all linked up in some way through our networks. But you have to know where you want to go, before you start nesting.'

Tongue-tied by their many questions, I shifted the attention away from me and towards them, and learned a bit about their careers. Lynn had spent her career working on issues of economic and social development, both internationally and in the United States. She has extensive experience of leading organisations and organisational units in both the public and private sectors, and is now a senior-level consultant. She also works with a number of charitable organisations and serves on the board of a couple of philanthropic organisations. Rodney is interested in the role of think tanks in policy analysis, not least their potential to provide alternative platforms for addressing present-day problems in the developing world. (I later learned that he had earned a fine reputation as a think-tank expert.) He serves on several policy institute boards and is a senior fellow of a research centre affiliated with a university. Both Lynn and Rodney have academic degrees and have maintained strong and active links to academia.

After a few weeks circling in and out of think tanks and trying to get my feet wet in the political jungle, I did learn a thing or two about practice and about the importance of ties and connections. Basically by making all sorts of mistakes. Not knowing the correct way to address people; unaware of the intricacies of networks; inexperienced in US and DC politics; and with no credentials – at least none that mattered in their world – I ran into many dead ends, stepped on a number of sore feet and failed to see a number of potential openings. But as we know, doing ethnographic fieldwork is, to a large degree, about putting oneself up for trial. It is basically about practising culture, or practising organisation, hopefully learning to do it better. I also realised that in the social world of think tanks, different social ties have different significance. While some referrals proved to be vital and served as an Open Sesame, others led me astray and sometimes into dead ends. While this trial-and-error exercise was extremely time-consuming, it also provided me with a great deal of learning material. The DC landscape was like a marketplace, in which the exchange of names, information and rumours was ongoing, day and night.

This chapter tells about my research in and among think tanks in Washington DC, and how I approached this interconnected and nebulous ethnographic field.[1] The node in this network became the Center for Global Development, or CGD. CGD provided me with a platform for a broader examination of the way think-tank experts influence decisions and policy-making without the ability to lobby in the strict sense of the word. In these efforts, the dense network of 'policy intellectuals' – think-tank experts, policy-makers, politicians, multilateral experts and corporate leaders – works like 'an economy of connections', in which connections become valuable capital in a competitive and politicised form of exchange. Equally important, 'the interactional ease of privilege' (Rahman Kahn 2011) works to mark distinctions. Figuring out the network, finding my way into it and experimenting with new ways of engaging with people, was not only a methodological enterprise; it provided some theoretical insights into the organisational world of think tanks.

THINK TANKS AND THE SWAY OF IDEAS

For someone fascinated by the gateways of organisations, the Janus-faced public image of think tanks raised my curiosity. They offer a haven for free and creative minds and serve as conduits for corporate profits. My interest in how organisations funded by corporate resources work to influence policy-making and politics in the broad sense of the word steered my gaze in the direction of think tanks. I had already wondered, during earlier fieldwork at Apple Computer (Garsten 1994) in the boom era of Silicon Valley high-tech firms, where all the profits made by early investors and by corporations went. Studying corporate-funded think tanks was one way of following the money. Although I was well acquainted with corporate environments from previous fieldwork, I was acutely aware that the intricacies of social networks around these 'brain boxes' would provide me with challenges tough enough to require me to sharpen my ethnographic tools.

The very notion of 'think tank' is evocative enough to capture the imagination of an organisational anthropologist. The term is said to have been coined in the USA in the 1950s, when it referred to organisations offering strategic advice to the military.[2] The word referred then to a separate and inaccessible room in which strategies and secret operations could be discussed, away from the prying eyes of a wider public (Rich 2004: 13; Smith 1991: xiii). Many of today's think-tank experts prefer the reverse image: as neutral and non-partisan institutions, with a high degree of transparency and openness. Think tanks maintain a degree of attractiveness through a sophisticated combination of opacity and transparency, of closed and open boundaries (see Garsten and Lindh de Montoya 2008; Hood 2006). The perceived opacity of think tanks has attracted a great deal of outside criticism. Critics point to their diffuse funding base, the informal interactions that think-tank experts have with political and business leaders, and the invisibility of decision-making processes as a deficit in public openness and a democratic problem.[3] Think tanks are also recognised, however, for bringing social problems to the attention of decision-makers, for increasing the visibility of urgent social problems and policy deficiencies, for providing platforms for open public debate and for providing alternative pathways for public influence on the political scene. Think tanks are also acknowledged for their capacity to engage in global issues and urgent social problems to the extent that the nation-state often fails to do (see McGann 2007; Rich 2004; Smith 1991; Stone 1996; Weidenbaum 2011).

Think tanks work to influence agendas outside regular decision-making channels. They disseminate scenarios of the future of the world and propose the best ways of getting there. Think tanks and the intellectuals who work there are part of a growing cadre of organisations and professionals engaged in producing global scenarios of cultural flows and borders that enter 'the public geocultural imagination', in Hannerz's (2009) sense of the term. But the scenarios produced in think tanks also capture the imaginations of politicians and policy-makers, often by way of seductive sound bites, like 'the clash of civilizations', 'the end of history', or 'the world is flat'.[4] In Anna L. Tsing's (2005) terms, they are engaged in scale-making activities. The resources at the disposal of think tanks, in the form of endowments, individual donations and corporate sponsorship, provide them with opportunities to pursue their ideas and exert influence on political decision-makers.

The presence of think tanks in the political arena is most noticeable in the USA. Stephen Barley (2010) has demonstrated how corporations systematically contributed to building an 'institutional field' during the 1970s and 1980s in order to exert greater influence on the US federal government, partly by way of founding and funding think tanks. The resulting network, comprising distinct populations of organisations and the relationships that bind them into a system, channels and amplifies corporate political influence, while simultaneously shielding corporations from appearing to exert direct influence on Congress and the administration. Organisation scholars, Barley (2010: 779) argues, focused as we have been on the way organisations are shaped by their environments, have accorded much less attention to the way organisations mould their environments. With the transformation of governance structures at the global level, and with the growth of think tanks around the world, there is all the more reason to examine how these organisations attempt to make a difference in the world of politics.

Think tanks have been conspicuous actors in US domestic and international policy for over a century, and they are better established in US society than they are in Europe.[5] The origins of US think tanks can be traced to traditions of corporate philanthropy established in the USA's Progressive Era – a period of flourishing social activism and reform from the 1890s to the 1920s – and to the sharp distinction between legislative and executive branches of government, the desire to bring knowledge to bear on governmental decision-making and an inclination to trust the private sector to 'help government think'. The early period of think-tank formation reflected a political environment that valued neutral expertise and placed trust in its potential for devising rigorous solutions to public problems (Rich 2004: 72).[6] The idea was that think-tank experts were well placed to provide robust and neutral research results, untainted by political influence.

Over the past three decades, in accordance with changes in the ideological and funding environment in the USA, we have seen a significant growth of think tanks. According to Barley (2010), 54 per cent of existing think tanks were founded during the 1970s and 1980s – two to three times more conservative than liberal think tanks. In fact, Barley (2010) claims that only 29 per cent of all thinks tanks are liberal; 42 per cent are conservative and 29 per cent are moderate. Think tanks with a more aggressive political agenda, particularly conservative ones, multiplied over this period (Rich 2004). Moreover, given the interest of business in the policy-making process, new sources of patronage have been made available to think tanks, particularly conservative ones (Rich 2004). 'Competition for ideas' (Weidenbaum 2011) has intensified, and the scene upon which think tanks operate is now crowded, with most of them concentrated in DC.[7]

Think tanks have generally evolved from producing painstaking research and objective writing to pursuing ideological agendas with a far-reaching impact on the battle of ideas (Rich 2004). As Weidenbaum (2011: 2) has noted, '[a]lthough they have been called "citadels for public intellectuals", those who work in those private, non-profit organisations do not just sit and think. They perform many important functions in the public policy process …' Think tanks are vital sources of information and expertise for people in the halls of Congress, for the large multilaterals and for the media. They sometimes set the agenda for key debates and issues, by focusing on emerging national and international concerns and by proposing other ways of dealing with well-known problems. Think tanks have emerged as organisations with wide-reaching impact beyond the Washington 'beltway'.[8]

Think tanks are in a position to wield a form of 'soft power', which works by way of attraction and mobilisation, agenda-setting and persuasion, rather than by coercion and sanction. Soft power – getting others to want the outcomes you want – co-opts people rather than coerces them (Nye 2004, 2011). It tends to work indirectly by shaping the environment for policy and the way in which a topic is framed. We may thus speak of soft power as relational, in that it relies on relationships cultivated to relevant others. It is also situational, in the sense that what is a valuable resource and how that resource is put to use in the wielding of power varies with the political and policy context.

Power has always been heavily reliant on personal associations, interlocking networks and linkages. In the global era, with information technology and many types of mediated communications readily available, opportunities for linkages and associations are burgeoning. Since C. Wright Mill's influential book, *The Power Elite* (1956), several scholars have described the intimate connections among elites in different spheres and have suggested that connectivity is becoming ever more complex with globalisation (see e.g. Rothkopf 2008; Stone 2001; Wedel 2009). Politicians, policy-makers and corporate leaders carefully nurture relationships with people they judge to be strategically positioned, in a field of diffuse and nomadic power.[9] Events such as the World Economic Forum Annual Meetings in Davos, the Boao Forum for Asia Annual Conference, the UN Global Compact Leaders Summit and other conferences around the world also contribute to knitting powerful people together.

The common political vocabulary, structured by such differences as those between state and civil society, public and private organisations, and coercion and consent, is unable to characterise the diverse ways in which power is exercised in advanced liberal democracies at the global level. As suggested by Rose and Miller (1992: 175), we need to relocate the state and the market, and the concept of politics and non-politics within an investigation of the 'problematics of government' and look more closely at how political power is exercised 'through a profusion of shifting alliances between diverse authorities'.

Central to an understanding of the way power works in contemporary forms of governance are the associations between entities construed as 'political', and their projects, plans and practices. Knowledge is pivotal for these activities, as it is through expertise that governance is executed, through attempts to influence, mobilise, encourage and direct (Rose and Miller 1992: 175). Consequently, the power that a particular think tank can acquire and execute is not power in an overt, formal and legal sense of the word, but rather power in the form of expertise and authority (cf. Cutler et al. 1999; Weber 1958). Through 'deep lobbying' – making use of networks and knowledge to shape the intellectual climate of decision-making – issues may be placed on the political agenda (Wallace-Wells 2003). 'There is a fine line', as one of my interviewees expressed it. 'We want to influence, but we do it by seeding ideas, not by lobbying.'

To analyse contemporary power, therefore, we must go beyond conventional understandings of organisations as bounded entities and the methodological formalism that has privileged the notion of 'one ethnography, one organisation', to look more seriously at interlocking practices, shifting alliances and new forms of connectivity among organisations. The ethnographic field may not be best conceptualised as being congruent with the boundaries of the organisation. More often, we find ourselves studying some type of 'anthropological problem', in Rabinow's (2003) sense of the term: problems that are not bounded by formal organisational entities or social units, but cut across them. Social interactions and relationships are constitutive of the organising process. A key feature of the world of think tanks is the continuous criss-crossing of formal organisational boundaries by way of nested practices and social interactions.

INTO CGD

My attempts to get closer to the practices of think-tank professionals eventually led me to CGD. The same woman who referred me to Lynn and Rodney had also suggested that I get in touch with Mike, one of the directors of CGD. Mike was only three referrals away from the initial contact I had in DC, and he became my key interlocutor and my main point of connectivity both in CGD and outwards. His curiosity about an anthropologist's ability to contribute to the understanding of the organisation opened several doors. In Westbrook's (2008) terms, the interlocutor (Mike) provided the navigator (me) not so much with a map of the culture, as with data that could be used to help me determine where I was and where I could go. The fact that think-tank people are engaged in activities that resemble those of the anthropologist – attempting to understand the environment in which they operate, to find ways to interpret and make sense of what is transpiring, and to communicate their insights – provided a common point of entry.[10] A key methodological concern emerged: to maintain a continuous awareness of the differences that may underlie the surface similarity in our reasoning, to engage with interlocutors around shared concerns and concepts, but to articulate my own analytical position, to find my own place on the map. An 'adjacency', in the terminology of Rabinow et al. (2008: 55–61), a certain amount of untimeliness in a fast-moving field, seemed necessary.

Following a conversation with Mike, I ventured to ask if CGD would consider hosting me for the remainder of my fieldwork in DC. I reasoned that my understanding of the operations of think tanks in the policy arena would be significantly enhanced by the opportunity to follow issues and practices on a day-to-day basis and over time. My request was favourably received, and I was offered the opportunity to be their guest for some three months and was given my own office space. This meant that I could participate in all kinds of meetings and events in the organisation, and talk with and interview staff. The Communications and Outreach Team, in which I was hosted, comprised a dynamic group of young people in charge of making the research results of CGD more visible and available to the media, to people 'on the Hill' (Capitol Hill – a metonym for the US Congress) and to a wider audience. Considering my interest in the way knowledge is produced, packaged and disseminated, this was an ideal vantage point.

CGD is an independent non-partisan and non-profit think tank, geared towards influencing policy for global development. CGD had just celebrated its tenth birthday when I arrived at the site. The organisation was founded in 2001 by Edward W. Scott Jr, C. Fred Bergsten and Nancy Birdsall. Ed Scott, a former technology entrepreneur, a philanthropist and former senior US government official, took the first initiative, based on the conviction that he wanted to make a contribution to improving the world. He provided the vision and a significant financial commitment that made the creation of the Center possible. Fred Bergsten, director of the Peterson Institute for International Economics, an influential DC-based think tank, had the necessary standing in the area to put the vision into action. He lent to the cause his formidable reputation in policy circles and among academics. He also provided the new organisation with an initial platform within the Peterson Institute, about 100 metres from the present-day site of CGD. Nancy Birdsall, a former head of the World Bank research department and executive vice-president of the Inter-American Development Bank, with a solid academic background, was recruited to become the first president of CGD. Her intellectual leadership and personal charisma attracted a cadre of researchers and other professionals dedicated to CGD's mission.

The dynamic duo – Chair of the Board Ed Scott and President Nancy Birdsall – represents and embodies the dual 'thinking and doing' focus of CGD: to produce top-level research and to create an impact on policy-making. This double ambition is also expressed in the CGD slogan, 'Think + Do = Influence & Impact'.[11] The emphasis on 'rigorous research' and 'thinking' lies at the heart of CGD, and the academic profile is a central aspect of the organisation. Based on research and policy analysis, the people at CGD want to 'turn ideas into action'. CGD is, in this sense, a 'think and do tank', combining research and analysis with an ambition to influence policy-making in its areas of engagement.

CGD houses a large number of experts, or fellows, most of whom have academic backgrounds and PhD degrees. Many of them have experience of working in the government administration, Republican or Democratic. The majority, however, had been recruited from one of the big multilaterals, like the World Bank. While these experts are all affiliated with CGD, not all of them are resident members. At the time of my fieldwork, there were 48 experts associated with CGD, about 20 of whom were non-resident fellows, and one-quarter of whom were visiting fellows. Most of the non-resident fellows had previously spent time at CGD as visiting fellows or as resident experts. During this time, there were 11 research assistants who worked with the senior experts on specific projects. Research assistants are typically younger college graduates, for whom a couple of years in an organisation like CGD serves as valuable experience before they embark on a PhD programme or apply for a more senior position elsewhere. The entire staff of 87 comprised executive, finance, operations, communications and outreach people; research assistants; resident, visiting and non-resident fellows; and programme staff, approximately 60 of whom were physically present most of the time. Also part of the organisation was a distinguished Advisory Group, consisting of people well connected and experienced in the DC policy world, and an equally illustrious Board of Directors. Donors may join the CGD Society network and gain preferred access to the Center's public conferences, events and informal meetings. Financial contributors may also join the Partners Council, which is a non-governing membership body, with participants supporting CGD through financial contributions, by attracting other potential supporters and by serving as advocates for CGD's mission in their professional and social communities.

CGD is a loosely integrated organisation, with boundaries to the outside environment that are continuously in flux.[12] Forms of affiliation vary from permanent to short-term, and members' degree of engagement in the organisation varies significantly. From within CGD, a vast and dense network of contacts connects it with other think tanks, corporations and foundations; with Congress and the administration; with multilaterals, NGOs and universities. From this viewpoint, CGD may be seen as an assemblage of people, resources and ideas, extending over and beyond the physically located and formally bounded organisation into a mesh of trans-organisational ties with other experts, business leaders, policy-makers and politicians. The trope of the 'inside' (Marcus 1998), aspiring to get 'inside' an organisation, an activity so cherished by anthropologists, thus proved not altogether satisfactory. Straddling the network was equally, if not more, important.

TURNING IDEAS INTO ACTION

At CGD, research is undertaken on a wide range of topics relating to the impact of policy on people in developing countries. There are research programmes on aid effectiveness and innovation, climate change, global governance, global health and education, migration, private investment and access to finance, and the links between trade and poverty reduction. Research topics can evolve in various ways. They may emerge from the interests and expertise of scholars, the priorities of the leaders, available funding opportunities and interests of strategic partners. It is often a combination of available funding opportunities and the priorities of senior management paired with scholarly ambitions that eventually channels resources into a programme.

But how do these educational activities translate into influence? CGD, like most US think tanks, is organised under US corporate law on the same terms as charities and educational organisations, as 501(c)3 organisations. As such, they are not permitted to use more than 5 per cent of their total resources for lobbying and political advocacy. Hence, they must be inventive in finding ways of educating and informing public officials about critical issues. CGD works actively to ensure that their research products and policy recommendations reach policy-makers, advocates and public-opinion leaders, and continuously experiment with new, more effective ways to turn ideas into action. CGD produces an extensive range of print and online materials, such as books, peer-reviewed working papers, essays, policy briefs, congressional testimony and short policy memos addressed to specific policy-makers. Policy recommendations and analytic findings are adapted in format and length to suit diverse audiences. The experts also write their own opinion editorials (op-eds) and may also have their own web pages. Online engagement is crucial. CGD has a lively website and a presence in such social media as Facebook and Twitter. Its members produce policy blogs, in which senior experts provide their views on topical issues and advocate policy changes. Trying to get an overview, let alone to stay abreast of the production of documents, as 'artifacts of knowledge practices', in Annelise Riles' (2009: 7) terms, was a daunting but crucial task. Moreover, CGD organises a range of events that feature the work of its experts and other influential policy thinkers, with the aim of reaching a wider audience of policy-makers, academics, diplomats, analysts, advocates and journalists.

Among the varied audience groups that CGD targets, the US Congress deserves special mention. The critical role that Congress plays in shaping, funding and overseeing US global development policies requires CGD's policy outreach team to work to ensure that the Center's research and analysis is readily accessible to audiences on Capitol Hill. A great deal of effort goes into ensuring that the experts are given the opportunity to provide testimony on development issues before the House and Senate Committees – testimonies that serve as critical milestones in the work of experts. The experts are also encouraged to submit written statements on relevant topics for the Congressional Record and to create opportunities for participating in discussions with members of Congress and their staff.

So, how are they faring? It is difficult to present evidence of the influence of think tanks on policy. As noted by Weidenbaum (2011: 87), 'there is an inevitable amount of puffery in the claims of individual think tanks, especially when they are raising money or reporting to their supporters'. It is clearly a temptation for think-tank experts to claim credit for the public policy statements of nationally known legislative figures. And because they cannot lobby in the strict sense of the term, their influence must come through the shaping of agendas and perceptions through education and the dissemination of information.

A distinction is made at CGD between influence and impact. Influence is the less tangible but nonetheless valuable change in the way key actors frame or approach a pressing problem. Impact refers to specific changes that can be largely or partially attributed to their work. Impacts are listed on the web page and highlighted in seminars, web features and blogs. The impact most discussed during my fieldwork was 'Shaping the Financial Access Agenda'. It was claimed that CGD is shaping the international agenda on ways to increase access to financial services for poor people and for small and medium-sized businesses in the developing world – which is seen as a key to shared global prosperity. In June 2010, the G-20 Summit in Toronto had adopted Principles for Innovative Financial Inclusion that closely mirrored those of a CGD task force report, 'Policy Principles for Expanding Financial Access' released in 2009 and led by Senior Fellow Liliana Rojas-Suarez. The fundamental and often frustrating question of how to measure impact and influence in the public policy arena was a constant concern that fuelled activities with a certain spark. The 'So what?' question is never far away.

FEATURES AND WONKCASTS

On my second day at CGD, I was invited to attend the weekly Communication Team meeting. The meeting is convened in order to coordinate the planning of upcoming events, to help members decide which expert is to be featured on the web site and what the lead story of the week will be, and to pick up on unforeseen events. We were seated in the kitchen area that Tuesday morning – an open, light area with large windows overlooking the greenery of Dupont Circle, adjacent to the library area and to the open-office landscape. The team comprised close to 20 people, including research assistants, most of whom were present. Mike greeted everyone, and introduced me as their in-house anthropologist, who was going to be their guest over the next couple of months. He said he expected everyone to greet me with their usual warm hospitality. Introductions around the table followed, with team members briefly presenting themselves, their backgrounds and their areas of responsibility. Most of them were relatively young college graduates in their mid-to-late twenties, sparkling with talent and ambition. I had a difficult time recalling all their names, but over time, as things settled into some sort of daily rhythm, I received a relatively good overview of who did what and of their educational and professional experiences and aspirations.

Mike moderated the discussion with elegant ease and focus. First on the agenda was Kate, who reported on upcoming events, like the Richard H. Sabot Lecture held annually to honour the life and work of Richard 'Dick' Sabot, 'a respected professor, celebrated development economist, successful Internet entrepreneur and close friend of the Center for Global Development'.[13] That year Esther Duflo, professor at the Massachusetts Institute of Technology and co-founder of the Abdul Latif Jameel Poverty Action Lab (J-PAL), had been invited to give the Sixth Annual Richard H. Sabot Lecture. Her lecture was to draw upon her latest book, co-authored with Abhijit Banerjee and entitled *Poor Economics: A Radical Rethinking of the Way to Fight Global Poverty* (Banerjee and Duflo 2011). When this event had been properly planned for, the next board meeting, which was also in the pipeline, was carefully discussed.

Next in line was Miranda, who reported on noteworthy events in the wider policy community. There were mentions of a couple of reports that had recently emerged from the United Nations Population Fund and the World Bank. A few staff members had just returned from a research visit to Pakistan and a wrap-up of the insights gained on this trip was provided. Mike then reported on other significant policy events that had occurred over the past week, and discussed how they related to the expert feature he was intending to do this week. 'When is Earth Day?' Mike queried. 'We need a nice package for the Watson Kit', he explained, Watson being the expert who, it was planned, would be highlighted in the upcoming feature. Attention then turned to the content of blogs over the past few days, and the traction they had provided. Back on track again, Mike made a swift decision to bump Watson back one week and to feature Clark instead. Clark's recent report was more clearly in line with the recent events and newscasts, focused as it was on the role of private enterprise in the developing world. His recent report on how private investments could help fund development of public goods in the developing world was more acutely topical. 'Does anyone have picture ideas for the feature?' Mike asked. 'Something that carries a sense of crisis, something concrete and appealing, since the report is so abstract. Could you, Jamie, write a blurb for the report?' When the feature was settled, the attention again turned to Kate, who provided an outline of the upcoming events for the next week. Among the items covered were a meeting at the World Bank and another at the International Monetary Fund.

Mike then turned our attention onto the 'Wonkcast': 'We need to think about possible Wonkcasts. Something post-Pakistan.' 'What on earth is a Wonkcast?', I asked myself. Jamie, who was in charge of publications, later explained to me that:

> The Wonkcast is the name we came up with for the podcast. So that's the weekly audio interview that Mike does, usually with one of our fellows, but sometimes with a visitor. So we tried to come up with a name that – something more interesting I guess than CGD's podcasts. So I think it was Mike's idea of the Wonkcast, and I can't remember who came up with, but he liked it.

I asked him whether 'wonk' actually meant something, and was told that:

> Well, wonk, it plays off – it might be someone who spends much time studying and has little or no social life, but policy wonks are people who are I guess kinda technocratic and into the details of policies and kind of – I don't know [what] the word [is] – it's probably something like nerd.... Yeah. So there are a lot of wonks in DC, and I guess we are – we house a few of them.

So, in the Global Prosperity Wonkcast, Mike interviews CGD experts and others on innovative, practical policy responses to poverty and inequality in a globalising world. This interview is then placed on the website.

Mike then went around the table again, asking for concrete information about what every member was doing during that week. Mary Jane, director of policy outreach, who was the one who kept in close contact with people on the Hill, dominated the discussion. She told about the possible government shutdown, what she had gleaned from sources in Congress and the possible implications of a shutdown. Mike emphasised that it was necessary to acquire all the information possible regarding the predicted shutdown and its implications. 'Could you cover this in a blog, Mary Jane?' Mary Jane replied that she was already onto it.

CONCLUSION: OF CONNECTIVITY AND CAPITAL – AND EXPERIMENTATION

As in most think tanks, the professional networks of people at CGD extend far beyond the organisation in which they are housed. Maintaining both strong and weak ties, in Granovetter's (1973) sense of the term, to relevant others is key. The revolving door phenomenon of DC – the movement of people between their roles as legislators and regulators in the political administration, the industries affected by the legislation and regulation, and such organisations as think tanks or lobby organisations – builds upon and feeds the connectivity of individuals across organisations. The ethnographic field is, in essence, a relational one, delineated by the reach and depth of network connections.

The networks of think-tank professionals constitute something like 'an economy of connections', in which referrals and references take the form of valuable symbolic capital in a highly competitive and politicised form of exchange. This is an economy, in the sense that social connections and referrals are provided as gifts between trusted parties. The connection may provide access to yet other valuable resources, like information, attention, or a job opportunity, which may, in the long run, translate into financial resources. Introductions and referrals to high-ranking, influential people are given as gifts, in the sense that they are tokens of a relationship that is seen as valuable enough to invest in and in which there may be an anticipation of reciprocity. In return, the recipient of the gift is expected to recognise the value in the act of the giver, to provide the giver with information about the unfolding of the contact and, most important, to be ready to assist with a useful connection in the future. Ideally, recurrent giving serves to circulate and redistribute valuables, in the form of connections, within the community of professionals, contributing, over time, to the development of a dense network of connections around specific policy areas.

These gifts differ in their value. The gift of a connection from someone with prominent credentials is more beneficial than a connection from someone with fewer credentials or someone who carries a less valuable brand name. My first experience of doing fieldwork in Washington DC was, indeed, as an outsider to this 'economy of connections'. My academic credentials from Sweden counted for little in this community, and to squeeze into the exchange circle as an outsider took some effort, perseverance and strategising. Once I got the hang of it, however, and had something to offer in return, connecting became an easier game.[14]

This gift economy is intertwined with the organisational structures of society, erecting 'pillars of social capital' (Bourdieu 1986) that attach to key positions in organisational hierarchies. The social capital that derives from resources linked to a durable network of relationships of mutual recognition provides the members with the backing of credentials which, in Bourdieu's (1986: 51) words, 'entitles them to credit, in the various senses of the word'. The 'economy of connections' is thus an economy in two ways: as a system of exchange of valuables (connections and their translations into other resources) and as investment and interest in the cultivating of certain relationships.[15]

The existence of networks of connections within and among organisations is not a natural or a social given, but the product of investment strategies, aimed at establishing or maintaining social relationships that can be used in the short or long term and that imply durable obligations (Bourdieu 1986: 52). With continuously changing organisational boundaries and positions, an 'economy of connections' takes shape, in which market logics and sociality are at once emphasised.

In my first attempts at nesting myself into the network of policy intellectuals in DC, I learned about the networks, their nodes, the exchange of gifts and the building of social capital, basically by testing and making mistakes. What I have labelled 'ethnography by failure' boils down to a way of learning by practice and experimentation. One of the distinct advantages of ethnographic fieldwork is that it allows and indeed encourages us to do just that. Justin, who works as a research assistant for one of the experts, expressed a similar idea when I interviewed him, asking him what advice he would give to a brand new research assistant starting work at CGD. Justin says:

> I guess a piece of advice would just be to let yourself branch out, experiment.... Think tanks are wonderful for being able to take longer to complete a project than the private sector would endure. And this is a good chance for you to look at – develop – your own research style when you don't have the pressures of being in grad school, more classes or teaching or any of this sort of stuff. So it's good to take time to figure out your own ways of doing things and to make mistakes and then learn from them, because you're not going to have ... CGD is an extraordinarily relaxed environment. Not many other places are going to be like that, so this is a good time for you to experiment and figure out what's best.

Experimentation. Ethnographic fieldwork, just like work in a think tank, is all about stepwise refinement.

NOTES

1. The research project is part of the research programme Organising Markets, funded by Riksbankens Jubileumsfond. All informant names are pseudonyms.
2. The origins of the term are unclear. See, for example, Dickson (1971), Rich (2004), Smith (1991), for slightly different views.
3. With regard to the field of nuclear weapons policy, Gusterson (2009) posits that a number of organisations perform what he calls 'an audit function' in regard to government policy. These organisations are hybrids, operating partly as think tanks and partly as advocacy NGOs.
4. The expression 'the clash of civilizations' was proposed by political scientist Samuel P. Huntington. It suggests that people's cultural and religious identities will be the primary source of conflict in the post-Cold War world. This thesis was developed in a 1993 *Foreign Affairs* article entitled 'The clash of civilizations?', in response to Francis Fukuyama's (1992) book, *The End of History and the Last Man*, and expanded on by Huntington in *The Clash of Civilizations and the Remaking of World Order* (1996). Fukuyama's view was that the advent of western liberal democracy may signal the end point of humanity's sociocultural evolution and the final form of human government. The expression 'the world is flat' emanates from the international bestselling book by Thomas Friedman, *The World Is Flat: A Brief History of the Twenty-first Century* (2005), which analyses globalisation, primarily in the early twenty-first century. The title is a metaphor for viewing the world's commerce as a level playing field, where all competitors in the global market are seen to enjoy equal opportunities, and where historical and geographical divisions are becoming increasingly irrelevant.
5. According to McGann (2007), about 40 per cent of the world's think tanks are located in North America. Twenty-three per cent are found in Western Europe, 12 per cent in Asia, 8 per cent in Eastern Europe and 6 per cent in Africa. In the USA alone, there are 1736 think tanks, half of them created since 1950.

6. Smith (1991: xv) also notes the linkage between the growth of think tanks and the Scientific Management movement.
7. Think tanks tend to be clustered in the area around Dupont Circle and lobby firms on K Street. Thus there is a sense in which the population of organisations in DC show a particular spatial mapping.
8. Geographically, the term 'beltway' refers to Interstate 495, the Capital Beltway, that encircles Washington, DC. The idiom 'inside the beltway' has a political meaning, in that it suggests that officials of the US federal government, its contractors and lobbyists, think-tank experts, and the media which cover them, are somewhat insulated from the interests and priorities of the general population. I often heard this term used by people in think tanks and by others.
9. See Faubion (2009) for an insightful discussion of 'classical' and 'new' forms of connectivity in novel designs of ethnographic fieldwork.
10. This is an example of what Holmes and Marcus (2005) have called 'para-ethnography'.
11. See: http://www.cgdevl.org/section/about/ (accessed 20 April 2012).
12. Think tanks therefore resemble what Ahrne and Brunsson (2011) have described as 'partial organisations'. As partial organisations, they make use of some, but not necessarily all, the organisational elements that characterise a complete, formal organisation, and they exist in a partly organised environment.
13. See: http://www.cgdev.org/section/about/sabot (accessed 19 May 2012).
14. Melissa Fisher (2012) experienced similar challenges to access in her fieldwork among female Wall Street investors; her way into the field was largely dependent upon the right person providing her with the right connections.
15. See Steege (2007) for a fascinating account of how the 'economy of connections' became a way to secure one's survival in post-war Berlin.

REFERENCES

Ahrne, A. and N. Brunsson (2011) 'Organization outside organizations: The significance of partial organization', *Organization*, Vol. 18, No. 1, pp. 83–104.

Banerjee, A. and E. Duflo (2011) *Poor Economics: A Radical Rethinking of the Way to Fight Global Poverty* (Philadelphia, PA: Public Affairs).

Barley, S. R. (2010) 'Building an institutional field to corral a government: A case to set an agenda for organization studies', *Organization Studies*, Vol. 31, No. 6, pp. 777–805.

Bourdieu, P. (1986) 'Forms of capital', trans. R. Nice, in J. E. Richardson, ed., *Handbook of Theory of Research for the Sociology of Education* (New York, NY: Greenwood Press).

Cutler, A. C., V. Haufler and T. Porter, eds (1999) *Private Authority and International Affairs* (New York, NY: State University of New York Press).

Dickson, P. (1971) *Think Tanks* (New York, NY: Atheneum).

Faubion, J. D. (2009) 'The ethics of fieldwork as an ethics of connectivity, or the good anthropologist (isn't what she used to be)', in J. D. Faubion and G. E. Marcus, eds *Fieldwork Is Not What It Used to Be: Learning Anthropology's Method in a Time of Transition*. (Ithaca, NY: Cornell University Press).

Fisher, M. (2012) *Wall Street Women* (Durham, NC: Duke University Press).

Friedman, T. L. (2005) *The World Is Flat: A Brief History of the Twenty-First Century* (New York, NY: Farrar, Straus and Giroux).

Fukuyama, F. (1992) *The End of History and the Last Man* (New York, NY: Free Press).

Garsten, C. (1994) *Apple World: Core and Periphery in a Transnational Organizational Culture*, Stockholm Studies in Social Anthropology 33 (Stockholm: Almqvist & Wiksell International).

Garsten, C. and M. Lindh de Montoya, eds (2008) *Transparency in a New Global Order. Unveiling Organizational Visions* (Cheltenham: Edward Elgar Publishing).

Granovetter, M. S. (1973) 'The strength of weak ties', *American Journal of Sociology*, Vol. 78, No. 6, pp. 1360–1380.

Gusterson, H. (2009) *The Sixth Branch: Think Tanks as Auditors*. Working paper, March (New York, NY: Social Science Research Council).

Hannerz, U. (2009) 'Geocultural scenarios', in P. Hedström and B. Witrock, eds, *Frontiers of Sociology*. Annals of the International Institute of Sociology 11 (Leiden: Brill).

Holmes, D. and G. E. Marcus (2005) 'Cultures of expertise and the management of globalization: Toward the re-functioning of ethnography', in A. Ong and S. J. Collier, eds, *Global Assemblages: Technology, Politics and Ethics as Anthropological Problems* (Malden, MA: Blackwell).

Hood, C. (2006) 'Conclusion', in C. Hood and D. Heald, eds, *Transparency: The Key to Better Governance?* (Oxford: Oxford University Press).

Huntington, S. P. (1993) 'The clash of civilizations?', *Foreign Affairs*, Summer.

—— (1996) *The Clash of Civilizations and the Remaking of World Order* (New York, NY: Touchstone).

Marcus, G. (1998) *Ethnography through Thick and Thin* (Princeton, NJ: Princeton University Press).

McGann, J. G. (2007) *Think Tanks and Policy Advice in the United States: Academics, Advisors and Advocates* (New York, NY: Routledge).

Mills, C. W. (1956) *The Power Elite* (New York, NY: Oxford University Press).

Nye, J. S. Jr (2004) *Soft Power: The Means to Succeed in World Politics* (New York, NY: Public Affairs).

—— (2011) *The Future of Power* (New York, NY: Public Affairs).

Rabinow, P. (2003) *Anthropos Today: Reflections on Modern Equipment* (Princeton, NJ: Princeton University Press).

Rabinow, P. and G. E. Marcus, with J. D. Faubion and T. Rees (2008) *Designs for an Anthropology of the Contemporary* (Durham, NC: Duke University Press).

Rahman Kahn, S. (2011) Privilege: *The Making of an Adolescent Elite at St. Paul's School* (Princeton, NJ: Princeton University Press).

Rich, A. (2004) *Think Tanks, Public Policy, and the Politics of Expertise* (Cambridge: Cambridge University Press).

Riles, A. (2009 [2006]) 'Introduction: In Response', in A. Riles, ed., *Documents: Artifacts of Modern Knowledge* (Ann Arbor, MI: University of Michigan Press).

Rose, N. and P. Miller (1992) 'Political power beyond the state: Problematics of government', *British Journal of Sociology*, Vol. 43, No. 2, pp. 173–205.

Rothkopf, D. (2008) Superclass: *The Global Power Elite and the World They are Making* (New York, NY: Farrar, Straus and Giroux).

Smith, J. A. (1991) *The Idea Brokers: Think Tanks and the Rise of the New Policy Elite* (New York, NY: Free Press).

Steege, P. (2007) *Black Market, Cold War: Everyday Life in Berlin, 1946–1949* (Cambridge: Cambridge University Press).

Stone, D. (1996) *Capturing the Imagination: Think Tanks and the Policy Process* (Portland, OR: Frank Cass).

—— (2001) 'The "policy research" knowledge elite and global policy processes', in D. Josselin and W. Wallace, eds, *Non-state Actors in World Politics* (London: Palgrave).

Tsing, A. L. (2005) *Friction: An Ethnography of Global Connection* (Princeton, NJ: Princeton University Press).

Wallace-Wells, B. (2003) 'In the tank: The intellectual decline of AEI', *Washington Monthly*, December.

Weber, M. (1958) 'The three types of legitimate rule', trans. H. Gerth. *Berkeley Publications in Society and Institutions*, Vol. 4, No. 1, pp. 1–11.

Wedel, J. R. (2009) *Shadow Elite: How the World's New Power Brokers Undermine Democracy, Government, and the Free Market* (New York, NY: Basic Books).

Weidenbaum, M. (2010) 'Measuring the influence of think tanks', *Society*, Vol. 47, pp. 134–137.

—— (2011) *The Competition of Ideas: The World of Washington Think Tanks* (New Brunswick, NJ: Transaction).

Westbrook , D. A. (2008) *Navigators of the Contemporary: Why Ethnography Matters* (Chicago, IL: University of Chicago Press).

10
Working connections, helping friends
Fieldwork, organisations and cultural styles

Brian Moeran

INTRODUCTION: NETWORKING AS AN OPPORTUNITY

If there is one thing that has not just influenced, but almost dictated, the course of the various periods of fieldwork that I have conducted over the years, it is connections.[1] There are some societies in which nothing can be accomplished without such particularistic linkages (Hannerz 1980: 192). Japan, on which the fieldwork accounts presented here focus, is a case in point.

But there are also certain social situations in which particularistic linkages play a crucial role. Without doubt, one of these consists of the, in one way or another 'foreign', anthropologist entering and negotiating his way through a social field. It is through contact with certain people that he (or she) is granted entry into a particular community or organisation and allowed to conduct fieldwork among the people there. It is through the connections that he then makes that he talks to one person rather than another, is invited to one event rather than another, finds himself involved in one project, not another, and pursues some lines of enquiry more fully than others, during the course of his, ideally long-term, participant observation. To an outsider stumbling blindly about in an unknown social field, connections are everything. Often serendipitous, they may also be purposely strategic, taking the fieldworker in unexpected, as well as planned, directions. Connections ultimately form the basis for quality in ethnographic research. They might be said to be more or less directly responsible for the development of anthropological theory. They also constitute a crucial aspect of the organisation of organisations. As Japanese businessmen often remark: 'corporations are people' (*kigyō wa hitonari*).

One aim of this chapter is to show how – in the context of Japan's advertising and ceramic art worlds – connections partly 'cut across enduring groups and institutions' and partly 'cover other areas of the local landscape' (Hannerz 1980: 174). Although nowadays, following on from a long anthropological tradition, it is common to refer to such connections as 'networks', we should, I think, distinguish between the two. Connections pertain to the process of network*ing*, while networks themselves assist us in 'abstracting for analytical purposes more or less elaborate sets of relationships from some wider system' (Hannerz 1980: 172). In other words, connections are what people *practise*, while networks are how they analyse them *theoretically* (Moeran 2005: 111). It is the connections made, rather than the overall networks *per se* (Kanter and

Eccles 1992: 521–522), which form the basis of everyday business behaviour and the anthropologist's endeavours in the corporate field.

Another aim of this chapter is to reveal ways in which individuals use organisational affiliations to make connections and pursue aims that may be personal and/or institutional, either consecutively or at the same time. Connections can thus undermine the structural stability of a single organisation, while providing opportunities for a change in its position vis-à-vis the field as a whole. In this respect, networking is a crucial force for change. It provides, once again as Japanese businessmen like to say, an 'opportunity' (*kikkake*) to try out something new.

USING PEOPLE

How much does the anthropologist use people for his, or her, own ends? How much is he himself used? And how consistent are his experiences with those with whom he comes into contact in the field? My fieldwork in Japan, in an advertising agency as well as in the ceramic art world, sheds some light on the various ways in which connections work.

Japanese often distinguish between what they call, in English, 'wet' and 'dry' relations, usually bemoaning their perception that interpersonal relations in Japan tend to be 'wet', whereas those in Europe or the USA are 'dry'. As one newspaper journalist put it:

> If you're going to get involved in pottery, you have to do so objectively. It's no good getting caught up with any one person through *tsukiai* – whether it's a critic, potter, department store representative, or whatever – because then you get involved with *every*one. There are just too many cliques, too many factions, too many likes and dislikes, to allow you to do business that way. All sorts of rumours, stories, and bits of gossip come into your ear. Some of it you store away because you think they might be useful. The rest you discard because you've already heard it. If you're going to be really successful, you've got to be like the three monkeys: see no evil, speak no evil, and hear no evil. *Tsukiai* doesn't allow that.

The two examples that follow illustrate the distinction between 'wet' and 'dry' nicely, although the 'dry' relation described here is by no means characteristic of the advertising industry as a whole, while among the numerous 'wet' relations of the ceramic art world, occasional 'dry' patches were to be found.

As an example of 'dry' relations, I will trace the development of a 'connection' between a senior manager on the agency's board of directors, whom I will call Yano, and myself, the fieldworker who was by then also a professor at London University. It is of interest because, unlike my earlier relationships with people when I studied the folk art movement in Japan (Moeran 1997), my acquaintanceship with Yano was developed entirely in a professional organisational context – with the important exception of our very first contact.

This I have already recounted in some detail (Moeran 2005: 89–96), but it bears partial retelling for the purpose of this chapter. On one of my trips to Tokyo before starting fieldwork in Asatsū, the advertising agency that had accepted me as researcher, I paid a courtesy call on its CEO, Masao Inagaki. As I was leaving, one of Inagaki's assistants asked me if I had time to meet a Mr Yano, who was managing director of accounts and whose son was going to London to study.

I was ushered into a meeting room and a few minutes later a slightly haggard-looking man in his early to mid fifties entered and introduced himself. After a few pleasantries surrounding my forthcoming research in the agency, Yano informed me that his son was going to study in England for a few months later on in the summer. Moreover, as we quickly established, he was by chance going to be at my own institution, the School of Oriental and African Studies, London. Could I possibly keep an eye on the boy during his stay there?

'Of course,' I replied. In the context of the endless 'give-and-take' that characterised Japanese society, I was already calculating that if I were to do Yano a favour before I started my fieldwork, he might well do me one back later on during the course of my research. At the same time, I wondered vaguely whether Inagaki had thought to make use of the fact that Yano's son was going to study at the institution by which I myself was employed to test my grasp of Japanese etiquette. After all, in situations of uncertainty, those concerned tend to be 'cautious about extending themselves for people whose reputation for honouring interpersonal debt is unknown' (Burt 2000: 288).

Anyway, I thought little more about it until a couple of months later when there was a gentle knock on my office door and a young Japanese man hesitatingly introduced himself as the son of Yano. Having made sure that he was settled in all right, I invited him out for a chat and some snacks in a bar somewhere near the British Museum, and several hours later we parted the best of friends (it is amazing what a bottle of Chablis can do for a tongue-tied young Japanese man in a foreign country).

On my next trip to Tokyo Yano insisted on meeting me and made effusive apologies for my having wasted several hours of my precious time on his 'insignificant son'. It seemed that the father was particularly impressed by the fact that I had ordered a bottle of Chablis for his son to share with me – a possibility that I have to admit to being at least partially conscious of when I selected this particular, comparatively expensive, offering from the wine list. Just how conscious, though, is hard to tell. Sometimes we know exactly what we're up to and calculate very precisely how to give off an impression; at other times, however, we're less aware of how calculating we are, even though the activity is still going on in that way (Goffman 1959: 17).

By the time I started fieldwork in Asatsū, therefore, I had in Yano an influential supporter in the company. Inagaki himself made sure that everyone in the agency knew about my being there as a researcher, first by having me introduced at the first-Monday-of-the-month morning meeting for all employees, and then by arranging for me to be taken round every single department of the agency and introduced to all those at their desks. The fact that my entry into Asatsū had been sanctioned at the highest managerial level meant that I was well looked after as I moved from one department to another, and from one division to another. But, although I had access to all kinds of information and detail concerning the agency's day-to-day activities, it did not mean that I had access to its closely guarded secrets. This was where the favour I had done for Yano came into play.

The first part of his 'repayment' came when, a couple on months into my fieldwork, I was assigned to the accounts division headed by Yano, who immediately arranged for a desk to be placed at an angle to his own, opposite his secretary. It was here that I sat for the month that I was nominally studying account handling (in fact, the desk remained in place for me to use during the rest of my fieldwork as and when I so wished). By being so placed, I was able to listen in on informal, but often quite sensitive, discussions about clients between Yano and his senior staff, as well as on his telephone conversations, the gist of which he would often relay to me and comment on, sometimes to give vent to his frustration at a client's unexpected way of doing business (Moeran 2005: 68–69).

The second part came after I had mentioned one day how difficult it was to understand how the agency managed to secure clients in the first place, as well as what went on during speculative or competitive 'presentations'. Over the next two to three weeks, Yano arranged for me not only to participate in preparations for what turned out to be a successful presentation to a major Japanese electronics firm, which I called Frontier (Moeran 2007), but also to witness a speculative presentation to a soft drinks manufacturer, as well as a couple of other lesser presentations (none of which was immediately successful).

The fact that I was able to take advantage of Yano's initial introduction to the Frontier account team by coming up with a successful tagline for the proposed campaign had two immediate effects. First, it redounded to his own credit, since it was he who had brought me on to the account team in the first place, and he who was the managing director of the accounts division that won the Frontier account. As a foreign university professor who had (with a little help from some friends in a Belgian bar) come up with a good idea, I unwittingly provided him with social and cultural capital. This he felt bound to repay, by allowing me to sit in on other presentations. Even though it was often too late for me to play a part in their build-up, Yano made sure to ask me what I thought about them, what the mood was like and so on.

At the same time, however, and this was an integral part of the second effect mentioned above, Yano began to treat me less as a 'professor' and more as an 'ad man' (though he never failed to call me 'sensei' or 'teacher'). This meant that both he, and a lot of other employees in the agency who heard about the role I had played in helping win the Frontier account, no longer confined themselves to front-stage information, institutions and ideal practices when talking to me, but shifted to back-stage discussions of the gossip and personalities in the world of advertising, and the tactics and strategies that the agency adopted when courting clients and dealing with the media.

All of this led to our embarking upon a series of reciprocal exchanges that shifted from the purely instrumental to an affective relationship between us. When I needed information about a particular account, Yano would tell me who to talk to, and on occasion call up the person concerned and ask him to talk 'frankly' to me (in other words, he hinted that it was all right to give me back-stage stuff, rather than front-stage formalities).[2] When he needed a 'foreign professor' to add a bit of cultural capital to an expensive lunch or dinner in the company of a (would-be) client, he would ask whether I might possibly be able to take the time off from my research to join him. Of course, I never refused, given that everything was grist for the fieldwork mill.

Although Yano prevailed upon me to give the new recruits a two-hour lecture during their three-week training course in the spring, I gained far more from our professional relationship than he did from mine. But what was interesting about it was that, having got over the initially rather obvious instrumentality of our 'give-and-take', we were able to engage without much prior thought or obvious calculation in exchanges that were of mutual benefit to us and that enabled us to enjoy each other's company in and around the agency's offices.

Indeed, my relationship with Yano was nothing like the one I had experienced with Sakakura Inoshige, my closest 'informant-cum-friend' in the pottery community of Sarayama where I had conducted fieldwork some years earlier, and where 'wetness' often prevailed as I found myself involved in pottery, forestry and rice agriculture, extended family and community relations, the local school and PTA, a land deal, hostesses in the local bars, softball tournaments and singing competitions (Moeran 2010). It is here, I think, that a clear distinction needs to be made between traditional 'frame-based' fieldwork in rural or other communities and what often amounts to 'network-based' fieldwork in business or government organisations of one sort or another (Moeran 2005). In the former, we are invited as fieldworkers to observe and participate in multiple roles – of family and household, work, community, politics, religious practices and so on – both inside and outside the community itself. In the latter, we are not. Unlike with Sakakura, I never once visited Yano's home, nor met his family, nor knew his religious beliefs, nor which political party he voted for. We hardly talked about anything other than work-related matters. This is not to say that we only talked about advertising: far from it. We would discuss as wide a range of topics as I had done in the company of Sakakura, but we would do so because they impinged in one way or another on something with which Yano was involved at work. In this respect, our relationship was confined to our single roles: his as an ad man, mine as researcher. It was wonderfully 'not tacky' and 'dry'.

NETWORKING AT WORK

Let me now address in more general terms how people employed by, or affiliated with, different kinds of Japanese organisations make use of interpersonal connections (known as *tsukiai* in Japanese) to further both individual and organisational ends, and how such connections reflect on seemingly unrelated symbolic and cultural ideals (such as the judgement of 'art'). For this purpose, I will discuss the ceramic art world in Japan, which I studied for over a year way back in 1981. For reasons that should become apparent, I was at the time reluctant to publish the results of this period of fieldwork, but feel now, 30 years later, that no great harm will come of it. So, let us don our water wings and dive into some wetness!

My anthropological fieldwork was on the production, marketing and aesthetic appraisal of contemporary ceramic art in Japan.[3] The research question asked was simple enough: how did an aspiring potter get selected as the holder of an important intangible cultural property (*jūyō mukei bunkazai*) – the highest honour awarded to a traditional artist-craftsman in Japan, and popularly referred to in the media as a 'national treasure' (*ningen kokuhō*)? The answer was also simple, on the surface at least: by exhibiting his or her (mainly his) work in department stores.

I therefore spent a large proportion of my early fieldwork attending the one-man gallery shows and group exhibitions that were held on a regular basis in Japanese department stores – located in various cities in the southern island of Kyushu, where I was plugged into a network of ceramic artists (some of whom were happy to call themselves simply 'potters'), as well as in the capital, Tokyo, where they all ultimately aspired to hold their own exhibition. What I quickly discovered was that the ceramic art world was built on a quadripartite structure, of which two parts consisted overtly of individuals (potters and critics, with collectors as additional players), and the other two of organisations (newspaper publishers and department stores, with gallery owners as additional players). More slowly, I came to realise that individual actors often had organisational, and organisations individual, aims in mind. What united them was their common practice of networking.

In order to earn themselves a 'name', potters needed to exhibit their work. For this they needed department stores, since museum exhibitions were reserved almost entirely for dead artists. But how were they to persuade a store to exhibit their work? Here interpersonal connections came to the fore. A potter had several networking strategies from which to choose. He (or she) could get an introduction from a (more famous) potter to whom he had been apprenticed; or from a well-known professor at the art school where he had studied. In the latter case, the professor concerned was often well known because of the art school to which he was attached, and the school, similarly, well known because of the professor. There was thus a 'mutual consecration' (Bourdieu 1993) between individual and organisation that could then be manipulated by an aspiring lesser-known potter.

Alternatively, a potter could join a regional potters' association, first exhibiting his work in a group exhibition arranged by the association's (more senior) chairman, and then using connections made there to hold his own one-man show. He could also work through the association to have his work accepted – and ultimately awarded a prize – in one of the numerous juried exhibitions held annually in department stores throughout the country. Here, an organisation was used by a potter for the recognition and advancement of individual work.

This last strategy required the intervention of a critic. Pottery critics were invited to give advice to potters' groups and associations of all kinds, since they were often invited to act as judges of work submitted to national exhibitions. They could therefore 'pre-judge' pots and advise potters on what to submit to a particular exhibition and then make sure that some of them, at least, had their work accepted.[4] Different critics affiliated themselves to different groups of potters around the country and tended to establish 'fiefdoms' in particular regions. Senior potters acted in a similar manner. A famous ceramics professor at the Tokyo University of Art, for example, was said to have had a strong influence on which potters in the Kantō region around Tokyo had their work accepted, and awarded prizes, at the National Crafts Exhibition (Dentō Kōgeiten) held in Mitsukoshi department store every autumn.

Many of the critics enlisted to juried exhibitions were employed as curators in national, prefectural and private museums around the country. Their organisational affiliation, therefore, established their judging 'credentials', although they freely admitted that taste was extremely individual (something potters latched on to as justification for a lack of success in juried exhibitions). At the same time, however, they would engage in a protracted power game during judging, when they did their best to promote potters in their particular 'fiefdoms'. This was essential if they were to maintain their positions as aesthetic 'advisers'.

But the power that they wielded in terms of a potter's (in)ability to move up the art ladder also promoted and strengthened an 'art for art's sake' philosophy among many potters who wished to deny the importance of interpersonal connections. In this way, tsukiai, which was often little more than self-interested manipulation on the part of both potters and critics, ironically sustained the classic distinction in cultural production between 'art' and 'commerce' (Bourdieu 1993).

Mention of commerce brings us to department stores and the dealers who often supplied them. Japanese department stores have long been involved in cultural events of one sort or another so that their involvement in putting on art exhibitions from the 1960s was not unexpected. However, precisely because they were commercial enterprises, department stores had to make use of newspaper companies to act as intermediaries when negotiating the loan of art objects from (particularly foreign) museums. While stores provided the necessary financial outlay for exhibitions of all kinds, therefore, newspapers acted as cultural 'sponsors' by promoting them in their daily editions and by producing expensive colour catalogues for visitors to purchase.

For both shows and catalogues, of course, art objects were needed. Some of these, as intimated, came from museums of art, but many others were owned by individual collectors who, for the most part, wished to remain anonymous (often, it was said, because of tax evasion). Precisely because it was difficult to ascertain where art objects were to be found, newspaper companies made use of critics to approach collectors for loans, since it was the critics who knew precisely who had bought and owned what. This use of connections, however, did not necessarily contribute to an objective 'standard' of taste since what was selected for public exhibition and critical appraisal depended on personal friendships, not on a 'disinterested aesthetics'.

This situation was exacerbated by the fact that the – primarily Tokyo-based – critics would also rely on national and regional newspapers to introduce them to well-known potters in different parts of the country, since newspapers made it their business to publicise cultural activities in general and had numerous contacts in Japan's ceramic art world. This meant that newspapers would in turn call on particular critics to curate shows on their behalf, and the critics would then adopt the easiest path by choosing the work of those with whom they had connections and ignoring those with whom they did not. This itself led to the latter allying themselves with a different newspaper and/or critic, so that various potter–critic–newspaper factions came into being (often with a preferred department store being involved). Likes and dislikes of individual people were thus transformed into organisational alliances.

One of the perceived problems in this respect concerned a newspaper's choice of which individual potter's show to sponsor. Informants suggested that, at times, the person employed within the department arranging cultural exhibitions would favour one potter rather than another, because of some form of *tsukiai* (ranging from family connections to having attended the same university or having been born in the same prefecture). This was particularly true of regionally based newspapers, which could not criticise local potters' work or evaluate it objectively precisely because somebody somewhere would make use of his or her connections to bring some form of pressure to bear.

While interpersonal ties were consciously developed between potters and department stores, the latter were always in search of new 'talent'. Because they did not have sufficient manpower to do this, they would often develop relations with a pottery dealer or gallery owner who had his own 'stable' of potters (Thompson 2008). A number of large exhibitions, therefore, were arranged by entrepreneurial dealers who, like *bunraku* black-robed puppeteers, pulled the necessary strings to make the theatre unfold while being totally invisible.

There was, however, no *quo* without the *quid*. Anyone doing business with a department store found himself, at some stage or other (but particularly at a New Year's party), being obliged to purchase something (diamonds, a fur coat, a suit and so on) in return, so that he would repay in part the financial reward already reaped (and anticipated for the year to come). This principle of circulation, based on a sense of indebtedness (*giri*) between individuals and organisations, extended to potters who, at the end of a one-man exhibition, were often obliged to purchase an art object to show their 'gratitude' to a store for exhibiting their work in the first place. These and numerous other examples revealed that networking was in fact little more than an intricate form of bribery which had to be employed by any potter wishing to be appointed a 'national treasure'. To succeed you had to be 'wet'.

CONNECTING CONCLUSIONS

What do these two ethnographic descriptions tell us about doing fieldwork in organisations? First of all, as I remarked at the beginning of this chapter, connections are everything. The people whom a fieldworker meets, and to whom she is passed on, open up a field of 'local knowledge' that enables enquiry, reflection, analysis and, when appropriate, redirection of enquiry. Such local knowledge encompasses informants' ideas about themselves, the organisations for which they work, and the worlds in which they live and of which they try to make sense. It allows us to identify which individual actors and organisations are important, and in what ways, as well as to structure them in a field of competing positions.

Second, I have suggested that the main challenge faced by a fieldworker doing anthropological research in an organisation is how to move beyond the 'front stage' of information and ideal practices in a particular firm and industry, to 'back-stage' gossip and actual ways of doing what has to be done. This shift, when it occurs (and it is clear from some anthropological writings that it by no means always does so), takes place in many different ways.

In Asatsū, the shift from front to back stage demanded a useful input on my part. So long as I remained an academic researcher, asking innumerable questions, the answers to which I wrote down in one pocket notebook after another, I skimmed nicely along the surface of the world of advertising. I was little more than a journalist conducting an 'in-depth' report. However, once I showed that I could actually make a contribution to a campaign by coming up with a successful tagline for a potential client, I came to be seen as, in part at least, an 'ad man' and not just a 'university professor'. This recognition led to a marked change in my relationships with people I had already met, as well as to a large number of new connections. What marked out the latter was that they came directly to me to seek my help, whereas I had previously had to make all the running and go and seek out the help of others. By being accepted back stage, I found myself immediately involved in numerous relationships that were characterised from the start by a 'balanced reciprocity'.

In the world of ceramic art, I was fortunate enough to have the backing of a respected museum curator and a renowned professor of modern art, thanks to an earlier involvement with the English potter Bernard Leach. These connections opened doors that would otherwise have remained firmly closed: for example, my being able to witness first-hand the judging of a national ceramics exhibition, from selection of pots to awarding of prizes. But I was still little more than an, albeit persistent, journalist. It was a chance connection, followed by friendship, with a pottery dealer, Reisuke Miyamoto, which transformed the nature of my research. Whereas hitherto my questions had been met by department store managers with an almost identical story of the Japanese people's insatiable thirst for culture that was fulfilled by stores as a gift of gratitude for all the money consumers had spent therein, I now found myself visiting stores on their closing days (when exhibitions were changed) and, literally back stage, hearing the most unexpected gossip and detail about the potters whose work was being exhibited front stage during the rest of each week. The fact that I was present as Miyamoto's 'assistant' and not as a 'researcher' allowed my informants to drop their front-stage masks and reveal their back-stage personae.

What is common to these last two examples is the fact that, in each case, I was able to transform myself, like a chameleon, from an academic researcher to a more or less normal member of the 'working world' I was studying. As a result, I became more 'observant participant' than 'participant observer' (Wacquant 1995: 494). In both cases, I was extremely fortunate. By choosing to study an advertising agency, I found myself doing fieldwork in an organisation that openly called for novelty, innovation, creativity and a sense of difference, and which put its employees together in different combinations in account teams as a means towards achieving these ends. This was the opportunity offered to me, as well as all the agency's regular employees – an opportunity that I was able to make the most of (with a little bit of help from my friends). And, just as the agency formulated and pursued a single organisational business strategy from the myriad goings-on of its numerous account teams, so was I able to develop an anthropological theory about the structure of accounts from the various projects in which I was lucky enough to participate (Moeran 1996).

In the ceramic art world, precisely because Miyamoto was a fast-thinking entrepreneur who had gained the respect of potters, critics, media journalists *and* department store managers, he was able to get everyone to agree to my holding my own pottery exhibition and then pushed it through to a successful conclusion. This not only led to my experiencing first-hand hitherto only partly noticed problems like pricing and display; it also helped me develop a theory of values that has characterised much of my ensuing research on advertising, fashion magazines and trade fairs (Moeran and Strandgaard Pedersen 2011).

The need for a fieldworker to engage successfully in an identity transformation brings me to my third and final point. Organisations of all kinds – whether a potters' association, department store, newspaper publisher, or advertising agency – tend to establish boundaries around themselves. Some, especially in a Japanese context where the distinction between insider and outsider is the most pervasive form of social classification (Martin 1964), are more closed than others. This is why entry becomes such an important issue for the prospective fieldworker.

But entry into an organisation is insufficient in itself to guarantee successful research. Every organisation consists of sub-groupings of one sort or another. A department store, as its name implies, is made up of different departments, and marks strong boundaries between permanent and temporary staff, in terms of gender and age, as well as between visible (perfume, food, menswear and so on) and invisible (event planning, *gaishōbu*, or external sales and so forth) activities. An advertising agency distinguishes first and foremost between its different divisions (account services, media buying, marketing, creative and so on), which themselves tend to be stratified according to whether they bring in or spend money. But the agency is also structured into numerous account teams, each of which deals exclusively with a single client's account and recruits personnel for this purpose from its different divisions.

The fieldworker thus finds himself obliged to negotiate his way anew every time he moves – as I did once a month in Asatsū – from one division to another within an advertising agency, and renegotiate his acceptance (or lack thereof) every time he joins an account team for one purpose or another. The same was true of every pottery exhibition that I attended in a different department store, sponsored by a different newspaper and juried by a different set of critics. This process of negotiating and renegotiating one's acceptance as an 'insider' is not limited to the fieldworker, but in many ways is participated in by *all* personnel employed in an organisation – especially in those with the kind of matrix structure used by Asatsū. What became clear during the course of my fieldwork there was that it was extremely rare for members of an account team *not* to know, or know of, one another beforehand. There was always somebody there who was the 'contact' person for an otherwise unknown member of the team, somebody whose presence and assuring word facilitated the inclusion of the newcomer (who in some cases was myself).

Connections, then, not only facilitate entry into an organisation, but further movements into different parts of that organisation. Of course, other mechanisms are brought into play to ensure that all employees feel that they are fully fledged members of a company: a monthly address by the CEO, an annual marathon race, a three-week training course for all new recruits and so on. But connections perform an extremely important part in this process.

At the same time, however, connections take employees *outside* their organisation – especially in the ceramic art world, or in an industry like advertising, which is based upon building networks and developing new ideas with potential and existing business partners. There are two aspects of this external form of connection that are worth noting here. First, we find ourselves engaging with how connections 'resolve conflicts between structural principles' (Firth 1955: 2). If, as in Japanese society, the principal form of social organisation is the 'in-group', and if that 'in-group' is a company whose business it is to do business with other companies, the sociological challenge is to create a set of mechanisms that allows individual members of a company to move beyond the established boundaries of his 'in-group' and make contact with other companies (forming their own 'in-groups'). That mechanism is – as I have shown in my account of the ceramic art world – *tsukiai*, or interpersonal connections, with their supporting concepts of university, age and regional ties (Moeran 2005: 107–108). Both internally and externally, therefore, companies can in some respects be seen as social networks.

The fact that a company is a network of people interacting within and across organisational boundaries means that it is sometimes hard, both for observers and for participants to distinguish between actions performed as part of the role of – say – a senior account manager of an advertising agency, and those carried out by an individual called Yano. In the ceramic art world, actors constantly and purposely confused the two, with the result that what constituted 'art' itself came to consist of, on the one hand, high aesthetic ideals (based on perceptions of craftsmanship and beauty) and, on the other, a mish-mash of material, social, situational, use and economic values (Moeran 2012).

In this respect, while overtly used for 'in-group' ends, connections are potentially dangerous. Because he was a senior account manager, Yano could develop relations with his opposite number in a potential client company and bring in a lucrative account. But, precisely because he was Yano and not Tanaka or Yamashita, he could also have developed a special relationship, friendship even, with his opposite number that could have worked against his agency if, for one reason or another, Yano had decided to move to a new agency and take his clients' accounts with him. (He didn't, but others like him did.)

The more emphasis is laid on connections in a particular social field, the more dangerous they are likely to be. Because some kinds of organisations – advertising agencies or department stores, for instance – stake their survival on the supply of products (advertising campaigns or artworks), they have to employ people (account executives or art gallery personnel) whose job it is to keep in continuous contact with their suppliers (advertising clients or artists). They thus end up as 'betwixt and between' their own organisations and those with whom they spend all their time and energy liaising.[5] Consequently, they may have a conflict of loyalties when forced to choose between 'in-group' company and 'out-group' connection. Like account executives in an advertising agency, editors, for example, will often take their authors with them when they move from one publishing house to another. Similarly, it was not impossible for a department store employee to become independent and set up his own gallery. Connections thus undermine the structural stability of single organisations, but provide opportunities for change in the ordering of positions occupied by organisations within a field as a whole.

A second aspect of external relations between individual and company concerns how individual connections are transformed into alliances between organisations. Here I am concerned with the relationship between connections built on particularistic ties, on the one hand and, on the other, organisational networks aimed at achieving universalistic ends. In the advertising industry, as in many other business organisations, a formal relation between agency and client usually starts out as an informal connection between individual members thereof and *not* between the organisations concerned. In other words, organisational network alliances (such as the newspaper–potter–critic–department store alliances mentioned earlier) are driven by individual connections.

How does this come about? There are several variations, but what usually happens in advertising is that an account executive makes contact with the advertising manager of a particular company (usually through connections), and proceeds to 'woo' him over several months or years, until the advertising manager is prepared to let the account executive's agency participate in a competitive presentation for his company's advertising account.

All this time, the account executive relays news of the potential account's progress to his department or divisional head. When it appears that the advertising manager concerned is thinking of moving beyond an individual connection to a more general, business relation at a company level, the account executive's divisional head will take steps to set up a friendly meeting over dinner and drinks with his opposite number in the potential client's company. If the two men concerned get on reasonably well, they may then agree to establish an informal connection at the most senior management level – between each organisation's CEO.

This triple connection between agency and client serves a double function. First, it ensures that, if the agency's presentation is successful (and usually by this stage it is), the relationship established between the two companies is at a proper organisational level, underpinned by operational and management personnel relations. Second, it acts as insurance against the loss of business should the account executive in charge of the client account, for some reason, fall out with the advertising manager, or if, as is more likely, the manager is promoted and a new incumbent takes his place. By developing multiple connections, a company is more likely to be able to sustain its formal business relationship with another company.

What conclusions are we to draw from this account? That making connections reveals power – the power of individuals to associate themselves with this or that organisation, with this or that famous personality, or with this or that event, and to reap the benefit accruing therefrom. Making personal or organisational connections also impacts on cultural style. For example, an advertising manager's association and friendship with one advertising executive rather than another, resulting in the hiring of one advertising agency rather than another, leads to one advertising campaign being different in content from what might have emerged if he had formed a different friendship with a different advertising executive working for a different ad agency. So, too, with the set of choices made by a young apprentice potter who chooses this, rather than that, 'master', who himself is aligned with one, rather than another, pottery style and association, itself linked with one critic, rather than another, with his stable of collectors, all of whose likes and dislikes influence the kind of work that the apprentice potter learns to make and exhibit. The power of social connections thus becomes the power of cultural styles.

ACKNOWLEDGEMENT

I would like to thank the Strategic Research Council of Denmark for making available the time that enabled me to write this chapter as part of the ©reative Encounters research programme on the socio-economic organisation of creative industries.

NOTES

1. As Malcolm Chapman (2001: 32) observes: 'many business researchers rely upon the exploitation of previous contacts, friendships, and the like, for first access to a company'.

2. I have made frequent use of the masculine pronoun 'he' (and its related grammatical forms) because in Asatsū at that time, it was men, rather than women, who did accounts work and who occupied *all* managerial positions (except for one, the director of marketing) in the agency.
3. The research in question was funded by the School of Oriental and African Studies, University of London, and the Economic and Science Research Council, UK, in 1981–1982.
4. In some exhibitions, potters were judges. This encouraged certain kinds of factionalism (for which Japanese society is famous [Nakane 1972]), which themselves sustained particular ceramic styles and so hindered aesthetic innovation.
5. Entrepreneurial jobs which require 'agency' (not just in advertising, but brokers in corporate acquisitions, for example, or real estate deals) are by their very definition 'betwixt and between' and rely heavily on connections in order to be able to function successfully. Such brokers find themselves working now for, now against, each party to a transaction, in order to ensure that the transaction itself is concluded and that they themselves may benefit. Miyamoto's preparations for my own pottery exhibition provide an excellent example of this (Moeran 2012).

REFERENCES

Bourdieu, P. (1993) *The Field of Cultural Production* (Cambridge: Polity Press).
Burt, R. (2000) 'The network entrepreneur', in R. Swedberg, ed., *Entrepreneurship: The Social Science View* (Oxford: Oxford University Press).
Chapman, M. (2001) 'Social anthropology and business studies: Some considerations of method', in D. Gellner and E. Hirsch, eds, *Inside Organizations: Anthropologists at Work* (Oxford: Berg).
Firth, R. (1955) 'Some principles of social organization', *Journal of the Royal Anthropological Institute*, Vol. 85, Nos 1/2, pp. 1–18.
Goffman, E. (1959) *The Presentation of Self in Everyday Life* (New York, NY: Anchor Press).
Hannerz, U. (1980) *Exploring the City: Inquiries toward an Urban Anthropology* (New York, NY: Columbia University Press).
Kanter, R. and R. Eccles (1992) 'Making network research relevant to practice', in N. Nitin, and R. Eccles, eds, *Networks and Organizations: Structure, Form and Action* (Boston, MA: Harvard Business School Press).
Martin, S. (1964) 'Speech levels in Japan and Korea', in D. Hymes, ed., *Language in Society and Culture* (New York, NY: Harper and Row).
Moeran, B. (1996) *A Japanese Advertising Agency: An Anthropology of Media and Markets* (London: Curzon).
—— (1997) *Folk Art Potters of Japan* (London: Curzon).
—— (2005) *The Business of Ethnography: Strategic Exchanges, People and Organizations*. (Oxford: Berg).
—— (2007) *Ethnography at Work* (Oxford: Berg).
—— (2010 [1985]) Ōkubo *Diary: Portrait of a Japanese Valley* (London: Routledge).
—— (2012) 'A business anthropological approach to the study of values: Evaluative practices in ceramic art', *Culture and Organisation*, Vol. 18, No. 3, pp. 195–210.
Moeran, B. and J. Strandgaard Pedersen, eds (2011) *Negotiating Values in the Creative Industries: Fairs, Festivals and Competitive Events* (Cambridge: Cambridge University Press).
Nakane, C. (1972) *Japanese Society* (Berkeley, CA: University of California Press).
Thompson, D. (2008) *The $12 Million Stuffed Shark: The Curious Economics of Contemporary Art and Auction Houses* (London: Aurum).
Wacquant, L. (1995) 'The pugilistic point of view: How boxers think and feel about their trade', *Theory and Society*, Vol. 24, No. 4, pp. 489–535.

11
Messy logic
Organisational interactions and joint commitment in railway planning

Åsa Boholm

INTRODUCTION: REOPENING DECISION-MAKING[1]

In the planning of a piece of technical infrastructure, such as a railway tunnel, a new road, a huge bridge or some other 'engineering artifact' (Suchman 2000), decision processes over time are shaped by the alignment of networks of organisational actors. Coordination of action and adaptive expectations among relevant organisational actors are crucial to the realisation of plans. However, organisational decision-making often follows a 'messy' logic of practical and material considerations, negotiations of what is to be considered to be of value, and not least, post-hoc rationalisations (Brunsson 2007).

Through a case study of decision-making in railway planning in Sweden focusing on the interaction of a number of private and public organisations, this chapter revisits from an ethnographic perspective what, in the public administration literature, is labelled inter-organisational 'joint action' (Pressman and Wildavsky 1973). Implementation of policies requires decision-making processes involving communication, interaction and coordination of administrations and organisations (O'Toole Jr 2003; Pressman and Wildavsky 1973; Winter 2003). Hence decision-making is intrinsically social; it depends on power relationships and is influenced by expectations of the intentions of co-decision-makers (Flyvbjerg 1998). The classic study from 1973, *Implementation: How Great Expectations in Washington are Dashed in Oakland*, by Jeffrey Pressman and Aaron Wildavsky, identifies crucial conditions that explain why policy programmes crumble when implemented. A key factor is the presence of many participating actors, interconnected within a complex institutional framework. The 'complexity of joint action' draws from the interplay of heterogeneous organisational actors having diverse goals and working methods. Furthermore, the sequencing of critical decision points according to an 'assembly line structure' of interdependence (O'Toole Jr 2003: 147) offers veto points to key actors, instantiated by regulatory and bureaucratic constraints. Decision processes therefore involve numerous critical points where decision problems, alternatives, benefits, losses and values at stake, must be re-assessed, negotiated and agreed on. Organisational decision-making to implement policy can therefore be viewed

169

as a 'shared cooperative activity' (Bratman 1992) in which decisions are nested in past decisions that condition current commitments, thereby framing what new decisions can or cannot be made. Path dependency deriving from actor interdependency, the need for action coordination and the role of an actor's 'adaptive expectations', in that they must plan their own actions in light of how they understand other actors' planning, is therefore a key feature of the organisational decision process (Pierson 2000).

Decisions constitute a crucial dimension of organisational action; they have highly significant ordering effects that serve to stabilise (Brunsson 2007). A fundamental idea in Niklas Luhmann's (1995, 2005) work on decisions and decision-making is that decisions instigate action in that they create expectations about future action. However, as Luhmann notes, there is an analytical gap between decision and action, since actions do not follow from decisions in any logical or causal sense. A decision indicates commitment to future action by confirming an intention to act (see Bratman 1999, 2007); in doing so, according to Luhmann a decision 'absorbs' uncertainty about future courses of action. As it confirms an intention to act, a decision directs future action by accepting the premises for a decision and using them as conditions for new decisions to follow (Luhmann 2005: 96). However, the temporal continuity of decisions generating succeeding decisions from the original premises can be broken; decisions are often reconsidered and changed, so that new choice horizons are created from which new decisions arise. This is part and parcel of the reflexivity of the human mind (that is, reasoning and communicating according to multi-layered external and internal perspectives on self and other) within an 'ecology of life', enabling the adaptive planning of action in the face of changing environment and life circumstances (Ingold 2000).

In everyday life, reopening decisions is not a major problem. We often change our decisions and intentions to act, due to new information as well as altered preferences and priorities, and by re-evaluating decision stakes, options and benefits (Bratman 1999). In collective action, however, when we do things together with others and depend on their actions to reach goals, changed decisions are more problematic. The case presented here concerns an organisational decision process regarding the creation of a material structure, an 'engineering artifact' (Suchman 2000), namely a road/railway crossing. The decision is clear-cut, since there is only one problem and two alternative solutions: a road and railway must not cross on the same level (according to transport policy goals for road safety), so the road should cross the railway line either under the tracks or on a bridge going over them. The decision problem must be solved and no third alternative is available.

In inter-organisational railway planning, the reopening of a decision (Kleindorfer et al. 1993: 12–3) can be problematic, since decisions are nested, and have consequences for other decisions, by means of physical, technical and logistical parameters. In railway planning, therefore, capacity is limited to accommodate ambiguity deriving from conflicting interpretations or goals, since in the case investigated here, the road must cross either under or over the railway line. To reach a bona fide policy solution, the organisational actors (representing various authorities and stakeholders) must agree on one solution, and the choice will have consequences, including logistical ones, for further planning.

By using an ethnographic approach the chapter explores decision-making within a context of 'complex joint action', to use the concept launched by Pressman and Wildavsky (1973). A basic question asked is how organisational interactions within networks influence changes of decisions and decision contexts. Of specific interest is how a decision can be reopened and how it might transform over time without there being any explicit annulments of the old decision in favour of the new one. We will examine the social conditions necessary for decision reopening, especially how organisational actors' expectations about the planning of others affect their understanding of prior decisions and their motives for reopening and putting the issue on the decision table again. This actualises sense-making, reaching agreement, and the assigning of responsibility and accountability in organisational decision-making (Vidaillet 2008). We will do this by exploring the nested structuring of a temporal trajectory of decisions emerging in the planning of a new railway route. By following the shifting framing of a decision problem through a planning process, this study addresses the reframing of the decision premises of a railway planning 'problem' and how this contributes to the restructuring of a choice horizon (Luhmann 1995: 297).

CASE BACKGROUND

In 2004 the Swedish government decided to invest SEK 10 billion (about EUR 1 billion) to upgrade road and rail capacity on the Norway–Väner Link north of Göteborg in western Sweden. One rationale for the investment was to support the SAAB car industry in Trollhättan from the threat by General Motors (the then owner of SAAB) to move car production abroad. This deal is popularly described as the 'Trollhätte package' and one of its ingredients is the upgrading of the existing single-track railway between the cities of Göteborg and Trollhättan to a double-track line that would allow X2000 trains to run at speeds of around 200 km per hour. The new railway line promises reduced travel time, shorter intervals between departures, commuter stations and environmental benefits. Among several sub-projects is a route comprising approximately 14 km of double-track rail, including three tunnels 124–200 metres long and a 400 metre bridge. The route traverses rural farmland as well as hilly areas covered with dense pine forest, and it passes through two rural communities of just over 500 inhabitants each. The area is rich in archaeological and historic heritage and in natural conservation sites, including the Slumpån River that passes through a spectacular canyon. The railway currently crosses the canyon on a steel bridge, built in the 1950s, which will be replaced by a new railway bridge; the construction and building of this bridge in a highly sensitive natural environment presents a major challenge for the project. Building started in 2009 and the line is scheduled to be ready for traffic in December 2012.

Another challenge for the project is that the railway line crosses an open landscape of pasture that, according to geological investigations, consists of unstable clay. This particular landscape was noted in the railway investigation to be of unique value. The new railway line will cross several roads where all level crossings must be replaced by overpasses or underpasses to avoid collisions between road traffic and trains. One road is the 2018, which will cross the railway line where it passes through open pasture a few kilometres north of the community of Upland. The passage through forested hills calls for several tunnels and deep mountain cuttings. The local communities and municipality generally favour the project and the selected route. Some citizens and affected landowners are critical, but mostly regarding specific features that affect their own interests concerning access to land, land use and crossings with roads in the area. (The last issue has been a major source of local contention.)

The study builds on fieldwork conducted between March 2007 and mid autumn 2008 by means of participant observation of project planning meetings, reference group meetings (including authorities such as the County Administrative Board, the municipality, the regional public transport company and the Road Administration), and consultation meetings with stakeholders, all concerning planning for the railway project. The meetings were documented in field notes taken during observation. Data also include internal documents, minutes, official reports, National Rail Administration (henceforth 'Rail Administration') handbooks and standards, and records of informal discussions with officials, planners, designers and consultants. In all, 23 meetings were observed.

NESTED DECISIONS

Land use planning for infrastructure facilities such as railways, for power plants, for waste disposal facilities or for other technological facilities, actualises many possible consequences. Planning must take into account an array of intended outcomes, unwanted side-effects and uncertainty (Boholm and Löfstedt 2004). Furthermore, the societal benefits or harms associated with a project, including risks to humans and the natural environment, are seldom understood and prioritised according to a single frame of reference (Boholm 2009). Planning entails complex joint action (Pressman and Wildavsky 1973) involving many stakeholders, local communities, citizens and authorities with diverse sectoral responsibility, power resources and rationales for making decisions (Flyvbjerg 1998). The coordination and cooperation of organisational actors over time is crucial for successful ordering of the material 'engineering artifact' (Suchman 2000).

Railway infrastructure is state owned in Sweden, and the national government determines investments in new lines and decides whether to upgrade or close down existing lines. The Rail Administration is responsible for the railway system, including provision of railway tracks, the signalling system and electricity for trains, while the trains are run by private or state-owned companies that rent rail capacity from the Rail Administration. (The Rail Administration was an independent government authority up to 1 January 2009, after which several Swedish transportation authorities were merged to form the Swedish Transport Agency). In 2001, the Rail Administration production unit was deregulated and opened to market competition. Railway planning is regulated by the Railway Building Act (Swedish Railway Building Act 1995: 1649) and the Environmental Code (Swedish Environmental Code 1998: 808), while numerous other regulations and standards apply to a variety of railway planning responsibilities – technical, organisational, economic, legal and environmental. The Railway Building Act states that consultation with affected property owners, municipalities and regional boards, and 'others who might have a substantial interest in the matter' (Swedish Railway Building Act 1995: 1649: ch. 2, section 5), is mandatory. Although providing stakeholders with certain legal rights, railway planning adheres to a Swedish technocratic regulatory style of consensual negotiation between governmental interests and elite stakeholders but involves limited public participation (Löfstedt 2005).

The regulatory framework for railway planning establishes a number of major official decisions, such as licensing, as veto points (O'Toole Jr 2003) that bear on the legality of a project. Large decisions grow out of numerous internal negotiations that involve the Rail Administration (including officials, planners and experts), consultants, agencies, governmental bodies (including municipalities and County Administrative Boards), and various stakeholders (including local residents). Major decisions that require legal licensing call for successive decisions in which planners are expected to consider various factors: benefits to society, local communities and the environment; negative consequences, risks and uncertainties; technical alternatives and solutions; costs in terms of time and money; and – last but not least – legal and administrative demands and conditions. 'Large decisions generate nested series of smaller ones. This is the typical "decision in principle" followed by elaboration and implementation in ever more narrowly focused choices' (Langley et al. 1995: 271).

The railway planning stage is preceded by an investigation to identify several alternative spatial corridors for the railway line. These alternatives are described, compared and assessed in terms of their consequences for traffic and society, environment, landscape and building technique. The railway investigation also includes viewpoints and opinions on the alternatives from a broad array of stakeholders (that is, other authorities, local citizens, and interest organisations). After the Rail Administration has selected one corridor as the 'best' alternative for a future railway line, it presents the supporting arguments and applies to the government for a permit to continue with detailed planning of the chosen corridor. This railway planning stage includes the design of the line, bridges, tunnels, barriers, road crossings and electrical installations, taking into consideration land use, landscape and the environment. The plan must also take into account safety issues regarding future train traffic, technical installations (for example, overhead lines for electricity and signal systems), construction logistics and construction facilities (for example, construction roads and locations for storing excavated material), along with organisational, technical, economic and property rights issues. An environmental impact assessment according to the Environmental Code is mandatory. The property rights of owners are topical in this stage. Consultation with property owners, municipalities, regional boards and other authorities are vital to the process of formulating the railway plan.

The railway planning process results in a substantial document that precisely describes the design of the line. The law requires that the plan be made public if it entails substantial consequences for the environment, public health or nature resources, or if it encroaches on private property. After being made public, the railway plan can be legally approved by the Rail Administration Board on the condition that the County Administrative Board has no objections. The County Administrative Board is the public administration unit at the regional level with a mandate to coordinate various interests from a national perspective. It has supervisory powers to ensure that legal requirements are met, and it is an environmental licensing authority issuing permits and setting conditions for permits for activities that are potentially harmful to the environment, in accordance with the Environmental Code.

Like other railway projects, the studied railway planning project is managed by a project leader responsible for ensuring that the consultants deliver a plan according to the contracted agreements. The Division South of the Rail Administration has contracted planning services, in this case for the railway plan, the environmental impact assessment and the so called 'systems document' describing the new railway line in detail, from the firm Rail Administration Consulting (RAC). RAC was founded in 1998 and its competency in railway projecting and planning formerly belonged to the Rail Administration. Since 2001, RAC has operated on the market, competing with other consultancies for rail planning contracts from the Rail Administration. The project leader is accountable to the Rail Administration hierarchy and is responsible for the financial and time planning of the project. Other Rail Administration officials taking part in the project include various experts on economics, environmental monitoring, quality control, information technology, purchasing, safety and traffic control. The Rail Administration specialists possess competence in, for example, technical coordination, environmental impact assessment, and property and land management. The Rail Administration Environmental Impact Assessment (EIA) co-coordinator and the land negotiation specialist participate in the project on a regular basis. The RAC head consultant is responsible for delivering the following: plans for the physical routing of the railway line; designs for the signal system and contact cables, railway bridges, tunnels and overpasses or underpasses; and the EIA document and all investigations pertaining to it, such as risk assessments and impact on flora, fauna, landscape and cultural heritage.

BUREAUCRATIC SOCIAL INTERACTION

Railway planning is carried out under strict organisational and bureaucratic conditions, involving administrative logic (including schedule, budget and legal constraints) and decision logistics, with a strong interdependency between decisions within a formal sequential planning process. Numerous planning problem-solving decisions must be made for the process to continue. The planners spend much of their working time in meetings that constitute the *modus operandi* of railway planning, since they serve to coordinate planning and action to ensure that agreement is reached regarding the interests of authorities, stakeholders and expert advisers. The railway project planning group is multi-professional and incorporates a broad range of expertise. At meetings, participants can express reservations and articulate demands, making viewpoints and positions transparent in a semi-public space. Much of what is discussed at meetings concerns cooperation and the coordination of planners' intentions and actions.

Inside the Group of Planners: The Project Meetings

Apart from numerous smaller meetings to coordinate work and discuss solutions for specific tasks, the project meetings considered matters relevant to the entire project. These meetings were generally monthly and fulfilled several functions: coordinating planning among specialists and sub-tasks, detecting critical issues by including a broad competency in discussions, and allowing the Rail Administration project leader to control and supervise the planning process in terms of scheduling, cost and consultant 'deliverables'. The meetings were structured using a formal agenda, provided by the RAC contract manager, which included a checklist covering numerous items; every meeting included going through this list to check whether or not the issues had been dealt with, and the current status of each item was noted.

The project meetings were led by the Rail Administration's project leader and the RAC contract manager. The meeting agenda came with the invitations, which were emailed to participants in advance. A project meeting normally included RAC project leader and contract manager, the Rail Administration land negotiator, EIA co-coordinator and occasionally other 'in-house' Rail Administration experts with competences in relevant fields; additional participants included consultants subcontracted by the RAC in the fields of, for example, geology, tunnelling, hydrogeology or environmental assessment. A total of 50 consultants were contracted by RAC to complete various tasks pertaining to the railway planning project; not all were present at all the project meetings. These consultants included experts in geology, hydrogeology, tunnel engineering, railway construction technology, risk assessment and 'comprehensive' planning (that is, competence in how various parts are integrated into a whole planning document). The project meetings covered a wide range of perspectives: practical, technical, theoretical, political, administrative, organisational, legal and informational. The issues discussed included construction and design of roads, tunnels and bridges, flora and fauna, the behaviour of wild animals, landscape characteristics and values, geological investigations of ground conditions, farming and agricultural conditions, future traffic safety, stakeholders and their claims, and what opinions other authorities might have on the project.

I attended the project and reference group meetings regularly. The participants took little notice of me; however, when controversial remarks or comments were made around the table, someone might ask me jokingly: 'Are you writing this down?' At the meetings, I took a seat at the conference table along with the others and opened my notebook. I never considered using a laptop for note taking because I wanted my presence to be as inconspicuous as possible. I took notes almost constantly during the meetings, even when the topics under discussion were highly detailed and technical and seemingly far from what I was interested in. Since the meetings were also attended by a secretary who took minutes, which were distributed to all participants including myself, I could compare my own much more detailed notes with the minutes. A problem I initially encountered was the highly specialised nature of the topics of discussion, the unfamiliar expert terminology and internal jargon. After a while, I became more accustomed to this world of expertise and to the technical aspects of railway planning, and was able to follow more easily the subjects discussed, at least in broad terms.

Communicating with Other Planners: The Reference Group Meetings

Another type of meeting was the reference group meeting, a forum for various outside actors and stakeholders, such as the County Administrative Board, the municipality where the railway was to be built, represented by a senior official from the technical and planning administration in charge of municipal planning and zoning issues, and by officials from the environmental administration in charge of environmental protection and biodiversity, the regional public transportation company, and the Road Administration, together with leading project members, such as the Rail Administration project leader, the Rail Administration environmental expert, the RAC project leader and the contract manager. While the County Administrative Board and the municipality were represented at every reference group meeting during the study period, the regional public transportation company and the Road Administration participated only occasionally. The reference group meetings were chaired by a Rail Administration official who had led the pre-investigation of the studied railway line project. The chair was thus well acquainted with the project background, and he demonstrated this knowledge by occasionally intervening to remind discussants of past concerns and considerations.

The minutes of the reference group meetings were distributed to participants, and each meeting started by reviewing the minutes of the previous one. These minutes were sometimes revised if someone thought that what had been recorded was not entirely accurate. The minutes were not considered official documents; rather, they constituted semi-official documentation for internal use that confirmed project status and history and, most importantly, displayed the various actors' positions and concerns regarding the myriad issues discussed. The reference group took an interest in many matters, such as the transformation of the old railway line into a cycling route, what to do about central Upland and the area near the future station area, how to access local bathing lakes, how to organise the transportation and storage of excavated materials, and how to design road underpasses and overpasses.

What To Do with Road 2018?

Preliminaries

The railway investigation planning stage, which aimed to identify, specify and weigh the alternative routes for the proposed line, had included substantial consultation with the County Administrative Board, municipalities, public authorities, stakeholder organisations and members of the public. In the railway investigation report the open landscape north of Upland was identified as possessing value that should be protected from encroachment by the new railway line. This landscape was described as follows:

> North of Upland is vast open landscape around the Lillån watercourse. The landscape is essentially a flat outer part of the canyon landscape surrounding Slumpån.... The landscape is characterised by long unbroken views. Farms are situated at the edges bordering on the forest. (my translation)[2]

Later in the same section on environmental impact, the report characterises the open agrarian landscape as follows:

> The landscape has great potential as a source of knowledge of the agrarian and settlement history of the area.... In general, this district has been treated gently by modern society. The major change in the landscape was the construction of the railway in the nineteenth century, when the station in Upland was built.... The railway was located on ... ancient farmland dating to prehistoric times. (my translation)[3]

To protect the 'open agrarian landscape', the railway investigation report argued that road 2018 must cross under the railway line to minimise its visibility in the landscape: 'The public road 2018 needs to be relocated under the railway. The line of the road and its design need to be investigated in greater detail in further planning' (my translation).[4]

This decision regarding road 2018, set forth in the railway investigation report, posed a complicated decision problem in the railway planning stage. We will now examine in detail how the planners came to disconnect their upcoming decision concerning road 2018 in the railway planning stage from the previous decision in the railway investigation stage, and how they succeeded in reopening the decision that road 2018 must pass under the railway line.

Road 2018 is Going Under

At a project meeting early in the railway planning process on 24 April 2007, one Rail Administration official stated, referring to the railway investigation of road 2018, that it would be 'advantageous to have the road passing under the rail track'. However, he also noted that ideas diverged within the project as to whether this was actually the 'best' alternative, since 'geotechnology wants to have it pass over the track, but an overpass would be too dominant in the landscape'. At this project meeting, a conflict between preserving the undisrupted view of the landscape and geotechnical considerations was implicit, since the dominant view was that the railway investigation decision should determine further planning.

At the next project meeting, on 29 May 2007, when the road was discussed again, the RAC project leader stated: 'We are going under.' In discussing a local landowner who wanted to modify the railway route to accommodate a private road, the Rail Administration's environmental coordinator emphasised the value of the area: 'The open landscape is Upland's most valuable asset. This area must not be unnecessarily subdivided. There must be access to the area for walking. It is very beautiful down there.' The underpass solution was not questioned at this meeting and, at the reference group meeting on 11 June 2007, the RAC project leader stated explicitly: '2018 is not going over! We are going under.' No objections were raised.

However, two months later, at a project meeting on 22 August 2007, the solution for the 2018 underpass was discussed more thoroughly; this time, the conflict between the value of the open landscape and the geotechnological issues hinted at the earlier April project meeting were openly addressed. The RAC project leader said: '2018 goes under. The Road Administration has looked into this. There may be geotechnical problems. The underpass road would be expensive. It will go into stiffer clay. The groundwater can be lowered with pumps.' It was now recognised that there were geotechnical problems to be solved, but it was not suggested that the decision should be reopened due to these problems. A discussion followed about what technical investigations and measurements would be needed, and about local landowners, who had started asking questions about what was going to happen with the road and railway crossing. At this juncture, four months after road 2018 had first been raised as an issue at a project meeting, the underpass solution emerged as problematic due to several factors: geotechnological difficulties, groundwater, economic factors and local resident concerns. However, these problems appeared solvable and the underpass solution was not questioned.

At the reference group meeting on 18 September 2007, at which participants discussed the upcoming EIA public consultation meetings for the railway plan, the RAC project leader stated that road 2018 was going under the railway but that groundwater was a problem. It was also mentioned that a Road Administration representative would be present at the public consultation meetings to inform about the alternatives for the roads and crossings (as noted earlier, the project involves several road crossings apart from 2018). A hydrogeological expert would attend the consultations to answer questions about groundwater. The Road Administration representative pointed out that the arguments for roads going over or under the railway line had to be clear. After discussion of road/railway crossings, the County Administrative

Board official raised a question and said that he had a message from Deputy County Governor Göran Bengtsson, who had given:

> clear signals regarding the Trollhättepaketet [the 'Trollhätte package deal'] that the County Administrative Board should be supportive and adaptable. We are the long arm of the state. Göran Bengtsson has spoken to the department. This does not have to be in any notes.

By this statement, the County Administrative Board official signalled that his administration was not intending to make trouble, meaning vetoing the railway plan, but was committed to mutual action (Bratman 1992, 1999). After further discussion about the roads, the RAC project leader commented regarding 2018: 'Of course it is possible to construct a bridge, but there would be terrible embankments. The County Administrative Board would have a fit. The line is kept as low as possible in the open landscape. It is under 2 metres [high].' The chair commented on this, saying that the solution reached by the railway investigation was excellent: the road passing *under* the railway. This was the first time at a project meeting or reference group meeting that the road overpass alternative was even mentioned (although rejected).

Snow, Rain and Hydrogeology

A month later, at the public consultation meeting in Upland on 23 October 2007, the solution for road 2018 was one of the issues presented. The Rail Administration message was that the road should go under the railway at a depth of 8 metres; a higher profile was undesirable, since the train traffic would then produce too much noise. Interestingly, the 'open' quality of the landscape was not mentioned at the public consultation meeting as a decision parameter for the underpass; the focus was instead on the disturbing noise of train traffic. Presumably, this negative effect was deemed to be of more interest to local residents than the 'open' landscape quality, understood to be of more concern to the County Administrative Board. Lively discussion ensued, and there were many comments and questions from the many local residents in attendance (around 100 people had come to the meeting) about road 2018. Issues raised related to risks of flooding during heavy rains and of snow drifting in winter into the road underpass.

At a project meeting just a few days after the EIA consultation meeting of 26 October 2007, lessons from the two EIA consultation meetings were reviewed and discussed among the planners. The solution for road 2018 was discussed extensively and, as can be seen from the following dialogue, the process was now moving towards reopening the rail investigation decision.

RAC consultant: The consultation meeting wants 2018 to go over. There were a lot of questions about snow and water.
Rail Administration project leader: This will be difficult with the County Administrative Board!

Geologist: The preferable solution is for the road to cross on a bridge. On the west side, there is a small hill with firm ground. The problem is hydraulic – pressure from the ground. The road will cut into rock. A trough solution [for the underpass] must be sealed. It must be watertight. The rock can be blasted, but then water can leak under the trough. We can permanently lower the groundwater table, but that might affect the surroundings. I have always believed that the road should go over.

Rail Administration project leader: I think this has gone very far!

Geologist: There are no tightening layers of clay.

Rail Administration project leader: We ought to have given geology a higher priority from the beginning.

Someone: What is the cost?

Geologist: It costs money to build an embankment. The embankment must be high and must be strengthened. All alternatives cost money. [The embankment] will not affect the railway line or the groundwater. If we go under, there will be wells, pumping stations, additional strengthening of the railway embankment, and maintenance measures for lowering groundwater. This is a risk.

Rail Administration project leader: We said earlier that there would be enormous embankments 8–9 meters [high]. The main argument was the open landscape.

Geologist: It is my duty to point out complications.

Rail Administration project leader: The values are the fields and the open landscape. We need to evaluate this very carefully. We need to sit in a group and decide on the best alternative.

EIA consultant: The problem with passing over was dealt with in the railway investigation.

Rail Administration project leader: Those who live nearby will have a huge bridge quite close.

A discussion developed about what a possible road bridge would look like.

Rail Administration project leader: The pre-investigations of the roads were poor. I was not involved. The one who did the railway investigation has quit. Can't we just make the railway plan public without including the roads? We need to sit down soon and take into account landscape and geotechnology and sharpen the arguments.

This meeting initially saw conflict between the geologist and the Rail Administration project leader. The geologist identified several difficulties pertaining to the underpass alternative, while the Rail Administration project leader was concerned about the change of course in the planning process, that is, reopening the decision to choose the underpass and the Rail Administration's commitment to the County Administrative Board on this issue. The County Administrative Board was expected to favour the underpass option, since it values the open landscape, which would be obscured by a huge road bridge. Another complication for the Rail Administration project leader was the local stakeholders, both those who favour an overpass, since they perceive the underpass as risky for traffic, and those who favour an underpass, since they live nearby and it would not encroach on their view. Economic considerations entered the discussion but did not resolve the choice, since both alternatives would be expensive. The project leader then distanced herself from the railway investigation, arguing that it was poor in quality and noting that the person in charge had left the organisation (leaving no one from the Rail Administration in a position to defend the underpass alternative). The matter was resolved consensually, via new meetings to determine what to do with the problematic crossing and to identify new arguments for and against the decision alternatives.

Re-evaluating the Open Landscape

At the next reference group meeting, on 30 November 2007, the Rail Administration chair noted that road 2018 was a 'difficult question'. When the road and underpass solution were discussed in more detail, the Rail Administration EIA coordinator said that the geotechnology was difficult due to the high groundwater table and that there was a risk of snow drifting in winter; she said that 'The Rail Administration has a problem, since it [that is, the road] will go under and geotechnology does not want that.' Some pictures were shown to illustrate what a road bridge over the railway would look like. The bridge depicted was said to be 6 metres high. The Rail Administration EIA coordinator, when looking at the pictures, said, 'I feel that the bridge gets [visual] support from the terrain behind it, if you look at it from the perspective of the meadows.'

This marked an important shift from the earlier position that a huge road bridge would be devastating to the landscape view. The initial argument in the rail investigation was that the landscape was an invaluable asset that must be protected, so an underpass was decided on for road 2018; a highly visible and aesthetically dominant construction such as a road bridge was deemed out of the question. The municipal official supported the new perspective on the road bridge as no longer in contradiction with the landscape, by saying that the solution for road 2018 was 'not a big issue' for the municipality. The Rail Administration chair then asked the County Administrative Board official the critical question, namely, what he thought about the matter, but did not receive an answer. This juncture marked a turning point for the decision about what to do with the 2018 crossing: the County Administrative Board, which, in the railway investigation, had expressed such strong concern for safeguarding the open landscape north of Upland, was now silent. Discussion continued about how to deal with road 2018, and the government officials from the County Administrative Board and the municipality clearly had no interest in starting a dispute over the solution for 2018.

At the project meeting three weeks later, on 18 December 2007, the possibility of an additional public consultation with local stakeholders regarding road 2018 was discussed, but no date was mentioned. The Rail Administration project leader hinted that a decision on road 2018 was going to be made by the administration 'this week'. The discussion about road 2018 continued at the project meeting on 29 January 2008, when the Rail Administration project leader announced that the administration had decided that road 2018 would cross over the rail track on a bridge. She also acknowledged that the other principal actors, the Road Administration and the County Administrative Board, had not yet taken a position: 'We will go over! The Road Administration is looking into this. The County Administrative Board is looking into it. If the County Administrative Board says stop, we have to accept that.' A public consultation meeting with local stakeholders regarding road 2018 was again on the agenda, but it was now discussed whether an additional consultation was actually needed; this could be taken to mean that, since other key actors were leaning towards the bridge crossing, no additional support from local stakeholders would be needed. At the reference group meeting a month later on 29 February 2008, some time was spent discussing road 2018, and it was announced that consultations with local stakeholders had been held. The Rail Administration project leader then summarised the decision problem:

> We recognise that it is not good to go under. We have lowered the profile [of the line] in this area. The geotechnological conditions are not good. There is a lot of water. And then there is the landscape. So we will go over instead. We have reported to the County Administrative Board and, luckily enough, the County Administrative Board has the same view.

The County Administrative Board official supported the project leader by stating that the issue of the open landscape had been reconsidered by the board: 'To dwell on landscape values – nothing to quarrel about.' The municipal official in charge of environmental monitoring, however, made the point that road 2018 constituted a delicate matter for the municipality due to local public concern.

Reopening and Closing the Decision on 2018

At this point, the road 2018 question seemed to have been settled in the project. The County Administrative Board was not prepared to fight the bridge proposal for road 2018 by advocating the protection of landscape values, which was what the Rail Administration officials had feared. The controversy between the geotechnical experts and the project leadership could then be resolved when it became clear that the County Administrative Board was unwilling to oppose the project on this issue.

Initially, the road 2018 underpass alternative, advocated by the County Administrative Board in the railway investigation phase to protect the open landscape, was not reconsidered in the railway planning project. Although the geotechnological experts voiced reservations about this alternative in the beginning, the technical arguments alone were not strong enough to reopen the decision at this juncture. A problem built up in the EIA public consultation processes when it became clear that the local stakeholders had strong arguments against the underpass (that is, risks of flooding and snow drifting), arguments that reinforced the geotechnical arguments (that is, high groundwater table, complicated and expensive technology, and uncertainty about the construction process). Resistance to the underpass solution from both the technical experts and the local stakeholders had built up and was becoming difficult to manage. A problem for the project was that the County Administrative Board was understood to be very much in favour of the underpass, since it wanted to protect the open landscape from the intrusion of a highly visible road overpass.

At the February 2008 reference group meeting the matter was closed, since it was clear that the County Administrative Board was unwilling to make an issue of protecting the open landscape. The County Administrative Board had come to a point at which it had to prioritise between (a) protecting the open landscape and (b) its commitment to the railway planning project. These two objectives were not in conflict in the railway investigation phase. The conflict emerged and mounted in the railway planning stage, when more detailed planning decisions were considered and when the board prioritised commitment to the project rather than the landscape. The 'stable alignment' (Suchman 2000) of the project was thereby resumed; the actors tacitly agreed that the decision that road 2018 should go under the railway line was reopened and a new decision was made: that it should go over. The decision, however, was not explicitly reopened. Instead, there was a transition from one decision state to another; arguments built up opposing the original decision, and actors organised to promote an alternative. When it was established that no forceful actors opposed the bridge alternative, choosing the bridge was established as a necessary step to continuing the project planning. So the reopened decision was not the outcome of a decision but of a changed decision context; the question of road 2018 became embedded in a different context, creating a new choice horizon and demanding another solution.

CONCLUDING DISCUSSION

Railway planning decision-making involving organisational actors such as officials, consultants and experts, organised within a highly regulated administrative setting characterised by strong demands for efficiency and legality, emerge through interaction and anticipation of the intentions of others. Expert competences as well as stakeholder interests and priorities are negotiated and balanced in accordance with an administrative logic of efficiency, that is, producing predefined outcomes given a set budget and timeframe and following standardised rules. In this network setting, decisions develop, interact and are redefined (Langley et al. 1995: 276) as negotiated interim achievements rather than definite final choices resulting from a rational process of assessing identified decision alternatives in accordance with set preferences, as assumed by normative social science planning theory.

This case shows how what initially appears to be a fairly simple decision problem (that is, mapping the pros and cons of the two alternatives and selecting the optimal one) turns out to be complicated in its implementation, given that the decision is part of a history of past decisions generating future decisions. The temporal trajectory of the problem, previous organisational decisions made, the existence of veto points, and the circumstance that decision-making is a shared cooperative activity involving several mutually committed interdependent organisational actors (Bratman 1992) who make decisions based on their interpretations of the commitments and intentions of other actors, add up to a complex social dynamic. The kind of interest-based calculation of 'hard facts' as the game theory model of group decision-making would predict is way off (Kleindorfer et al. 1993: 241).

As Carol Suchman (2000) has noted, the establishment of a temporarily stable organisational alignment between arrays of socio-technical elements is decisive for the progress of the planning process. Thus 'material stability is inseparable ... from the networks of social practice – of design, construction, maintenance and use – that must be put into place' (Suchman 2000: 316). Decisions serve to stabilise the project in terms of agreements on design, construction and technical solutions, modes of cooperation and responsibility, and schedule. All these decisions must fit together, so that reopening one could well change the project significantly.

Carrying out a complex joint action as an instance of cooperative activity requires some basic conditions for success (Bratman 1992: 328). Actors (or agents) must trust that they are responsive to each other's intentions; they must be committed to supporting and helping each other carry out the joint activity to realise a common goal. Communication between participants (that is, stakeholders and planners) is therefore crucial in railway planning. The actors must continually review their actions and ensure that the mutual responsiveness – the joint commitment to mutual support that conditions their joint activity – still exists. For the joint activity to continue, they also depend on continuous updates regarding the intentions and plans of the other actors in order to continue their own planning. In complex joint actions, decisions derive from negotiated agreements between various organisational actors that are reached only after considerable time and effort. This means, as the present case illustrates, that strong commitment underlies decisions. Apart from the formal and technical problems of reopening decisions, social and communicational consequences, such as loss of trust, arise from breaking agreements and violating commitments (Bratman 1999).

This study has approached decisions and decision-making via an open-ended enquiry (Strathern 2000: 285) into the flow of social interaction, seeking to understand the 'balancing' of action and accounting, doing and saying. The ethnographic study of decisions and decision processes within a bureaucratic format of social interaction contributes to a comprehensive understanding of intentionality and context in which 'the anthropologist's kind of ethnography grasps not just the contingency and unpredictability of social life, then, but how description and self-description contribute to it' (Strathern 2000: 287).

This approach sheds light on the practical reasoning (Bratman 1999) occurring in organisational decision-making, by conveying the actor and observer perspectives and their interaction in producing a social reality. The findings add to the understanding of decisions as interrelated according to a 'messy' logic of power rationalisation rather than a rational pattern of decisions and consequent actions, goals and their implementation (see Flyvbjerg 1998). The ethnographic approach adopted gives insight into how instances of actors' 'strategic agenda building' (Dutton 1986) and 'issue connectedness' (Langley et al. 1995: 270) noted in organisational studies are constituted by organisational interactions in social life.

NOTES

1. This work is funded by research grants from the Swedish Research Council, the Swedish Rescue Services Agency, the Emergency Management Agency, the Swedish Governmental Agency for Innovation Systems, the Swedish Road Administration and the Swedish Maritime Administration. I wish to thank Per Binde, Max Boholm, Hervé Corvellec, Annette Henning, Vicki Johansson, Ragnar Löfstedt and the editor Christina Garsten, for valuable comments and suggestions on versions of this chapter. The case study was presented at the 27th EGOS Colloquium in July 2011, at the workshop 'Deconstructing institutions: Meaning, technology and materiality', convened by Jannis Kallinikos, Hans Hasselbladh and Giovan Francesco Lanzara. I am thankful to the convenors and workshop participants for their constructive critique.
2. BRVT 2006:01, 2006-01-25, Norge Vänerbanan. Dubbelspår Velanada-Prässebo Järnvägsu-tredning inklusive miljökonsekvensbeskrivning (MKB), utställningshandling [BRVT 2006:01, 2006-01-25, Norway Vänerlink. Double track Velanda–Prässebo. Railway investigation including Enviornmental Impact Assessment (EIA), exhibition document], p. 37.
3. Ibid., p. 45.
4. Ibid., p. 37.

REFERENCES

Boholm, Å. (2009) 'Speaking of risk: Matters of context', *Environmental Communication: A Journal of Nature and Culture*, Vol. 3, No. 2, pp. 335–354.

Boholm, Å. and R. Löfstedt, eds (2004) *Facility Siting: Risk, Power and Identity in Land Use Planning* (London: Earthscan).

Bratman, M. E. (1992) 'Shared cooperative activity', *Philosophical Review*, Vol. 101, No. 2, pp. 327–341.

—— (1999) *Intentions, Plans, and Practical Reason* (Stanford, CA: CSLI Publications).

—— (2007) *Structures of Agency* (Oxford: Oxford University Press).

Brunsson, N. (2007) *The Consequences of Decision-making* (Oxford: Oxford University Press).

Dutton, J. E. (1986) 'Understanding strategic agenda building and its implications for managing change', *Scandinavian Journal of Management Studies*, Vol. 3, No. 1, pp. 3–24.

Flyvbjerg, B. (1998) *Rationality and Power: Democracy in Practice* (Chicago, IL: University of Chicago Press).

Ingold, T. (2000) *The Perception of the Environment: Essays in Livelihood, Dwelling and Skill* (London: Routledge).

Kleindorfer, P. R., H. C. Kunreuther and P. J. H. Schoemaker (1993) *Decision Sciences: An Integrative Perspective* (Cambridge: Cambridge University Press).

Langley, A., H. Mintzberg, P. Pitcher, E. Posada and J. Saint-Macary (1995) 'Opening up decision making: The view from the black stool', *Organisation Science*, Vol. 6, No. 3, pp. 260–279.

Löfstedt, R. E. (2005) *Risk Management in Post Trust Societies* (Basingstoke: Palgrave).

Luhmann, N. (1995) *Social Systems* (Stanford, CA: Stanford University Press).

—— (2005) 'The paradox of decision making', in D. Seidl and K. H. Becker, eds, *Niklas Luhmann and Organisation Studies* (Kristianstad: Copenhagen Business School Press/Liber).

O'Toole, L. J. Jr (2003) 'Interorganisational relations in implementation', in B. G. Peters and J. Pierre, eds, *The Handbook of Public Administration* (Los Angeles, CA: Sage).

Pierson, P. (2000) 'Increasing returns, path dependency, and the study of politics', *American Political Science Review*, Vol. 94, No. 2, pp. 251–267.

Pressman, J. L. and A. Wildavsky (1973) *Implementation* (Los Angeles, CA: University of California Press).

Strathern, M. (2000) 'Afterword: Accountability', in M. Strathern, ed., *Audit Cultures: Anthropological Studies in Accountability, Ethics and the Academy* (London: Routledge).

Suchman, L. (2000) 'Organizing alignment: A case of bridge building', *Organisation*, Vol. 7, No. 2, pp. 311–327.

Swedish Environmental Code(1998) SFS 1998: 808.

Swedish Railway Building Act (1995) SFS 1995: 1649.

Vidaillet, B. (2008) 'When "decision outcomes" are not the outcomes of decisions', in G. P. Hodkinson and W. H. Starbuck, eds, *The Oxford Handbook of Organisational Decision Making* (Oxford: Oxford University Press).

Winter, S. (2003) 'Implementation perspectives: Status and reconsideration', in B. G. Peters and J. Pierre, eds, *The Handbook of Public Administration* (London: Sage).

Section four

Opaque worlds

12
The profane ethnographer
Fieldwork with a secretive organisation[1]

Lilith Mahmud

INTRODUCTION: A PROFANE ASKING TO ENTER

The initiation of a neophyte into the mysteries of Freemasonry begins with three loud knocks on the temple's doors. It is not the neophyte herself who knocks but the Tyler, the protector of the lodge who stands guard at its threshold, and knocks to announce the intrusive presence of an uninitiated. The Freemasons inside will demand to know, as formula prescribes, who stands outside the temple's doors. Once again, it is the Tyler who will answer their call with a few simple words enchanted by the symbolic power of ritual: It is a profane asking to enter.

When I conducted ethnographic research on Freemasonry in Italy, I was a profane. My status as a non-Mason concerned some of my potential informants – the men and women Freemasons I met in preliminary fieldwork, as I first tried to establish the feasibility of my research project. They worried about my motivations and agendas, and about a profane's ability to understand their experiences in an esoteric society, whose rituals are open only to the initiated. As a profane, I too worried that I would never attain the depth of access that is the 'holy grail' of anthropological fieldwork.

Freemasonry is the most romanticised western 'secret society'. Although my informants rejected that title unequivocally, the image of their nefarious secrecy persists in Italian popular conspiracy theories portraying Masonic lodges as powerful networks made up of the country's elites. Other scholars, especially those familiar with Italy, appeared confused whenever they learned that I studied Freemasons. Surely, I must be studying Freemasonry historically through archival research. How else would one dare to study Italian Freemasons? Certainly not ethnographically, through participant-observation and interviews, 'hanging out' deeply around the lodges, as Renato Rosaldo once summed up the fieldwork experience.[2] How could a profane ethnographer in her right mind do fieldwork among the members of an organisation as powerful and secretive as Freemasonry?

In this chapter I invoke the Masonic notion of the 'profane' as both an emic category of my fieldwork and as a metaphor for the scholastic subjectivity of the ethnographer him- or herself. Drawing on 18 months of fieldwork I conducted among Freemason men and women in Italy between 2004 and 2006, I will reflect on my own status as a profane in relation to my informants

189

and on the meaning of this positionality for ethnographic methods. My hope is to trouble the line between insider and outsider that seems to persist as an anthropological trope, despite decades of reflexive and critical writings on anthropology's disciplinary formations.

Although the profane and the Masonic were rhetorically produced as dichotomous terms by Freemasons themselves, in my informants' everyday lives these were rather porous and flexible categories. Some people, for instance, were considered profane in some contexts but Freemasons in others, and there always seemed to be exceptions and ways around even the strictest rules. Taking the profane, then, not to be a static position but, rather, a processual enactment of becoming, resulting from complex negotiations of power, intimacy and belonging, I will use the profane to think about ethnographers' relations to our subjects of study.

The anthropology of secret societies has long been preoccupied with questions of belonging, intimacy and the making of ethnographic subjects (Evans-Pritchard 1976 [1937]; Luhrmann 1989; Murphy 1980), but contemporary ethnographers face new ethical, political and legal challenges when studying the secretive practices of bureaucratic organisations (Deeb and Marcus 2011; Herzfeld 1992; Wright 1994a). The structures of Masonic initiation follow closely patterns identified in studies of rituals and secret societies (Simmel 1906; Turner 1969). A neophyte is initiated to the status of Apprentice, the first degree of Freemasonry, then Fellow (second degree) and *Maestro* or *Maestra* (third degree Master Mason).[3] Depending on the rites of particular lodges, Master Masons may pursue up to 33 further degrees of initiation that transform the initiate's subjectivity and bond him or her to a community of practitioners.

Despite their esoteric practices, Masonic lodges are also in a bureaucratic and technical sense organisations like many others. The lodges' very existence, in the early twenty-first century, depends on their ability to establish their legality as non-profit cultural associations rather than secret societies, which are explicitly forbidden by the Italian Constitution. Lodges thus often employ accountants, lawyers, and PR firms; some have taxpayer ID numbers and contribute to charities to ensure their legitimacy in civil society. Each lodge has a charter, bylaws and elected or appointed officers administering its functions. Nonetheless, the actual location of most lodges and the identity of most Freemasons are secret. Temples are concealed within ordinary looking buildings and registered under the name of façade cultural associations.

Freemasonry's unique positioning as an Italian legal secretive organisation offers a productive site for thinking through the anthropology of secret societies and the anthropology of organisations. In this chapter I will thus return to some of the core debates of the discipline to ask new questions and reframe old ones about the making of communities, and about access and intimacy in the fieldwork encounter under neoliberal conditions, especially within larger ideologies of governance and transparency, which exercise pressures on political subjects, organisations and researchers across the globe (Garsten and Lindh de Montoya 2008; West and Sanders 2003).

Early on in my research I considered my profane status a methodological, ethical and epistemological 'problem' to be solved. By the end, however, I came to realise the unexpected richness and flexibility that the concept of profanity could afford me, and which ultimately enabled me to carry out this research. My contention is that, far from being a problem, standing in the space of the profane can paradoxically open up channels for increased trust, which are crucial to the development of ethnographic intimacy. I offer the profane as an analytical entry point to the study of a secretive complex organisation, even one that denies the title of 'secret society', to tackle some of the challenges of conducting fieldwork in highly contested and politicised sites.

THE MASONIC AND THE PROFANE

The distinction between the sacred and the profane has been explored at length in the anthropology of religion. Durkheim famously declared the two terms foundational to the elaboration of religious beliefs and rites, and posited an absolute separation between the two realms. 'The sacred and the profane', he wrote, 'are always and everywhere conceived by the human intellect as separate genera, as two worlds with nothing in common' (Durkheim 2008: 38). When Malinowski employed Durkheim's terminology in his study of the Trobrianders, he maintained the assumption that the sacred and the profane are two domains to be found 'in every primitive community', although he did not necessarily see them as antagonistic (Malinowski 1948: 1).

The absolutism and universalism of such pronouncements has been questioned by more recent anthropological scholarship. Talal Asad (1993), for instance, has refuted the cross-cultural applicability of anthropological notions of religion derived from European forms of Christianity. Even within the context of European religions, Jonathan Sheehan (2006) has challenged what he called the 'anthropological profane', a notion to which he contrasted alternative historical genealogies of the term *profane* (see also Tambiah 1990).

In Masonic terminology, profane denotes anyone who has not received a ritual initiation, as well as the social world outside the ritual space of a Masonic temple. From the Latin *pro fanum* (literally: in front of/outside the temple), the term *profane* is used in contrast to *Masonic*, and it can apply to people, places and concepts. Masonic rituals and regulations construct the profane and its opposite, the Masonic or the esoteric, as dichotomous and mutually exclusive. In everyday life, however, the Freemasons I met travelled back and forth between profane and esoteric spaces. For instance, my informants had profane jobs as lawyers, architects or journalists, in addition to their Masonic positions as Maestre, Tylers or Apprentices in their lodges. They had profane family members, while also having 'brothers' and 'sisters' in the lodges. Therefore, and despite the rhetorical distinction between profane and esoteric, the line between the two terms was often blurred in everyday life.[4]

Moreover, some people could be recognised as Freemasons in some contexts but they could be treated as profane in other settings. The clearest example of such context-specific attributions is the ambivalent status of women

Freemasons, whose inclusion in the lodges has been the subject of fierce controversy throughout the last three centuries, and whose very existence is often invisible and misrecognised.

Women's participation in Freemasonry has taken one of three possible forms. First, some women have joined 'adoption lodges' – auxiliary para-Masonic organisations for female relatives of Freemason men. The Order of the Eastern Star (ES), headquartered in the USA and with chapters worldwide, is one of the best known. In Italy, the ES is open to female relatives of members of the men-only Grand Orient of Italy (GOI), the oldest and largest Masonic organisation in the country. Second, some Masonic organisations formerly reserved for men have opened their doors to women. The Grand Lodge of Italy – Piazza del Gesù (GLDI), for instance, became a mixed-gender lodge after the Second World War. Third, some women have formed or joined women-only Masonic lodges, which often derive their legitimacy from lesser known histories of female figures in Freemasonry. For instance, the Grand Women's Masonic Lodge of Italy (GLMFI), a women-only lodge officially founded in 1990, traced its roots back to late nineteenth-century underground Masonic women's groups and to the more documented political history of women's Freemasonry in neighbouring countries, such as France.

The controversy surrounding women's initiation in Freemasonry is illustrative of larger patterns of differentiation of Masonic lodges in different contexts. Freemasonry began as an esoteric fraternal society in early eighteenth-century England for upper-class men, and it quickly spread worldwide, acquiring distinctive national traits over time (Jacob 1991; Mola 1992). Each country has one or more national Masonic organisations with local chapters ('lodges') in different cities. Lodges have generally maintained their pyramidal structure, and they continue to pursue humanist liberal values, such as liberty, fraternity and equality, under the spiritual guidance of a non-denominational higher power, known as the Great Architect of the Universe. However, lodges worldwide differ widely around issues of secrecy, exclusivity and membership, as the inclusion of women, racial minorities, lower classes, the disabled and former slaves have been topics of debate for the last three centuries (Clawson 1989).

Commenting on the great variety of Masonic formations throughout the world, a Maestro in the mixed-gender GLDI once said to me that 'all these little groups pop up like mushrooms claiming to be Freemasons, but we don't know who they are, and they give us all a bad name'. Although his comment was specific to the Italian context, where mass media often attribute political scandals to loosely defined Masonic influences (Mazzocchi 1994), it also underscored how tricky the question of legitimacy is for Freemasonry broadly. In the absence of any centralised authority, the umbrella term *Freemasonry* is claimed by a wide range of organisations worldwide.

There are two main ways for a Masonic lodge to be considered legitimate. The first is to be recognised by the United Grand Lodge of England (UGLE), the oldest lodge in the world. Since the UGLE only initiates men, any lodge open to women is by definition 'irregular', including the ones I studied.[5] Lodges that reject the UGLE's historical monopoly over the name of Freemasonry establish legitimacy instead by exchanging treaties of mutual friendship with other lodges. Just as countries do, Masonic lodges forge mutual fraternal bonds through complex international diplomatic efforts. The more treaties a lodge has, the more legitimate it is. As a result of these different paths to legitimacy, individual Freemasons might be considered brothers or sisters by lodges that recognise them but profane by other lodges.

The ambivalence of context-specific attributions of Masonic and profane became clear to me during the first Masonic gathering I ever attended, in what was my entry point to this research project. In April 2004 I attended a three-day convention in the Adriatic beach town of Rimini organised by the men-only GOI. With approximately 15,000 members, the GOI is the largest Italian lodge, and since the conference was technically open to anyone, it was an excellent opportunity for early reconnaissance.

A few months earlier I had learned to my great surprise that someone I considered an 'aunt' was married to a member of the GOI, and that she herself belonged to the ES, the auxiliary group for female relatives of GOI brothers. My surprise was due not only to the discovery that relatives of mine could be Freemasons but also to the fact that they would willingly admit it to me or anyone else. The pervasive secrecy characterising Masonic lodges in Italy, unlike elsewhere, is the result of complex political histories that have seen enormous tensions between Freemasonry and governmental or societal forces, including the Vatican and left-wing parties.[6] Having grown up in Italy, I was used to the dominant representations of Freemasonry there as an elite right-wing secret society running the country from behind the scenes.

Both my aunt and her husband belonged to an increasingly large minority among Italian Freemasons who believed Freemasonry's reputation could improve if Freemasons were less secretive. They were the ones who first encouraged my research project and invited me to attend the GOI's convention. My uncle explained to me that the then Grand Maestro of the GOI, Gustavo Raffi, had spearheaded a series of unprecedented policy changes to make Freemasonry more 'transparent'. One of these initiatives was an annual convention, open to the public, during which he would briefly open the temple's doors to let the profane witness a Masonic ritual.

One of the best-kept Masonic secrets in Italy is the location of temples, which only the initiated are supposed to know.[7] The fact that during preliminary fieldwork, still light-years away from the social and 'cultural' intimacy (Herzfeld 2005) that eventually came to characterise my ethnographic research, I found myself standing outside a Masonic temple was therefore by itself an extraordinary occurrence. To be sure, this was not one of the GOI's many splendid temples hidden throughout the historical landscape of Italy's urban centres. This *ad hoc* temple was built within the auditorium of the convention centre the GOI had rented out.

The ceremony was scheduled to start at 5 p.m. on the first day of the convention. Until then, everyone was busy mingling, attending panels, walking through the book exhibits and information booths. Crowds of elegant men and women were following arrow-shaped signs pointing in all directions to 'café', 'library', 'info desk', 'philately', 'temple'. We arrived around noon, and my uncle quickly put on a pair of white gloves, and tied a short, white apron embroidered with Masonic symbols around his suit pants. Excusing himself, he rushed ahead to join hundreds of other older men wearing dark suits, white gloves and short white aprons, all making their way through the large temple door on the opposite side of the hall. My aunt handed me a copy of the programme and told me that while the men were inside the temple 'doing their thing', we could attend any of the lectures listed on the brochure. First, though, she needed to stop by the ES booth to say hello to her sisters.

The Stars had set up a table right next to the large temple door. The women volunteers had come from all over Italy and many had never met before. In the imagined community of the Masonic convention, however, people treated strangers as long-time friends, exchanging business cards and three formulaic kisses on the cheeks. My aunt recognised several of her sisters from Rome, and we pulled up two seats to join in the conversation. Pointing toward the *ad hoc* temple, some of the sisters were complaining about only being allowed inside for the Grand Maestro's inaugural speech along with the profane. The doors of the temple served as the dividing line between Freemasons and the profane, and the Stars were clearly left sitting outside.

Over the next couple of days, I spent most of my time at the ES booth, helping them hand out brochures and participating in their conversations, which revolved around Masonic politics. The Grand Maestro had just been re-elected to a second five-year term. Several of the sisters felt ambivalent about his re-election, which many of their male relatives had fully supported. Although the sisters approved of the Grand Maestro's politics of transparency, many questioned his position against women in Freemasonry. Some of them swore he had told them personally that he would welcome women into the GOI, perhaps as an electoral promise, whereas others claimed with absolute certainty that they had always known him to be 'a misogynist'. Either way, the temple's doors did not seem any more open to women under Raffi's administration than they had been before.[8]

Shortly after 5 o' clock, two men wearing ritual aprons emerged from the large doors and invited the crowd in. It took almost half an hour for over a thousand people to be ushered in and seated in the enormous sloped theatre engulfed in darkness. I held the hand of one of the ES sisters, who held another's, so as not to lose each other, and together we made our way over to a group of empty seats. The sight was breathtaking. A projection of lights above us had replaced the barren concrete of the auditorium ceiling with the illusion of a starry night sky. Down on the main stage, an ornate throne served as the seat of the Grand Maestro, and behind it an illuminated projector screen displayed the blinding light of the rising sun. It was meant to represent the East, the Masonic esoteric Orient, from where the Grand Maestro would irradiate all of us with the power of his allocution. In front of the throne, a small altar holding a book and a square and compass stood on top of a black and white chequered floor. Hundreds of men in dark suits, white gloves and aprons sat on all sides of the stage and guarded the doors. The sisters and I sat at the back, with members of the press, friends and guests, and watched a supposedly secret ritual unfold before our eyes.

Delegations of foreign Masonic lodges marched into the temple in procession, carrying their insignia and paying homage to Grand Maestro Raffi. GOI members then performed some formulaic exchanges to signify the opening of the temple, the symbolic locking of its doors and the beginning of ritual work. With a bright light radiating from behind him, the Grand Maestro stood up from his throne and took the microphone. After welcoming all guests, including some politicians and city representatives, he proceeded to explain that this public opening of a Masonic temple was part of an explicit attempt to make Freemasonry better known to society. 'We have nothing to hide', he asserted firmly to an applauding crowd, 'and we have no debts to pay to the justice system.'

After the speech ended, guests were asked to leave the temple so that GOI brothers and the foreign Masonic delegations could finish their ritual work privately. Like all profane attendees, the Stars were banned too. Walking back to their booth, one of them told me how sorry she was that, unfortunately, they would not be able to show me the GOI's ritual today. She said that the ritual was incredibly beautiful, and that the two of them – looking at her sister, who was nodding along – had been hoping I would get to see it too. Noticing my confused look, the other sister quickly explained that the light technician, who was also in the GOI, was a friend of theirs. In the past, he had let them sneak into the light control booth above the auditorium to enjoy an unobstructed view of the ritual. Unfortunately, the technician had called in sick that day.

Back at the ES booth, the sisters continued to discuss the GOI's gender politics with a mixture of bitterness and sadness. They felt proud of their ability to elude the GOI's surveillance, sneaking up to watch the ritual right under the nose of the Tyler guarding the temple's doors. The small pleasure of an act of insubordination, however, did not erase the sisters' resentment toward the GOI, an institution that they otherwise supported and admired. As more sisters joined the conversation, their frustration and disappointment were palpable. They complained of watching foreign delegations welcome into the temple with great honours, while they sat in the back amidst the profane.

It was some time during that conversation that I first heard a reference to 'the Florence group'. In a moment of pathos, an ES sister confessed to the group that sometimes, when she got really fed up with her GOI husband, she thought about leaving and joining the Florence group. Others nodded silently. Whenever the Florence group was mentioned, it sounded like an escapist fantasy. My direct questions about what this Florence group was about, however, received no answers. Instead, I received an admonition not to talk too much about it, at least 'not here' at the GOI's convention. My aunt later whispered to me that the Florence group was a Masonic organisation of women not recognised by the GOI.

The next day, on a break from the ES booth, my aunt and I took a walk through the book exhibit area. Several esoteric presses were advertising their latest releases and selling discounted copies of their books. Every few steps we ran into people to greet, to meet and to kiss three times on the cheeks. In this ethnographer's paradise, I strolled around collecting business cards and offering brief descriptions of my project, in the hope that some of these contacts would prove useful later on. All of a sudden, my aunt pulled on my arm, and whispered, 'There she is, I'll introduce you.'

Chatting loudly, as she made her way through crowds and bookstands, was a tall and strong-looking woman of about 60 years of age with short blonde hair and wearing an elegant green suit. When my aunt introduced us and explained my project to her, the woman seemed very interested, and handed me two business cards: one with her personal address and information; the other listing her official status, as 'Paola Foggi, *Gran Maestra*' of the GLMFI.

That is how I first met Paola, the Grand Maestra who became a mentor to me for most of this project. In Rimini, she told me, she had only come as a 'private citizen' to accompany her husband, a GOI brother. She had not been invited as a representative of another Masonic organisation because the GOI did not recognise the women-only GLMFI. The Grand Maestra was thus standing outside the GOI's temple as a profane like the rest of us. She told me to give her a call. She was very interested in a project about women in Freemasonry, and she said she would be happy to introduce me to some of the sisters in her lodge.

The GOI convention was an entry point into my study of Freemasonry. A microcosm of Masonic experiences in Italy, the convention brought together a diverse set of interlocutors for my project, including Freemasons of different denominations, their family members and profane politicians, journalists, law enforcement authorities and scholars. Some of the tensions and conflicts characteristic of Italian Masonic experiences at the turn of the twenty-first century, and which later became central to my study, were brought to the fore at the convention itself. Where was the line to be drawn between the Masonic and the profane? What was the relationship between Freemasonry and the most nefarious side of Italian politics? How did women fit into the imaginary of this powerful and secretive brotherhood?

The category of the profane enacted at the convention was a highly flexible one. Most convention attendees were, in a way or another, Masonic affiliates whose participation in Freemasonry was an object of dispute. Moreover, and despite however strict the official rules may have been, the convention revealed that there were always ways around. Some of the Stars, for instance, had found an illicit path to the light control booth, from which they had observed a ritual forbidden to profane eyes. Members of other Masonic organisations not recognised by the GOI, including the Grand Maestra of the GLMFI, were also roaming through the convention site in an unofficial capacity, as if profane, and yet marked as figures of authority by the deferential attention they received from others. At the convention I thus realised that the status of profane depended on context and on power negotiations; even then, the boundaries between the profane and the Masonic were made porous by the various authorised and unauthorised crossings that took place repeatedly.

The convention also underscored the importance of timing in working with a secretive organisation. The timing of my project was undoubtedly one of its conditions of possibility. As the discourse of 'transparency' swept through Italy and many other countries over the last three decades (Garsten and Lindh de Montoya 2008; Vattimo 1992; West and Sanders 2003), it was right at the turn of the twenty-first century that a formerly secret society decided to deploy the logic of transparency to its advantage and refashioned itself into a non-profit cultural organisation hosting public conventions. The profane ethnographer thus came knocking on the temple's doors just as Italian Freemasons were planning strategies to open up their doors cautiously and intentionally, even if only partially, to the public gaze (Mahmud 2012a).

THE PROFANE ETHNOGRAPHER

When I returned to Italy in the summer of 2004, my first stop was the Florentine home of Grand Maestra Paola Foggi. At the convention I had met a large number of Freemasons, and I had received encouraging signs of interest in my project. I knew that in their haste to prove their transparency, Freemasons would be happy to answer a few questions, but would they really let me 'hang out' deeply with them for over a year?

Unlike the surveys and one-time interviews of journalists or sociologists, and unlike the archival studies of historians, anthropological fieldwork with its imperative of long-term participant-observation is often unfamiliar even to educated audiences. By meeting the Grand Maestra of the GLMFI, I was hoping to secure her approval to conduct ethnographic fieldwork.

As we sat in her living room having tea, Paola and I discussed what ethnography tries to capture of human experience, the stuff of life that can only be observed over time and that does not always translate easily into words. What is it like to be a woman Freemason? How do sisters and brothers relate to one another? How do they navigate the profane world, including their families of origin? How do they transmit knowledge and acquire cultural capital? What is their experience of secrecy?

The Grand Maestra nodded along in approval, and then she said that ethnography makes a lot of sense because someone's life cannot be captured in an interview. She told me that she and her sisters had weekly card games, and they often got together at somebody's mountain or beach home for the weekend, or had dinner parties at someone's house. She told me I would be welcome to spend time with them. Members of the men-only GOI and of the mixed-gender GLDI were usually there too, she informed me, and then proceeded to explain a very enlightening fact about Masonic relations in Italy. Even though different Masonic groups might not recognise each other formally, members of each have close friends and relatives in other groups. 'In the end,' she told me, 'everyone comes over for dinner.'[9]

Before concluding our meeting, Paola raised one final concern about my project: as a profane, I would never be allowed to witness the rituals of Freemasonry. There are initiations, funerals, rites of passage, ritual dinners. Those would all be closed to me, Paola warned me. Was I really sure that I wanted to study Freemasonry *from the outside*?

My answer to Paola was that I wanted to understand the workings of Freemasonry as a masculine social organisation that has had a conflicted relationship with the Italian state, and in which some Italian women – mostly upper-class, right-wing, educated, heterosexual white women – have found a site for a unique form of gender-based activism that falls outside the rubric of feminism. The specific content of Masonic esotericism was not my focus. Besides, lodge rituals have long been revealed in tell-all books authored by disgruntled former Masons or by profane spies. That afternoon in her apartment the Grand Maestra and I thus struck a deal: I would be writing a profane ethnography of Italian Freemasons.

The position of profane ethnographer I came to embody was the product of ongoing negotiations with my informants, starting in the Grand Maestra's living room and continuing in various forms through each and every subsequent field encounter. Many of my interlocutors asked me if I wanted to be initiated, and their question was deeply loaded. In an ideologically divided social world, where most profane commentators have been deeply critical of the lodges, my informants' offers to initiate me could be a test of my allegiances. Would I ultimately stand with the detractors or with the apologists? Could they trust me with their life histories, or would I use them against them? If I did not wish to become a Freemason, what would my refusal suggest about my own political commitments? Moreover, while Freemasons of all denominations claim that they accept 'anybody', the lodges have been widely criticised for their ongoing elitism and exclusivity. Why they would ask *me* to join – a racially marked Italian citizen of Eritrean descent conducting this research with the institutional backing of an elite American university – therefore required some further reflection on my subject position in the field, and on the humanist notions of inclusion underlying Masonic membership.[10]

My interlocutors suggested pragmatically that it would be easier to do my research as a Freemason. They insisted theirs was an esoteric society, not a social club. By choosing to remain a profane, I would miss out on what they considered the most important part of their organisation: the rituals. 'It would be like studying Catholics without ever going to Mass', a Maestra told me once. Could I really study Freemasonry as a profane? And what would be the point of doing that?

Underlying my informants' concerns for the wellbeing of my study were also some friendly rivalries among different lodges. Members of the women-only GLMFI and the mixed-gender GLDI, for instance, would at times ask me which type of Freemasonry I deemed best for women. Although I always deflected such questions, they provided me with an easy explanation for refusing to be initiated. An initiation is necessarily into a particular Masonic group. As a profane researcher I was free to travel through different lodges without taking sides. My informants understood the discursive power of 'objectivity' and 'independent' research, and most left it at that, although a few kept insisting that I could join *their* lodge after I finished my research.

Although my interlocutors' desire to initiate me might have been an attempt to control my research, I took seriously their concern that as a profane I could not enter the temples. For them, esoteric rituals were at the core of Freemasonry, and they suspected that my profane ethnography could only encompass its periphery. Their concern pointed to the difficulty of delineating the exact borders of a community of study.

As moments of both social rupture and social integration, rituals are necessary to imagine a community into being. Rituals, however, are not only the formulaic practices of an esoteric system of belief. There were also profane and social rituals that were equally important in giving Freemasonry its meaning. Going to the opera, attending art exhibitions or partaking in erudite conversations at semi-formal dinners were community-forming rituals that produced Freemasonry as a classed and gendered organisation in profane cultural terms. Both the social and esoteric rituals of Freemasonry were important for its existence as an Italian secretive organisation.

As it turned out, the dividing line between the Masonic and the profane that was supposed to limit the scope of my project was only drawn in pencil. Ethnographers are often exempt from dominant expectations put on other members of the community, and I too began to enjoy an 'honorary' status among my informants. Although I remained a profane, my interlocutors began to make increasingly frequent exceptions to their cosmological rules in order to allow me to cross the threshold of esoteric spaces and observe ritual works.

In addition to meeting my informants for drinks after work, at home with their families, at Masonic conferences and dinner parties, by the end of fieldwork I had also met them inside temples, at solstice celebrations and at ritual feasts. I even travelled with a group of sisters to a distant initiation path, where each step of the Masonic initiation ritual could be followed through a life-size forest of symbols (Mahmud 2012b). As a profane ethnographer I thus observed not only the social rituals of Masonic lodges but also many of their esoteric practices as well, although the latter were ostensibly off-limits to profane people like me. Every excursion into the esoteric was presented rhetorically as an 'exception' to our rules of engagement.

In the power relations characteristic of 'studying up' (Nader 1972), my informants were the ones to decide whether to break the rules. I was never in a position to initiate requests to enter esoteric spaces. In fact, I soon learned that explicit requests could be counter-productive. My interlocutors could shun me at any time if I seemed intrusive, as they had often shut down the persistent inquiries of journalists. As a rule of thumb, then, I thought it best not to push. Waiting patiently for someone (usually a high-ranking Freemason) to invite me to join her among the initiated, I learned to practise the gendered subjectivity of the quiet listener, nodding along, knowing that fewer words interjected at the right time in the conversation were much more effective than a series of nosey questions.

My silence was often the key that let me enter the esoteric world from which I was supposedly banned. If during an interview a Fellow Mason changed the subject away from esoteric practices, I followed her lead to more comfortable topics. If a Maestro explained to me the internal politics of his lodge, I simply pulled out notebook and pen to write down some notes without interrupting his flow. If a Maestra asked me not to disclose some of her confidences in my book, I reassured her that I would not publish anything against her will. That promise, which I have kept, did not stem solely from an ethical commitment to protecting my informants' privacy but also from a more humbling acknowledgment of the potential repercussions ahead 'when they read what we write' (Brettell 1993), especially when 'they' are members of an organisation romanticised to be as powerful as Freemasonry.

For this project to be possible, I had to learn to exercise a great deal of 'discretion', as my informants called the fine art of revealing and concealing knowledge at the same time (Mahmud 2012b). Some of my interlocutors made it no secret that, although they had nothing to hide, they agreed to let me study their organisation partly because I seemed 'discreet'. Moreover, social capital was another necessary condition of possibility for this profane ethnographer's entry into the field of a secretive organisation. Freemasons who might not otherwise have given me the time of day out of fear or lack of interest were willing to help my research because the Grand Maestra herself had vouched for me.

I remember sitting in Paola's living room, that summer afternoon. I watched her pull out her address book from a desk drawer. It was a thick old book with a black leather cover and pages turned yellow by age with post-it notes and business cards precariously held together by a stretched rubber band. I watched Paola search through the contacts of a lifetime and then make five or six phone calls on my behalf. 'I'm sending you a girl who's doing her thesis on women in Freemasonry. She's a doctoral student from Harvard University. Her uncle is in the GOI and I know her aunt, who's an Eastern Star. Listen, she'll give you a call later. Please talk to her and, if you can, try to give her a hand. It's a good project, and I think we should try to help her.'

First the Grand Maestra called her own sisters in the GLMFI. Then she called a friend of hers, a Maestro, in the mixed-gender GLDI, so that he could introduce me to his sisters and brothers. Those introductions, disguised in the language of exhortations to her fellow brothers and sisters to come to my aid, carried the full force of the Grand Maestra's authority. My initial contacts in 2004 followed a point-to-point network. Each new informant gave me the name and phone number of another. After I moved to Florence for 15 continuous months, starting in 2005, those one-on-one fieldwork encounters expanded into group activities and official events.

Initially I credited my access to Freemasonry to my fortunate connection with the Grand Maestra, whose authorisation of my project had trickled down to so many members of this pyramidal organisation. Later on, however, Paola corrected my impressions. Not even the Grand Maestra herself, she informed me, could have spoken to me so candidly about Freemasonry, had she not received prior authorisation from the Supreme Council. Freemasonry, she reminded me, is not a dictatorship. There is a system of checks and balances.

The Supreme Council, the governing board of many Masonic lodges, consisted of elected or nominated members selected among those at the 33rd degree of initiation. The Supreme Council's duties include nominating candidates for the position of Grand Maestra in election years. Apparently, some time between the GOI convention in April and our meeting at her house in July 2004, the Grand Maestra had put my project on the agenda of one of the GLMFI Supreme Council's monthly meetings, and the council had voted to allow the sisters to participate in my research.

It was therefore not only an economy of connections that made my entry into the field possible. The bureaucratic, institutional mechanisms that propel a Masonic lodge – just as they propel any other organisation – had blended with the informal, discreet workings of social and cultural capital to manufacture the particular subject position of the profane ethnographer. The profane ethnographer produced by both formal and informal systems of authority was not a settled status but, rather, an ongoing object of negotiations among a variety of social actors, myself included, as our investments and complicities matured over time in the highly politicised and contested field site of Italian Freemasonry. Being a profane ethnographer meant standing in a particular relation of power with my informants, one punctuated not only by our social differences – of race, politics, age – but also by institutional mechanisms, which mediated my ability to access their organisation.

CONCLUSION: OF MAGIC AND METHOD

What is then this ethnographer's magic, by which he is able to evoke the real spirit of the natives, the true picture of tribal life? (Malinowski 1984: 6)

In this chapter, I recounted some of my earliest encounters with Italian Freemasonry instead of later, richer and more ethnographically intimate moments of fieldwork. My reasons for choosing to focus on a public Masonic convention and on my initial agreement with the Grand Maestra of the GLMFI are twofold. First, by foregrounding two ethnographic episodes that appear less 'deep' than those that followed – both derived from preliminary fieldwork – I hope to challenge some of the disciplinary assumptions that especially in the study of secret societies posit a natural correlation between depth of access and depth of knowledge (see Gable 1997). Second, by looking back at Masonic encounters that occurred before I had enough knowledge to understand their implications fully, I follow a Masonic trope of knowledge production: the secret was always already in front of our eyes, but it is only in hindsight that we can understand it.

Whenever I have presented my work at academic conferences throughout the years, someone in the audience has invariably asked the question about access. How did I get in? The question was formulated with considerable trepidation by scholars familiar with the history of Freemasonry in Italy, where the lodges have been implicated in the worst political scandals of the last few decades. Was my project strictly historical and archival? To suggest that one could conduct fieldwork among Italian Freemasons would seem as preposterous as to suggest that one could study the *mafia* ethnographically.

Of course, anthropologists *have* studied organised crime groups like the *mafia* (Jacquemet 1996; Schneider and Schneider 2003). They have also studied political insurgents in times of war, human trafficking, secretive bureaucratic institutions and, of course, they have always studied secret societies, including Italian ones (Galt 1994). I therefore suspect that propelling the question of access is not so much a reasoned surprise for the topic itself, as much as it is a sceptical inquiry into the methodological validity of its attending fieldwork. Could fieldwork among a secretive and powerful European organisation be 'real' fieldwork? And if indeed it was 'real' fieldwork, undertaken with due diligence over an appropriate length of time by a participant observer of a community's daily life, then the inquirer's scepticism might give way to a prurient curiosity. How did I do it? What was the ethnographer's magic that unveiled the world of Italian Freemasons?

Akhil Gupta and James Ferguson have addressed the question of anthropological legitimacy through an analysis of what they called the 'fieldwork mystique' (1997), an ideological construction of the field as the natural and pre-discursive site for anthropological work. Fieldwork, at least in the interpretive school of anthropology, is often viewed as an incommunicable practice, to be experienced, rather than a method to be formally taught. And yet, the notion of 'real' fieldwork is often used to question the legitimacy of an anthropologist's work (see Weston 1997).

Alongside critical reviews of the 'field', the relationship of the ethnographer to her subjects of study has also been an ongoing topic of inquiry in anthropology. In the 1980s and 1990s, feminist, postcolonial and 'native' ethnographers shook the epistemological foundations of a discipline centred on the tropes of insiders and outsiders and on a 'field' site produced through practice as much as through the ethnographic writings that followed (Behar and Gordon 1995; Clifford and Marcus 1986; Visweswaran 1997). The anthropology of Europe grew in those years (see Goddard et al. 1994; Herzfeld 1987), alongside the anthropology of elites and of organisations (Marcus and Hall 1992; Pina-Cabral and Lima 2000; Wright 1994a) as a framework to reverse the trope of the anthropological gaze cast only on the poor, black/ brown, marginal other.

One of the main contributions of these debates has been a push to recognise the multiplicity of power relations that infuse the fieldwork encounter. In this vein, reflexive and post-reflexive writings have offered new conceptualisations of the ethnographer's positionality, using terms such as 'halfie' or 'native' or 'postcolonial' or 'split' selves to highlight the anthropologist's identity-based connections to her informants (Abu-Lughod 1986; Behar 1996; Kondo 1990; Narayan 1993).

Although the last two decades have seen increasing diversity among anthropology's subjects and practitioners, as well as renewed interest in fieldwork epistemologies (Holmes and Marcus 2005), it is remarkable how little has changed when it comes to the pedagogy of anthropological training and the codification of disciplinary authority in a set of field practices so loosely definable. Anthropologists' trade secrets, 'the ethnographer's magic' (Stocking 1983), continue to have an archetypal effect on current notions of methodological rigor. Learning to occupy the calculated position of the profane ethnographer was my answer to the riddle of the ethnographic method.

What makes the notion of the profane ethnographer different from the subject categories that emerged from the anthropological literature on reflexivity is that it emphasises a particular configuration of 'power/knowledge' (Foucault 1980) that privileges the informants' worldviews without necessarily locating the foundation of the fieldwork relationship in a shared identity. The profane is a category intelligible only from the perspective of the initiate; initiates are the ones who call others profane. Assuming my informants' viewpoint, then, the profane are those who have not received an initiation to embark on a self-cultivation path through the pursuit of esoteric knowledge, which will remake them into new subjects. Through ritual practice and schooling in esotericism, a profane could become a Freemason. Despite my interlocutors' essentialist claims about their identities, the condition of 'profane' is thus inherently temporary and relational. A profane always has the possibility of becoming an initiate, but initiates control access to the ritual initiation that marks the beginning of knowledge.[11]

When working with a secretive organisation, the temptation to reify *emic* boundaries of belonging that structure our informants' worldviews is great. A social world defined by an initiation ritual purportedly separating people into two groups, insiders and outsiders, lends itself to an essentialist analysis of intimacy; the profane might thus seem like a commonsensical category. What I learned, however, living among Freemasons, and occasionally crossing the threshold of an initiate space as an ethnographer turned 'honorary' sister, is that the profane is literally an outsider, but one etymologically defined by her degree of proximity. She is *right outside* the temple (*pro fanum*), standing so close to its doors that at times her outsiderness turns into a liminality, and her liminality is indeed the ethnographer's magic.

Victor Turner taught us that: 'the attributes of liminality or of liminal *personae* ("threshold people") are necessarily ambiguous, since this condition and these persons elude or slip through the network of classifications that normally locate states and positions in cultural space' (1969: 95). The profane ethnographer at the threshold of a secretive powerful organisation is also an ambiguous figure, whose status is not one end of a polarity but instead a positionality negotiated in a contested political field.

Most anthropologists are profane in relation to our subjects of study. Regardless of our educational degrees and linguistic proficiency, our informants often treat us like idiots – a predicament many of us welcome as the beginning of useful knowledge. The profane are not idiots, of course, but they are uninitiated, inherently lacking in status and knowledge. Their deficiency is not an ontological condition but a pedagogical one. My profanity thus made me a student and Freemasons my *maestri* of Masonic life. In this configuration of power/knowledge, my interlocutors could set the rules of engagement, and the profane ethnographer could appear to be a non-threatening, even sympathetic presence.

Working with a powerful secretive organisation in Europe – negotiating research ethics, institutional requirements, and the effects of transparency laws on the fieldwork encounter – made being a profane ethnographer not only necessary but also wise in my case. Allowing a profane to carry out ethnographic research could lend much credibility to the lodges, whose self-presentations as transparent, non-profit associations have been met with great scepticism by Italian media and law enforcement. My profanity thus proved valuable to my informants' political agendas.

In turn, it was my potentiality as a profane that, far from being a problem, turned out to be crucial to the development of ethnographic intimacy in my project. Although my decision not to join a lodge was initially a cause of concern, over time, as I became a stable presence in my interlocutors' lives, I discovered that the act of declining an initiation had made me more trustworthy in the eyes of many Freemasons. It showed that I was not interested in infiltrating the lodges to capture that esoteric 'secret' that many have been after for centuries. Paradoxically, it was my choice to remain a profane that increased the trust between us. Being a profane ethnographer thus turned out to be this ethnographer's magic.

NOTES

1. Fieldwork for this project was supported by the Wenner Gren Foundation for Anthropological Research and by the Social Science Research Council IDRF programme. I thank Tom Boellstorff, Christina Garsten, Michael Herzfeld, Rusaslina Idrus, Arthur Kleinman, George Marcus, Anette Nyqvist, Kris Peterson, Miriam Shakow, Mary Steedly and Kath Weston for their comments on earlier versions of this chapter, and all the Freemasons who shared their lives with me. None of them are to be blamed for my shortcomings.
2. The phrase 'deep hanging out' has become popular among anthropologists in the US to describe fieldwork informally. It was coined by Renato Rosaldo at a conference in 1994 (Clifford 1997: 188 n. 2).
3. I use the Italian words, *Maestro* (plural, *Maestri*) and *Maestra* (plural, *Maestre*) instead of the English 'Master' Mason in order to underscore the gender of these titles.
4. Freemasonry is not an organised religion. Lodges practice rituals in the name of a non-denominational higher power.
5. The United Grand Lodge of England uses several different criteria to grant its recognition to Masonic Lodges worldwide. There are therefore many men-only Masonic organisations, too, that are not recognised by the UGLE.
6. From the late 1960s to the mid 1990s, Masonic lodges were implicated in major political scandals, corruption and right-wing terrorism (Mola 2008; Rossi and Lombrassa 1981). As a result, Freemasons have been the subjects of widespread conspiracy theories depicting the lodges as secret societies of elite men plotting against the country's democratic process.
7. For many of my informants, the secrecy of their identities and locations was necessary for their own safety and privacy in a country that they perceived as hostile to Masonic experiences. In turn, it was precisely Freemasons' secrecy that was often used against them in media attacks meant to challenge the constitutionality of the lodges.

8. Anthropologists have shown that organisations are resistant to change, and often deploy an ideological notion of organisational 'culture' to justify their stands (Wright 1994b). Women's struggle for full inclusion in Freemasonry mirrors patterns of gender inequality found by anthropologists of organisations (Cockburn 1994; Kerfoot and Knights 1994).

9. Although the GOI did not officially recognise the GLMFI women's initiation, and treated them as if they were profane in formal contexts, the Grand Maestra assured me that behind the scenes GOI brothers had been very supportive toward her lodge. The sisters were thus an integral part of a Masonic community dominated by the historical legacy of the men-only brotherhood and its much larger membership.

10. In his ethnography of Communists and Catholics in Italy, David Kertzer (1980) argued that 'conducting participant-observation fieldwork in a situation of sharp sociopolitical polarisation means struggling to define a nonpartisan role in a setting in which there is no precedent for such a role' (1980: 21). Kertzer credited his subject position 'as an American and as a Jew' for his ability to navigate the conflictual milieu of his fieldwork (Kertzer 1980: 21).

11. That potentiality was very important in day-to-day fieldwork encounters. My interlocutors accepted my presence in their social worlds at least in part because I could, one day, be initiated. Anthropologists working with religious groups have also found that the potential for 'conversion' was an important motivation for their informants' acceptance of the ethnographer's presence (see Harding 2000).

REFERENCES

Abu-Lughod, L. (1986) *Veiled Sentiments: Honor and Poetry in a Bedouin Society* (Berkeley, CA: University of California Press).

Asad, T. (1993) *Genealogies of Religion: Discipline and Reasons of Power in Christianity and Islam* (Baltimore, MD: Johns Hopkins University Press).

Behar, R. (1996) *The Vulnerable Observer: Anthropology that Breaks Your Heart* (Boston, MA: Beacon Press).

Behar, R. and D. A. Gordon, eds (1995) *Women Writing Culture* (Berkeley, CA: University of California Press).

Brettell, C., ed. (1993) *When They Read What We Write: The Politics of Ethnography* (Westport, CT: Bergin and Garvey).

Clawson, M. A. (1989) *Constructing Brotherhood: Class, Gender, and Fraternalism* (Princeton, NJ: Princeton University Press).

Clifford, J. (1997) 'Spatial practices: Fieldwork, travel, and the disciplining of anthropology', in A. Gupta and J. Ferguson, eds, *Anthropological Locations: Boundaries and Grounds of a Field Science* (Berkeley, CA: University of California Press).

Clifford, J. and G. Marcus, eds (1986) *Writing Culture: The Poetics and Politics of Ethnography* (Berkeley, CA: University of California Press).

Cockburn, C. (1994) 'Play of power: Women, men, and equality initiatives in a trade union', in S. Wright, ed., *Anthropology of Organizations* (New York, NY: Routledge).

Deeb, H. N. and G. Marcus (2011) 'In the green room: An experiment in ethnographic method at the WTO', *PoLAR: Political and Legal Anthropology Review*, Vol. 34, No. 1, pp. 51–76.

Durkheim, E. (2008) *The Elementary Forms of Religious Life* (New York, NY: Oxford University Press).

Evans-Pritchard, E. E. (1976 [1937]) *Witchcraft, Oracles, and Magic among the Azande* (Oxford: Clarendon Press).

Foucault, M. (1980) *Power/Knowledge: Selected Interviews and Other Writings, 1972–1977* (New York, NY: Pantheon).

Gable, E. (1997) 'A secret shared: Fieldwork and the sinister in a West African village', *Cultural Anthropology*, Vol. 12, No. 2, pp. 213–233.

Galt, A. H. (1994) '"The good cousins" domain of belonging: Tropes in southern Italian secret society symbol and ritual, 1810–1821', *Man*, Vol. 29, No. 4, pp. 785–807.

Garsten, C. and M. Lindh de Montoya, eds (2008) *Transparency in a New Global Order: Unveiling Organizational Visions* (Cheltenham: Edward Elgar).

Goddard, V. A., J. R. Llobera and C. Shore, eds (1994) *The Anthropology of Europe: Identity and Boundaries in Conflict* (Oxford: Berg).

Gupta, A. and J. Ferguson (1997) 'Discipline and practice: "The field" as site, method, and location in anthropology', in A. Gupta and J. Ferguson, eds, *Anthropological Locations: Boundaries and Grounds of a Field Science* (Berkeley, CA: University of California Press).

Harding, S. F. (2000) *The Book of Jerry Falwell: Fundamentalist Language and Politics* (Princeton, NJ: Princeton University Press).

Herzfeld, M. (1987) *Anthropology through the Looking-glass: Critical Ethnography in the Margins of Europe* (Cambridge: Cambridge University Press).

—— (1992) *The Social Production of Indifference: Exploring the Symbolic Roots of Western Bureaucracy* (New York, NY: Berg).

—— (2005) *Cultural Intimacy: Social Poetics in the Nation-state* (New York, NY: Routledge).

Holmes, D. and G. Marcus (2005) 'Refunctioning ethnography: The challenge of an anthropology of the contemporary', in N. Denzin and Y. Lincoln, eds, *Handbook of Qualitative Research* (Thousand Oaks, CA: Sage).

Jacob, M. C. (1991) *Living the Enlightenment: Freemasonry and Politics in Eighteenth-century Europe* (New York, NY: Oxford University Press).

Jacquemet, M. (1996) *Credibility in Court: Communicative Practices in the Camorra Trials.* (Cambridge: Cambridge University Press).

Kerfoot, D. and D. Knights (1994) 'The gendered terrains of paternalism', in S. Wright, ed., *Anthropology of Organizations* (New York, NY: Routledge).

Kertzer, D. I. (1980) *Comrades and Christians: Religion and Political Struggle in Communist Italy* (Cambridge: Cambridge University Press).

Kondo, D. K. (1990) *Crafting Selves: Power, Gender, and Discourses of Identity in a Japanese Workplace* (Chicago, IL: University of Chicago Press).

Luhrmann, T. M. (1989) *Persuasions of the Witch's Craft: Ritual Magic in Contemporary England* (Cambridge, MA: Harvard University Press).

Mahmud, L. (2012a) 'In the name of transparency: Gender, terrorism, and Masonic conspiracies in Italy', *Anthropological Quarterly*, Vol. 85, No. 4, pp. 1179–1210.

—— (2012b) '"The world is a forest of symbols": Italian Freemasonry and the practice of discretion', *American Ethnologist*, Vol. 39, No. 2, pp. 425–438.

Malinowski, B. (1948) *Magic, Science and Religion, and Other Essays* (Boston, MA: Beacon Press).

—— (1984) *Argonauts of the Western Pacific: An Account of Native Enterprise and Adventure in the Archipelagoes of Melanesian New Guinea* (Prospect Heights, IL: Waveland Press).

Marcus, G. E and P. D. Hall (1992) *Lives in Trust: The Fortunes of Dynastic Families in Late Twentieth-century America* (Boulder, CO: Westview Press).

Mazzocchi, A. (1994) *La massoneria nella stampa italiana degli anni '80* [Freemasonry in the Italian Press in the 1980s] (Firenze: A. Pontecorboli).

Mola, A. A. (1992) *Storia della massoneria italiana dalle origini ai nostri giorni* [History of Italian Freemasonry from Its Origins to the Present] (Milano: Bompiani).

—— (2008) *Gelli e la P2: fra cronaca e storia* [Gelli and the P2: Between News and History] (Foggia: Bastogi).

Murphy, W. P. (1980) 'Secret knowledge as property and power in Kpelle society', *Africa*, Vol. 50, No. 2, pp. 193–207.

Nader, L. (1972) 'Up the anthropologist – Perspectives gained from studying up', in D. Hymes, ed., *Reinventing Anthropology* (New York, NY: Pantheon).

Narayan, K. (1993) 'How native is a "native" anthropologist?', *American Anthropologist*, Vol. 95, No. 3, pp. 671–686.

Pina-Cabral, J. D. and A. Pedroso de Lima, eds (2000) *Elites: Choice, Leadership and Succession* (New York, NY: Berg).

Rossi, G. and F. Lombrassa (1981) *In nome della 'loggia': le prove di come la massoneria segreta ha tentato di impadronirsi dello stato italiano: i retroscena della P2* [In the Name of the

'Lodge': Evidence of How Secret Freemasonry Has Attempted to Seize the Italian State: The Back Stage of the P2] (Roma: Napoleone).

Schneider, J. and P. T. Schneider (2003) *Reversible Destiny: Mafia, Antimafia, and the Struggle for Palermo* (Berkeley, CA: University of California Press).

Sheehan, J. (2006) 'Sacred and profane: Idolatry, antiquarianism and the polemics of distinction in the seventeenth century', *Past & Present*, No. 192, pp. 35–66.

Simmel, G. (1906) 'The sociology of secrecy and of secret societies', *American Journal of Sociology*, Vol. 11, No. 4, pp. 441–498.

Stocking, G. W. (1983) *Observers Observed: Essays on Ethnographic Fieldwork* (Madison, WI: University of Wisconsin Press).

Tambiah, S. J. (1990) *Magic, Science, Religion, and the Scope of Rationality* (Cambridge: Cambridge University Press).

Turner, V. W. (1969) *The Ritual Process: Structure and Anti-structure* (London: Routledge and Kegan Paul).

Vattimo, G. (1992) *The Transparent Society* (Baltimore, MD: Johns Hopkins University Press).

Visweswaran, K. (1997) 'Histories of feminist ethnography', *Annual Review of Anthropology*, Vol. 26, pp. 591–621.

West, H. G. and T. Sanders, eds (2003) *Transparency and Conspiracy: Ethnographies of Suspicion in the New World Order* (Durham, NC: Duke University Press).

Weston, K. (1997) 'The virtual anthropologist', in A. Gupta and J. Ferguson, eds, *Anthropological Locations: Boundaries and Grounds of a Field Science* (Berkeley, CA: University of California Press).

Wright, S., ed. (1994a) *Anthropology of Organizations* (New York, NY: Routledge).

—— (1994b) 'Culture in anthropology and organizational studies', in S. Wright, ed., *Anthropology of Organizations* (New York, NY: Routledge).

13
Communicative nature of money
Aligning organisational anthropology with technocratic experiments

Douglas R. Holmes

INTRODUCTION: GLASS

In the East End of Frankfurt along the banks of the Main stands a huge abandoned structure, the Großmarkthalle, the city's historic wholesale market. In March 2002, the European Central Bank (ECB) agreed to purchase the site from the city and an international urban planning and architectural design competition chaired by Lucas Papademos, former vice-president of the ECB, was launched to select a plan for the central bank's new headquarters.

On a winter afternoon in early 2005 I visited the Frankfurt City Museum to view the three finalists' models in the design competition. The winning design concept by the Viennese firm of Coop Himmelb(l)au had been announced a few weeks earlier by Jean-Claude Trichet, former president of the ECB. The press release praised the Coop Himmelb(l)au design as best meeting 'the functional and technical requirements specified by the ECB, and has features that reflect the ECB's values and transforms them into architectural language'. Papademos noted in his statement accompanying the earlier announcement of the finalists (20 February 2004) that the jury was looking for a 'visible icon' that expressed a very particular constellation of communicative values. He further described the distinguishing features of the Coop Himmelb(l)au design.

> Their design concept was viewed by the Jury as a powerful image, reflecting the values of the ECB, such as transparency, communication, efficiency and stability. It is also an appealing and sophisticated design, which is easily readable and establishes a strong and unique identity in Frankfurt's skyline. The high-rise is a sculptural hybrid of two towers connected by an atrium. We felt that this multi-purpose atrium reflected the values of transparency and communication. We believe this project to be compatible with the City's urban design concept for the whole river Main area. The Großmarkthalle itself is well preserved, both in terms of external visibility and its interior architectural articulation. (Papademos, 2004)

The design gave physical expression to the philosophy governing a new monetary regime; crucially, it sought to symbolise how the communicative practices like those operating within these institutions could be transformed into a public discourse mediated by transparency (Garsten and Lindh de Montoya 2008: 79–96; Grossman et al. 2008: 97–116).

In the case of the ECB, however, the monetary regime had far broader significance and far more radical aspirations. The text drafted by the winning firm that accompanied its architectural plan makes explicit that it aspired to create a dramatic cultural statement.

> Starting from a research base of urban sightlines and cones of vision, we proposed a polygonal-shaped double slab tower in the east–west orientation. The narrow side of the tower profile is a solitary figure seen from all of downtown Frankfurt's major viewpoints ... Its form and presence becomes an unmistakable fixture on the Frankfurt skyline ... By reinforcing the dynamic internal communication culture of the ECB the solution will create an unprecedented symbol in the urban context, representing the public dimension of the ECB within Europe and the world.[1]

In the city museum where the three finalists' scale architectural models were moved after their initial presentation and display across the Main at the architectural museum, I had a chance to closely examine these efforts to materialise ECB values.

I found the winning design arresting. Each of the main towers of the Coop Himmelb(l)au design had a distinctive translucence that addressed the key design brief of ECB: the transparency that is to be emblematic of the new European order. At the same time, each tower is anchored or otherwise linked to the dramatically renovated Großmarkthalle, symbol of the old economy of trade and commerce. The glass towers were, to my architecturally naive eyes, most captivating. Unlike the modernist skyscraper in which the structural elements are exposed, these towers seemed to be suspended by an invisible hand, as it were, their load-bearing elements obscured.[2]

Why all this glass? The translucent design is intended to symbolise the free movement of ideas and information countering (the historically correct) suspicion that central banks are resolutely secretive. It invites scrutiny, acknowledging that monetary policy operates in the world, in collaboration with markets and the public, and that communications mediate this collaborative operation. For all its translucence, the transparency signalled by the building is more than merely ephemeral; it forms a significant load-bearing element of an intellectual regime, a constellation of values, ideals and practices encompassing a *Kultur*. The architecture of the new ECB headquarters conveys an insistence that the soundness of the euro must be conceptualised and managed across a vast communicative field within which confidence is continually shaped and modelled as a public discourse. The euro was designed from the outset as a public currency with emphatic communicative features.

In my work with George Marcus we have sought to develop ethnographic strategies for examining the operation of complex technocratic institutions allowing us to explore two questions: (1) How are organisational designs derived from systems of ideas, from experiments driven by theory? (2) How are research functions assimilated within these technocratic realms to inform and to refine their organisational dynamics? Linking both of these questions is the concept of 'performativity': a concept that is decisive for a theoretically informed organisational anthropology (Callon 2007; Holmes 2009; Holmes and Marcus 2005).

In the middle of the last century there was a faith or hope that the social and behavioural studies – notably economics – might become predictive sciences. My claim is that, from the vantage point of the early decades of this new century, economic theories have been most consequential as a performative apparatus shaping institutions and economic thinking rather than underwriting a predictive science. J. M. Keynes (1971 [1923], 2007 [1936]), the philosopher of language John L. Austin (1961), and the social theorist Jürgen Habermas (1987, 1991) established the intellectual foundations of a performative economics in which data and representations of data have currency. In the brief, paradigmatic example that follows I examine how a series of monetary experiments pursued by Deutsche Bundesbank *in vivo* formalised an organisational ethos for central banking based on a '*Kultur* of inflation fighting'.

In what follows I examine how the Bundesbank's experiments not only imparted the constitutional principles for the creation of the ECB, but also established an organisation model for the operation of central banks globally (Bernanke and Woodford 2005; Bernanke et al. 1999). At the heart of these performative experiments – known narrowly and rather prosaically as 'inflation targeting' – is a radical premise: the public broadly must be recruited to collaborate with central banks in achieving the ends of monetary policy: 'stable prices and confidence in the currency'. In other words, the economists and technocratic officialdom of the Bundesbank (and small group of outside academic observers) orchestrated organisational experiments that endowed the Germany monetary system with a new communicative architecture and dynamic. My task has been to align my ethnographic inquiry with *their* organisational anthropology to demonstrate how *they* addressed and, to some degree resolved, deep and abiding questions of contemporary culture and political economy (Callon 1998, 2007; Holmes and Marcus 2008; Latour 2005; Riles 2011). This is the essence of what Marcus and I have termed 'para-ethnography', that is, the multiple genres of collaboration by which we draw on the intellectual acumen of our subjects, assimilating their critical insights and their interpretive analyses. The account that follows is, thus, an example of what we have advocated, an exploration of the intellectual strategies that constitute ethnographic practice in and of our time (Holmes and Marcus 2005, 2006, 2012).

MONEY TARGETS

It is only a slight exaggeration to say that the reason for all this glass, all this signalling of transparency, can be traced back to information contained in a technical publication of the other great institution in Frankfurt, the Deutsche Bundesbank. Broached for the first time in the bank's publication of 5 December 1974 is a target for the growth of money – 8 per cent – for the following year: a target that would serve as the bank's nominal anchor (Issing 1997). Articulating this single number publicly was meant to exert leverage on the development of prices in Germany in the face of the eclipsing of the last vestiges of the Bretton Woods agreement in March 1973 and the destabilising oil shocks in the early 1970s.

A little over a year after the end of the global monetary regime of fixed exchange rates pegged to gold and to the dollar, the Bundesbank sought to tether expectations about the value of the Deutsche Mark to a publicly announced target for the growth of money. In an era after the collapse of the tightly defined monetary rules of the post-Second World War era, the bank began experimenting with communicative strategies informed by theory – an updating of the 'quantity theory of money' – and continually modified in relation to the flow of economic and monetary research. By virtue of this experimentation in discretionary monetary policy the bank began enlisting the public as active participants in its *Kultur* of inflation fighting and, thereby, the Deutsche Mark began to attain distinctive communicative characteristics. The Bundesbank not only worked out what were to become the key features of a monetary regime, it also began to experiment fully with the performative nature of economic ideas and theory (MacKenzie 2006; MacKenzie et al. 2006; Miyazaki and Riles 2005; Muniesa and Callon 2007).

Money had acquired in the 1970s a nature that was initially difficult to discern let alone manage. The Bretton Woods rules had allowed for very limited discretion in the exercise of monetary policy.

Monetary coordination in Bretton Woods system centered on the construction of a new fixed exchange rate regime. In consultation with the IMF, member states agreed to set the value of their currencies at predetermined rates and promised to keep their currencies trading in international markets with a band of 2 percent (thus plus or minus 1 percent of the predetermined central rate) at all times. In practice, their dislike of exchange rate variability led the European countries to stay with a smaller margin of three-fourths of 1 percent (.75%) on either side of the dollar. Though not originally designed to do so, the Bretton Wood system soon evolved into a fixed exchanged rate system pegged to the dollar, which in turn pegged to gold at the fixed rate of $35 an ounce. (McNamara 1998: 74)

Central banks had to find new means to exercise their responsibility for managing the value of money without the monetary rules provided by the Bretton Woods system. The efforts largely failed; inflation became chronic. There were, however, a few important exceptions, notably the Bundesbank and the Swiss National Bank, which found a means to successfully impart soundness to money over extended periods of time (Beyer et al. forthcoming).

The 1957 design of the Bundesbank Act, particularly Article 3, mandated the 'safeguarding of the currency', and thus the achievement of price stability, as the overriding priority of monetary policy. The episodes of hyperinflation in the 1920s – incited by reckless, indeed, staggering increases in the printing of money – that had rent asunder the German social fabric and political order, opening the way for the destructive enthusiasms of National Socialism, established the exigencies of monetary policy. An inflation rate averaging 322 per cent per month over a 15-month period from August 1922 to November 1923 fuelled by an increase of currency in circulation by a factor of 7.32×10^9 provided an emphatic counter model (Salemi 2008).

Fighting inflation was thus not merely a technical matter of avoiding 'suboptimal economic performance', but a profound societal preoccupation that was key to the reconstruction of the German Federal Republic. The leadership of the Bundesbank knew that they could invoke the memory of a searing history to recruit the German people in their inflation-fighting campaign. They also embraced a theory, monetarism, to provide not only an intellectual framework for research and policy formulation, but also as a macroeconomic allegory that could render the relationship between monetary policy and prices plausible and coherent to the citizens of Germany. Making the economy 'speak', as it were, was the key step in the creation of this currency regime, but also instrumental for German people as a collectivity with a decisive historical experience (Blinder et al. 2001).

The Bundesbank thus began to experiment in the 1970s with a new framework by which it announced very specific goals for monetary policy and explicit outcomes for these interventions. By so doing the bank created a system of accountability, aligning its actions directly with public interests in a manner that was overt and transparent. Each year the banks' performance was exposed: did Bundesbank policies successfully control prices and thus retain the soundness of the Deutsche mark? A single measure of consumer prices, the German all-item consumer price index – itself an important innovation in the creation of a public currency – served as a standard for all to see (Shore and Wright 2000).

The bank's institutional independence demanded a new, 'non-political' basis of accountability and the 'scientific principles' of macroeconomics and monetary theory fulfilled this role. Data were the new idioms of credibility predicating the monetary regime on a deep analytic question: do broad measures of the supply of money contain information on the evolution of prices in the future? As we will see, the relevance of this question for macroeconomic adjustments shifted over time and became increasingly open to doubt.

What I argue below is that by working out the conceptual imperatives of the *Kultur* of inflation fighting, the Bundesbank endowed the Germany economy with a new communicative architecture and dynamic. This *Kultur* was not merely a compendium of affective predispositions modelled from a vexed historical experience, but rather a series of institutional innovations that reconfigured the nature of monetary policy in the last quarter of the twentieth century.

SYMBOLIC CAPITAL

The leadership of the Bundesbank, the Direktorium, had determined that in order to confer a stable value to the German currency, an evolving story about the present and the near future, rendered credible to the public by virtue of the artful and consistent communication of the central bank's officialdom, was needed. Soundness came to be mediated by an explicit anchoring of Bundesbank policy in a macroeconomic allegory focused on a broad measure of money, Central Bank Money (CBM), and its influence on changes in prices. Protagonists within the Bundesbank began to interpret systematically the nature of prices as a function of central bank communication. They knew that an intellectual regime was needed to legitimise these communications and thus to influence the evolution of expectations (Knorr Cetina 1999).

There was a particular reason for the Bundesbank to embrace monetarism in the early 1970s. The authority of Keynesian monetary and fiscal activism was in doubt, the inverse relationship between unemployment and inflation – known as the Phillips curve – had faltered (Lucas 1976). The apparent policy trade-off – 'less unemployment at the cost of finite boost in inflation' – was undercut by the experiences of the 1960s, in which inflation and unemployment appeared to develop simultaneously (Tobin 1999–2010). The Keynesian framework had offered policy-makers the promise that permanent levels of lower unemployment could be achieved by accepting a higher rate of inflation and vice versa. The outcomes of these activist policies in the 1960s and 1970s were dismal; not only did they fail to deliver their promised benefits, 'they helped to generate the inflationary pressures that could be subdued only at high economic costs' (Bernanke et al. 1999: 11; Bordo and Orphanides forthcoming; Orphanides 2002). These costs were manifest in the deep recessions and attendant unemployment of 1973–1974 and 1981–1982.

Milton Friedman (1968) provided an alternative analysis that appeared to explain these new circumstances and a policy regime to respond to them.

> Friedman convinced the economics profession in 1968 that if monetary policy persistently attempts to bring unemployment below 'the natural rate of unemployment' (the rate corresponding to Keynes's 'full employment'), it will only boost the inflation rate explosively. Friedman's further conclusion that monetary policy should never concern itself with unemployment, production, or other real variables has been very influential. (Tobin 1999–2010)

Friedman made another important assertion about the nature of monetary policy, notably that its effects on the real economy:

> set in only with lags that are both long and variable (that is, varying from episode to episode in essentially unpredictable ways). Consequently, Friedman argued that monetary policy, though powerful, is not a tool that can be used with precision. (Bernanke et al. 1999: 12)

Robert Lucas Jr (1986, 1995) further refined this critique by focusing on the role of expectations in limiting or excluding the possibility of activist monetary policy. The Lucas critique can be stated in terms of a metaphorical shift:

> [T]here is an important difference between rockets and the people who make up an economy, which is that people try to understand and predict the actions of their 'controllers' (the policy-makers), while rockets do not. More specifically, Lucas showed that the optimal control methods may be useless for guiding policy if they do not take into account the possibility that the public's expectations about the future will change when policies change. The public's expectations about the future, including expectations about future policy actions, are important because they affect current economic behavior. Consequently, Lucas argued, policy-making takes on elements of a strategic game between the policy-makers and the public. Analyzing such a game is a considerably more difficult problem than guiding a rocket. (Bernanke et al. 1999: 12)

Lucas, by introducing reflexive subjects who could assimilate the same models as policy-makers and thus anticipate their intervention, appeared to make control of the economy with any degree of precision perilous (Soros 1994, 2008).

Another source of uncertainty identified by Friedman was the:

> tendency of the public and politicians in modern democracies to take a myopic view of public policy issues. Given the pressures of frequent elections and the almost instantaneous reporting of poll results, it is difficult for politicians to appreciate that watchful waiting is sometimes the best policy. (Bernanke et al. 1999: 13)

Policy discretion – in this case the latitude to over-manipulate monetary policy – exercised by politically exposed central bankers would, in Friedman's view, inevitably undermine the credibility necessary for sustainable and consistent management of money and credit and thereby the control of prices.

These shifts in economic theory defined the *mise-en-scène* across which inflation targeting unfolded as an anthropological experiment in which culture served as the contextualising framework within which information was created and exchanged and, more broadly, the means by which the economy attained features that could sustain individual and collective action.

PRAGMATIC MONETARISM

The load-bearing elements of the Bundesbank monetary framework, forged as technical issues in macroeconomic theory, were translated into a series of pragmatic institutional imperatives that animated the bank's *Kultur* of inflation fighting. The framework depended on a public recruited to the task of anchoring the value of money, but a public that could also serve as an intellectual foil compelling officialdom at the bank to think through deep questions in monetary economics. Crucially, these deliberations allowed abstract, theoretical matters to re-emerge as a substantive basis of collaboration with various segments and strata of German society. In thinking through its relationship to the public, the bank's leadership refined and focused its internal practices of research and policy formulation for the purposes of creating a communicative field, a field within which the bank's narratives could circulate and thus influence expectations.

Supporting the simple articulation of a numerical target for the growth of money for the coming year was an active pedagogy. Technical issues in economics and monetary theory were re-crafted to speak directly to the German people. Initially these communications were directed to only a very tiny group of experts in business and finance, but increasingly these pedagogic narratives sought or acquired a broader audience. The Bundesbank tactfully revealed the data and analysis informing the bank's decision-making retroactively. Acute attention to the rhetorical nature of policy in shaping expectations was a central preoccupation, imparting an educative dynamic to monetary policy and to the symbolic economy of the Deutsche mark (Brenneis 1999). If, as Lucas suggested, the public can learn to anticipate policy moves, then central banks can respond by establishing a pedagogic framework that conveys not just information but a shared formula for interpreting monetary policy over time. Persuasion was built into the regime. What were the lessons that the bank sought to convey?

The central dictum of this pedagogy was reducible, in the first instance, to Milton Friedman's famous assertion that 'inflation is always and everywhere a monetary phenomenon in the sense that it is and can be produced only by a more rapid increase in the quantity of money than output' (1970: 85). In this model the growth of money and credit are the overriding issues for understanding inflationary forces at play in the economy. Since central banks can influence these monetary conditions their policies must be constrained by rules in order to control the evolution of prices.

> Strictly defined, the use of a money growth target means that the central bank not only treats all unexpected fluctuations in money as informative … but also, as a quantitative matter, changes the interest rate or reserves in such a way as to offset these unexpected fluctuations altogether … and thereby restore money growth to the originally designated target rate. (Friedman 1998: 5–6)

The Bundesbank used a measure of money that captured these dynamics in a very simple numerical form. 'The quantity equation states that the sum of real output growth and the inflation rate is equal to the sum of money growth and the change in (appropriately defined) velocity' (Bernanke et al. 1999: 57–58). The Bundesbank thus:

derives the target growth rate of the change of monetary aggregate ... by estimating the growth of the long-run production potential over the coming year, adding the rate of price change it considers unavoidable ... and subtracting the estimated change in trend velocity over the year. (Bernanke et al. 1999: 57–58)

An explicit target for money growth was derived that would support long-term economic expansion consistent with what were deemed acceptable increases in prices. By holding to this target through the management of short-term interest rates, the central bank insured, according to this model, the soundness of money.

This approach allows the Bundesbank to claim that it is not making any choice about the business cycle when it sets policy. It also de-emphasizes any public discussion of its forecasting efforts for the real economy, further distancing monetary policy from the conversations of expected fluctuations in output and employment. Thus the quantity approach serves to take certain items off the monetary policy agenda ... by limiting the list of central bank responsibilities. (Bernanke et al. 1999: 58)

In other words, the strategy radically delimited the focus of policy interventions, at least in terms of how it was revealed publicly.

The Bundesbank made its projections of prices prior to the formulation of its money supply target in the last quarter of each year. A rate of growth of the German all-item consumer prices index was calculated and plugged into the quantity equation to derive its targets for money creation for the following year. This target made it clear that controlling the supply of money was pursued in the interest of price stability consistent with the growth potential of the German economy in the medium term. By the mid 1980s the bank had shifted its projection of 'unavoidable' inflation to 'a medium term prices assumption of 2%' (Bundesbank 1995c: 80–81 quoted in Bernanke et al. 1999: 58). Inflation was thus designed into the monetary system, consistent with the growth potential of the German economy. The 2 per cent figure was arrived at in part to compensate for the tendency of the consumer price index to overstate inflation by underestimating increases in the quality of goods.

The targeting of money growth is, in fact, difficult and the Bundesbank modified its regime to account for these difficulties. Most notably, it shifted the measure of money it was targeting (from CBM to M3) as well as shifting from a fixed target to a target range (plus or minus 1 or 1.5 per cent) for money growth. There were also actual deviations from targets, significant deviations, during the German re-unification in 1991 that the bank carefully explained and justified. What the Bundesbank achieved over time was 'confidence that it can explain target deviations and re-definitions to the public [which] is reflected in the design [of] its reporting mechanisms' (Bernanke et al. 1999: 60). It is not mere explanation of the information transmitted to the public, but, again, a matter of active pedagogy designed into the monetary regime by which the Bundesbank gained the confidence of the German people. An intellectual regime thus came to legitimise the bank's statutory independence and research underwrote its credibility.

Confidence and credibility were also cultivated through networks of key figures in business, government, trade unions and the news media, with whom wage- and price-setting information, and economic data more generally, were continually exchanged. Vigorous rounds of speech making by senior officials of the bank, the regular publication of technical reports and data series, and the scrupulous attention paid to the bank's institutional independence and its constitutional accountabilities further enhanced this credibility. At every turn the bank's leadership formulated policies attuned to the political situations in Germany and in Europe. These officials did not hesitate in correcting any 'mis-understandings' of the bank's positions among political, business and labour leaders, nor were they shy about expressing their displeasure and rancour in very personal terms to participants involved in wage- and price-setting negotiations or to political leaders involved in determining German budgetary, regulatory and taxation policies if their actions threatened the soundness of the German currency.

Let me be clear, the Bundesbank was by no means perfect. It was capable of misjudgement, miscalculation, lack of candour and various policy infelicities. The bank's experiment in transparency was, by current standards, far from optimal (Nergiz and Eichengreen 2009). The Bundesbank did not publish forecasts nor did it publish any substantive accounts of its policy discussions. It was not forthcoming about the range of data and analytical models it employed in its policy deliberations. Indeed, we know now that the Bundesbank was employing more comprehensive analytical agendas than would be required solely for the care and feeding of the quantity equation. The bank was scrutinising rigorously just about every data series, every statistical report relevant to the performance of the German economy and carefully considering every alternative outcome of its policies and practices.

> Monetary targets were never the actual target of or even sole guide to policy ... the announced monetary targets were never slavishly followed in the sense of being an actual intermediate target variable in Germany. It is well-known that annual target ranges were missed around fifty percent of the time in Germany in the 1980s and 1990s. Far more significantly, the Bundesbank has, by its own account and as seen in the historical record, taken into account a much broader range of information than just money when setting policy. When inflation and monetary forecasts have diverged, the Bundesbank has responded to the former. Moreover, the Bundesbank has responded to a number of short-run shocks and challenges even when they have not directly affected inflation or money. (Posen 1997)

The bank further modified its framework as academic faith in monetarism for guiding macroeconomic adjustments was eclipsed: 'money plays no explicit role in today's consensus macro model and it plays virtually no role in the conduct of monetary policy' (King 2002: 162).

Otmar Issing, former board member of the Bundesbank and founding member of the executive board of the ECB, described how the aims of monetary analysis shifted as the latter institution assimilated them. Measures of money thus served as a basis for cross-checking analysis rather than as a meaningful standard in its own right. 'Real-time extraction of signals of medium-term inflationary or deflationary pressures from monetary developments' served as the means for overcoming the 'limited reliability of other indicators, such as the output gap, and the unavoidable limitations of economic analyses, such as macroeconomic projections'.[3]

COLLABORATIVE SYSTEM

Over four decades the bank built a *Kultur* that represented far more than a mechanism for setting targets for the growth of money and credit. Managing inflation and thus insuring the soundness of the Deutsche mark was achieved by means of a communicative system for endowing the future with discernible features. The Bundesbank created a framework for managing expectations by aligning its actions directly with public interests in a manner that was overt, if not entirely transparent. The load-bearing elements of the Bundesbank monetary framework depended, not solely (or necessarily) on a quantity equation, but on macroeconomic allegories by which the public was recruited to the task of anchoring the value of money. The careful parsing of abstract, theoretical matters in monetary economics in a manner that was coherent and plausible to the German public served as a basis of an institutional collaboration that drew on and shaped distinctive cultural sentiments. Again, what was framed as an experiment in monetary policy was, in fact, a far broader historical and anthropological experiment implicating German society in its entirety (Herzfeld 1993, 2004). Notably, the Direktorium of the bank was fully aware of the audacious scope of its endeavour: they understood that they were imparting novel communicative features to the Deutsche mark. They understood that confidence is always and everywhere mediated by culture, a culture that made the near- and medium-term future plausible for the German public (Abolafia 1998). How did this work?

DEMIURGE

Inflation fighting anchored cognitive balance sheets for individuals and households, for family owner-managers of the *Mittelstand*, for executives of large industrial manufacturers, for labour unions, for small exporters as well as for technocrats planning public expenditures and so on. Expectations about the development of prices became manifest in real plans for budgets, for investment, for stocking inventories, for expanding or contracting employment and, above all, for negotiating wages, for setting prices, for computing various commercial interest rates. The willingness of the German people to act in relationship to their expectations ratified and stabilised the future, conferring on it basic contours, if not precise characteristics. Faith – albeit contingent, informed by data and contextualised within econometric allegories – allowed for planning and allowed for the diverse expectations of every segment of German society, of every individual to yield action. The acumen of the bank's officialdom – notably figures like Hans Tietmeyer former President of the Bundesbank 1993–1999 – shaped and modelled the economy linguistically in a manner that could align the bank's agenda with the plans and the expectations of the public. Economic reality was made and tested continually by shocks and uncertainty – not least of which those attendant on Germany's re-unification – and relentlessly revised in concert with the German people.

The *Kultur* of inflation targeting anchored a vast communicative field in which the economy undergoes incessant analytical scrutiny and linguistic modelling by countless actors ratifying what monetary policy operates in the world, in collaboration with markets and the public, and that transparency sustains this collaborative regime (Holmes 2009). By means of subtle cultural intermediations, sentiments and expectations became overt bases for planning and for action. The gradual accretion of this experiment established the Bundesbank's symbolic capital, its store of confidence, but it also provided an emphatic example of how to design a European Central Bank (Scheller 2004).

ECB HABITUS

From the earliest negotiations on the ECB's institutional design, the incorporation of Bundesbank's *Kultur* was central to underwriting the credibility of the new institution and the new currency it was designed to manage, the euro (Trichet 2005). Transferring the Bundesbank's credibility to the ECB was the key for the new project. Within the first decade of its operation the ECB had gone considerably further than merely announcing targets for money growth; indeed, with a few notable exceptions, virtually every aspect of the introduction of the euro and the operation of the new central bank was conceptualised as operating within a vast communicative field. The ECB tries to be explicit about what it means by the term:

Transparency means that the central bank provides the general public and the markets with all relevant information on its strategy, assessments and policy decisions as well as its procedures in an open, clear and timely manner.

Today, most central banks, including the ECB, consider transparency as crucial. This is true especially for their monetary policy framework. The ECB gives a high priority to communicating effectively with the public ...

Transparency helps the public to understand the ECB's monetary policy. Better public understanding makes the policy more credible and effective. Transparency means that the ECB explains how it interprets its mandate and that it is forthcoming about its policy goals.[4]

Again, by communicating its goals in a transparent and consistent fashion, central banks seek to continually shape market expectations in advance of the need to take those disruptive and often painful actions attendant upon the conventional exercise of monetary policy. The cultural challenge of operating in the near future is, at least in theory, resolved through monetary policy that focuses on the management of expectations.

> The ECB publicly announces its monetary policy strategy and communicates its regular assessment of economic developments. This helps the markets to understand the systematic response pattern of monetary policy to economic developments and shocks. It makes policy moves more predictable for the markets over the medium term. Market expectations can thus be formed more efficiently and accurately. If market agents can broadly anticipate policy responses, this allows a rapid implementation of changes in monetary policy into financial variables. This in turn can shorten the process by which monetary policy is transmitted into investment and consumption decisions. It can accelerate any necessary economic adjustments and potentially enhance the effectiveness of monetary policy.[5]

Transparency is not merely about candour, openness or, more generally, democratic accountabilities, it is instrumental in defining future-oriented behaviour (Strathern 2000).

The basic argument of this chapter is that a distinctive kind of knowledge is being 'created' in or mediated by central banks, knowledge that exceeds what is typically understood as 'economic'. The architecture of the new ECB headquarters conveys an insistence that the soundness of the euro must be conceptualised and managed across a communicative field within which confidence is continually shaped and modelled as a public discourse. Again, the euro was designed from the outset as a public currency with emphatic communicative features. The staggering fiscal crises that emerged in Europe in early 2010 demonstrated, ironically, how radical these features are (Connolly 1995).

DISSONANT EXPERIMENTS

Issues of public debt, fiscal policy, financial stability, economic restructuring and their relationship to the euro were exposed and they became part of an expansive political debate across Europe, most excruciatingly in Greece, Ireland and Portugal. The crisis imposed a new, dissonant dynamic on the euro. The technical workings of the euro were linked openly to the operation of public and private finance, which in turn became aligned with the predicaments – the intimate predicaments – of European citizens (Herzfeld 2004). Assumptions regarding employment, social welfare and taxation were disrupted and the features of a discernible future obscured, if not, erased.

The conduct of public finance by a number of member states and the oversight capabilities of EU institutions were thoroughly discredited by the crisis, imperilling not merely a European financial order, but, far more importantly, a constitutional order (Issing 2011; Schäuble 2011). Threatening the European project is, ironically, the possibility that the euro will attain a status as a fully public currency, un-tethered from the narrative management of technocrats and animated by rancorous political dynamics that obscure the future and undercut faith and credit (Comaroff and Comaroff 2003; Garsten and Lindh de Montoya 2008: 283–289). To the extent that the historical struggles of our time are technocratic in nature, not only is an organisational anthropology vital, it is – as I have argued above – fully implicated in those struggles (Marcus 2008; Riles 2011).

NOTES

1. See: http://www.ecb.int/ecb/premises/html/coop-concept.en.html (accessed 12 July 2009).
2. See: http://www.ecb.int/ecb/premises/construction/html/index.en.html; http://www.coop-himmelblau.at/site/.
3. See: Issing 2005: www.ecb.int/int/press/key/date/2005/ html/sp050603.en.html (accessed 12 June 2005).
4. See: http://www.ecb.int/ecb/orga/transparency/html/index.en.html (accessed 12 July 2009).
5. See: http://www.ecb.int/ecb/orga/transparency/html/index.en.html (accessed 12 July 2009).

REFERENCES

Abolafia, M. Y. (1998) 'Markets as cultures', in M. Callon, ed., *The Laws of the Markets* (Oxford: Blackwell).

Austin, J. L. (1961) *Philosophical Papers*, edited by J. O. Urmson and G. J. Warnock (Oxford: Oxford University Press).

Bernanke, B. and M. Woodford, eds (2005) *The Inflation-targeting Debate* (Chicago, IL: University of Chicago Press).

Bernanke, B., T. Luabach, S. F. Mishkin and S. A. Posen (1999) *Inflation Targeting: Lessons from the International Experience* (Princeton, NJ: Princeton University Press).

Beyer, A., V. Gaspar, C. Gerberding and O. Issing (forthcoming) 'Opting out of the great inflation: German monetary policy after the break down of Bretton Woods', in M. Bordo and A. Orphanides, eds, *The Great Inflation* (Chicago, IL: University of Chicago Press).

Blinder, A., C. Goodhart, P. Hidebrand, D. Lipton and C. Wyplosz (2001) *How Do Central Banks Talk?* Geneva Report on the World Economy No. 3 (Geneva: International Center for Monetary and Banking Studies).

Bordo, M. D. and A. Orphanides, eds (forthcoming) *The Great Inflation* (Chicago, IL: University of Chicago Press).

Brenneis, D. (1999) 'New lexicon, old language: Negotiating the "global" at the National Science Foundation', in G. E. Marcus, ed., *Critical Anthropology Now: Unexpected Contexts, Shifting Constituencies, Changing Agendas* (Santa Fe, TX: School of American Research Press).

Callon, M. (1998) 'An essay on framing and overflowing: Economic externalities revisited by sociology', in M. Callon, ed., *The Laws of the Markets* (Oxford: Blackwell).

—— (2007) 'Performative economics', in D. MacKenzie, F. Muniesa and L. Siu, eds, *Do Economists Make Markets?* (Princeton, NJ: Princeton University Press).

Comaroff, J. and J. Comaroff (2003) 'Transparent fictions or, conspiracies of a liberal imagination: An afterword', in H. G. West and T. Sanders, eds, *Transparency and Conspiracy: Ethnographies of Suspicion in the New World Order* (Durham, NC: Duke University Press).

Connolly, B. (1995) *The Rotten Heart of Europe: The Dirty War for Europe's Money* (London: Faber and Faber).

Friedman, B. (1998) *The Rise and Fall of Money Growth Targets as Guidelines for U.S. Monetary Policy*. NBER Working Paper No. 5465 (Cambridge, MA: National Bureau of Economic Research).

Friedman, M. (1968) 'The role of monetary policy', *American Economic Review*, Vol. 58, No. 1, pp. 1–17.

—— (1970) *The Counter-revolution in Monetary Theory*. Institute of Economic Affairs, *Occasional Paper 33* (London: Institute of Economic Affairs).

Garsten, C. and M. Lindh de Montoya (2008) 'Introduction: Examining the politics of transparency', in C. Garsten and M. Lindh de Montoya, eds, *Transparency in a New Global Order: Unveiling Organizational Visions* (Cheltenham: Edward Elgar).

Grossman, E., E. Luque and F. Muniesa (2008) 'Economies through transparency', in C. Garsten and M. Lindh de Montoya, eds, *Transparency in a New Global Order: Unveiling Organizational Visions* (Cheltenham: Edward Elgar).

Habermas, J. (1987) *The Theory of Communicative Action*, Volume 1: *Reason and the Rationalization of Society*; Volume Two: *Lifeworld and System: A Critique of Functionalist Reason*, trans. T. McCarthy (Boston, MA: Beacon).

—— (1991) *The Structural Transformation of the Public Sphere: An Inquiry into a Category of Bourgeois Society*, trans. T. Burger (Cambridge, MA: MIT Press).

Herzfeld, M. (1993) *The Social Production of Indifference: Exploring the Symbolic Roots of European Bureaucracy* (Chicago, IL: University of Chicago Press).

—— (2004) *Cultural Intimacy: Social Poetics in the Nation-state* (London: Routledge).

Holmes, R. D. (2009) 'Economy of words', *Cultural Anthropology*, Vol. 24, No. 3, pp. 381–419.

Holmes, D. and G. Marcus (2005) 'Cultures of expertise and the management of globalization: Toward the re-functioning of ethnography', in A. Ong and S. Collier, eds, *Global Assemblages* (Oxford: Blackwell).

—— (2006) 'Fast capitalism: Para-ethnography and the rise of the symbolic analyst', in M. Fisher and G. Downey, eds, *Frontiers of Capital: Ethnographic Perspectives on the New Economy* (Durham, NC: Duke University Press).

—— (2008) 'Collaboration today and the re-imagination of the classic scene of fieldwork encounter', *Collaborative Anthropologies*, Vol. 1, pp. 136–170.

—— (2012) 'Collaborative imperatives: A manifesto, of sorts, for the re-imagination of the classic scene of fieldwork encounter', in M. Konrad, ed., *Collaborators Collaborating: Counterparts in Anthropological Knowledge and International Research Relations* (Oxford: Berghahn).

Issing, O. (1997) 'Monetary targeting in Germany: The stability of monetary policy and the monetary system', *Journal of Monetary Economics*, Vol. 39, No. 1, pp. 67–79.

—— (2011) 'Slithering to the wrong kind of union', *Financial Times*, 8 August, http://www.ft.com/intl/cms/s/0/c4159b34-c1a8-11e0-acb3-00144feabdc0.html#axzz1UUUNwEPr (accessed 3 October 2011).

Keynes, J. (1971 [1923]) *A Tract on Monetary Reform*, Volume 4: *The Collected Writings of John Maynard Keynes*, edited by D. Moggridge (Cambridge: Cambridge University Press).

—— (2007 [1936]) *The General Theory of Employment, Interest and Money* (Basingstoke: Palgrave).

King, M. (2002) 'No money, no inflation – The role of money in the economy', *Bank of England Quarterly Bulletin*, summer, pp. 162–177.

Knorr Cetina, K. (1999) *Epistemic Cultures: How the Sciences Make Knowledge* (Cambridge, MA: Harvard University Press).

Latour, B. (2005) *Reassembling the Social: An Introduction to Actor-Network Theory* (Oxford: Oxford University Press).

Lucas, R. Jr. (1976)'Econometric policy evaluation: A critique', in K. Brunner and A. Meltzer, eds, *The Phillips Curve and Labor Markets, Carnegie-Rochester Conference Series on Public Policy* (New York, NY: American Elsevier).

—— (1986) 'Adaptive behavior and economic theory', *Journal of Business*, Vol. 59, No. 4, pp. 401–426.

—— (1995) 'Monetary neutrality [Nobel] prize lecture', *Economic Sciences*, 7 December, pp. 246–265.

MacKenzie, D. (2006) *An Engine, Not a Camera: How Financial Models Shape Markets* (Cambridge, MA: MIT Press).

MacKenzie, D., F. Muniesa and L. Siu (2006) 'Introduction', in D. MacKenzie, F. Muniesa and L. Siu, eds, *Do Economists Make Markets?* (Princeton, NJ: Princeton University Press).

Marcus, G. E. (2008) 'The end(s) of ethnography: Social/cultural anthropology's signature form of producing knowledge in transition', *Cultural Anthropology*, Vol. 23, No. 1, pp. 1–14.

McNamara, K. (1998) *The Currency of Ideas: Monetary Politics in the European Union* (Ithaca, NY: Cornell University Press).

Miyazaki, H. and A. Riles (2005) 'Failure as an endpoint', in A. Ong and S. Collier, eds, *Global Assemblages* (Oxford: Blackwell).

Muniesa, F. and M. Callon (2007) 'Economic experiments and the construction of markets', in D. MacKenzie, F. Muniesa and L. Siu, eds, *Do Economists Make Markets?* (Princeton, NJ: Princeton University Press).

Nergiz, D. and B. Eichengreen (2009) *Central Bank Transparency: Causes, Consequences and Update*. NBER Working Paper 14791 (Cambridge, MA: National Bureau of Economic Research).

Orphanides, A. (2002) 'Monetary-policy rules and the great inflation', *American Economic Review*, Vol. 92, No. 2, pp. 115–120.

Papademos, L. (2004) 'Introductory statement'. ECB, 20 February, http://www.ecb.int/press/key/date/2004/html/sp040220.en.html (accessed November 2012).

Posen, A. (1997) *Lessons from the Bundesbank on the Occasion of Its 40th (and Second to Last?) Birthday*. Working Paper 97-4, Peterson Institute for International Economics, http://www.iie.com/publications/wp/wp.cfm?ResearchID=153 (accessed 10 February 2012).

Riles, A. (2011) *Collateral Knowledge: Legal Reasoning in the Global Financial Markets* (Chicago, IL: University of Chicago Press).

Salemi, M. K. (2008) 'Hyperinflation', in Library of Economics and Liberty, Concise Encyclopedia of Economics, http://econlib.org/library/Enc/Hyperinflation.html (accessed 12 April 2010).

Schäuble, W. (2011) 'Why austerity is only cure for the eurozone', Financial Times.com, 5 September.

Scheller, H. (2004) *The European Central Bank: History, Role and Function* (Frankfurt am Main: European Central Bank).

Shore C. and S. Wright (2000) 'Coercive accountability: The rise of audit culture in higher education', in M. Strathern, ed., *Audit culture: Anthropological Studies in Accountability, Ethics and the Academy* (London: Routledge).

Soros, G. (1994) 'The theory of reflexivity', paper delivered to the MIT Department of Economics World Economy Laboratory Conference, Washington, DC, 26 April.

—— (2008) *The New Paradigm for Financial Markets: The Credit Crisis of 2008 and What It Means* (Philadelphia, PA: Public Affairs).

Strathern, M. (2000) *Audit Culture: Anthropological Studies in Accountability, Ethics and the Academy* (London: Routledge).

Tobin, J. (1999–2010) 'Monetary policy', in *The Concise Encyclopedia of Economics*, http://www.econlib.org /library/Enc/MonetaryPolicy.html (accessed 9 August 2008).

Trichet, J-C. (2005) 'Monetary policy strategies: A central bank panel', paper presented at the Federal Reserve Bank of Kansas City Symposium, Jackson Hole, Wyoming, 25–27 August.

14
Not being there
The power of strategic absence in organisational anthropology

Tara A. Schwegler

INTRODUCTION: RETROSPECTIVE ACCOUNTS

This chapter begins with a simple question: who has the right to speak authoritatively for organisations, in this case, the Mexican federal government? If, as scholars have noted, one of the defining features of modern bureaucracy is its ability to coordinate complex behaviour (Ahrne 1994), then an apt corollary is that it also synthesises the views of many into a single voice. Yet, as I interviewed Mexican government officials about the genesis and development of the New Law of Social Security, I encountered multiple, competing accounts. When I tried to reconcile these accounts through repeated interviews, I became a conduit for ongoing contestations between officials at the Ministry of Finance and the Mexican Social Security Institute, or IMSS – the two primary parties in the reform – over who had prevailed in the process, to the extent that my interlocutors would arm me with anecdotes and questions to pose to their colleagues. Though the reform had been adopted three years before, they continued their spirited exchange as if it were yesterday, an unmistakable clue that there was something more at stake in these accounts than I initially realised.

This chapter explores the methodological ramifications of these irreconcilable accounts for the anthropological study of organisations, as well as the unconventional method – 'strategic absence' – that led me to them in the first place. Because I was unable to directly observe the formal negotiations in which the details of the policy were hammered out between the Ministry of Finance and IMSS, I was forced to rely on retrospective accounts by officials involved. In this chapter, I reflect on how the inability to engage in direct observation may be productively deployed to generate multi-faceted data that adumbrates nuances of the political field that may otherwise remain submerged – a point that has profound ramifications for our understanding of the Mexican federal bureaucracy and the methods anthropologists use to study it. Direct observation is a trademark method of anthropology, and yet anthropologists almost instinctively understand that many social phenomena are not directly observable. My intent here is not to declare the primacy of absence or presence, but rather to draw attention to the countless permutations of absence and presence that may illuminate the social, political and economic processes in which anthropologists are most interested.

This chapter unpacks the retrospective accounts of government officials in the Ministry of Finance and IMSS in order to probe their broader theoretical and methodological implications. While the Mexican government exhibits many of the characteristics of a classic Weberian bureaucracy (1978 [1968]) – such as strict hierarchical relations, clearly defined roles and impersonal authority – it nevertheless contains idiosyncratic elements, the most conspicuous of which is a high rate of turnover. The officials who were directly involved in the New Law of Social Security were mid- and high-level government officials in the Ministry of Finance and IMSS, and the political profiles of these officials could not be more different: from 1992 to 2000, the Ministry of Finance was dominated by US-trained Mexican economists, or technocrats, distinguished from traditional bureaucrats by their educational credentials (Babb 2001; Centeno 1994). In contrast, IMSS was the stomping ground of career politicians with deep ties to the dominant party, the Party of the Institutional Revolution, or PRI. Although the Ministry of Finance was the most influential agency in the President's cabinet at the time, IMSS had accumulated political resources that the Ministry of Finance needed in order to broker support for the reform effort. Since the formal structure of the bureaucracy counterbalances the influence of the two agencies on the policy-making process, it cannot account for the persistence of the competing accounts. I contend that these accounts are not casual reflections, the detritus of political confrontations; rather, they are integral components of the political field that enable government officials to contest the formal structure of the organisation and thereby elevate their authority in future political negotiations. Indeed, one of the great contributions of anthropology to the study of organisations is the recognition that the informal structure of the organisation plays a critical role in the articulation of power relations (Britan and Cohen 1980; Wright 1994). Of course, this form of contestation cannot completely overcome gross imbalances of institutional power, but it can be mobilised to blunt their impact on policy negotiations. The analytical consequences of this phenomenon are twofold. First, it suggests that although the formal organisational structure establishes power relations within the government, there are significant grey areas in which power relations are uncertain or ambiguous, making them likely sites for contestation (Hoag 2011). Second, it shows that, in the Mexican case, bureaucracy paradoxically contains conflict by sustaining it, a perfect complement to the modus operandi of the Mexican political system in which groups are encouraged to allocate spoils rather than reach a definitive ideological consensus (González-Rossetti and Mogollon 2000; Randall 2006).

THE FLEXIBLE STABILITY OF MEXICAN FEDERAL GOVERNMENT

The Mexican federal government epitomises a strict hierarchical organisation, with rituals of subordination inscribed in the daily habits and physical movement of its occupants. In a country where more than half the population works in the informal sector, acquiring a government job, however menial, is viewed as a clear sign of success, and it is not unusual for low-level civil servants to carry business cards that attest to their position within the organisation. Not unlike Weber's ideal type of a rational bureaucracy, specific roles are clearly delineated, and the formal protocol frequently compromises the ability of the organisation to be agile and expedient (Herzfeld 1993). All organisations exert forms of control over their constituents and, in the Mexican bureaucracy, time is the instrument of choice. There is an unspoken rule that subordinates cannot go home for the evening until the individual to whom they report has left the office, a practice that has the effect of holding employees hostage while their bosses attend after-hours meetings that often run late into the night. I unwittingly abetted this practice when I met with officials at the end of the day and would leave their offices to see their entire staff sitting idle at their desks. Ostensibly, this ensures that staff will be available to support the official if a meeting results in urgent requests; however, in practice, it functions to assert the control of the organisation over the time of its employees.

Nevertheless, the informal character of the bureaucracy is just as important to the everyday functioning of organisation as the formal structure, if not more so (Britan and Cohen 1980; Heyman 2004). In Mexico, unique historical circumstances have conspired to produce an idiosyncratic blend of co-optation, patronage and power-sharing that characterises the informal structure of Mexico's federal government (Randall 2006). Unlike in Weber's description of the ideal type, in which skill and qualification determine access to mid- and upper-level positions in the bureaucracy, in the Mexican system, moving up depends on knowing the right people. In this arrangement, access to material resources is governed by patron–client relations orchestrated through political cliques called *camarillas* (Camp 2006; Centeno 1994). Dating back to the nineteenth century (and perhaps even earlier), *camarillas* unite individuals with common political interests under the leadership of a mentor who navigates through the bureaucracy and brings members of his *camarilla* with him as he moves through the ranks (Camp 1990). *Camarillas* provide essential job security in an atmosphere of frequent bureaucratic turnover: unwavering support for their mentor is the ticket to political mobility for *camarilla* members who cannot risk getting left behind when new appointments are made (Smith 1979).[1] In this way, *camarillas* lend an almost vertiginous feel to the formal structure of the Mexican bureaucracy, with vast swirls of people moving in tandem with their leader as his political fortunes rise and fall, resulting in de facto turnover that not only prevents the accumulation of political expertise, but also politicises even the most quotidian of government functions.

The corporatist structure of the PRI (the dominant political party from 1929 to 2000) and the principle of no re-election further augment the role of patron–client relations in the Mexican government. Although the Mexican Revolution officially ended in 1920, violence raged on as members of the competing revolutionary factions vied for primacy, culminating in the assassination of President-elect Álvaro Obregón in 1928. In a desperate bid to turn the corner on political strife, previous President Plutarco Elias Calles (1924–1928) established the PNR, or Party of the National Revolution, by incorporating the revolutionary factions under one umbrella, effectively institutionalising the conflict (Smith 1992). Thus, from its inception, the PNR (the name was changed to PRI in 1946 by President Lázaro Cardenás) was designed to contain dissenting views rather than reconcile them, a distinction that has had a profound impact on the political landscape in Mexico. In the Mexican context, the adage, 'You are either with us or against us' rings startlingly true. Over time, the PRI's preferred strategy has been to offer political or economic opportunities to potential rivals in order to ensure their compliance with the party's objectives, resulting in a distinctively 'pragmatic approach to policy decisions and analysis' (Randall 2006: 15). Through trial and error, opposition groups have learned that failing to accept the first offer can result in political marginalisation or, in some cases, repression.

The principle of no re-election has helped the PRI distribute power among the elite factions that comprise it and thereby preserve the long-term stability of Mexico's corporatist pact. Designed to prevent the accumulation of political power by a single individual, the principle of no re-election enshrined in the Mexican Constitution of 1917 applies to all elected officials and bars officials from seeking more than one elected term in office. In response to this limitation, the PRI has evolved an informal practice of power-sharing to staunch excessive competition among party factions (Smith 1992). Accordingly, the party gives each faction an opportunity to govern by rotating the presidential nomination among them (up until 2000, being named the PRI candidate was synonymous with winning the election). The price for participation is the tacit agreement not to contest the legitimacy of the PRI nominee once selected (Centeno 1994). Therefore, from an organisational perspective, the goal for bureaucrats within the system is to maximise their spoils when their patron is in office, a season of plenty that lasts for six glorious years and then comes to an abrupt end.

Once in office, the President wields wide-ranging discretionary authority that frequently circumvents the formal structure of the bureaucracy and lends a distinctly personalistic character to political life. The President not only sets the political agenda, he also determines the way in which political work is accomplished (Camp 2006). Upon assuming office, the President generally modifies the bureaucratic structure to signal his policy priorities and to designate the key players who will participate in the process, a practice that enables him to mould the political field to his advantage at the cost of substantial turnover and political expertise. While lower-level bureaucrats are less vulnerable to the vagaries of the political process, most mid- and high-level officials are either directly or indirectly affected by changes in political administration since the scope of the President's power to appoint extends deep into the mid-level of the federal bureaucracy. Historically, when the President has been unable to accomplish his political aims through the formal structure of the government, he has had the prerogative to sidestep it entirely and pursue political conciliation through informal pacts among political actors (Camp 2006). Taken together, the authority granted to the

President by formal decree and historical circumstance has yielded a federal bureaucracy that is both structurally robust and highly variable.

LEARNING MORE BY SEEING LESS

Much has been written about the ontology of 'being there' in anthropological field research (Geertz 1988; Hannerz 2003). It is a cruel reality indeed that, prior to the paradigm-shattering work of Bronislaw Malinowski in the early 1900s, many of the classics that now count as vestigial anthropology were based on research conducted *in absentia*. Despite the amount of field data contained in Emile Durkheim's *The Everyday Forms of Religious Life* (1995 [1912]), Durkheim belonged to the generation of the armchair ethnographer, who interpreted the data sent to him by his research assistants. Of course, *someone* was actually *there* in the field – just not Durkheim himself. But it is unfair to single out Durkheim for a practice that, at the time, was considered perfectly reasonable. If the data was understood to be raw fact, then it made no difference whether the analyst himself had actually collected it. And we should not forget that Malinowski's commitment to live among the primitives was not greeted with universal enthusiasm – there were quite a few who argued that being physically present made it more difficult for the anthropologist to maintain objectivity towards his informants. Perhaps the most powerful archetype of being there is Marcel Griaule's work with the Dogon. Griaule's field methods rested profoundly on the metaphor that 'seeing is believing', an epistemological construct with a long history in western scientific thought (Rorty 1979). Griaule stationed observers at strategic points throughout the field site in almost paramilitary fashion so that he could have line of sight to anything and everything that took place in the village (Kuper 2003). Despite the uncomfortable parallel to espionage, there is an inescapable allure to Griaule's work that continues to nourish the anthropological fantasy of omniscience.

The exigencies of contemporary anthropological investigation, however, have forced participant-observation to stretch to accommodate ever-evolving field contexts. As people and objects become increasingly mobile, anthropologists have followed suit, deftly manoeuvring through multiple field sites in an effort to understand social, political and economic phenomena that are highly elusive from a static point of view (Hannerz 2003; Tsing 2005). In the absence of a physically discrete field site, anthropologists of policy 'study through' the complex tangle of overlapping networks that radiate from a single policy, nimbly bouncing back and forth among various actors and 'actants' (Latour 2005) directly or indirectly involved in the process (Wright and Reinhold 2011; see also Gusterson 1997; Powell and Schwegler 2008; Wedel et al. 2005). This form of mobile inquiry enables the anthropologist to discern how specific ideas mobilise collective action across distinct constituencies and thereby attend to the contingencies and ideological slippages that fall through the cracks of less flexible methods (Schwegler 2008b; Shore et al. 2011). Participant-observation in a single government office would undoubtedly yield potent insights about organisational dynamics, but it would be ill-suited to explain the genesis and development of specific policies (Schwegler 2012). These emergent types of inquiry problematise the role of place as the defining locus of participant-observation, shifting the emphasis from geographically defined groups to specific phenomena (Gupta and Ferguson 1997). Rapid technological innovation further disrupts place-based participant-observation by dispensing with the notion of a discrete field site altogether. For a growing number of anthropologists, there may be no 'there' in which to set up shop because their informants are not physically contiguous in any meaningful way, such as participants in on-line communities (Boellstorff 2008; Kelty et al. 2009). This does not mean that place is irrelevant but, rather, that it is not the primary container of field research.

While contemporary anthropologists have grappled with how long and in what capacity they should be present in various locales, they have not systematically addressed the possibilities of strategic absence in field research. Unfortunately, the binary opposition between absence and presence embedded in the debate over 'being there' obscures the many permutations of long-term participant-observation and mobile inquiry that may facilitate eclectic and emergent field strategies (Kelty et al. 2009; Wedel et al. 2005). Presence has been the linchpin of anthropology for so long that it seems near anathema to question what it might obscure. Yet in my work with Mexican bureaucrats, I discovered that strategic absence interspersed with presence could be productively deployed to gather meta-discursive data that might otherwise escape the conventional gaze because its effect of the political field was perceptible only in hindsight. In my situation, presence and strategic absence were essential complements: It would have been difficult if not impossible to detect the references to previous engagements had I not been physically immersed in the field site to collect rich, contextual data. Similarly, I would not have been able to cultivate the necessary political connections to obtain the interviews in the first place had I attempted to conduct field research remotely. There is no magic formula or immutable rule to determine how and in what proportion presence and strategic absence should be combined; rather, my point here is to suggest that jiggling with some of the fundamental assumptions of the fieldwork encounter can yield new and provocative methodological strategies. In the next section, I detail how I arrived at the particular combination of presence and strategic absence described in this chapter.

SIMULATING PRESENCE THROUGH STRATEGIC ABSENCE

When I was an undergraduate economics major at the University of Chicago, I met several Mexican graduate students in economics who later assumed mid-level positions in the Mexican government after completing their PhDs. I thus had the good fortune to have a small group of key informants already ensconced in government prior to my arrival in the field. Fully cognisant of the difficulties of securing access to mid- and upper-level government officials (Conti and O'Neal 2007; Marshall 1984; Schwegler 2008b), I knew that my informants' connections would weigh heavily on my choice of a policy to study. Shortly after arriving in the field, it became clear that the New Law of Social Security fulfilled the two most important selection criteria: (1) it was the one to which I would have the most direct access by virtue of my informants' networks and (2) it exemplified the application of economic expertise to social welfare reform, an analytically auspicious combination. There was just one problem: the New Law had already been developed, meaning that I would not be able to directly observe the negotiation process.

I reasoned that the next best thing to being there would be to gather retrospective accounts of key meetings from their participants. After collecting all of the narratives, I would compare them to identify gaps and disjunctures and then conduct repeat interviews to reconcile inconsistencies and chart the discursive path of technical disagreements. By design, this approach was eminently physical – through the process of negotiating actual landscapes to obtain interpretations, I would be traversing the disagreements in physical space, spatially and temporally reproducing the dynamics of the discrete meetings. I planned to supplement the individual interviews with observations of participants' interaction at meetings on another topic so that I could become familiar with communicative styles and conventions (Schwartzman 1989). These observations would form the backdrop against which I would situate the retrospective accounts of the New Law of Social Security. The strategy was predicated on approximating presence, of finding a viable way to simulate the tone and texture of the meetings.

When I was collecting accounts, I assumed that they would be additive, in the sense that they would gradually build on one another until a complete picture of the meeting emerged. Yet the more accounts I collected, the murkier the meetings became. Not only did each participant seem to think that he had the upper hand, but, to make matters worse, they disagreed on what the critical issues were. It was only after I started noticing meta-pragmatic cues sprinkled in the accounts that I realised that my participants were actually re-creating the debates *through* me. They were not simply relating the past; they were talking to one another through me, continuing to jockey for the upper hand through their dialogic accounts (Schwegler 2008a). As Bakhtin (1982: 143–144) argues, utterances are freighted with the 'ossified remains' of previous utterances, with the implication that every utterance, however unwittingly, is situated within a broader dialogic history from which it can never break free. By juxtaposing participants' accounts, then, I was not simply comparing moments in time but, rather, a vast dialogic history. When applied to political negotiation, Bakhtin's theory of dialogue suggests that political struggles are recursively linked and ongoing, meaning that previous political contests form the discursive building blocks of future ones. In this vein, the meaning of specific political episodes must be interpreted through the lens of the history of relationships between political actors. To assert the primacy of one's interpretation of the past is to simultaneously project an image of future power relations and thereby to implicitly transform them. Thus, direct observation of the meetings would not necessarily get any closer to the essential truth of 'what happened' because the outcome of the meetings and larger political struggles is continually revisited through present political struggles.

My field experience demonstrates that policy-making meetings and their subsequent re-interpretation are the loci of multiple, overlapping negotiations of meaning and power. As they attempt to define a policy problem, Mexican policy-makers invoke competing discourses that imply distinct sets of social, political, economic and cultural assumptions, or political rationalities. In the case of the New Law, the IMSS team framed the policy problem with the metaphor of the corporatist state by emphasising the need for intergenerational solidarity and equality, whereas technocrats defined it more narrowly as a budget problem exacerbated by the inefficiency of a bloated state agency. Anthropologists of policy have traced the often uncanny permutations of political rationalities that emerge from the inherently messy and elliptical policy-making process (Greenhalgh 2008; Mosse and Lewis 2005; Schwegler 2008a; Shore and Wright 1997). Alongside the negotiation of the policy content is a meta-negotiation of the power relations that are substantiated through reference to previous political engagements. These contests reconfigure the political field and are an essential practice in asserting and contesting the formal structure of the bureaucracy. Schwartzman (1989: 36) notes that 'successive interpretations of meetings may serve to legitimate or delegitimate meeting content, social relations, or cultural systems'. Paradoxically, these retrospective accounts temporally displace conflict through their fundamental irresolution. The informal structure of the bureaucracy contains sufficient ambiguity that it is often impossible to completely dismiss any specific version since all are plausible yet refutable interpretations of the political field. Much like indirect language (Brenneis and Myers 1984), these accounts do not eliminate conflict but, rather, sublimate it, transforming direct confrontation into a spatially and temporally removed discourse of power relations.

BUILDING POLITICAL CONSENSUS THROUGH INCOMMENSURATE REALITIES

To understand the nature of the working disagreements, it is necessary to understand the key players vis-à-vis the New Law of Social Security. Although numerous government agencies, labour unions, business groups and international agencies took part in the initial discussions and subsequent negotiations – which lasted approximately six years! – three groups within the Mexican government were integral to the development and socialisation of the policy: the Ministry of Finance, IMSS and the Centre for the Strategic Development of Social Security, CEDESS (Centro de Desarrollo Estrategico para la Seguridad Social/Centre for the Strategic Development of Social Security).

During the genesis and development of the New Law of Social Security (approximately 1990–1997), the Ministry of Finance was the most influential ministry in the presidential cabinet and a key stakeholder in all policy decisions. The period from 1982 to 2000 demarcates a special era in Mexican politics in which US-trained Mexican economists, or technocrats, dominated the public sector, and nowhere was their presence more conspicuous than the Ministry of Finance.[2] Technocrats fitted a distinct social, educational and professional profile that distinguished them from previous generations of bureaucrats in several respects. First, technocrats had excellent educational credentials: whereas prior to the 1980s, Ministry of Finance officials held undergraduate degrees in economics from the National Autonomous University of Mexico (UNAM), technocrats held advanced graduate training, usually PhDs, from the most prestigious universities in the US, generally Harvard, Yale, the University of Chicago and MIT (Centeno and Maxfield 1992). Hailing from upper-class families in Mexico City, most technocrats attended elite private secondary schools and moved in privileged social circles. Finally, by virtue of their training, technocrats were globally oriented: they spoke impeccable English and moved comfortably through transnational policy networks, effortlessly glad-handing officials from the US Treasury, the International Monetary Fund and even Wall Street bankers (Babb 2001). Their presence in the administrations of Miguel de la Madrid (1982–1988), Carlos Salinas (1988–1994), and Ernesto Zedillo (1994–2000) was formidable: 'nearly one in four officials in the [de la Madrid] administration had studied in the US' (Babb 2001: 179), lending an unprecedented international bent to Mexican economic policy.

The dominance of the technocrats left a distinctive mark on the form and tone of political negotiations. Under the leadership of technocrats, the Ministry of Finance gained notoriety as the crucible of neoliberal economic reforms in Mexico, having presided over the privatisation of numerous state enterprises and the liberalisation of trade, investment and agricultural policy (Golob 1997). Yet these reforms were the visible manifestation of a deeper transformation in Mexican politics instigated by the rise of technocrats. Comparatively younger than their counterparts in the government, Mexican technocrats came of age during the devastating debt crisis of 1982, and many of them cite the profound economic instability they experienced as their primary motivation for pursuing graduate study in economics. Thus, unlike 'Eurocrats', who seek to impose a universal European culture (Shore 2000), Mexican technocrats perceive themselves as doing quite the opposite: mastering the discourse of economics so that they can be more effective negotiators on behalf of Mexico vis-à-vis the international economic community (whether this is the actual effect they have had is another matter entirely). The policies espoused by technocrats dismantled many of the features of the developmentalist state and exacted a substantial political toll on historically powerful actors, namely labour unions and old-guard politicians. For better or worse, Mexico's political stability in the twentieth century has frequently been attributed to the success of the corporatist model (Smith 1992), and the parties marginalised by technocrats were loath to relinquish their political influence. For their part, older, politically experienced bureaucrats had risen to prominence through dedicated service to the PRI and loyalty to their patrons, and they felt that technocrats not only flouted Mexico's political traditions but also exhibited dogmatic adherence to the ideology of neoliberal economics with almost reckless disregard for other considerations (Centeno 1994).

It was in the context of this epic struggle over the future of Mexico's political modus operandi that the New Law was negotiated. At the helm of the Ministry of Finance was Pedro Aspe, an MIT-trained economist and mentor to numerous technocrats. Aspe's chief of advisers was Alejandro Reynoso, an IT-trained economist who, by all accounts, was the consummate technocrat in that he had an impressive command of the technical issues but a low tolerance for political wrangling. In 1990, Reynoso was one of the lead investigators of a study of the financial position of IMSS which revealed that it had amassed a sizeable budget deficit and was on track to fall even deeper into the red as Mexico's population aged (Queisser 1998). At the most basic level, IMSS constituted a sizeable drain on public finance, and it was incumbent upon the Ministry of Finance to staunch the ever-increasing flow of state funds to IMSS to fund what technocrats viewed as overly generous benefits that were at best inefficient and at worst (depending on one's assumptions) a form of political cronyism. Improving IMSS's cash flow not only conformed to the broader political programme of economic liberalisation, but was also essential to put Mexico in good standing with international financial institutions and investors who, for better or worse, held substantial sway over Mexico's economic future.

At a deeper level, however, technocrats at the Ministry of Finance were taking aim at what they perceived to be the misappropriation of state funds for political purposes. Since its inception in 1943, IMSS collected and housed all payroll deductions with little or no direct oversight by the Ministry of Finance, an arrangement that resulted in expansive discretionary power. Moreover, since IMSS had a large base of taxpayers relative to the number of retirees during most of the twentieth century, it accumulated significant reserves that it used to finance a wide range of social programmes and services designed to improve the quality of life for IMSS beneficiaries (Queisser 1998). In addition to the cross-subsidies within IMSS, it was widely suspected by technocrats at the Ministry of Finance that loose accounting standards had led to the misuse of funds and outright embezzlement. IMSS developed strong ties to the PRI and has been the target of allegations of impropriety and political cronyism. For example, some officials claim that IMSS had become the voice of the party in isolated rural areas and showered peasants with cash gifts in order to garner their support for the ruling party. Thus, with the pension reform, the Ministry of Finance saw an opportunity not only to tighten fiscal discipline and eliminate what they perceived to be wasteful spending, but also to dismantle the corporatist structure of the Mexican political system.

Shrewd and experienced politicians, IMSS bureaucrats were well aware of the potential organisational impact of the proposed reform on their political clout. Since its inception, IMSS was 'the centerpiece of the corporatist arrangement with politically organised social groups' and had enjoyed dispro-portionately larger budget allocations in comparison to other agencies through the 1990s (González-Rossetti and Mogollon 2000: 41). One technocrat acerbically characterised IMSS as 'insurance against social revolution', a quip that powerfully conveys the extent to which access to IMSS benefits had been used to pacify would-be opposition (personal interview, 2 February

2000). The profile of bureaucrats at IMSS contrasts sharply with that of the technocrats: the IMSS had a long tradition of recruiting bureaucrats from the rank and file of the PRI as a reward for loyal service to the party, and IMSS bureaucrats enjoyed generous benefits and privileges. In contrast to most government agencies in Mexico, the IMSS union, SNTSS, encompasses the entire staff of IMSS – including mid- and upper-level officials – and affiliated health and administrative workers across the country. With 350,000 members and control over most positions within IMSS (including high-level positions), SNTSS is a prodigious force in Mexican politics that can effectively counteract the influence of the President in social welfare policy (Madrid 2003). Enjoying substantial collective action resources and links with the PRI, IMSS was ready to advance its two highest priorities: replenishing its operating budget and preserving its autonomy to the greatest extent possible.

The political landscape seemed to tilt strongly in favour of the Ministry of Finance, but IMSS held a critical bargaining chip. Highly trained and determined to restore the fiscal stability of IMSS, technocrats nonetheless lacked the political experience and networks to effectively negotiate with the corporatist groups ensconced in the union. All the technical elegance in the world would not be enough to mobilise the support of the necessary political actors. For that, the Ministry of Finance would have to rely on the cooperation of IMSS, specifically, its newly appointed director, Genaro Borrego. Having served as the governor of the state of Zacatecas and as executive director of the PRI prior to assuming the directorship of IMSS, Borrego was a savvy politician with wide-ranging political networks.

In March 1993, Pedro Aspe met with Genaro Borrego to inform him of the grim state of IMSS finances. Borrego listened carefully, but he was somewhat wary of the neoliberal zeal of the technocrats in the Ministry of Finance. While he respected Aspe's technical skill, he worried that a narrow focus on IMSS's budgeting would overlook other systemic problems with the calculation and administration of IMSS benefits. In his view, the problems at the IMSS were not solely macro-economic, but micro-economic as well. In order to effectively communicate with the Ministry of Finance team, however, Borrego would have to create his own think tank, CEDESS, staffed by social scientists with expertise in social and labour policy. The explicit purpose of CEDESS was to articulate an internal point of view on the reform of IMSS and to ensure that the wide scope of problems that afflicted it – not just those singled out by the technocrats – were addressed in the reform effort. Quite simply, it was formed to ensure that IMSS had a voice in the process. Institutionally speaking, CEDESS occupied a liminal role in the policy-making process – it was an autonomous organ of IMSS, and Borrego worked hard to maintain a veil of secrecy around CEDESS. Most IMSS officials did not know that CEDESS existed, nor that it was drafting alternative reform proposals (personal interview, 4 February 2000). One member of CEDESS gleefully described how he lived a 'double life', working days in IMSS and moonlighting at CEDESS in the evening (personal interview, 2 February 2000).

From an organisational perspective, the Ministry of Finance and IMSS were mutually dependent upon one another, yet as I worked my way through the bureaucracy, I discovered that officials at both agencies were loath to acknowledge their joint ownership of the reform process. For their part, Ministry of Finance officials typically described a division of labour in which Finance was responsible for the content of the reform and IMSS was responsible for negotiating support for the reform:

> In Mexico, everything was arranged through IMSS. That was a political point. Everything was presented through IMSS. The reform was designed at Hacienda, and Solis, who was at CONSAR, personally played a very important role. IMSS was convinced that the people at Hacienda were very capable – Santiago Levy and Carlos Noriega designed the programme with the participation of IMSS. (personal interview, 4 January 2000)

While at first his comments seem to recognise the importance of IMSS in the process, he ends up ascribing an implicit hierarchy of values to the work performed by both teams. His comments suggest that the Ministry of Finance did all of the heavy lifting with little to no input from IMSS (in fact, he does not acknowledge the role of CEDESS at all) and that IMSS was simply the public face of the reform. Any seeming involvement by IMSS was, by this account, choreographed to appease the power brokers in the union. His remarks establish the technical and political as mutually exclusive domains and, consequently, discursively exclude the possibility of IMSS meaningfully contributing to the technical discussion.

Perhaps not surprisingly, the relevant stakeholders at IMSS took issue with this interpretation of the respective roles of IMSS and Finance in the reform process. Gabriel Martinez, director of finance at IMSS, offered the following counter-explanation of the relationship between IMSS and the Ministry of Finance:

> At the end of 1993, the director of IMSS, Genaro Borrego, began to make proposals for reforms. He formed a group of representatives from the Ministry of Finance, the Ministry of Labour, and the Ministry of Commerce to talk about social security. He invited me to work here in December 1994 … By 1995, IMSS was a major part of the reform process. IMSS is a strong institution, and although people criticise social security, they still respect it. The director of IMSS is a very experienced politician. He has been a federal representative, party President [PRI], and governor of Zacatecas. There was an effort at IMSS to show that this was not a Finance proposal to unions, but an IMSS proposal. (personal interview, 2 February 2000)

This rebuttal discursively reframes the nature of the relationship between IMSS and Finance by juxtaposing the political weight of IMSS against the unpopularity of the Ministry of Finance at the time. Whereas the Ministry of

Finance officially downplayed the importance of political negotiation in the reform effort, the IMSS official underscores the dependence of the Ministry of Finance on IMSS's political prowess. What initially seemed a hierarchical relationship between technical skill and political finesse has been recast as a mutual dependence.

When I noticed this pattern, I initially tried to determine which of the two was the effective driver of the reform and ultimately concluded that the two interpretations are incommensurate: there is no way to resolve this debate because there is no way to definitively establish the importance of technical vs. political prowess. It is a bit like arguing that air is more important than water for human life: one is not terribly useful without the other. By the same token, a technically elegant reform will not be effective if it is politically infeasible. The fact that participants continued to resurrect this debate even after the reform had been passed, however, prompted me to hypothesise that the debate itself is performing political work. By continuing to assert the primacy of their team, each participant is not only projecting power in the past, but into the present and future as well, discursively framing himself as having the upper hand in political engagements. The very incommensurability of the accounts is, consequently, the way that the two interpretations can peacefully cohabit. The participants in the reform process reached a political consensus, albeit a consensus built on working disagreements.

The retrospective interviews took an unexpected turn when the participants began talking directly to one another through me. One of the benefits of this approach, I surmised, was that the participants were no longer in the heat of the reform and would be able to step back and take a more thoughtful, global view of the political negotiations. In an interview a member of CEDESS, who later assumed a position in the revenue department of the Ministry of Finance, offered the following explanation of the expenditure concessions that the Ministry of Finance was attempting to extract from IMSS:

> It had been originally proposed that IMSS assign to AFORES resources that before were destined to the title of social loans, which is itself debatable. The funds were being used to build buildings, auditoriums, theatres, vacation centres for IMSS personnel, social centres where baking classes are offered. Places where women go to chat in the afternoon over coffee. Originally, it had been proposed that those activities disappear and that the money be channelled to the pension system. In reality, it wasn't done. We wanted to make that spending transparent, and originally, that spending was supposed to disappear ... That was not done. You can ask Gabriel [Martínez] if IMSS is carrying out its promises. (personal interview, 2 February 2000)

His comments vividly convey the dominant outside view of IMSS as a bastion of populism, illegitimate spending and corruption. The fact that he encouraged me to ask Gabriel Martínez directly (he knew that I would be interviewing Martínez a few days later), however, adds a new discursive dimension to his comments. He clearly believes he already knows the answer, so his interest is not purely informational. Instead, he seems to want to let Martínez know (indirectly) that he has not forgotten the IMSS's empty promises and will continue to push for them to be fulfilled, a warning that has some teeth given that both he and Gabriel inhabit positions to affect IMSS's spending.

For his part, Gabriel Martínez did not seem terribly ruffled by this perception. A University of Chicago-trained economist, Martínez, was hired by Borrego in 1993 when, according to Borrego's trusted assistant, Borrego realised that he would need an economist on his side to negotiate with the cadre of PhD economists entrenched at the Ministry of Finance. Martínez is as technically proficient as they come, and he relished pointing out what he identified as the gratuitous application of neoclassical economic theory to no apparent end. When confronted with his colleague's question, Martínez fired back:

> The Ministry of Finance and the Bank of Mexico do not understand why social security exists except to keep the poor at bay. Social policy in Mexico has been viewed as preventive expenditure against social upheavals – this is why it was instituted and this is why the government continues to support it. (personal interview, 4 February 2000)

Martínez's response turns Dávila's argument on its head by asserting that IMSS is carrying out populist spending by virtue of an implicit mandate from the government to keep the masses happy, whatever the cost. While Martínez does not necessarily agree with the discretionary funding, he clearly thinks that it is a legitimate extension of the government's traditional strategy to mitigate opposition. His remark intimates that the spending problem at IMSS was not the result of greedy IMSS officials, but the consequence of government policy that does not adequately address the needs of its people and must resort to alternative methods.

As they rehashed the technical arguments made during the policy negotiations, Martínez and Dávila not only attempted to vindicate the past but also to lay the groundwork for future struggles for authority. These retrospective accounts temporally displace conflict through their fundamental irresolution. In this case, the structure of the bureaucracy is sufficiently ambiguous to admit multiple, contesting views regarding who was the main driver of the reform process to coexist. Both are plausible, refutable interpretations of the political field and, as such, can continue indefinitely, suggesting that the point of the exercise is not to reach a decisive agreement about the past but, rather, to wrangle about the present and the future.

CONCLUSION: THE ILLUSION OF BUREAUCRATIC INERTIA

Organisations exhibit both centripetal and centrifugal forces (Ahrne 1994; Wright 1994), but the study of bureaucracy tends to focus on the former without recognising the methodological implications of the latter. The formal hierarchy of the bureaucracy is engineered to defuse conflict through the transparent distribution of power, yet my field experience suggests that, in practice, bureaucracies manage and sustain conflict. In the Mexican federal government, bureaucrats and technocrats actively contest the formal distribution of power by discursively framing current political contests through conflicting accounts of previous political engagements, thereby challenging the formal structure of power relations. Yet it is exceedingly difficult to assess the validity of the interpretations because they are incommensurate: they reference distinct discursive spaces that do not naturally intersect. In the case of the New Law of Social Security, it is impossible to definitively state that the Ministry of Finance or IMSS was the more powerful agency since both draw on different political and material resources and have experienced historical vicissitudes in organisation visibility and influence. The net effect, then, is that multiple interpretations cohabit in a single policy, sustaining political consensus through working disagreements. Paradoxically, the fact that the interpretations cannot be fully reconciled is the key to their efficacy.

The existence of these structural idiosyncrasies implies that, rather than being seen as a rigid monolith, the Mexican bureaucracy is perhaps better understood as a flexible equilibrium subject to contingency and interpretation. This nuanced view of bureaucratic relations underscores the high stakes of policy negotiations. When I initially designed my research plan, I concentrated on the substantive negotiations among officials with regard to the scope, discursive framework and content of social security policy. I envisioned directly observing policy-making meetings so that I could determine how government officials reached a consensus on the definition of the policy problem and universe of possible solutions. It was only when I was unable to personally witness those meetings that I discovered that the explicit negotiation of policy paradigm and content was a subset of broader, implicit negotiations of bureaucratic position and influence.

This accidental discovery has far-reaching methodological implications for the anthropology of organisations. Far from being a missive on the relative virtues of absence versus presence in the field, this chapter reflects on the fact that tried-and-true anthropological methods may not always capture the crucial dynamics of organisational behaviour. In the case of my research, if I had not uncovered the discursive significance of retrospective accounts, I would have inadvertently privileged the technocrats' account, thereby re-enacting their dominance as a self-fulfilling prophecy. Thus, a commitment to an organisational framework must be accompanied by an equally strong commitment to a flexible methodology that constantly challenges the spatial, temporal and epistemological assumptions that implicitly structure field research. Accordingly, the anthropologist must be prepared to experiment with a vast array of methods and adjust her tactics as the project evolves (Wedel et al. 2005). Inert though it may seem, bureaucracy is in constant motion. If the anthropologist stands still to observe it, it will pass her by.

NOTES

1. Low-level civil servants are members of state workers' unions and can thus use collective action to ensure their job security (González-Rossetti and Mogollon 2000).

2. The Ministry of Finance had very little decision-making authority until the watershed moment in the rise of the new breed of technocrats occurred in 1976 when then-President Jose López-Portillo folded the Ministry of Finance into the Office of the President (effectively, the Chief of Staff) to create a super-ministry, the Office of Planning and Budget (SPP), with disproportionately high access to political and material resources (Bailey 1980).

REFERENCES

Ahrne, G. (1994) *Social Organizations: Interaction Inside, Outside, and Between Organizations* (Thousand Oaks, CA: Sage).

Babb, S. (2001) *Managing Mexico: Economists from Nationalism to Neoliberalism* (Princeton, NJ: Princeton University Press).

Bailey, J. J. (1980) 'Presidency, bureaucracy and administrative reform in Mexico: The Secretariat of Programming and Budget', *Inter-American Economic Affairs*, Vol. 34(summer), pp. 27–59.

Bakhtin, M. M. (1982) *The Dialogic Imagination: Four Essays*, edited by M. Holquist and C. Emerson (Austin, TX: University of Texas Press).

Boellstorff, T. (2008) *Coming of Age in a Second Life: An Anthropologist Explores the Virtually Human* (Princeton, NJ: Princeton University Press).

Brenneis, D. and F. Myers (1984) *Dangerous Words: Language and Politics in the Pacific* (New York, NY: New York University Press).

Britan, G. and R. Cohen, eds (1980) 'Toward an anthropology of formal organizations', in *Hierarchy and Society: Anthropological Perspectives on Bureaucracy* (Philadelphia, PA: Institute for the Study of Human Issues).

Camp, R. (1990) 'Camarillas in Mexican politics: The case of the Salinas cabinet', *Mexican Studies/Estudios Mexicanos*, Vol. 6, No. 1, pp. 85–107.

—— (2006) *Politics in Mexico* (New York, NY: Oxford University Press).

Centeno, M. (1994) *Democracy within Reason: Technocratic Revolution in Mexico* (University Park, PA: Pennsylvania State University Press).

Centeno, M. and S. Maxfield (1992) 'The marriage of finance and order: Changes in the Mexican political elite', *Journal of Latin American Studies*, Vol. 24, No. 1, pp. 57–85.

Conti, J. and M. O'Neil (2007) 'Studying power: Qualitative methods and the global elite', *Qualitative Research*, Vol. 7, No. 1, pp. 63–82.

Durkheim, E. (1995 [1912]) *The Elementary Forms of Religious Life* (New York, NY: The Free Press).

Geertz, C. (1988) *Works and Lives: Anthropologist as Author* (Stanford, CA: Stanford University Press).

Golob, S. (1997) '"Making possible what is necessary": Pedro Aspe, the Salinas team, and the next Mexican "miracle"', in J. Domínguez, ed., *Technopols: Freeing Politics and Markets in Latin America* (University Park: Pennsylvania State University Press).

González-Rossetti, A. and O. Mogollon (2000) *Enhancing the Feasibility of Health Reform: The Mexico Case Data for Decision-making Project*, Document no. 41 (Washington, DC: Agency for International Development).

Greenhalgh, S. (2008) *Just One Child: Science and Policy in Deng's China* (Berkeley, CA: University of California Press).

Gupta, A. and J. Ferguson (1997) 'Discipline and practice: The "field" as site, method, and location in anthropology', in A. Gupta and J. Ferguson, eds, *Anthropological Locations: Boundaries and Grounds of a Field Science* (Berkeley, CA: University of California Press).

Gusterson, H. (1997) 'Studying up revisited', *Political and Legal Anthropology Review*, Vol. 20, No. 1, pp. 114–119.

Hannerz, U. (2003) 'Being there ... and there ... and there! Reflections on multi-site ethnography', *Ethnography*, Vol. 4, No. 2, pp. 201–216.

Herzfeld, M. (1993) *The Social Production of Indifference: Exploring the Symbolic Roots of Western Bureaucracy* (Chicago, IL: University of Chicago Press).

Heyman, J. (2004) 'The anthropology of power-wielding organizations', *Human Organization*, Vol. 63, No. 4, pp. 487–500.

Hoag, C. (2011) 'Assembling partial perspectives: Thoughts on the anthropology of bureaucracy', *PoLAR: Political and Legal Anthropology Review*, Vol. 34, No. 1, pp. 81–94.

Kelty, C., H. Landecker, E. Kayaalp, A. Potoczniac, T. Stringer, L. Naficy et al. (2009) 'Collaboration, coordination, and composition: Field work after the internet', in J. Faubion and G. Marcus, eds, *Fieldwork Is Not What It Used to Be: Learning Anthropology's Method in a Time of Transition* (Ithaca, NY: Cornell University Press).

Kuper, A. (2003) 'Anthropology', in T. Porter and D. Ross, eds, *Cambridge History of Science: The Modern Social Sciences* (New York, NY: Cambridge University Press).

Latour, B. (2005) *Reassembling the Social: An Introduction to Actor-Network Theory* (Oxford: Oxford University Press).

Madrid, R. (2003) *Retiring the State: The Politics of Pension Privatization in Latin America and Beyond* (Stanford, CA: Stanford University Press).

Marshall, C. (1984) 'Elites, bureaucrats, ostriches, and pussycats: Managing research in policy settings', *Anthropology and Education Quarterly*, Vol. 15, No. 3, pp. 235–251.

Mosse, D. and D. Lewis, eds (2005) *The Aid Effect: Giving and Governing in International Development* (London: Pluto).

Powell, M. and T. Schwegler (2008) 'Unruly experts: Methods and forms of collaboration in the anthropology of policy', *Anthropology in Action: Journal for Applied Anthropology in Policy and Practice*, Vol. 15, No. 2, pp. 1–9.

Queisser, M. (1998) *The Second-generation Pension Reforms in Latin America* (Paris: OECD).

Randall, L. (2006) *Changing Structure of Mexico: Political, Social, and Economic Prospects* (New York, NY: M. E. Sharpe).

Rorty, R. (1979) *Philosophy and the Mirror of Nature* (Chicago, IL: University of Chicago Press).

Schwartzman, H. (1989) *The Meeting: Gatherings in Organizations and Communities* (New York, NY: Plenum Press).

Schwegler, T. (2008a) 'Take it from the top (down)? Rethinking neoliberal economic knowledge and political hierarchy in Mexico', *American Ethnologist*, Vol. 35, No. 4, pp. 682–700.

—— (2008b) 'Trading up: Reflections on power, collaboration, and ethnography in the anthropology of policy', *Anthropology in Action: Journal for Applied Anthropology in Policy and Practice*, Vol. 15, No. 2, pp. 10–25.

—— (2012) 'Navigating the illegible state: The political labor of government in Mexico', in K. Coulter and W. Schumann, eds, *Governing Cultures: Anthropological Perspectives on Political Labor, Power, and Government* (New York, NY: Palgrave Macmillan).

Shore, C. (2000) *Building Europe: The Cultural Politics of Integration* (New York, NY: Routledge).

Shore C. and S. Wright, eds (1997) *Anthropology of Policy: Critical Perspectives on Governance and Power* (New York, NY: Routledge).

Shore, C., S. Wright and D. Però, eds (2011) *Policy Worlds: Anthropology and Analysis of Contemporary Power* (London: Berghahn Books).

Smith, P. (1979) *Labyrinths of Power* (Princeton, NJ: Princeton University Press).

—— (1992) 'Mexico since 1946: Dynamics of an authoritarian regime', in B. Leslie, ed., *Mexico Since Independence* (New York, NY: Cambridge University Press).

Tsing, A. (2005) *Friction: An Ethnography of Global Connection* (Princeton, NJ: Princeton University Press).

Weber, M. (1978 [1968]) *Economy and Society: An Outline of Interpretive Sociology*, Vol. 2 (Berkeley, CA: University of California Press).

Wedel, J., C. Shore, G. Feldman and S. Lathrop (2005) 'Toward an anthropology of public policy', *Annals of the American Academy of Political and Social Science*, Vol. 600, pp. 30–51.

Wright, S., ed. (1994) *The Anthropology of Organizations* (New York, NY: Routledge).

Wright, S. and S. Reinhold (2011) 'Studying through: A strategy for studying political transformation. Or, Sex, lies and British politics', in C. Shore, S. Wright and D. Però, eds, *Policy Worlds: Anthropology and the Analysis of Contemporary Power* (New York, NY: Berghahn Books).

15
Momentum
Pushing ethnography ahead

Christina Garsten and Anette Nyqvist

INTRODUCTION: WEIGHT AND SPEED

There is both a physical phenomenon and a bodily sensation that one experiences after having pedalled hard up a hill on a fixed-wheel bike. Thighs burning from exhaustion, looking at a stretch of level road ahead after the climb, feet moving fast from the power accumulated on the way up the hill. There is a powerful push as the bike moves ahead faster and the rider maintains the effort. There is momentum: the force gained by a combination of accumulated mass and velocity.

Anthropological studies in and among complex organisations have reached such a point of momentum: the impressive weight of decades of ethnographic inquiry combined with the more recent speed of the development of these forms of engagement paves the way for a smooth and powerful continuation ahead. With the help of qualitative and ethnographic tools, human organising and social institutions in formal organisations are no longer novel. An impressive mass of experience in conducting ethnographic fieldwork has been assembled: in and of government authorities and bureaucracies of various levels, in and of the vast assortment of non-governmental organisations and in and of corporations, ranging from the largest multinationals to the tiny family-owned corner store. The study of human organising is, and has always been, at the very core of the discipline.

Organisations are vital, continuously evolving entities. In many ways, bureaucracies, corporations and other types of organisation impact upon us and influence, even shape, the way we conduct our lives. Conversely, organisations are, of course, human constructs and, as such, are placed at the centre of what has always been of anthropological interest: how social patterns and forms are shaped by human actions, and how human action is shaped by organisations. In short, organisations connect individuals with larger structures and coordinate human action. They make possible the swing from individual to social, from idea to impact, and from sentiment to collective feelings.

Typically, and to put it simply, the anthropological perspective on organisations is broader than that of organisational theory. An anthropological inquiry in and of organisations favours a processual approach. It highlights issues of power, ideology and politics, identity and belonging. The anthropological perspective on organisations entails studies of culture and studies of systems of meaning-making, and it pays simultaneous attention to the complex and the particular in these processes. It does not take the formal boundaries of organisations for granted, either as sites for empirical research or as borders in actual practice. The anthropological eye sees organisations as circuits for the flows of people, ideas and artefacts, and as conduits for influence, power and control (Wright 1994).

Much has happened since the Hawthorne studies of the 1930s. The anthropological approach to the study of organisations has accumulated both weight and speed: it has gained momentum. Looking to the future, we have identified three themes salient to anthropological studies in and among complex organisations. They concern the very sites of our inquiry, how we engage with the field and the tools we use to conduct our studies.

SITES OF COMPLEXITY

As anthropologists, we attend not merely to look at the way organisations connect individuals to larger structures, we also attend to the way connections are forged between organisations of various types and sizes. Individuals are connected to organisations through various types of membership: as citizens, customers, employees or members (Ahrne 1994). And different types of organisations are connected to each of these individuals and to each other. An intricate web of interconnectivity extends far and wide, connecting people to the world and vice versa.

It *is* complicated. And it is probably impossible and pointless to breach or grasp, let alone attempt to study such vast interconnectivity in its entirety. The gist, rather, is to identify specific sites – hot spots – where the complexity is rendered visible and made tangible in one way or another. For the ethnographer, the general idea, then, is to place oneself and the study in the thick of it – where the action is. Organisations are such strategic sites of connectivity, but we can also distinguish locations where various types of organisational forms meet and interact. The anthropologist studying organisations is not necessarily bound, therefore, to stay in one place, but may be prone to follow, trace and explore the intricacies and complexities that comprise, emerge from or pass through the organisation in question. Conducting ethnographic studies in and among complex organisations requires that, as anthropologists, we aim for the interface at which organisations overlap and/or individuals and organisations interact. We focus our attention at a nexus, at a specific point of interaction or critical intersection where ideas meet.

The fact that many of the contributions to this volume include ethnographic inquiry in, of, between and among organisations requires that we pay attention to boundaries. A pivotal function of organisations is to set and uphold the boundaries between members and non-members and between a given organisation and others (Paulsen and Hernes 2003). Boundaries evoke strong feelings of belonging, exclusion, hope and frustration. They act as levers for what counts – what is really at stake. The ethnographer is not restrained to work within such boundaries, of course, but could well make use of boundary-setting practices in the analysis of organisational activity. And instead of being bound by the erected boundaries, several of the authors in this volume describe how they balance on borders. By balancing on the border, ethnographers can positively provoke and highlight their own positionality in the field in relation to interlocutors, while drawing attention to essential protected resources.

Because organisations are complex, interconnected entities that continuously work to establish boundaries around themselves, defining what is and what is not, who is in and who is out, ethnographic attention to the creation and negotiation of boundaries is essential. When the informants are busy with work at and of boundaries and borders, so is the ethnographer. Border work encompasses a balancing act on boundaries, walking on lines, transgressive ethnography in which the researcher is poised on a threshold, with one foot in the door and one outside. Straddling the boundary while traversing it and making use of it is a significant characteristic of ethnography in and among complex organisations. Defining existing boundaries, the shaping or negotiation of boundaries and utilising them empirically and analytically is at the heart of ethnographic inquiry at these sites of complexity. Yet one can sometimes learn just as much by *not* getting inside the boundaries, as shown by Lilith Mahmud and Tara Schwegler (chapters 12 and 14).

The ethnographer's positions at such sites are neither stable nor singular, but rather mobile and multiple, in-between positions where, as Renita Thedvall in particular notes (chapter 7), entries are multiple and punctuated and must be negotiated time after time. The dividing lines and boundaries are rarely permanent, but processual and porous, and the ethnographer is also enabled by a certain agility and flexibility.

Yet another aspect of the complexity of these ethnographic sites is the significant difference between the positions of informant and researcher, which is ambiguous at times and may be challenging to define and uphold. All of this calls for a stronger emphasis on the various forms of engagement in the ethnographic study of and among these sites of complexity.

FORMS OF ENGAGEMENT

The forms of entry into any organisation are necessarily multiple. You can be born into a nation-state and a family or acquire citizenship and kinship at a later point in life. You can enter a corporation by way of inheritance or through a long series of interviews and tests. You can be elected into a non-governmental organisation, pay membership fees or merely sign your name on a membership list. For all individuals, there are many, many ways to enter organisations, some of which actually define the type of organisation it is. Conversely, there are many ways to exit an organisation. In most nation-states, people must work hard to rid themselves of their citizenship, but it is much easier in most countries to obtain a divorce. Opting out of a voluntary organisation can be either easy or difficult, depending on the organisation: a religious sect versus a sports association, for example.

The complexity of organisations calls for heightened attention and innovation with regard to the forms of engagement available to ethnographers. The dispersed, transient and intertwined complexity of organisational forms invites equally dispersed, transient and intertwined ethnography with multiple foci that allow the researcher to track, trace and follow processes. An assortment of forms for accessing organisations from within and for engaging with informants have evolved and continue to emerge continuously. Ethnographers still seek first-hand experience and set out to gain it within the complexity of organisations, something which accentuates classical anthropological issues of balancing distance and proximity. These issues become more pronounced because the study of organisations often involves studying 'at home' and 'sideways' (Hannerz 2006), and researchers can find themselves on common ground with and in similar predicaments to the researched. Researcher and informant may have similar backgrounds, social positions and educations, and may share a professional interest in issues of culture, knowledge and power. Researcher and informant may even share the same vocabulary and use similar concepts to describe and discuss their concerns (Holmes and Marcus 2005). In many ways, such proximity, even overlap, enables the researcher to gain better access, deeper understanding and thicker ethnography. But such similarities also call for greater attention to differences and sensitivity to distinctions between the etic and emic.

Some of the new or improved forms of engagement emerging from ethnographic endeavours regarding complex organisations are variations of a collaborative approach. Here the researcher and informant engage with each other in ways that resemble the relationships of colleagues. Researcher and informant engage in dialogues and conversations over joint interests and utilise each other's similar yet slightly different skills and projects. The researcher is asked to contribute to the work task of the informant and the informant to the project of the researcher. In situations in which researchers become co-workers and informants are collaborators, it is crucial that the classic anthropological concerns of insideness and outsideness are accorded extra attention. And for the ethnographer this novel collaborative field situation calls for a swift and appropriate juggling of statuses: constantly attending to the hat that should be worn, while simultaneously noting which hat the informant cum collaborator is wearing that day, at that meeting or at that moment. It is in these instances that anthropology may well be conceptualised as a study *with* rather than *of* and perceived as both a way of *knowing* and of *being*.

Another form of engagement, similar to that of the collaborator but different in decisive ways, is that of the apprentice – a role which also involves certain co-worker aspects. The apprentice is on the inside to learn from more experienced people how things are done. Ethnographers may, as several of the contributors here have done, acquire apprenticeship positions in the organisation in which they are conducting ethnographic fieldwork. Or, as yet others have described, they may conceptualise their position in the field as that of an apprentice rather than that of a collaborator. Ethnographers who engage in and with the field *as if* they are apprentices are actively and openly learning from the more experienced members of the organisation and picking up tricks of the trade. Apprentice-ethnographers observe and test various practices by trial and error. As Christina Garsten demonstrates (chapter 9), they are learning by doing through ethnography by failure – by making mistakes. Apprenticeship as a form of engagement includes collaboration, and the ethnographers must juggle their dual roles of researcher and co-worker. The apprenticeship approach may call for an embodied ethnography, however, in which appearance, vocabulary and practice are not so much a given prerequisite as attained through trial and error and observant participation.

Yet another variation of the co-worker approach to ethnography is to assume the role of assistant – more of an observer with a purpose than a participator in the making. The assistant is able to be close enough to observe and learn but not close enough to practise the tricks of the trade. At the other end of the continuum of roles is that of the expert. Anthropologists entering large-scale organisations, such as business corporations or multilateral organisations, have sometimes done so by holding the status of 'expert', a role that is not always as glorious as it sounds when an organisation is simply utilising external experts in their strategic activities. The organisation may temporarily hire or engage experts on crucial topics for which they possess no long-term, in-house competence. The hat of the 'expert' is sometimes placed on the ethnographer's head to provide a legitimate slot for entry into the organisation. This position may come with different expectations: that the ethnographer will make expert contributions or contribute academic insights. As Jakob Krause-Jensen (chapter 3) suggests, ethnographers need to be alert to how they are gaining access into an organisation and what their position may entail.

Adaptations to and developments of the long-term and participatory approach of traditional anthropology, based on interpersonal relations, certainly seems to be an appropriate research method in contemporary, formal and complex organisations. Engagement is still key, but as the sites of investigation are increasingly mobile and dispersed, the ethnographer's form of engagement must follow, which entails a heightened attentiveness to twists and turns in the field and an openness to the unexpected. As Brian Moeran (chapter 10) emphasises, the *practice* of networking, as opposed to network as an analytical concept, is valuable for researchers conducting ethnographic studies in and among complex organisational forms. A readiness to make and follow connections seems pertinent for the forms of engagement currently being developed and tested.

It must be noted that although the examples provided here – collaborator, apprentice and assistant – may seem to be relevant forms of engagement only in a business setting, this is not the case. All types of organisations are peopled by individuals who hold specific positions; we are suggesting that we must be open to connecting with these individuals in their specific roles and that we can do this in a number of ways. It seems that the transient and transforming, intertwined, multi-dimensional character of organisations is reflecting itself in a creative and exploratory manner in the number of novel variations of engaging ethnographically. These variations are emerging as anthropologists continue to strive for new, improved adaptations of our trademark research tools. These are exciting times. Let us open the toolbox.

THE ETHNOGRAPHIC REPERTOIRE

In an increasingly mobile and interconnected world movement, agility, adaptation and mobility must be included in the ethnographer's repertoire. With heightened attentiveness and openness to the unexpected, it seems to be useful to take serendipity seriously when investigating the various social forms in and among complex organisations.

Prefixes such as 'multi-' and 'co-' are key. Ethnographers now cooperate and collaborate and coexist in multi-sited, multi-dimensional fields of research. Ethnographic engagements need to be polymorphous, as Gusterson (1997) called it; we must be able to coexist with and adapt to other 'life forms'. The ability to assimilate and adjust to their surroundings like chameleons seems to be a valuable skill for ethnographers. And ethnographers interested in the study of organisations may also benefit from having the knack of changing direction at short notice, trying a different route, while never losing sight of the previous path. Halvard Vike introduces the image of ethnographer as a nomad (chapter 8). Today the ethnographer's repertoire includes split vision and multi-tasking, the ability to hold multiple positions and a willingness to study not only up and down, sideways and through, but also across and between in multi-dimensional criss-crossing ethnographies.

Ethnographers' portfolios are expanding. They must be nimble and able to think on their feet. An accumulated range of resources now enables the researcher to shift positions swiftly and smoothly – to go with the flow easily, to move around within fields and to sashay in and out of them. In ever-changing organisational forms, the ethnographer must have the ability to sit still, to sit in silence and discreetly observe at one moment and, in the next moment, to shift position and partake actively in a pertinent practice, while maintaining exploratory conversations with collaborators in and out of the field.

Panta rhei – everything flows, moves and changes – and one can never step into the same river twice. Place, in the sense of a singular and permanent site is no longer the main focus of contemporary anthropology – especially not organisational anthropology. For the methodology to mimic the field, the ethnographer's repertoire is now as mobile and dispersed as the organisation under study. Rather, the main focus is the issue at hand, the actual practice, which includes a focus on discourse, objects and the fashioning of ideas.

A lesson learned from studying organisations is that they all, including the state, the business corporation, and the charity organisation, tend to use tools for simplification (Scott 1998). They tend to want to speak dogma using buzzwords, to see through rose-coloured glasses, and to steer through the use of numbers and abbreviations. As ethnographers, we can contribute a richer narrative. The field is evolving with increasing speed, the methodology and approach is mature and able. As the weight and speed accumulates, there is momentum.

CURIOSITY

For all the excitement that awaits an anthropologist engaging with organisations, there may still remain a degree of hesitation and awkwardness. For the PhD student, this feeling may linger around questions like, 'What if my informants show up at the public defence of my thesis?' The professor may ask, 'What if they actually read what I write, and start to debate my findings in the news media?' Questions like these may sound like academic vanity. But they may also be about ethics and the ways in which we represent and deal with our material. They may also indicate a forlorn innocence in relation to the fields in which we collect our ethnographic data.

As for vanity, well, this is something we will have to learn to shake off or live with. Our informants and interlocutors will increasingly want to comment on, question, debate and refute our findings. As uncomfortable as this may be, it will, in the end, spur us to sharpen our tools further. The ethical aspects must be taken seriously, continuing a narrative with a long history in the discipline of anthropology. Different times have had their different formats and different genres for representing and making sense of the locals and the field. Subsequently, they have been questioned. We can therefore expect and should welcome interference from the field in the form of dialogue and exchange. A large portion of our awkwardness about engaging in organisational contexts has to do with the fact that ethnography often has been done from a position of privilege. When the chances are slim that our informants will read what we write and comment upon it publicly, much less provide an alternative interpretation, we can be relatively relaxed. We can retain the engaged distance of watching, participating and evaluating, with a return ticket safe in our pocket.

Yet we do not always get to enjoy this comfortable position of being somewhere else when we engage with organisations. As shown by several contributors to this volume, and as Emil A. Røyrvik (chapter 5) has explicitly reminded us, our interlocutors can and will provide us with their viewpoints. In our present situation, we may often do better by acknowledging our reliance on our interlocutors' willingness to engage, on their analyses and interpretations and on their comments on our research. The ethnographer has always been a certain kind of broker, bringing varied systems of meaning into juxtaposition, blending revelations and insights from various locations and contexts and bringing another world home to Academia. Hopefully – and here is where the broker ethnographer needs to work – something is being offered in return. We are not suggesting here that we should go native, lose sight of our academic goals or compromise our intellectual freedom. But it may be the case that academic goals can as easily be furthered by properly engaging with interlocutors. It is, after all, a chance to test our preliminary findings, our arguments and our results.

Properly engaging with interlocutors is also a test of our anthropological curiosity. Most ethnographers do fieldwork because we are curious about ourselves and about other people, in our local whereabouts and in distant places. We should welcome responses from our interlocutors, the challenges, and their differing views. Assessing the validity of our findings and ensuring multivocality requires multiple views. Organisational actors, prepared as many of them are to deliver opinions, analyse complex happenings and deal with masses of data, can assume valuable roles as partners in research. This terrain still remains largely unexplored.

CONTRIBUTIONS

In this volume, we have emphasised the value of anthropological perspectives on and ways of researching organisations. Anthropologists share this interest in organisations with many other disciplines – with organisation theory, sociology, management, political science and others. We find ourselves, therefore, at a disciplinary interface that is confusing, bewildering and productive. As with interlocutors, we believe curiosity is best served not by flirting with these disciplines from a distance, but by seriously taking them into account. In many of the contributions to this book, one can easily trace influences from critical management theory and new institutionalism. In part, this cross-fertilisation is the result of following where curiosity leads, rather than maintaining strict disciplinary boundaries. As outlined in chapter 1, there have been several points at which anthropology and organisation theory have approached each other: around the discovery of the social system, the notion of institution and the concept of organisational culture, to name a few. We believe we are now at a point at which we can engage more intensely with organisation theory, and that both sides have much to gain from it.

We have already highlighted some of the areas in which we believe that anthropology has much to offer organisation studies. We would like to add a short note on other partly unexplored territories. Anthropology's sensitivity to local ways of life and the ways they interlink with larger systems and influences invites us to explore the role of organisations in scale-making projects of various kinds (cf. Tsing 2005). Organisations contribute actively in globalising processes. They are often shapers of globalisation processes, and act as conduits for the diffusion of norms, financial resources and formats for shaping the world.

Corporations produce global grammars for organising across large territories. The standards, procedures and reporting formats they produce are performative at a global scale, and have an impact on actions at local levels. To trace the practices of producing and using these scalar technologies, we need to abandon the methodological formalism of confining our study to one organisation in one locality. The intricate connectivities and layering of influences require a simultaneous recognition of the formal boundaries of the organisations, and the many ways in which practices move up and down the scale of impact. At a time when powerful scalar arrangements are being entrenched by organisational actors with transnational reach, an examination of the politics of scale appears to be one of the more urgent contributions that anthropology could make to organisation theory. The selective omission of formal organisational boundaries, the entangling of the macro and the micro, and the wariness with regard to doctrines should serve the cause well.

Another compelling area to delve in to more deeply is the seeming innocence of small-scale technologies of organisations. The spheres of everyday practices are vital for learning about organisations. What appear to be banal practices, like getting a statement signed or notarised, undergoing an audit, completing a recruitment test, are, in fact, infused with significance (see, for example, Power 1997; Strathern 2000). Organisations and our perceptions of them are shaped largely by routine procedures and repetitive activities. Take, for example, the seemingly mundane activity of meetings within organisations. As Åsa Boholm, Anette Nyqvist and Renita Thedvall show (chapters 11, 6 and 7 respectively), each in a different way, any meeting is packed with critical and intricate social and political activities. Because these procedures are so ordinary and so commonplace, they are also often considered apolitical and non-consequential (cf. Ferguson 1994). It is through these putatively innocent little practices that the very political tasks of state agencies are made possible, however, and through which they aggregate into scalar technologies. Anthropologists have a keen eye for small-scale rituals and the meanings that people attach to them. What does filing actually mean, for instance? What kind of knowledge is stored? How is it packaged and structured? What does the practice of communicating through bullet points do to people's self-perceptions as performers in an organisation? And, as explored by Gavin Hamilton Whitelaw (chapter 2), what do routine movements behind the counter in a convenience store do to one's physiology – from the nimble fingers required for sorting money to hours of standing in one spot? And what does a person learn to look for routinely when standing behind the counter? From within an organisation, we learn to see things from a certain perspective.

The anthropological engagement in organisations foregrounds why organisations favour certain ways of thinking and acting, and why they produce classificatory schemes. As we are well aware, large-scale projects like state buildings and business planning require simplification and ordering of things into slots. Classificatory schemes may be empowering for those in charge. To know how many publications are produced annually in department A in relation to university goals, is to be at an advantage. To know how many customer phone calls were being responded to by employee B, allows one to be in charge. To know that job-seeker C has a certain disability classification, means to be in control of a portion the job-seeker's future. We may view these classificatory systems as forms of rationality that can be analysed as practices that create and shape idealised templates for representing local realities – but also for abstracting them and turning them into 'facts' (cf. Rose 1999). These templates, despite seeming evidence to the contrary, have a moral form and content, because they address people who are classified within the bureaucracy in relation to that bureaucracy's specific intentions. Moreover, the language of abbreviations, numbers and slots embodies conceptions about the subjects. For anthropologists and organisation scholars, they offer insights into the epistemologies of organisations, something that both Peter Fleming (chapter 4) and Douglas Holmes (chapter 13) convincingly show in their respective contributions to this book. The comparative perspective, so essential to anthropology, teases out the local part of management ideologies *and* points to the universality of power struggles and organisational attempts.

It is time to enjoy the power of the momentum achieved so far, to enjoy the ride with the speed and velocity gained. Anthropology has an advantage in approaching organised life.

REFERENCES

Ahrne, G. (1994) *Social Organizations: Interaction Inside, Outside and Between Organizations* (London: Sage).

Ferguson, J. (1994) *The Anti-Politics Machine: 'Development', Depoliticization, and Bureaucratic Power in Lesotho* (Minneapolis, MI: University of Minnesota Press).

Gusterson, H. (1997) 'Studying up revisited', *Political and Legal Anthropology Review*, Vol. 20, No. 1, pp. 114–119.

Hannerz, U. (2006) 'Studying down, up, sideways, through, backward, forward, away and at home: Reflections on the field worries of an expansive discipline', in S. Coleman and P. Collins, eds, *Locating the Field: Metaphors of Space, Place and Context in Anthropology* (Oxford: Berg).

Holmes, D. and G. E. Marcus (2005) 'Cultures of expertise and the management of globalization: Toward the refunctioning of ethnography', in A. Ong and S. J. Collier, eds, *Global Assemblages: Technology, Politics, and Ethics as Anthropological Problems* (Oxford: Blackwell).

Paulsen, N. and T. Hernes, eds (2003) *Managing Boundaries in Organizations: Multiple Perspectives* (Basingstoke: Palgrave Macmillan).

Power, M. (1997) *The Audit Society: Rituals of Verification* (Oxford: Oxford University Press)

Rose, N. (1999) *Powers of Freedom: Reframing Political Thought* (Cambridge: Cambridge University Press).

Scott, J. (1998) *Seeing Like a State* (New Haven, CT: Yale University Press).

Strathern, M. (2000) *Audit Cultures: Anthropological Studies in Accountability, Ethics, and the Academy* (London: Routledge).

Tsing, A. L. (2005) *Friction: An Ethnography of Global Connection* (Princeton, NJ: Princeton University Press).

Wright, S., ed. (1994) *Anthropology of Organizations* (London: Routledge).

Notes on contributors

Åsa Boholm's research interests cover a broad spectrum of areas, ranging from historical anthropology, political symbolism, ritual and religion, to environmental anthropology and risk research. She has published on cultural dimensions and conceptual meanings of risk, and on the communication, regulation and management of technological risks in the public domain and in relation to organisational practice. Her regional specialisation covers Sweden and Italy. She is Professor of Social Anthropology at the University of Gothenburg, formerly at the School of Public Administration and the Center for Public Sector Research, and since 2011 at the School of Global Studies.

Peter Fleming is Professor of Work and Organisation at Queen Mary College, University of London. He researches new forms of power and neo-managerialism, particularly focusing on the power relations and resistance that underlie them. He is the author of several books, including *Dead Man Working* (Zero, 2012), *The End of Corporate Social Responsibility* (Sage, 2012) and *Contesting the Corporation* (Cambridge, 2007).

Christina Garsten researches globalisation processes in corporations and markets. She currently studies the role of think tanks in setting agendas for global governance. Earlier works have focused on transnational organisational culture, on organisational visions of transparency and accountability for transnational trade, and on policy changes towards flexibility and employability in work life. Field experiences in organisational life have also incited her to explore the mix of humour and boredom that often permeates it. She is Professor of Social Anthropology at Stockholm University and Chair of the Board at Score (Stockholm Centre for Organizational Research).

Douglas Holmes is Professor of Anthropology at Binghamton University. His forthcoming book, *Economy of Words: Communicative Imperatives in Central Banks* (Chicago, 2013), examines experiments pursued by five central banks that underwrite the creation of this new monetary regime: what he terms a 'public currency'. His first book, *Cultural Disenchantments* (Princeton, 1990), explores cultural and political economy in north-east Italy. His second book, *Integral Europe* (Princeton, 2000), investigates configurations of radicalism – fusing left- and right-wing agendas – incited by European integration. He continues an ongoing collaboration with George E. Marcus that seeks to re-function modalities of ethnographic inquiry.

Jakob Krause-Jensen's research focuses on the ethnographic study of management practices. After having focused on value-based management in business organisations (Bang & Olufsen), he has more recently researched the implications of introducing private sector ideas (lean management) into public sector institutions (family counselling). He is currently Associate Professor at the Department of Education, Aarhus University. While he has no intention of giving up studying management ideas and practices in their particular ethnographic setting and broader cultural context, he is currently trying to get 'back to business', that is looking for additional field sites where informants wear suits.

Lilith Mahmud is a feminist anthropologist whose research focuses on gender, secrecy, transparency, power, elites, nationalism and critical studies of Europe. Her fieldwork among women Freemasons in Italian Masonic lodges is the basis of her forthcoming book on the making of humanist fraternity in the context of a highly contested and secretive brotherhood. She earned her PhD in Anthropology from Harvard University and she is an Assistant Professor in the Department of Women's Studies, the Department of Anthropology, and the PhD Program in Culture and Theory at the University of California, Irvine.

Brian Moeran is a social anthropologist whose research has focused on different aspects of cultural production (ceramics, advertising, women's fashion magazines, incense and books), primarily in Japan, but also in other parts of Asia and Europe. He is particularly interested in creative processes and in how these are constrained by material, technical, aesthetic, social and other factors. He is Professor of Business Anthropology at the Copenhagen Business School and founding editor of the online *Journal of Business Anthropology* (www.cbs.dk/jba). He is looking forward to at least partial retirement from February 2013 when he will go back to making pots.

Anette Nyqvist's research interests are on issues of power at the nexus of statecraft and market-making. For her PhD she studied the remaking of Sweden's national pension system and her current research is on financial and political strategies of institutional investors. Anette is a researcher at Score (Stockholm Centre for Organizational Research) and a lecturer at the Department of Social Anthropology at Stockholm University. While she has no intention of abandoning research of power where politics and finance meet, Anette is currently looking for additional fields where informants do not wear suits.

Emil André Røyrvik's focus of research is on ethnography and anthropological theory in the context of management, organisation and political economy. He has written about issues like the knowledge economy, industrial management, and the financialisation and crisis of capitalism, and is broadly concerned with contemporary post-democracy and economic globalisation. He is a Senior Research Scientist at SINTEF Technology and Society, Scandinavia's largest independent research organisation.

Tara Schwegler's research focuses on the intersection of state power and forms of expert knowledge in the policy-making process. She conducted field research among Mexican technocrats in order to observe the role of economic knowledge in social security reform in Mexico. A former Collegiate Assistant Professor at the University of Chicago, Tara is currently an Experience Design Strategist at a major financial services company. Working in the financial sector has exposed her to many uncanny parallels between corporate and public organisations, which will undoubtedly become the subject of future research. It seems that she will always be where the suits are.

Renita Thedvall is based in the field of policy and organisational anthropology and has a particular interest in how policies around, for example, quality in work or fair trade are developed, shaped and framed via indicators or standards. Currently, she is working on how the lean management model is negotiated, discussed and implemented, and operates in public pre-schools. She is a senior lecturer and Director of Studies at the Department of Social Anthropology and a senior research fellow at Score (Stockholm Centre for Organizational Research) at Stockholm University.

Halvard Vike is Professor of Social Anthropology at the University of Oslo. He has carried out extensive research on local politics, planning, public organisations, history, gender and cultural heritage in Norway, and is currently working on issues relating to comparative political culture. His previous publications include *The Conscience of Power* (*Maktens samvittighet*, Gyldendal Akademisk 2002), 'Culminations of complexity' (in *Anthropological Theory*, Vol. 2, No. 1, 2002), 'L'État de la morale et la morale de l'état' (*Ethnologie française*, Vol. 39, No. 2, 2009), and 'Cultural models, power, and hegemony' (in David Kronenfeld et al., *A Companion to Cognitive Anthropology*, Wiley-Blackwell 2011).

Gavin H. Whitelaw's research focuses on issues of commerce, work, food and consumer culture in contemporary Japan. He earned his doctorate in anthropology at Yale University. His dissertation on the cultural life and human ecology of Japan's convenience stores is currently a book manuscript. He is an Assistant Professor of Anthropology at International Christian University (ICU) in Tokyo, where he teaches in the university's College of Liberal Arts and Graduate School. He also serves as Coordinator for the Japan Studies Program. When Gavin is not visiting convenience stores, he can be found foraging in the wooded fringes of western Tokyo.

Index

Compiled by Sue Carlton

Page numbers followed by 'n' refer to end of chapter notes